TIZIANO TERZANI

A Fortune-Teller Told Me

Earthbound Travels in the Far East

Flamingo
An Imprint of HarperCollinsPublishers

For Angela, always

Flamingo
An Imprint of HarperCollins*Publishers*
77–85 Fulham Palace Road,
Hammersmith, London w6 8jb

Published by Flamingo 1998
9 8 7 6

First published in Great Britain by
HarperCollins*Publishers* 1997

Author photograph by Vincenzo Cottinelli

ISBN 0 00 655071 1

Set in Postscript Monotype Bembo

Printed in Great Britain by
Clays Ltd, St Ives plc

CONTENTS

	Map	vi
1	A Blessed Curse	1
2	A Death that Failed	11
3	On Which Shore Lies Happiness?	18
4	The Body-Snatchers of Bangkok	32
5	Farewell, Burma	46
6	Widows and Broken Pots	64
7	Dreams of a Monk	78
8	Against AIDS? Raw Garlic and Red Peppers	93
9	The Rainbow Gone Mad	111
10	Sores under the Veil	126
11	The Murmurs of Malacca	138
12	An Air-Conditioned Island	152
13	A Voice from Two Thousand Years Ago	169
14	Never Against the Sun	185
15	The Missionary and the Magician	198
16	Hurray for Ships!	215
17	The *Nagarose*	229
18	Buddha's Eyelash	242
19	The Destiny of Dogs	259
20	A Ship in the Desert	274
21	With my Friend the Ghost	283
22	The Peddlers of the Trans-Siberian Railway	304
23	Better than Working in a Bank	312
24	The Rhymeless Astrologer	322
25	TV for the Headhunters	329
26	New Year's Eve with the Devil	339
27	The Spy who Meditates	353
	Epilogue: And Now What?	369
	Index	371

CHAPTER ONE

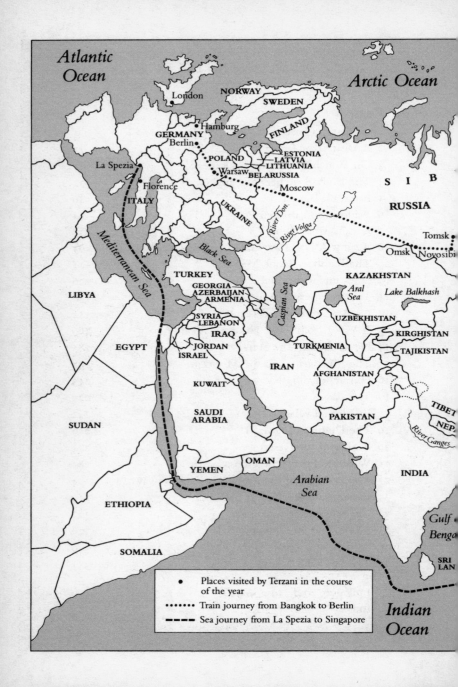

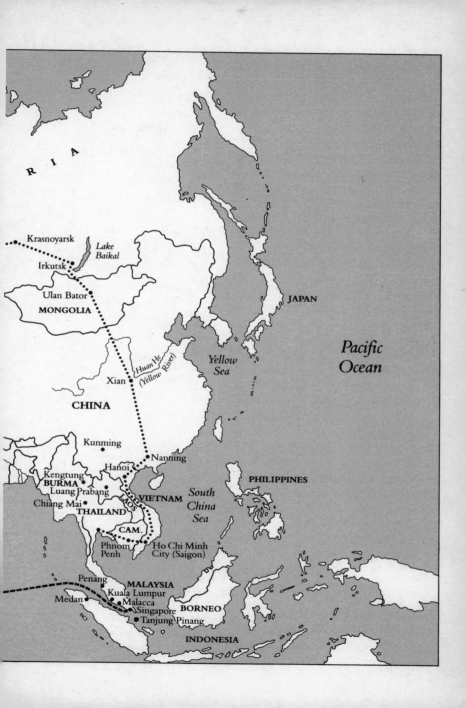

A Blessed Curse

Life is full of opportunities. The problem is to recognize them when they present themselves, and that isn't always easy. Mine, for instance, had all the marks of a curse: '*Beware! You run a grave risk of dying in 1993. You mustn't fly that year. Don't fly, not even once,*' a fortune-teller told me.

It happened in Hong Kong. I had come across that old Chinese man by sheer chance. When I heard his dire words I was momentarily taken aback, but not deeply disturbed. It was the spring of 1976, and 1993 seemed a long way off. I did not forget the date, however; it lingered at the back of my mind, rather like an appointment one hasn't yet decided whether to keep or not.

1977 . . . 1987 . . . 1990 : . . 1991. Sixteen years seem an eternity, especially when viewed from the perspective of Day One. But, like all our years (except those of adolescence), they passed very quickly, and in no time at all I found myself at the end of 1992. Well, then, what was I to do? Take that old Chinese man's warning seriously and reorganize my life? Or pretend it had never happened and carry on regardless, telling myself, 'To hell with fortune-tellers and all their rubbish'?

By that time I had been living in Asia solidly for over twenty years – first in Singapore, then in Hong Kong, Peking, Tokyo, and finally in Bangkok – and I felt that the best way of confronting the prophecy was the Asian one: not to fight against it, but to submit.

'You believe in it, then?' teased my fellow-journalists – especially the Western ones, the sort of people who are used to demanding a clear-cut yes or no to every question, even to such an ill-framed one as this. But we do not have to believe the weather forecast to carry an umbrella on a cloudy day. Rain is a possibility, the umbrella a precaution. Why tempt fate if fate itself gives you a sign, a hint?

When the roulette ball lands on the black three or four times in a row, some gamblers count on statistical probability and bet all their money on the red. Not me: I bet on the black again. Has the ball itself not winked at me?

And then, the idea of not flying for a whole year was an attraction in itself. A challenge, first and foremost. It really tickled me to pretend an old Chinese in Hong Kong might hold the key to my future. It felt like taking the first step into an unknown world. I was curious to see where more steps in the same direction would lead. If nothing else, they would introduce me, for a while, to a different life from the one I normally led.

For years I have travelled by plane, my profession taking me to the craziest places on earth, places where wars are being waged, where revolutions break out or terrible disasters occur. Obviously I had held my breath on more than one occasion – landing with an engine in flames, or with a mechanic squeezed in a trapdoor between the seats, hammering away at the undercarriage that was refusing to descend.

If I had dismissed the prophecy and carried on flying in 1993, I would certainly have done so with more than the usual pinch of anxiety that sooner or later strikes all those – including pilots – who spend much of their lives in the air; but I would have carried on with my normal routine: planes, taxis, hotels, taxis, planes. That divine warning (yes: 'divination', 'divine', so alike!) gave me a chance – in a way obliged me – to inject a variant into my days.

The prophecy was a pretext. The truth is that at fifty-five one has a strong urge to give one's life a touch of poetry, to take a fresh look at the world, reread the classics, rediscover that the sun rises, that there is a moon in the sky and that there is more to time than the clock's tick can tell us. This was my chance, and I could not let it slip.

But there was a practical problem. Should I stop working for a year? Take leave of absence? Or carry on working despite this limitation? Journalism, like many other professions, is now dominated by electronics. Computers, modems, fax play a paramount role. Snappy, instantaneous television images transmitted by satellite have set new standards, and print journalism, rather than concentrating on reflection and the personal, limps after them in the effort to match the invincible immediacy (and with it the superficiality) of TV.

During the days of the Tiananmen massacre, CNN was broadcasting live from the square in the centre of Peking, and many of my colleagues preferred to stay in their hotel rooms and watch television rather than go out and see what was happening a few hundred yards away. That was the quickest way of keeping up to date, of following events. Moreover, their editors were seeing – thousands of miles away – the same images on their screens; and those images became the truth, the only truth. No need to look for another.

How would my editors react to the idea of having an Asia correspondent who, on a whim, took into his head not to fly for a whole year? What would they think of a man who in 1993 suddenly became a journalist from the beginning of the twentieth century, one of those who would set off at the outbreak of a war and would often arrive when it was already over?

My chance to find out came in October 1992, when one of the two editors-in-chief of *Der Spiegel* passed through Bangkok. One evening after dinner, without much beating about the bush, I told him the story of the Hong Kong fortune-teller and announced my intention of not travelling by plane in 1993.

'After what you've told me, how can I ask you to fly to Manila and cover the next *coup d'état*, or to Bangladesh for the next typhoon? Do as you think best,' was his reply. Magnificent as usual, my faraway masters! They saw that this caprice of mine might give rise to a different kind of story, one that might offer the reader something the others lacked.

Der Spiegel's reaction obviously took a load off my mind, but still I did not finally commit myself to the plan. The prophecy would take effect at the beginning of the new year, and I intended to make my decision at the very last moment, the stroke of midnight on 31 December, wherever I might find myself.

Well, I was in the Laotian forest. My celebratory feast was an omelette of red ants' eggs. There was no champagne to see the New Year in; instead I raised a glass of fresh water, and solemnly resolved not to yield for any reason, at any cost, to the temptation of flying. I would travel the world by any possible means as long as it was not a plane, a helicopter or a glider.

It was an excellent decision, and 1993 turned out to be one of the most extraordinary years I have ever spent: I was marked for death, and instead I was reborn. What looked like a curse proved to be a blessing. Moving between Asia and Europe by train, by ship, by car, sometimes even on foot, the rhythm of my days changed completely. Distances became real again, and I reacquired the taste of discovery and adventure.

Suddenly, no longer able to rush off to an airport, pay by credit card and be swept off in a flash to literally anywhere, I was obliged once again to see the world as a complex network of countries divided by rivers and seas that required crossing and by frontiers that invariably spelt 'visa' – a special visa, what is more, saying 'surface travel', as if this were so unusual as to cast suspicion on anyone who insisted on it. Getting from place to place was no longer a matter of hours, but of days or weeks. I had to avoid making mistakes, so before starting out I pored over maps. No longer were mountains beautiful, irrelevant frills seen from a porthole, but potential obstacles on my way.

Covering great distances by train or boat restored my sense of the earth's immensity. And above all it led me to rediscover the majority of humanity whose very existence we well-nigh forget by dint of flying: the humanity that moves about burdened with bundles and children while the world of the aeroplane passes in every sense over their heads.

My undertaking not to fly turned into a game full of surprises. If you pretend to be blind for a while, you find that the other senses grow sharper to compensate for the lack of sight. Avoiding planes has a similar effect: the train journey, with its ample time and cramped space, re-animates an atrophied curiosity about details. You give keener attention to what lies around you, to what hurtles past the window. In a plane you soon learn not to look, not to listen: the people you meet, the conversations you have, are always the same. After thirty years of flying I can recall precisely no one. On trains, on Asian ones at least, things are different: you share your days, your meals and your boredom with people you would otherwise never meet, and some of them remain unforgettable.

As soon as you decide to do without planes, you realize how they impose their limited way of looking at things on you. Oh, they diminish distances, which is handy enough, but they end up diminishing everything, including your understanding of the world. You leave Rome at sunset, have dinner, sleep a while, and at dawn you are in India. But in reality each country has its own special character.

We need time if we are to prepare ourselves for the encounter; we must make an effort if we are to enjoy the conquest. Everything has become so easy that we no longer take pleasure in anything. To understand is a joy, but only if it comes with effort, and nowhere is this more true than in the experience of other countries. Reading a guidebook while hopping from one airport to another is not the same as the slow, laborious absorption – as if by osmosis – of the humours of the earth to which one remains bound when travelling by train.

Reached by plane, all places become alike – destinations separated from one another by nothing more than a few hours' flight. Frontiers, created by nature and history and rooted in the consciousness of the people who live within them, lose their meaning and cease to exist for those who travel to and from the air-conditioned bubbles of airports, where the border is a policeman in front of a computer screen, where the first encounter with the new place is the baggage carousel, where the emotion of leave-taking is dissipated in the rush to get to the duty-free shop – now the same everywhere.

Ships approach countries by slowly and politely entering the mouths of their rivers; and distant ports become long-awaited goals, each with its own face, each with its own smell. What used to be called airfields were once a little like that. No more. Nowadays airports have the false allure of advertisements – islands of relative perfection even amid the wreckage of the countries in which they are situated. They all look alike, all speak the same international language, that makes you feel you have come home. But in fact you have only landed at the outskirts of a city, from which you must leave again by bus or taxi for a centre which is always far away. A railway station, on the other hand, is a true mirror of the city in whose heart it lies. Stations are close to the cathedrals, mosques, pagodas or mausoleums. On reaching them you have well and truly arrived.

Despite the limitation of not flying, I did not stop doing my job, and I always managed to arrive in time where I needed to be: for the first democratic elections in Cambodia, for the opening of the first line of communication – by land! – between Thailand and China via Burma.

And that summer I did not forgo my annual visit to my mother in Italy. I travelled the historic route by train from Bangkok to Florence: over thirteen thousand miles, passing through Cambodia, Vietnam, China, Mongolia, Siberia and so on – a journey which in itself was not exceptional in the slightest, only that nobody had done it for a long time. It took a month, accompanied by the clickety-clack of the wheels and the varied whistles of different countries' locomotives, to cross what still looks on the map like a small fraction of the earth.

I returned to the East from La Spezia, this time with my wife Angela, in a battered ship of the Lloyd Triestino line, by the great classical route through the Mediterranean, the Suez Canal, the Red Sea, the Indian Ocean and the Straits of Malacca to Singapore. We were the only two passengers on board. The rest was a cargo of two thousand containers and a very Italian crew of eighteen men.

If I had not invented the excuse of the fortune-teller, I would have done nothing of all this, and 1993 would have been a year like so many others, without one of the events that signal the passage of time.

How many great stories can there be in the life of a journalist? One or two, if he is lucky. I have already had my share of such luck: I was in Saigon in the spring of 1975 when the Communists arrived and ended the Vietnam war, which for my generation was what the Spanish Civil War had been for the generation of Hemingway and Orwell; and in the summer of 1991 I was in the bowels of the USSR when the Soviet empire fell to pieces and Communism died. Perhaps one day, if I am really lucky, I may have a chance to witness another great event, but until then I have to sharpen my curiosity on things that are less obvious, less striking.

With the decision not to fly I also took another, a logical extension of the game. I decided that wherever I might go that year I would seek out the most eminent local fortune-teller, the most powerful sorcerer, the most revered oracle or seer or visionary or madman of the place, ask him to look into my future, and try to learn something of my fate.

They came in all shapes and sizes. Every meeting was a new adventure, and along the way I collected dozens of warnings and much wise advice about how to live, as well as oils, amulets, pills, powders and prescriptions guaranteed to protect me from various dangers. I carried them all with me, and at the end of the year I was weighed down with gadgets, little bottles and paper packets. The power of each was linked with some taboo that had to be observed on my part: in every system, religious or otherwise, the dispensation of a benefit is always indissolubly connected with some effort to be made, some merit to be gained. An excellent principle, I believe, though in practice I was forced to limit my performance of these 'duties'.

If I had obeyed all the warnings and prohibitions, my life would have been much more complicated than I had already made it by renouncing flight. On an Indonesian island I met a *bomoh*, an expert in black magic, who told me I must never, never, piss against the sun. Another said not to piss against the moon. In Singapore a shaman, a woman who spoke in rhyme in ancient Chinese, counselled me never again to eat dog or snake. Another seer told me never to eat beef, another to remain strictly vegetarian for the rest of my life. An old lama in Ulan Bator read my whole destiny in the cracks in a sheep's shoulderblade burnt in a slow fire of dried cow-dung, and then handed me a little packet of dried, perfumed grasses from the Mongolian plain, to be used like smelling-salts in the event of danger. A Buddhist monk outside Phnom Penh splashed me, fully dressed as I was, with the same water he used to treat local epileptics.

Many of the fortune-tellers were just colourful characters, at times out-and-out charlatans just trying to make a living. Some, however, were truly remarkable, with a rare understanding of the human condition, an unusual psychic gift that enabled them to read other people's minds or to see 'scars' undetectable by the normal eye. Some left me wondering if indeed they had an extra sense. Is it possible? Is it possible that over the millennia man has lost through disuse certain capacities which were once natural to him, and which survive today in only a few individuals?

The history of the world is full of prophecies and portents, but we tend to feel, especially in the West, that all this belongs to the past. In Asia, however, the occult is still invoked to explain current events at least as often as economics or, until recently, ideology. In China, in India, in Indonesia, what we call superstition is still very much part of everyday life. Astrology, chiromancy, the art of reading the future in a person's face or the soles of his feet or the tea leaves in his cup, play a very substantial role in the life of the people and in public affairs, as do the practices of healers, shamans and the masters of *feng-shui*, the cosmic geometry. The name to give a child, the purchase of a field, the sale of a portfolio of shares, the repair of a roof, the date of a departure or a declaration of war, are governed by criteria that have nothing to do with our logic. Those criteria determine how millions of marriages are arranged, how thousands of buildings are planned and constructed. Political decisions which affect whole populations are based on the advice of individuals expert in consulting the occult.

People have always searched for the meaning of life, trying to comprehend its mystery and find a key to the future, and to influence their fate. Chinese, as a written language, was born not as a means of communication between men, but as a way of consulting the gods. 'Should I make war on the neighbouring state or not?' 'Will I win the battle or not?' A king wrote these questions on a flat bone which was then pierced with a red-hot needle. The divine answer appeared in the cracks caused by the heat – one had to know how to read them. Those bones, with those ideograms of 3500 years ago, are the first known Chinese 'manuscripts'.

Today the Chinese, especially those in the South-East Asian diaspora, still constantly interrogate their gods, for example by tossing up two pieces of wood shaped like large beans in order to receive counsel from heaven. If both pieces fall face up, the answer is yes, face down means no, one up and one down means try again.

The old fortune-teller's prophecy offered me a chance to learn about the different ways in which people seek this kind of advice, to explore new paths of knowledge, to look into the mysterious world of intuition and suggestion that so often beckons to us but is seldom taken seriously. My study of superstition was also a response to a changing Asia: I wanted to see what remained of that 'mysterious East' which has for centuries attracted so many Westerners. The newspapers say Asia is going through a period of boom, that the next century will be Asia's. This excites the bankers and financiers who see the world through the graphics on their highly sophisticated computers. But in reality Asia is not only a continent experiencing joyous economic growth: it is also killing itself by pursuing a model of development which it has not itself chosen, a model imposed upon it by the logic of profit which today seems inexorably to dominate all human behaviour.

Ancient cities are being bulldozed to make room for anonymous 'modern' developments; a whole popular culture is being pushed aside by the irresistible force of new models from abroad, spreading by satellite to the remotest hut in the Burmese jungle or on the Mongolian plain. A fearful wave of materialism is engulfing everything and everyone. Yet even among the young in Asia, as a reaction against this tendency and the immense disorientation it has produced, there is a revival of interest in the old beliefs, in the occult, in phenomena that have their roots in tradition.

Perhaps this is happening all over the world. Now that social groups are becoming increasingly fragmented and the natural world is ever more receding from people's daily lives, now that all problems are supposed to be solved by science alone, now that death is no longer lived chorally as it still was when I was a boy, but has become a taboo more and more excluded from life, people are more perplexed than ever about their destiny, and look for solace, understanding, friendship and hope wherever they can find it. That is why the East, with its aura of exoticism, has again become a source of inspiration for many young Western people, who look to Eastern religions and practices for the answers they no longer seem to find in schools or churches at home. More than the great philosophers of the home-grown variety, Oriental mysticism, Buddhism and Asian gurus seem to be able to help those who want to escape the prison of consumerism, the bombardments of advertising, the dictatorship of television. Western youth, coming from a super-organized world, where everything is guaranteed, where even their desires seem dictated by an interest which is not their own, is more and more interested in exploring Oriental paths of spirituality.

On various occasions while travelling in Asia I have seen European figures cloaked in the orange or purple robes of Buddhist monks, but I had never taken much interest in their stories. This year I had a reason to stop and listen; and thus I met, for example, a former journalist, like me a Florentine, who had taken the vows of a Tibetan monk, and a young Dutch poet who had chosen an austere life of meditation in a temple south of Bangkok. Both, in different ways, were victims of the disorientation of our time. It is certainly because of this disorientation that in European telephone directories the pages listing chiromancers, astrologers and seers are growing thicker and thicker. Their clientele is no longer limited to credulous ladies, to the gullible, the lonely or the ignorant; this was another discovery I made. In the course of the year I realized that my curiosity about this twilight world was shared by a huge number of people; people you would never suspect, people who would open up and tell their stories only when I admitted that I meant to take my prophecy seriously. It may be a platitude, but the problem of destiny, of good or evil fate and how to deal with it, sooner or later arises in everyone's mind.

The pages that follow are the story of this strange journey, of my year with my feet on the ground . . . or should I say less than ever on the ground? That would be nearer the mark, for never have I flown without wings as I did in those thirteen months. A year of thirteen months? Yes, but that will be the easiest of my explanations.

The conclusion? 'I never go to fortune-tellers. I like to be surprised by life,' was the sibylline reply of an elderly lady in Bangkok when I asked her how many times a month she consulted them.

In my case the surprises came precisely because I *did* go to a fortune-teller. His prophecy lent me a sort of third eye with which I saw things, people and places I would not otherwise have seen. It gave me an unforgettable year, which I began by sitting in a basket on an elephant's back in Laos and ended by sitting on a meditation cushion in a Buddhist retreat run by an ex–CIA agent.

His prophecy also – saved me from an air crash. On 20 March 1993 a UN helicopter in Cambodia went down, with fifteen journalists on board. Among them was the German colleague who had taken my place.

CHAPTER TWO

A Death that Failed

The occult and I had always had a cold and distant relationship. The reasons, as for so many other things, are rooted in my childhood. In fact the estrangement began very early.

They placed a small photograph of a soldier at the bottom of a bowl of water, then covered my head with a big towel and made me sit there in the dark, bent over the bowl, with my eyes fixed on the quivering half-length image under the water. All around me the women sat silently, waiting.

It was my grandmother's idea. She said an innocent soul had to be used, and apparently I fitted the bill. The séance took place in 1943 at our home in Monticelli, a working-class quarter of Florence. We had a neighbour called Palmira whose son had disappeared that winter in Russia during the retreat, and I was to discover if he was alive or dead, and try to see what he was doing at that moment.

I would have been glad to say I saw him eating at a table in a wooden hut with snow all around, but all I could make out was that sober, unsmiling face that fluttered with my every breath. The little black-and-white photo reminded me of others that I had seen on marble crosses in the Soffiano cemetery, but I didn't want to say that. The episode is one of the clearest images I retain from my childhood, and I well remember the disappointment when they took the towel off my head and poured the water away. Palmira retrieved her photo and dried it with a handkerchief. One of the women said that if the attempt had failed it might be because I had somehow lost my innocence – unlikely, as I was barely five years old at the time. But then, who knows? Perhaps it had succeeded after all: Palmira's son never did return from Russia.

Since that first experience, in the course of my life I have had no more than a normal, sceptical curiosity about the uncertain world beyond appearances; and instinctively I have always found some rational way to explain inexplicable things that sometimes took place before my eyes. Later, when I had children, I had more and more need of such explanations, because children constantly demand to 'understand'.

Once in Delhi, where I had brought the family to celebrate my fortieth birthday (being keen to plant a symbolic seed in India, and thereby announce, formally, my intention of going to live there one day), an old Sikh came up to Saskia and Folco. They were eight and nine years old at the time. 'If you like,' he said, 'I'll guess your grandfather's name.' Incredulous, they handed him a few rupees, whereupon he asked them several questions and, to their amazement, wrote the letter G on a piece of paper: my father's initial, his name being Gerardo. I was hard put to convince them that behind this, like so many other Indian 'miracles', from people buried alive to ropes standing on end, there must be a trick: they had probably suggested the letter somehow in their answers to his questions. But no! They were certain that at the very least the man had read their minds. Then a couple of years later, while we were on holiday in Thailand, we were all witnesses to an event where there was no question of a trick.

We were staying on the island of Phi Phi with Seni, a Thai journalist who was an old friend of ours, and his girlfriend Yin. Phi Phi was a tropical paradise with blue sea, white sand, and huts of bamboo and straw, until it too was invaded by electricity, fax machines and concrete hotels with swimming pools. We were about to get into a boat to go and see the great, mysterious caves where for centuries the local people have gathered one of the foods most prized by the Chinese, swallows' nests. Suddenly Yin realized that she had left her camera in their hut. 'Wait,' she said, 'I'll telephone Seni.' Telephone? There was no such thing on the island! Yin moved away, her head in her hands and her eyes closed, as if she were making a great effort of concentration. A few seconds later, Seni appeared in the far distance, like a little black dot running across the white sand. 'The camera! Yin, you forgot the camera!' Coincidence? Of course it was. No shadow of doubt crossed my mind.

Folco, on the other hand, was highly excited. The boat, the sea, the mysterious caves with towering bamboo poles which the local boys climbed to collect the precious nests, no longer interested him now that there was the possibility – for him proven – of telepathic communication. He spent the day 'doing exercises', and in the evening, before dinner, he told us he would direct his thoughts to his mother, who had had to go to Florence. 'What's she doing at this moment?' Saskia asked him. 'Sleeping,' he said. 'I see her sleeping, with a blue light all around her.' In Italy it was then early afternoon, there is no blue light in our house, and his mother never sleeps after lunch.

A week later, however, Angela came back from Florence and told us that on that particular day she had gone to Il Contadino, our country retreat in a village called Orsigna in the Tuscan Apennines. For once, right after lunch, she had taken a short nap in the children's room, the one with blue curtains. A paranormal son? More likely just a successful game.

Like everyone else, I had heard and read about prophecies that had come true, about people who could do incredible things – fly, levitate, see into the past or the future – but I had never given them much weight. If even one of them were true, I asked myself, how could we go on living normally? If fate is written in our palms, or in the stars, how can we go on catching buses, turning up at the office and paying the electricity bills? Should we not chuck the life we lead and devote ourselves utterly to the study of these phenomena? But people go about their business, trains run, the post arrives, newspapers appear daily. I told myself that the paranormal world is the invention of a few, that it is the product of the distorted imagination, an expression, like others, of man's need to believe in something beyond appearances; I need not bother about it. Thus for years I had lived in Asia without paying much attention to the occult side of things. I had visited temples and anchorites, I had heard all sorts of stories, but I had never allowed myself to be too impressed. Then, too, whenever I had occasion to check on one of those odd stories I always found something that seemed not to fit. Reality never quite squared with what I had been told.

In all my years in Asia I had never had my horoscope cast or consulted any of the numerous fortune-tellers, for whom I had always felt an instinctive distaste. When I was a boy, just after the war, gypsies would often stop at our house and ask to read my mother's palm. She would refuse and bolt the door, saying they were all thieves who would hypnotize us and carry off the little we had. Her outbursts obviously had an effect on me.

Nor had I wanted to go to that fateful fortune-teller in Hong Kong. We had just moved there from Singapore, and in the British colony we had found a very old Chinese friend from Shanghai, a fellow student in the 1960s at Columbia University in New York. His wife, a well known cinema director, was a granddaughter of the last warlord of Yunnan. Like all good Chinese she loved to gamble and was extremely superstitious. Once in a while she used to go to Macao and – like me – spend entire days playing blackjack, baccarat, and especially fan tan, that very simple but addictive game in which the croupier empties a bowlful of buttons onto the table and then slowly divides them into groups of four with an ivory chopstick. One has to guess the number of buttons that are left over at the end: none, one, two or three? The charm of the game is that you can follow it from on high, standing at a railing, and you place bets and collect your winnings by lowering and raising a little wicker basket on a string.

Every time she went to Macao, before taking the hovercraft my Chinese friend would go and consult her fortune-teller to find out whether those were auspicious days or not. 'He's one of the best in Hong Kong. He's someone you should get to know. Come along with me,' she said, finally overcoming my resistance.

The man lived in one of the many old tumbledown beehive-tenements of Wanchai. The doors of the flats were left wide open even at night to let in air, but they had big padlocked grilles to keep thieves out. We climbed several flights of stairs before arriving at a grille like all the others. I saw the red glow of a little altar on the floor, with a bowl of rice and some tangerines offered to the tutelary deities and ancestors. I recall a pleasant smell of incense. Behind an old iron desk sat a Chinese man of about seventy. He wore a sleeveless vest and his head was shaven like a monk's. His bony hands were resting on some old books and an abacus.

I stood to one side as the old man gave my friend the advice she sought. Then, pointing in my direction, he said in Cantonese, a dialect I did not understand, 'He's the one I'm interested in.' And I gave in.

First he measured the length of my forearm with a string, then he felt the bones of my forehead, asked me when I was born and at what time of day, made a few calculations on his abacus, looked into my eyes and began to speak. I was expecting the typical vague formulae used by fortune-tellers, which one can interpret at will, pull this way and that like a rubber band, and if one so desires always succeed (more or less) in squaring with reality. Had he said, 'You are married but there's another woman in your life,' I might have thought, 'Ah, perhaps that's the one he means.' Had he said, 'You have three children,' I could have enjoyed playing with the idea that besides Folco and Saskia I might have sown another somewhere in the world. But when my Chinese friend began translating I could not believe my ears: '*About a year ago you were about to die a violent death, and you saved yourself by smiling . . .*' Yes, that was true enough, but how could this old man I had never seen describe so exactly an episode which only I knew about, which even my Chinese friend had never heard mentioned before?

It had happened in Cambodia, exactly a year before. I had left the country a few days before the fall of Phnom Penh on 17 April, and in Bangkok, in that haven of peace and luxury that is the Oriental Hotel on the Chao Paya River, I was grinding my teeth at the thought of those friends and colleagues who had stayed put to see what was happening in Phnom Penh when the Khmer Rouge moved in. My not being there with them struck me as a terrible personal defeat, which I was not prepared to accept. I rented a car, drove to the Thai city of Aranyaprathet on the Cambodian border, and on the morning of 18 April I walked across the iron bridge that spans the frontier. What I had in mind was the crazy, stupid, reckless notion – proof of how little I then knew about the Khmer Rouge – that from there I would find a way of getting as far as Phnom Penh. And off I set along the road on foot.

I passed crowds of panic-stricken Cambodians racing in the opposite direction, cars crammed to overflowing with people and baggage, horns blaring. They were all terrified, all trying to escape to Thailand. One of them waved to me to turn back, but I took no notice. I had just reached the centre of Poipet when the Khmer Rouge, in single file, began entering the town. The government soldiers threw away their arms, took off their uniforms and fled. There was no resistance, no shooting. The first Khmer Rouge troops passed by as if they had not seen me, but a second group grabbed hold of me, turned their machine guns on me and shoved me up against a wall in the market square. Yelling something that sounded like 'CIA, CIA! American, American!' they prepared to shoot me.

Until then I had seen the Cambodian guerrillas only as corpses abandoned after a battle beside a road or a rice field. These were the first that I saw alive: young, fresh from the jungle, with dry, grey, dusty-looking skin and fierce eyes, red from malaria. 'CIA! American!' they kept shouting. I was sure they were going to shoot me. I thought it would be a quick and painless death, and worried only about how the news would reach my home, what suffering it would cause my family. Instinctively I reached into my shirt pocket and took out my passport. Smiling pleasantly, and speaking for some reason in Chinese, I said: 'I am Italian. Italian. Not American. Italian.'

From the cluster of spectators behind the guerrillas a man with pale, almost white skin – no doubt a local Chinese trader – stepped forward and translated into Khmer: 'I am a journalist, don't kill me . . . wait till a political cadre comes, let him decide . . . I'm Italian.' And I went on smiling, smiling, waving my passport. The Khmer Rouge lowered their guns and entrusted me to a very young guerrilla who scrutinized me curiously for hours. Now and then he would run the barrel of his big Chinese pistol around my face and over my nose, my eyes.

Towards sunset an older guerrilla arrived on the scene, evidently the leader. Without even looking at me he talked with his men for a few very long minutes, then turned to me and said in perfect French that I was welcome to liberated Cambodia, that these were historic days, the war was over and I was free to go.

Later that evening I was again between the beautiful cool linen sheets of the Oriental Hotel in Bangkok. 'If somebody aims a gun at you, smile,' I have told my children since. It seemed to me one of the few lessons in life I could give them.

But the encounter left me with something more than a 'lesson in life'. The real fear, as always, came later. For months I had nightmares; I often relived the scene in slow-motion, and not always with a happy ending. Obviously the experience had left its mark.

But how had the old Chinese fortune-teller, in his musty little Hong Kong flat, managed to see that mark? If I had been slashed with a knife or wounded by a bullet, my skin would have shown a scar that anybody's eye could have seen. But with what eye had he seen the scar that the Khmer Rouge had left inside me, not even I knew where? Was it mere coincidence? This time it really was hard to believe.

After looking into my past, the old man spoke of my relations with the five natural elements, fire, water, wood, metal and earth. 'You love wood,' he said. That is true: whenever I can I surround myself with wooden objects, and of all perfumes I like sandalwood best. 'You are happy if you live near water.' That is true: in Hong Kong we always had a view of the sea, and in Italy, at the country retreat in Orsigna, we hear the rushing of a mountain stream.

Then came the prophecy that was to rule my life for a year: '*Beware!*' said the old man: '*You run a grave risk of dying in 1993. You mustn't fly that year. Don't fly, not even once.*' He added, '*If you survive an air accident in that year, you'll live to be eighty-four.*'

There is no connection between the precise description of past events and the accurate prediction of the future, but obviously the one lends credibility to the other. For that reason, as I discovered later, almost all fortune-tellers use the same system, and thus I could not get the old man's words out of my head. His 'guess' about my past could not be accounted for by statistical probability. This story of a close encounter with death could not be brushed off as equally likely to be true or false for anyone who entered his little room in Wanchai. It was not like telling a woman 'You have children' or 'You have no children.' My experience in Poipet put me absolutely outside the range of the average.

And if in some way of his own the old man had hit on the truth, and could see backward to 1975, might he not perhaps also be able to see ahead to 1993?

Put that way, the question was not the sort that can easily be ignored; and the idea of spending a year looking for an answer attracted me immensely – especially in the few days leading up to that portentous deadline.

On 18 December 1992 I flew from Bangkok to Vientiane. On the twenty-second, on board a small, jolting Chinese-made plane, I arrived in Luang Prabang, the ancient royal capital of Laos.

CHAPTER THREE

On Which Shore Lies Happiness?

In one of the many fine passages in Hermann Hesse's *Siddhartha*, the prince – soon to become Buddha, the Enlightened One – is sitting on the riverbank. It strikes him that once the measurement of time is waived, the past and the future are ever-present – like the river, which at one and the same moment exists not only where he sees it to be, but also at its source and at its mouth. The water which has yet to pass is tomorrow, but it already exists upstream; and that which has passed is yesterday, but it still exists, elsewhere, downstream.

Sitting high on the Wat Pusi hill in Luang Prabang in the golden peace of sunset, I looked down at the heart-stirring confluence of the small, impetuous Nam Khan River and the broad, majestic Mekong, and thought of Siddhartha's vision. It seemed to me that that conjunction and mingling of muddy waters was, like life – mine included – made up of so many streams. It seemed that past, present and future were no longer distinguishable one from another: they were all there, in that relentless flow. Fifty-five years had slipped away like the great river rolling towards the China Sea; the rest of my time on earth was already welling up in the Himalayan slopes, already underway, moving towards me along the same channel, clearly defined and counted to the last hour. If I had had a higher perch than that hill I might have been able to see more of the river, in both directions. And thus could I have seen more past, more future?

I was alone, and as can happen when one is surrounded by nature, far from any other human presence, the mind slips free of the bonds of logic, and the imagination runs wild. The most absurd thoughts arise at the threshold of consciousness. Yes: perhaps what we call the future has already happened, and only because our view is limited do we fail to see it. Perhaps that is why some people can 'read' it as easily as we see the light of a star which has been extinct for centuries.

18

Perhaps the secret lies in breaking away from the dimension of time – time as we normally conceive it, made up of years, hours, seconds.

Laos was an ideal psychological preparation for my decision not to fly, and thus in a way to place myself outside time. As a country it has for years instinctively chosen to do just that. Without access to the sea, sheltered by impenetrable mountains that isolate it from China and Vietnam, protected by the Mekong which separates it from Thailand without a single bridge to link its two banks, Laos, despite wars, invasions and pressure from its neighbours, has continued in its ancient, detached rhythm of life. Though even there the calendar says one is in the twentieth century, the mind of the Laotian people remains in an epoch all their own, and they have no intention of leaving it.

In recent years the Thais have built superhighways leading to their bank of the Mekong, and have suggested to the Laotians in a thousand ways that just one bridge would enable them to link up with the Thai road system, giving them direct access to Bangkok and creating a point of easy access for tourists loaded with dollars. The Laotians have remained unconvinced. 'No, thanks. We don't need a bridge,' they have replied every time. 'We want to carry on living our own way.'

Sadly, however, that way of life is on the wane. Not because the Lao have suddenly changed their minds, but because in our day a country at the crossroads between modernization *cum* destruction and an isolation that would preserve its identity has no real choice: others have chosen on its behalf. Businessmen, bankers, experts from international organizations, officials of the UN and half the world's governments are passionate prophets of 'development' at all costs. They believe unanimously in a kind of mission not far removed from that of the American general in Vietnam who, after razing a Vietcong-occupied village to the ground, said proudly: 'We had to destroy it to save it.'

The same thing is happening to Laos: in order to save it from underdevelopment, the new missionaries of materialism and economic progress are destroying it. The hardest blow has been dealt by the Australians. With the kindest intentions, their government has built a fine big bridge over the Mekong River. It has cost the Laotians nothing – except their last virginity. With their innate suspicion of everything new and modern, they are already calling it 'the Bridge of AIDS'.

At heart the Lao belong to the past, and it is only by the accident of being located in the middle of Indochina that they have been forced to live amidst the violence of the contemporary world. They have paid a very high price for it. To supply the Vietcong guerrillas in South Vietnam, the Hanoi Communists opened through the forests of Laos what became famous as 'the Ho Chi Minh Trail'; and to close that path, between 1964 and 1973 the Americans 'secretly' dropped more bombs on Laos than fell on Germany and the whole of occupied Europe during the Second World War: two million tons of explosive.

Even now, in peacetime, Laos is prevented by its geographical position from living the life it desires. It is forced to become 'modern', to serve as a link between China and Thailand, a corridor between two powerful neighbours obsessed with the idea of progress.

Still, for the moment, one need only set foot in Laos to feel that there is something uniquely poetic in the air. The days are long and slow, and the people have a tranquil sweetness that is not found elsewhere in Indochina. The French, who well knew the peoples they ruled, used to say: 'The Vietnamese plant rice, the Khmer stand there and watch, and the Laotians listen to it growing.'

I set foot in Laos for the first time in the spring of 1972. On a small balcony of the Hotel Constellation in Vientiane a blonde hippie girl was smoking a marijuana joint so strong you could smell it all the way up the stairs. Seeing me approach, she whispered to me, as if to confide a secret formula for understanding all things, 'Remember, Laos is not a place; it is a state of mind.'

Indeed, I never forgot it, and twenty years later I wanted to see Laos again before it too became 'a place' – a place like all the others, lit by neon, full of plastic and cement. I found a journalistic excuse in two news items: one on the opening of the Ho Chi Minh Trail to tourism, the other on the construction of the great trans-Asian motorway from Singapore to Peking. The Laotian section, after the building of the Mekong bridge, was to run through the old royal capital, Luang Prabang, cutting in two one of the most peaceful and romantic places in Asia, one of the last refuges of the old charm of the Orient.

I found Luang Prabang as fascinating as I remembered it, huddled in its moist green valley, surrounded by peaks that seem painted by a Chinese brush, dominated by the hill of Wat Pusi from which the temples, built in artful disorder on the strip of land between the Mekong and the Nam Khan, shine with a seemingly eternal splendour.

At dawn I saw once more the moving spectacle of hundreds of monks as they issued from their monasteries and filed along the cobbled main street to receive offerings of food from the population kneeling on the pavements. Yes, that very street: the one destined to become part of the Asian superhighway. Fortunately, I learned, some old residents had found the courage to oppose the project, and the governor himself had pronounced in favour of an alternative route. Will Luang Prabang be saved, then? Not at all. Another plan, opposed by no one, will transform the present modest landing strip into a large airport capable of receiving jumbo jets full of tourists.

What an ugly invention is tourism! One of the most baleful of all industries! It has reduced the world to a vast playground, a Disneyland without borders. Soon thousands of these new invaders, soldiers of the empire of consumerism, will land, and with their insatiable cameras and camcorders they will scrape away the last of that natural magic which is still everywhere in this country.

In Asia, when an old man sees a camera pointed at him, he turns away and tries to hide himself, covering his face. He believes the camera will deprive him of something that is his, something precious which he will never recover. And is he not perhaps right? Is it not through the wear and tear of tens of thousands of snapshots taken by distracted tourists that our churches have lost their sanctity and our monuments their patina of greatness?

Tibet, to protect its spirituality, for centuries forbade anyone to cross its borders; that is how it preserved its very special aura. There it was the Chinese invasion that broke the spell; in the name of modernization, of course. One of the most disturbing bits of news I have read in recent years is that the Chinese, to facilitate (what else?) tourist access, have decided to 'modernize' the lighting of the Potala, the Dalai Lama's palace-temple, and have installed neon lights. This is no accident: neon kills everything, even the gods. And as they die, the Tibetan identity gradually dies with them.

The great Japanese writer Junichiro Tanizaki, in a particularly moving passage about the disappearance of the old Japan that has been swept away by modernity, eulogizes the shadows that contributed so greatly to creating the atmosphere, and thereby the soul, of the traditional houses of wood and paper. The dim interior of the Potala served the same purpose: you had to penetrate the recesses of that extraordinary palace in penumbra, and only by degrees did you discern, by the flickering light of butter lamps, the grimaces of the ogres and the benign smiles of the Buddhas. Neon holds nothing back. It clips the wings of anyone who still yearns to let his spirit take flight.

At the beginning of this century Pierre Loti arrived with the trepidation of a pilgrim at Angkor, in Cambodia, on a cart pulled by black oxen, to ask hospitality of the monks who lived in the temples. Twenty years later Cook's Travel Agency were organizing tours and dance shows by night amid the ruins, and selling centuries-old stones to tourists as souvenirs.

The man who in 1860 'discovered' Angkor for humanity – and for tourists – paid for that conquest with his life. Few know that his grave is still there, east of Luang Prabang. I wanted to go and pay my respects to that adventurous scientist, whose story had always fascinated me. His name is Henri Mouhot. He was a French naturalist who travelled in Indochina when it had just become a colony. His plan was to go up the Mekong to China. Before setting out he had read an account written ten years earlier by a monk who had seen strange ruins in the jungle not far from the town of Siem Reap.

In a letter Mouhot tells how one day he was walking through the forest, humming *La Traviata* to keep himself company, when suddenly, amid thick foliage under gigantic trees, he felt himself observed by two . . . four . . . ten . . . a hundred stone eyes, all smiling at him. I have often tried to imagine what he felt at that moment, a moment that made his journey and his death worthwhile. After spending some time amid the ruins of Angkor, Mouhot resumed his walk northward. He passed through Luang Prabang, but while he was marching along the Nam Khan River, beyond the village of Naphao, he fell ill. On 19 October he wrote, 'I am stricken by a fever.' Then for some days there are no entries in his diary, till on the twenty-ninth we come to the last words, written in a shaky hand: 'My Lord, have mercy on me.' Mouhot died on 10 November 1861. He was thirty-five years old.

Going to visit him was a much simpler matter: it took half an hour by car from Luang Prabang towards Ban Noun, then about ten minutes on foot down an escarpment, and up an overgrown path. When I reached the grave I felt as if Mouhot were dying at that very moment. Nothing had changed. The river ran with the same quiet murmur, the forest whispered with the same thousand voices, and in the distance a solitary woman was walking with a wicker basket on her shoulders – a woman of today, but also a woman of then, over 130 years ago.

The grave is where Mouhot died, in a fold of the hillside about thirty yards above the bed of the Nam Khan, as if his companions had wished to make sure the current would not carry him away. There is a mound of cement, behind which a great tree stands guard. To the left, waving like a banner, is a tall, joyous tuft of green bamboo.

The Italian poet Ugo Foscolo was right, in his poem in praise of tombs. They are a great inspiration, and I have always felt attracted by these simple, touching traces of life left by Westerners as they travelled the world. How many hours I have spent in Asian cemeteries for the foreign dead – in Macao, Chiang Mai, Nagasaki, Yokohama – trying to feel my way into the lives of these people who died far from home, trying to retrace the stories locked within the few formal words carved in stone. Ships' captains struck down by fever when barely in their twenties, young mothers who died in childbirth, sailors from one ship who succumbed in the space of a few days, obviously to a sudden epidemic. Sometimes an old man, mourned by children and grandchildren, whose life – so the epitaph says – was an example to many others. Adventurers, missionaries, traders: unknown names.

What is the strange fascination of tombs? Can it be that they really hold something more than bones? Perhaps with the memory of the dead there also remains some stamp of their presence. Perhaps the stone itself is imbued with their history. The grave of Mouhot, a silent, solitary presence, forgotten on the bank of the Nam Khan, truly seemed to speak. The mere fact of my going there had somehow given it life. Or was it that without the dimension of time, this past was always there, present for anyone willing to be moved, to be inspired?

I had chosen Laos as my last destination of 1992 because it was a place from which, if I decided not to fly, I knew I could easily return overland to Bangkok. From the first moment my visit was marked by curious new thoughts. The fact that in some way I had begun looking into the less usual side of experience made me notice all sorts of things that would have escaped me at other times. Suddenly, everything appeared to have a link with the other world; people whose acceptable social faces were all I normally saw now revealed a second nature, and moreover, one that was much more in tune with what interested me.

On my last day in Luang Prabang I took a boat up the Mekong to the caves of Tham Ting with their seven thousand Buddhas. During the war these famous caves in the steep mountainside high above the river had come under fire from the Pathet Lao, the Communist guerrillas who controlled the whole surrounding area, and I had never succeeded in getting there. By now many of the old statues had been stolen and sold to Bangkok antique dealers, but I wanted to go there nonetheless. Was my future not symbolically flowing down the Mekong towards me? I wanted to go and meet it.

In the main cave a group of Laotians were kneeling before a stone Buddha, enquiring about their future. I did the same. The process is simple. Slowly, with hands joined, you shake a boxful of little bamboo sticks until one of them falls to the ground. Each stick bears a number corresponding to a slip of paper with a message. Mine was eleven, and the message was:

> *Shoot your arrow at the giant Ku Pan. You will certainly kill him. Soon you will have no more enemies and your name will be known in every corner of the earth. Your people need you and you must continue to help them. If you go in for business you will lose every penny. You will have no illnesses. Travel is a very good thing for you.*

I did not think much of this, but later, when I pulled the little scrap of paper out of my pocket during the Christmas dinner at the French embassy in Vientiane, it was like the spark that ignites a great blaze. Soon, around that very formal table served by silent waiters in livery, the talk was all about fortune-tellers, prophecies and magic. Everyone had a story, an experience to tell. Perhaps because we were dining by candlelight, in a great white house surrounded by bougainvillaea and orchids, nestling in a mysterious garden populated with old statues of explorers – or perhaps because Europe and its logic seemed further away than ever – it was as if my slip of paper had opened a Pandora's box and this were an hour of unwonted confessions.

'A fortune-teller really changed my life,' said a beautiful, elegant woman of around forty, recently arrived from Paris, who sat opposite me. While still at university she had become pregnant by a fellow student, who had died immediately afterwards in a skiing accident. A common friend had stayed by her side, and a great love had developed between them. But one day this friend's mother had been to a fortune-teller who had said, 'Your son is about to become the father of a child which is not his, and he must absolutely not do it. It would ruin his life.' When the mother told her son this he was so shocked that he called off the wedding. 'And that,' said a gentleman sitting to the right of the ambassador's wife, 'is how I became the father of that child.'

This sounded to me like a typical case: the mother had somehow got the fortune-teller to say what she herself could not say to her son, and thus, through the authority of the occult, obtained the result she wanted. But the other diners were rather impressed, and the woman herself was totally convinced of the fortune-teller's powers. As for my fortune-teller in Hong Kong, everyone agreed that I must heed his warning and refrain from flying.

At dawn I left, by air, for the Plain of Jars, a strange valley amid the mountains of northern Laos, which is scattered with huge, mysterious stone vessels, some over seven feet high, all beautifully carved. But by whom? To hold what? Anthropologists say they were funerary urns of an ancient population of Chinese origin, now extinct, but the Laotians prefer to believe their legends. 'They are amphoras for wine,' they say. 'The giants made them. At the top of the mountain there is an enormous stone table where, from time to time, the giants meet for their banquets.' But no one had ever managed to reach it.

I spent three days in the region. The ripe opium poppies were beginning to shed their red, purple and white petals, and women were cutting open the bulbs to collect the precious sticky black juice in old bowls. The Muong, the mountain people, were celebrating their New Year. Young people were at their most popular sport: playing ball as a way of finding a mate. In each village rows of girls in traditional dress stand for hours on end opposite rows of boys and throw cloth balls back and forth while chanting an old ditty: 'If you love me, throw better. If you want me, improve your looks.'

I was accompanied by a very special guide, Claude Vincent, a cultivated Frenchman of about fifty who had lived in Laos since he was a boy. He had married a Laotian woman, and remained in the country even after the Pathet Lao seized power in 1975. In the years of the war we had often met, but had never known each other well; for him I was one of the many journalist-vultures who descended on Laos, attracted by its dead. Now it was different, and Claude wanted to make me understand his love for a land to whose ancient, beautiful soul he is fervently attached.

I realized this when, tired after an afternoon exploring the Plain of Jars, we retired for the night to an inn without electricity or water. We talked about the Communists: wherever they went, in China as in Cambodia, the first thing they did was to abolish the popular traditions. They fought against superstition, eliminated fortune-tellers and banned the old ceremonies. I asked Claude how the Pathet Lao had behaved. In reply he told me about something that had happened to him a few years before.

It was a Sunday in 1985 in Vientiane, and Claude and his family planned to have a picnic on the bank of the Mekong. One of his nieces was very excited about the trip, but she went down with a high fever and they decided to leave her at home. She was terribly upset and insisted that she *must*, absolutely *must* go to the river. Not to take her was out of the question.

They found a place on the bank, the adults eating and the children playing by the water. Only when it was time to go did they realize that the little girl was no longer there. They searched for her everywhere, but she had vanished. In desperation they consulted a famous clairvoyante, who went into a trance and told them: 'Next Friday, at 3.45 in the afternoon, go to the bend in the river. There, in front of the pagoda, you'll find her. She will have blue marks on her body: one under her arm and one on her chest.' The family went, and at the appointed hour the child's body floated to the surface, bearing the blue marks described by the woman.

Claude told me that the clairvoyante had made contact with the Spirit of the River and asked it to yield up the child's body in return for the sacrifice of seven chickens and a pig. The family's problem

Martyrs', and annual ceremonies would be held in their memory. Their story would be taught in schools. For the Laotians history does not bear this kind of meaning. In that hole are not the remains of their relatives, but only ghosts that have saturated the walls with wailing, suffering, horror. From this they must simply keep away.

In their vision of the world the relation between cause and effect is not the same as in ours. Shortly before my visit, near the Plain of Jars, a group of American experts had spent some weeks looking for MIAs (Missing in Action), pilots of planes shot down during the war whose deaths had never been verified. They dug in the jungle, sifting the earth to retrieve the least splinter of bone, and spent their evenings in Phongsovane. The Laotians did not show the least hostility towards them. Nobody even tried to show them one of the many children who even today are born deformed because of the chemicals released there by the Americans a quarter of a century ago.

The wife of the photographer of Phonsovane held one of these in her arms – a three-year-old child with a large square head and stubby hands with the fingers all stuck together. 'Karma,' she said, Buddhistically attributing the horror of that child to some sin committed in his previous life.

To go from Xianhuang to Pakse' in southern Laos I had to take another plane: the usual bouncing Chinese-made Y-21 with a pilot, a co-pilot, seventeen seats and a baggage compartment where the only toilet was. When I boarded the plane it was crammed full of mysterious floppy blue plastic sacks: they were in the aisle, on the empty seats, stacked to the ceiling in the baggage-toilet, piled against the emergency exit. I tried to lift one: very heavy. They were full of meat – pork and beef. In Vientiane meat costs twice as much as in the Plain of Jars, and thus it was that the pilots supplemented their meagre socialist wages. I remembered how, a few weeks earlier, in an airfield in the north, a Russian Antonov, just back from an engine overhaul, had been unable to take off and had caught fire. All the passengers had saved themselves by climbing out in time.

I wondered how anyone could get out of this plane, as every escape route was blocked by those heaps of flaccid bundles. I disliked the thought that if disaster struck, my flesh would be mixed with the meat in the sacks and nobody would be able to tell who had been who. But then I thought with relief of the Americans. I had heard that in the labs in Hawaii where they send what they find in their search for the MIAs, the Americans can determine whether a bone fragment belonged to one of their soldiers or not.

The sky grew dense and grey, and we threaded through heavy rainclouds and flashes of lightning among the steep, dark green mountains. The landscape had an extraordinary primitive beauty, but I could not enjoy it. Between one bounce and another I vowed that if this plane ever landed in Savannaket, where it was due for a stop-over, I would get off and continue my journey by boat. And so I did.

The Mekong was flat and undramatic, its opaque surface broken now and then by great bubbles of mud. We glided slowly between the two banks that summed up the contradiction I would have liked to resolve: on the left the Laotian shore with villages shaded by coconut palms, dinghies moored below rough bamboo ladders, oil lamps gleaming softly in the silence of evening; on the right, the Thai shore with neon lights, canned music and the distant rumble of motors. On one side the past, from which everyone wants to tear the Laotians away, on the other the future towards which all and sundry believe they must rush headlong. On which shore lies happiness?

On 31 December I was in the forest of Bolovens, on a high plateau three thousand feet above sea level, with the Mekong to the west, the Annamite range to the east, and the Khmer plain to the south. This was the most heavily bombed region in the history of the world, because it was the assembly point for all the supplies coming from Hanoi along the Ho Chi Minh Trail before they were redirected, either towards Cambodia in the direction of Saigon or towards central Vietnam. Not one building has remained standing from the colonial period, not one pagoda, not one village. Everything was demolished in the relentless earthquake of American bombs. Nature itself has been obliterated: the forest has become a scrubland, and even today you seldom hear a bird's call. Only here and there on the fertile red earth have some Japanese and Thai companies begun to revive the famous coffee plantations.

I stayed in a wooden hut built over a waterfall. The roar of the water was deafening, and I spent New Year's Eve pleasantly awake, imagining the strange 1993 that had reached its birth-hour. An omelette of red ants' eggs seemed perfectly suited to marking the occasion. By the time the hands of my watch casually swung past midnight, the decision not to fly had turned into an obvious one. With that slow, ancient descent by boat along the Mekong my days had already acquired a new rhythm. And yet I felt as if I were doing something bold, almost illicit. After a lifetime of sensible decisions, I now allowed myself a choice based on the most irrational of considerations. The limitation I was imposing on myself made no sense at all.

On the morning of 1 January 1993, to give my decision a symbolic flourish, I took my first steps of the new year on the back of an elephant. The route to Pakse' crossed a valley which long ago had been the crater of a volcano. The grass was tall and very green, punctuated here and there by brilliant silvery plumes of the *lulan* that barely stirred in the wind.

The elephant basket was shaky and uncomfortable, but its height gave me a perfect opportunity to enjoy the world from a different perspective.

CHAPTER FOUR

The Body-Snatchers of Bangkok

The car waiting for me in Takeck, on the Thai frontier post opposite Pakse', was like a time machine. It picked me up at the edge of ancient Laos, remote and still virginal, and in a few hours brought me back to the vulgar modernity of Bangkok – dirty, chaotic, stinking, where the water is polluted and the air lead-poisoned, where one person in five has no proper home, one in sixty, including newborns, is HIV positive, one woman in thirty works as a prostitute, and someone commits suicide every hour.

They call it 'the City of Angels', and perhaps it was once. The houses were built on piles, the streets were canals and the people went about by boat. The few streets on *terra firma* were lined with tall trees whose branches made tunnels of cool shade over the little traffic there was. The gilded spires of the pagodas soared above the houses and the palaces, even that of the king, who at the beginning of the century had called in an Italian architect to build him a throne hall.

Bangkok has never been a beautiful city, but it used to have charm; it was exotic. Sometimes the tropical heat was suffocating, but often a light breeze wafted in from the sea and up the Chao Paya River to blow unobstructed over the houses.

Among the flesh-and-blood human beings involved in the countless wheeler-dealings of a city that has long been known for its luxurious vices and its unsolved mysteries lived many other beings: invisible ones, born of the imagination, of the people's love and fear. Like the other peoples of the region, the Thais call these beings *phii*, spirits.

To propitiate the *phii* and keep them quiet so they would not bother ordinary mortals, shrines were erected in their honour in every corner of the city, in every street, in front of every house. The

32

people were assiduous in leaving them food, little wooden elephants, plaster figurines of dancing girls, a glass of alcohol, cakes, sweet-scented garlands of jasmine.

Whenever they laid the foundations of a new house or dug a well, they immediately built a little altar to the Earth Spirit to apologize for the disturbance caused, and begged its protection in times to come. These apologies and prayers were regularly renewed with fresh offerings. If the felling of a tree proved unavoidable, its *phii* ceremoniously received a request for the use of a saw against it.

The *phii* of the plot of land where the old Erawan Hotel was built was so happy with the way it had been treated that it took to performing miracles, and today its temple is still one of the most frequented and most popular in Bangkok. One of its specialities is to aid the conception of male offspring, and thousands of sterile women have come to it with all sorts of offerings; some dance around it semi-nude at night.

In the course of the past ten years Bangkok has been overwhelmed by the craving for modernity, and gigantic building works have turned the entire city upside down: the canals have been covered over and transformed into asphalted roads; magnificent century-old trees have been felled; entire streets of old houses have been swept away by bulldozers, and dozens of skyscrapers, with their deep-set steel and cement foundations, have been erected in their place. The earth has been opened, turned over, drilled, pulverized, and although here and there someone has taken the trouble to apologize to the *phii*, the disturbance has been so tremendous that many of them are very angry. The city is now swarming with these invisible presences, which take their revenge by driving people mad and causing frightful disasters. At least, that is what the old residents of Bangkok believe.

In September 1990, barely a week after we had arrived in Bangkok, a tanker full of liquid gas overturned right in the middle of the city, not far from where we lived. A cloud of death enveloped dozens of cars and houses, a spark set off an explosion, and more than a hundred people were burnt to a cinder.

A few months later, in the early afternoon, we heard a deafening roar and saw a dense, black cloud rise sky-high in the port district. A chemical depot had exploded, killing dozens of people. It is still not known what chemical products were involved, but since then more than two thousand people who found themselves in that pestilent cloud have suffered from inexplicable skin diseases and difficulty in breathing. Many children have been born deformed.

Disasters came one after another. One of the most dramatic was a fire in a doll factory where 190 girl workers were burned alive. To prevent the possibility of theft the management had padlocked every exit, and the girls were trapped.

Bangkok now lives under a malign spell, a city bewitched by the evil eye. People say it is too built up, that from the weight of all the skyscrapers it is sinking several inches every year, and will soon be swallowed up by the sea. Already it is hotter, because the cool coastal breeze of past years is blocked by new buildings. And there is a water shortage. But what is it that most worries the politicians and the leader writers of the local papers? That the poor have nothing to drink? No. Rather that the 'massage parlours' – as brothels in Thailand are coyly termed – lack sufficient water to wash the private parts of their numerous customers.

For every disaster there is an immediate, obvious, rational explanation: gas explodes because the safety regulations are not observed; factories are firetraps because instead of paying for proper fireproofing the bosses prefer to pay bribes to the officials who are supposed to check that the laws are obeyed. And yet it is the *phii* explanation that rings truest, because it sums up the essence of what is happening not only in Bangkok but in many other parts of the world: nature is taking revenge on those who fail to respect her, and who, out of pure greed, destroy every kind of harmony.

In Bangkok, we moved into the most beautiful and enchanted house we have ever lived in, an oasis of old Siam amid the horror of so much cement. Yet it had no altar in which to house the spirit of the place.

'Here the spirit is very much alive, and you really must feed it every day,' we were told by the American writer Bill Warren, the previous tenant. The 'spirit' was an enormous meat-eating turtle, almost three feet across, that lived in the pond on which the house is built.

I was happy: the house was on water, as the Hong Kong fortune-teller had recommended, and the turtle, for one like me who has lived so long among the Chinese, is the symbolic quintessence of a positive force. Legend has it that a turtle can live for centuries, which is why the Chinese have always erected steles bearing imperial edicts

34

on the backs of great stone or marble turtles. And in the Chinese tradition the turtle has another great merit: it is the symbol of the cosmos. The lower part of the shell is a square, the earth; the upper part is a sphere, the heavens. The turtle has always been used in divination because, enclosing this totality, it holds the key to time and space, and thus can understand the past and read the future.

Our turtle was another victim of progress. It had lived for heaven knows how many years in the city's canal system; then, when the canals were cemented over, and the water that formerly ran past and under the house became a stagnant pond, it remained there, trapped.

On our arrival the turtle decided to hide, and even though we rebaptized the place 'Turtle House' in its honour, it continued to make itself scarce. We knew it was around somewhere, because now and then one of our ducklings would disappear, but it did not seem to feel at ease with us. Similarly the people who worked at Turtle House; they began complaining of one ailment after another: the gardener coughed nonstop, the cook could not stand on her feet, and my secretary had a constant headache. Some of their relatives had road accidents; two died. Clearly our arrival had thrown the order of things out of kilter, and we had to find a way to restore harmony.

Some Thai friends suggested that Angela and I should present ourselves to the Emerald Buddha, the *phii* of all the *phii* of Bangkok, and announce to him that we had arrived in Thailand and would like to stay there for a few years; others advised us to have Turtle House exorcized to rid it of all possible negative influences.

We did not think twice: one morning we went to Wat Prakeo, the big temple on the river in front of the Royal Palace, to prostrate ourselves before the famous statue of Buddha; and on 9 April, Angela's birthday, we had nine monks come to the house. In their hands they held a very long white thread with which one of them encircled the house and the pond, then they sang some beautiful litanies, sprinkled holy water over everyone and everything, and ate before noon, as is required of them, the vegetarian food we had prepared.

After that, and after a swarm of wild bees had come and built an enormous honeycomb on a tree in the garden – a symbol of great good luck for the house – all troubles ceased.

★   ★   ★

But now I was facing a difficult year. I had assumed that even if I could move only very slowly, I would be able to get around by boat. I could not have been more wrong.

Bangkok is a port: hundreds of ships dock there every day, and several times a week the local newspapers publish a thick supplement listing the names and destinations of all the vessels and the times at which they load cargo. We began telephoning around for information about sailings to the Philippines, Vietnam, Hong Kong and Singapore. We may as well have been asking for the moon. I talked with chief clerks, chairmen and managing directors. No use. The politest would say, 'No, not us. But try another line.' Or, 'Yes, we used to carry passengers, but now . . .' Impossible. Ships no longer transport anything but goods, preferably sealed in containers which are loaded and unloaded automatically by computer-operated cranes.

To stave off the temptation to give up the whole project I began telling everyone about the Hong Kong fortune-teller and my decision not to fly for a year. This reinforced my commitment, but above all I attracted the sympathy of various Thai friends who suddenly felt 'understood'. The fact that I had taken a Chinese fortune-teller's prophecy seriously meant that I had entered into their logic, that I had accepted the culture of Asia. This flattered them, and they declared their willingness to help me, even if only with suggestions and advice. One of the most commonly repeated was: 'Don't worry. Try to acquire some merits!'

The underlying idea of acquiring merits is that fate is not ineluctable: a fortune-teller's predictions must be taken as a warning, or as indicating a tendency, but never as a sentence without appeal. Suppose a fortune-teller sees that you are about to fall gravely ill? Or that someone in your family will soon die? No need to despair. Make offerings in a temple, help an unfortunate, free some caged animals, adopt an orphan, pay for the construction of a *stupa* or donate a coffin to a poor man, and you will deflect what is otherwise coming for you. Obviously one must be guided by a professional in the choice of the quality, quantity and object of the merits to be acquired, but having done this, one's destiny has to be examined anew, or rather, it is returned to the hands of the person concerned. Fate is negotiable; you can always come to an agreement with heaven.

Despite all the advice I was given, it was difficult to get an answer to the simple question: 'Who is the best fortune-teller in Bangkok?'

I had the impression that everyone wanted to keep his favourite to himself. And then too, they are all convinced that the best fortune-tellers are to be found not among themselves but somewhere else. The Thais say the best are in Cambodia, the Cambodians say India, the Chinese that nobody can equal the Mongols, the Mongols believe only in the Tibetans, and so on. It is as if each one, conscious of the relativity that surrounds him, wants to preserve the hope that the absolute exists elsewhere. 'Ah, if only I could go to that fortune-teller in Ulan Bator!' a Javanese will say, thus keeping alive the hope that in some other place the key to his happiness can surely be found.

My case was simpler: I was in Bangkok and I wanted to see a fortune-teller there. I wanted to begin my flightless year by recon-firming my fate, by having my future read again. After all, since my encounter with the Hong Kong fortune-teller I had consulted none other.

Since none of my Thai acquaintances was able to recommend a fortune-teller, my friend Sulak Sivaraksa came to mind. He is Thai-land's leading philosopher, twice nominated for the Nobel Peace Prize. A convinced Buddhist, he has been a persistent critic of the way his country is abandoning its traditions, and he never misses a chance of attacking those he believes have strayed from the traditional Buddhist path. The Thai establishment does not care for him, and because of his outspokenness he has been accused of *lèse-majesté*, a crime that no longer exists elsewhere, and has spent some time in prison. The last time they arrested him I went to see his wife, thinking she would be distraught. Not at all! She had consulted a fortune-teller who had assured her that in a few days Sulak would be released. That is just what happened: the fellow had named the day and the hour. I decided to consult him.

I knew where he lived, and that he was blind. I needed an interpreter, but I did not want to take my secretary or anyone who knew anything about me: he or she might, even if unconsciously, give the fortune-teller a clue as to my trade or my family. So I telephoned an agency that provides secretaries for visiting businessmen. Pretending to be a guest at the Oriental Hotel, I made an appointment to meet my escort in the hotel lobby. The woman who arrived was about fifty, plump, with big glasses. She was delighted at the idea of not having to translate clauses of contracts and conversations about buying and selling.

The fortune-teller lived in the heart of Chinatown, and the Oriental Hotel's cream-coloured limousine, with a driver in white gold-braided livery, crept at a snail's pace into the marvellous, chaotic Vorachak quarter which is still one of the noisiest and liveliest parts of Bangkok – still unchanged, thank God, with its thousands of shops selling hardware, pumps, curtains, nails, coffins, sweets; with its myriad smells of incense wafting from little altars at the back of every hole in the wall, or balsam from the pharmacies; with the usual teeming crowds of overseas Chinese in their black shorts, immutable with white undershirts pulled up over their bellies, as if to air the navel and to stimulate the *qi* – the vital force – which, according to them, has its true centre there.

The fortune-teller lived at the far end of a tangle of little streets reachable only by foot. Finally we found his house. But it was not a house, exactly: through a big iron grille that opened on to the street we entered a large room that doubled as shop and home, where goods and gods cohabited. On one side, among the sacks of rice, was an old iron desk. Behind it, on a cane chair, was a blind man. More perching than sitting, he was massaging his feet, as the Chinese do, convinced that the bodily organs, from the heart to the lungs, the intestines to the liver, are controlled from there; it is enough to know the right points to touch. His eyes were blank. Where the pupils should have been were white spots that seemed always turned skywards. On the desk was a small teapot, a dish of tangerines – a symbol of prosperity – and an empty turtle-shell. The room was filled with a strong smell of incense from a large altar in one corner, full of statuettes made of gilded wood and representing gods and ancestors, the dead not as they were in life, but as they would have liked to have been. This is a curious tradition among the southern Chinese. An uncle failed the Imperial examination? Never mind: after death he is represented as a mandarin. Another had dreamed of being a policeman? After death he appears on the ancestral altar in uniform, with a rifle slung over his shoulder. Many of the fortune-teller's statuettes held raised swords, as if to protect him in his blindness. An old woman in green silk pyjamas, perhaps his wife, had just finished eating at a round table. She put wicker covers on the pots with the remains of her meal and sat down on a stool at the sink and began washing up.

Slowly, as if he did not want to hurry our relationship, the blind man began whispering something. My assistant translated. It was the usual question, to which I gave the usual reply: 'I was born in Florence, Italy, on 14 September 1938, at about eight in the evening.'

He seemed satisfied, and began performing some strange calculations with his fingers in the air. His sightless eyes, still raised to heaven, brightened as if he had a great secret with which to capture my attention. His lips whispered a sort of nonsense rhyme, but he said nothing intelligible. A Chinese girl in white pyjamas ran in, handed something to his wife and dashed off, first joining her hands over her bosom in salutation to all the impassive ones on the altar. An old clock on the wall ticked for long minutes. I had the impression that the blind man was searching for something in his memory, and had found it.

At long last his mouth opened. '*The day you were born was a Wednesday!*' he announced, as if he expected to surprise me. (Right. Bravo! A few years ago he might have impressed many people with that calculation, done entirely by memory. Now it seemed much less impressive. My computer does the same thing in a few seconds.) His satisfaction was touching, but I was disappointed and my interest flagged. I listened to him absent-mindedly. '*You have a good life, a healthy body and a lively mind, but a very bad character,*' he said. '*You are capable of great anger, but you are also able to calm down quickly.*' Generalities, likely to be true for anyone sitting before him, I thought. '*Your mind is never still, you are always thinking about something, which is not good. You are very generous to others.*' Again, true for almost anyone, I told myself.

I had placed a small tape recorder on the table, and took notes as well, but I suspected I was wasting my time. Then I heard the woman translate: '*When you were a child you were very ill, and if your parents had not given you away to another family you would not have survived.*' My curiosity revived: true, as a small child I was not very healthy. We were poor, it was wartime and we had little to eat; I had lung trouble, anaemia, swollen glands. '*From the age of seven to twelve you did well at school, but you were often ill and you moved house. From seventeen to twenty-seven you had to study and work at the same time. You have a very good brain, capable of solving various problems, and now you have no worries because you studied engineering. From the age of twenty-four to twenty-nine you went through the most unhappy period of your life. Then everything went better.*'

It is true that as a child I was often ill, but not that I began working at seventeen. It is not true that we moved house, but the years between twenty-four and twenty-nine were the most unhappy of my life: I had a job with Olivetti, and thought of nothing but getting away, but did not know how. As for engineering, I studied law.

I was not impressed: it looked like a typical case, where the fortune-teller's pronouncements have a fifty-fifty chance of being true. My mind wandered. I looked at his hands, which were caressing the turtle-shell on the desk. I heard his continuous whispered calculations, like a computer sifting its memory. Obviously he was mentally shuffling cards. But perhaps his real strength was instinct. Being blind, not distracted by the sight of all the things that distracted me, perhaps he was able to concentrate, to sense the person he had before him. Perhaps his instinct told him that my attention was wandering, because he suddenly broke off the singsong recital.

'*I've bad news for you,*' he said. For an instant I was worried. Was he going to warn me about flying? '*You'll never be rich. You'll always have enough money to live, but never will you become rich. That is certain,*' he declared.

I almost laughed. Here we were, in the middle of the Chinese city where everyone's dream is to become rich, where the greatest curse is just what the fortune-teller had told me. For the people here it really would be bad news, but not for me: becoming rich has never been my aim.

Well then, what would interest me? I asked myself, continuing my silent mental dialogue with the blind man. If I do not want to be rich, what would I like to be? The answer had just taken shape in my head when it came to me from him, still reading his invisible computer. '*Famous. Yes. You'll never become rich, but between the ages of fifty-seven and sixty-two you will become famous.*'

'But how?' I asked instinctively, this time aloud.

The translation had hardly reached him when he lifted his hands and, with a widening smile on his lips, began tapping an imaginary typewriter in mid-air. '*By writing!*'

Extraordinary! The blind man could of course guess that anyone sitting before him would like to be famous, but what gave him the idea that I might do so by writing? Why not by starring in a film, say? Had I perhaps told him? Told him mentally, in no actual language

– there was none we had in common – but in that language of gestures comprehensible to anyone who could . . . see?

Unconsciously, internally, at the very moment when I asked, 'But how?' I answered the question and mentally made the gesture of a hand that wrote. Could it be that the blind man 'read' this gesture and immediately repeated it with his hands? Is there any other explanation of this brief sequence?

He felt that he had regained my attention, and continued. '*Until the age of seventy-two you'll have a good life. After seventy-three you'll have to rest, and you'll reach the age of seventy-eight. From now on never try your hand at any business dealings or you'll lose every penny. If you want to start something new, if you want to live in another country, you must absolutely do it next year.*'

Business is something I have never thought about. As for changing countries, I knew I wanted to go and live in India, but definitely not before May 1995, when my contract with *Der Spiegel* and the lease on the Turtle House were due to expire. And then? It would depend on various circumstances if I could then move. To go next year was impossible, in any case.

'*Be careful; this year isn't good for your health,*' said the blind man. Then he stopped and did some more calculations with his fingers in the air. '*No, no, the worst is over. You were through with all that was bad at the beginning of September of last year.*'

At this point it seemed only right to let him know why I had come to him, and to tell him about the prophecy of the Hong Kong fortune-teller. The blind man burst out laughing, and said, '*No, definitely not. The dangerous year was 1991; you did then indeed risk death in a plane.*' He was not mistaken. I shuddered at the memory of all the ghastly planes in which I had flown that summer of 1991 in the Soviet Union, when I was working on my book *Goodnight, Mister Lenin*.

For a moment I had a sense of disappointment. Perhaps it was only because he knew I was firm in my resolve not to fly that he saw no danger in the future. As I told myself this, I realized how readily the mind will perform any somersault to rationalize what suits it.

We thanked the man, paid, and left. In the little square we found the limousine with the driver in his fine white uniform. 'Well?' the woman asked me. I did not know what to say. The strangest thing the blind man had told me was that as a child my real parents had given me to another family, and that only thanks to this had I survived. What a risk he took in saying such a thing! In the vast majority of cases it cannot be true, as it was not true in mine. Or perhaps it was? The Oriental Hotel's car inched slowly through the traffic; my thoughts flew rapidly and delightfully in every direction.

There can be no doubt that I am my mother's son. Where else would I have got this potato nose, which has re-emerged identically in my daughter? Yet it is equally true that in a certain sense I have never belonged to the family I grew up in. I felt this from an early age, and my relatives recognized it too, jokingly saying to my father: 'But that one, where did you ever dig him out from?'

The blind man had got the facts wrong, but he had hit on something profoundly true. One only had to interpret, to focus on that part of us that goes beyond our physical being, and ask where it comes from. In my case it does indeed come from 'another family', that is to say from another source than the genes that determine the shape of my nose, my eyes, and even certain gestures which now, the older I grow, I recognize more and more as those of my paternal grandfather.

In the tenor of my parents' ways there was not so much as a germ of the life I have lived up till now. Both of them came from poor, magnificently simple people. Calm people, close to the earth, chiefly concerned with survival – never restless or adventurous, never looking for novelty as I have always done since childhood. On my mother's side they were peasants who had always worked other people's land; on my father's side, stonecutters in a quarry that is still called by their name. For centuries the Terzanis have chiselled the paving stones of Florence, and – it was said – those of the Palazzo Pitti. Nobody in either family had ever gone regularly to school, and my mother and father's generation was the first that had learned, barely, to read and write.

Where then did I get my longing to see the world, my fetish for printed paper, my love of books, and above all that burning desire to leave Florence, to travel, to go to the ends of the earth? Where did I get this yearning for always being somewhere else? Certainly not from my parents, with their deep roots in the city where they were born and grew up, which they had left only once, for their honeymoon in Prato – ten miles from the *duomo*.

Among all my relatives there was not one to whom I could look for inspiration, to whom I could turn for advice. The only ones I felt indebted to were my father and mother, who I saw literally go without food to allow me to study after primary school. What my father earned never lasted to the end of the month, and I well remember how sometimes, holding my mother's hand and trying not to be seen by anyone who knew us, I would go with her to the pawnbroker in the Via Palazzuolo with a linen sheet from her trousseau. Even the money for a notebook was a worry, and my first long trousers – new corduroy ones, good for summer and winter, indispensable for secondary school – were bought by instalments. Every month we would go to the shop to hand over the amount due. It is hard to imagine today, but the pleasure of putting on those trousers is one I have never felt again with any other garment, not even those made to measure for me in Peking by Mao's own tailor.

As I grew up I had a great affection for my family and its history, but I never felt any real affinity for them – as if I really had been put there by accident. My relatives were irritated by the fact that I studied and did not start working at a very young age, as they had all done. A brother of my father's, who dropped in every evening before dinner, used to say: 'What's he done today, the layabout?' Then he would trot out the wisecrack that so offended my mother: 'If he carries on like this he'll go farther than Annibale!' Annibale was a cousin, another Terzani, who had gone far indeed. Since boyhood he had worked as a city street cleaner, walking the tram tracks with a spade and rake to clear away the horse droppings.

Why did I practically flee from home when I was fifteen, to go and wash dishes all over Europe? Why, when I arrived in Asia, did I feel so much at home that I stayed there? Why does the heat of the tropics not tire me? Why do I sit cross-legged without discomfort? Is it the charm of the exotic? The wish to get as far away as possible from the poverty-stricken world of my childhood? Perhaps. Or perhaps the blind man was right, if he meant that something in me – not my body, which I certainly got from my parents, but something else – came from another source, that brought with it a baggage of old yearnings and homesickness for latitudes known to me in some life before this one.

Slumped in the back seat of the Oriental Hotel's car, I let these thoughts whirl around in my head, and amused myself by chasing them as if they were not mine. Could it be that I believed in reincarnation? I had never thought seriously about it. But why not? Why not imagine life as a relay race in which, like the baton that passes from hand to hand, something not physical, not definable, something like a collection of memories, a store of experiences lived elsewhere, passes from body to body and from death to death, and all the while grows and expands, gathering wisdom and advancing towards that state of grace that concludes every life: towards illumination, in Buddhist terms? That would help to explain my difference from the Terzani clan, and to interpret the blind man's statement that as a child I was passed from one family to another.

At times we all have the disquieting sensation of having already experienced something that we know is in fact happening for the first time, of having already been in a place where we are sure we have never set foot. Where does this feeling of *déjà vu* come from? From a 'before'? That would surely be the easiest explanation. And where have I been, if there is a 'before'? Perhaps somewhere in Asia, an Asia without concrete, without skyscrapers, without superhighways. So I pondered as I watched the dull, grey streets of Bangkok as they slid past the window, suffocated by the exhaust of thousands and thousands of cars.

My interpreter lived on the outskirts of the city, and I had offered to see her home. The car entered a bit of motorway I did not know. 'A very dangerous stretch, this,' she said. 'People die here all the time. Do you see those cars?' In the shadows of an underpass I saw two strange vans with Thai writing on them, and some men in blue overalls standing nearby. 'The body-snatchers,' said the woman. It was the first time I had heard the word in Bangkok. The story behind it was grisly.

According to popular belief, when a person dies violently his spirit does not rest in peace. And if, in the moment of death, the body is mutilated, decapitated, crushed or torn to pieces, that spirit becomes particularly restless; unless the prescribed rites are quickly performed it goes to join the enormous army of 'wandering spirits'. These spirits, along with the evil *phii*, constitute one of the great problems of today's Bangkok. Hence the importance of the 'body-snatchers', volunteers from Buddhist associations who cruise around the city collecting the bodies of people who have died violently. They put the pieces together and perform the appropriate rites so that the souls may depart in peace, and not hang about playing tricks on the living.

Apart from murder victims and suicides, the most obvious candidates for becoming wandering spirits are those killed in road accidents. That is why the Buddhist associations station their vans at the most notorious black spots on the roads, and why their men stand guard, tuned to the police radio frequencies, ready to rush to corpses at a moment's notice. And they really do rush, for this kind of work has become so profitable that the charitable associations are in fierce competition, and each tries to take away more corpses than the others so as to get more donations from the public. The first to arrive has the right to the body, but the men from the different associations often come to blows over a dead person. Sometimes they carry off someone who isn't dead yet. To advertise their public service each association holds special exhibitions with macabre colour photographs of the victims, clearly showing the severed heads and hands, so that they can press for generous donations.

That evening Bangkok really felt to me like a city from which there was no escape. Despite the competitive zeal of the body-snatchers, the number of angry *phii* is constantly increasing. Finding no peace, they wander about creating disasters. In vain have thousands of bottles of holy water been distributed by the Supreme Command of the Armed Forces of Thailand to exorcize the evil eye from the City of Angels, which the angels all seem to have forsaken.

CHAPTER FIVE

Farewell, Burma

In January I heard that the Burmese authorities at the frontier post of Tachileck, north of the Thai town of Chiang Mai, had begun issuing some entry visas 'to facilitate tourism'. You had to leave your passport at the border and pay a certain sum in dollars, after which you were free to spend three days in Burma and travel as far as Kengtung, the ancient mythical city of the Shan.

This scheme was obviously dreamed up by some local military commander to harvest some hard currency, but it was just what I was after. I was looking for something to write about without having to use planes, and this was an interesting subject: a region which no foreign traveller had succeeded in penetrating for almost half a century was suddenly opening up. By pretending to be a tourist I could again set foot in Burma, a country from which as a journalist I had been banned.

In Tachileck the Burmese had probably not yet installed a computer with their list of 'undesirables', so Angela and I, together with Charles Antoine de Nerciat, an old colleague from the Agence France Press, decided to try our luck. We came back with a distressing story to tell: the political prisoners of the military dictatorship, condemned to forced labour, were dying in their hundreds. We brought back photographs of young men in chains, carrying tree trunks and breaking stones on a riverbed. Thanks to that short trip we were able to draw the attention of public opinion to an aspect of the Burmese drama which otherwise would have passed unobserved. And I had gone there by chance – or rather because of a fortune-teller who told me not to fly.

This is one aspect of a reporter's job that never ceases to fascinate and disturb me: facts that go unreported do not exist. How many massacres, how many earthquakes happen in the world, how many ships sink, how many volcanoes erupt, and how many people are persecuted, tortured and killed. Yet if no one is there to see, to write, to take a photograph, it is as if these facts had never occurred, this suffering has no importance, no place in history. Because history exists only if someone relates it. It is sad, but such is life; and perhaps it is precisely this idea – the idea that with every little description of a thing observed one can leave a seed in the soil of memory – that keeps me tied to my profession.

The two towns of Mae Sai in Thailand and Tachileck in Burma are linked by a little bridge. As I crossed it with Angela and Charles Antoine, I felt once again that tremor of excitement, so pleasing but rarer as time goes on, of setting foot where few had been and where perhaps I might discover something. This had been a forbidden frontier at one time. There was said to be a heroin refinery just a few dozen yards inside Burmese territory. With good binoculars, you could make out a sign in English: 'Foreigners, keep away. Anyone passing this point risks being shot.' Now in its place is one proclaiming in big gold letters: 'Tourists! Welcome to Burma!'

So, Burma too has yielded to the common fate. For thirty years it tried to resist by remaining isolated and going its own way, but it did not succeed. No country can, it would seem. From Mao's China to Gandhi's India to Pol Pot's Cambodia, all the experiments in autarchy, in non-capitalist development with national characteristics, have failed. And what is more, most have left millions of victims.

At least the Burmese experiment had a fine name. It was called 'the Buddhist way to socialism'. This was the invention of General Ne Win, who took power in 1962 and imposed a military dictatorship. He tried to spare Burma the severity of the Communist regime that ruled China on the one hand, and the American-style materialist influence that was taking root in Thailand on the other. Ne Win closed the country, nationalized its commerce and imprisoned his opponents, claiming that only in that way could Burmese civilization be protected. In a certain sense he was right, and ultimately this bestowed legitimacy on his dictatorship. In Ne Win's hands Burma did indeed preserve its identity. The old traditions survived, religion flourished, and the way of life of the forty-five million inhabitants was not thrown into confusion by industrialization, urbanization and mindless aping of the West. By these means a country like Thailand has indeed been developed, but it has also been traumatized.

The Rangoon authorities did not want too many foreigners to 'pollute the atmosphere'; they doled out visas sparingly, allowing only seven-day visits. Those who went there came back feeling that they had seen a country still untouched by influences from the rest of the world. Burma was a fascinating piece of old Asia, a land where men still wear the *longyi*, a sort of skirt woven locally; where even women smoke the *cheroot*, strong green cigars rolled by hand, and not Marlboros; a land where Buddhism is still a living faith and the beautiful old pagodas are still places of living worship, not museums for tourists to stroll around.

That Burma is now about to disappear, too. After a quarter of a century of uncontested power, Ne Win handed over the reins to a new generation of military men, who have imposed a dictatorship more brazen, more violent and murderous, but also more 'modern', than the former paternalistic one.

One had only to walk through the market in Tachileck to see that the new generals who are now the masters in Rangoon have dropped all pretence of following 'a Burmese path'. They have decided to put a stop to the country's isolation, and have adopted as a model of development the one that for decades has been knocking at their door, as at those of the Laotians, the Khmer and now the Vietnamese: Thailand.

Tachileck has already lost its Burmese patina. It has fourteen casinos and numerous karaoke bars. Heroin is on sale more or less openly. The largest restaurant, two discotheques and the first supermarket are owned by Thais. No transaction takes place in the local currency, the kyat. Even in the market the money they all want is that of Bangkok, the baht.

It is the military and the police who organize tourist visas, who change dollars, who procure a jeep, a driver and an interpreter. I took it for granted that the interpreter assigned to me was a spy, and I managed to get rid of him by offering him three days' paid holiday. In the market I had been approached by a man of about fifty who seemed more trustworthy. He was a Karen – a member of an ethnic minority hostile to the Burmese; a Protestant, and hence used to Western modes of thought; and he spoke excellent English. Meeting him was a rare piece of luck, because Andrew – a name given him by American missionaries – was a mine of information and explanations.

'Why are the hills so bare?' I asked as soon as we left Tachileck.

'The Thais have cut down the forests.'

'Whose houses are those?' I enquired at the first village we came to, where several new dwellings stood out glaringly among the old dark wooden ones.

'They belong to families who have daughters working in the brothels in Thailand.'

'And those cars?'

'They are on the way from Singapore to China. The Wa, they're no longer headhunters. They're smugglers.'

'In heroin?'

'Only in part. Here in the south they're in competition with Khun Sa, the real drug king.'

We drove into the mountains, which still looked as if they were hiding a thousand mysteries. In the old maps this part of the world was labelled the 'Shan States' because the Shan, who came from China in the twelfth century to escape the advancing Mongols, formed the bulk of the population. The whole region was a sort of living museum of the most varied humanity. Apart from the Shan there were dozens of other tribes living there, each with its own language, its own customs and traditions, its own way of farming and hunting. The encounter with these different groups, of which the Pao', Meo, Karen and Wa tribes became the best known, was one of the great surprises that greeted the first European explorers in the region.

The long necks of the 'giraffe women' of the Padaung, like the tiny bound feet of Chinese women, exemplified Asia's bizarre aberrations. Even today, the Padaung judge a woman's beauty by the length of her neck. From birth every girl has big silver rings forced under her chin. By the time she is old enough to marry her head will be sixteen to twenty inches above her shoulders, supported by a stack of these precious collars. If they were removed she would die of suffocation: her head would fall to one side and her breathing would be cut off.

For centuries the Shan have resisted every attempt on the part of the Burmese to dominate them, and have managed to stay independent. The British too, when at the end of the nineteenth century they arrived from India to extend their colonial power, recognized the authority of the thirty-three *sawbaws*, the Shan kings, and left them to administer their rural dominions, which bore names like 'the Kingdom of a Thousand Banana Trees'.

In 1938 Maurice Collis, a sometime colonial administrator who became a writer, visited the Shan States and tried to bring to the attention of the British public this unknown wonder of the Empire. Kengtung, with its thirty-two monasteries, struck him as a pearl, and he found it absurd that no one in London seemed to have heard of it. The book he wrote, *The Lords of the Sunset* – as the *sawbaws* were called, to distinguish them from the 'Lords of the Dawn', the kings of western Burma – is the last testimony of a traveller in that uncontaminated world of peasant kings, where life had been the same for centuries, its rhythm that of old ceremonies, its rules those of feudal ties. I had brought that fifty-five-year-old book with me as a guide.

The road that took us to Kengtung was in places little more than a cart track, barely ten feet wide and full of potholes, often perilously skirting the edge of a precipice, but it was obviously of recent construction.

'Who built it?' I asked Andrew.

'You'll see them soon.' Andrew had realized that we were not normal tourists, but that did not seem to worry him. Quite the contrary.

After a few miles Andrew told the driver to stop near a pile of timber at the side of the road. We had scarcely got out of the jeep than we heard a strange clanking sound from the brushwood, like chains being dragged. Yes – chains they were. They were around the ankles of about twenty emaciated ghosts of men, some shaking with fever, all in dusty rags, moving wearily in unison like an enormous centipede, with a long tree trunk on their shoulders. The chains on their feet were joined to another around their waists.

The two soldiers accompanying the prisoners made us a sign with their rifles to drop our cameras.

'They're missionaries. Don't worry,' said Andrew. It worked. A couple of cigarettes added conviction.

The prisoners put down the trunk and stopped. One of them said he was from Pegu, another from Mandalay. Both had been arrested five years before, during the great demonstrations for democracy: political prisoners, doing forced labour.

It is strange to stand before such an atrocity, be obliged to take mental notes and discreetly snap a few photos, trying to avoid risks and not to give those poor devils more problems than they already had; and then to realize that you have not even had the time to feel compassion, to exchange a word of simple humanity. You suddenly find yourself looking into an abyss of pain, you try to imagine its depths, and all you can think of asking is, 'And those?' pointing to the chains.

'I've had them on for two years. One more and I'll be able to take them off,' said the young man from Pegu. He was one of the lucky ones: he was wearing a pair of old socks that slightly mitigated the contact of the iron rings with his flesh. Others, lacking such protection, had ugly wounds on their ankles.

'And malaria?'

'Lots,' said the young man from Mandalay, turning mechanically to his neighbour, who was shaking, yellow and puffy-faced. His bony hands were covered in strange stains, like burns. The prisoners – about a hundred in all – lived in a field not far away. Soon we were to see their companions, also chained, breaking stones on the riverbed. These too were guarded by armed soldiers, who would not allow us to stop.

Since the coup in 1988, the massacre of the demonstrators and the arrest of the heroine of the pro-democracy struggle Aung San Suu Kyi, the Rangoon dictators have continued to terrorize the country and to stifle any expression of dissent at birth. Tens of thousands, especially young people, have been arrested and sent to forced labour, used as porters in the army or in fields mined by the guerrillas. Political prisoners are thrown in with common criminals in this forgotten tropical gulag.

'There are camps like this everywhere,' Andrew said. 'Private firms acquire contracts for road-building, and go to the prisons for the men they need. If they die they go back and take some more.' He had heard that to build the 103 miles of road from Tachileck to Kengtung several hundred men had already died.

It took us seven hours to cover those 103 miles, but by the time we arrived in Kengtung the use of that road was clear to us: it was

Burma's road to the future. Though its original purpose had been to finance the dictatorship and to provide an umbilical cord linking Burma with the neighbouring countries that shared its goals – China and Thailand – by now the road lived by a logic of its own, and served all sorts of people for all sorts of traffic. Communist ex-guerrillas, recently converted to opium cultivation, use it to move consignments of drugs; the Wa, former headhunters, to smuggle cars, jade and antiques; Thai gangsters to top up their supply of prostitutes with young Burmese girls. Thanks to its isolation Burma has, so far, staved off the AIDS epidemic, so these girls, often only thirteen or fourteen years old, are in great demand for the Thai brothels, where thousands of them are already working. At the end of 1992 about a hundred who tested HIV positive were expelled and sent home. Rumour has it that the Burmese military killed them with strychnine injections.

We arrived in Kengtung at sunset. After many miles of tiresome ascents and descents, through narrow gorges between monotonous mountains where the eye never had the relief of distance, we suddenly found ourselves in a vast, airy valley. In the middle of it white pagodas, wooden houses and the dark green contours of great rain trees were silhouetted like paper cutouts against a background of mist that glowed first pink and then gold in the setting sun. Kengtung was evanescent, incorporeal like the memory of a dream, a vision outside time. We stopped; and perhaps, from the distance, we saw the Kengtung of centuries ago, when the four brothers of the legend drained the lake that once filled the valley, built the city, and erected the first pagoda. There they placed the eight hairs of Buddha, which the Great Teacher had left when passing through.

The town was at supper. Through the open doorways of the shop-houses, with dogs on the thresholds, we could see families sitting around their tables. Oil lamps cast great shadows on walls dotted with photographs, calendars and sacred images. There was no traffic on the streets; the air was filled with the quiet murmur of evening's isolated voices and distant calls.

A fair was in progress in the courtyard of a pagoda. People crowded around the many stalls, lit by small acetylene lamps, to buy sweets and to gamble with large dice that had figures of animals instead of numbers. Wide-eyed children peered through the forest of hands holding out bets to the peasant croupiers. In the shadows, at the feet of three large Buddhas smiling timidly in bronze, a group of the faithful were gathered in meditation. Some women, their long hair gathered in off-centre chignons, had lit fires on the pavements and were cooking sugared rice in large bamboo canes.

There was nothing physically breathtaking about Kengtung – no particularly impressive monument, temple or palace. Its touching charm lay in its atmosphere, in its tranquillity, in the timeless pace of life without stress.

Is it strange to find all this beautiful? Is it absurd to worry that it is changing? In appearance everything is fine these days in Asia. The wars are over, and peace – even ideological peace – reigns, with very few exceptions, over the whole continent. Everywhere people speak of nothing but economic growth. And yet this great, ancient world of diversity is about to succumb. The Trojan horse is 'modernization'.

I find it tragic to see this continent so gaily committing suicide. But nobody talks about it, nobody protests – least of all the Asians. In the past, when Europe was beating at the doors of Asia, firing cannonballs from her gunboats and seeking to open ports, to obtain concessions and colonies, when her soldiers were disdainfully sacking and burning the Summer Palace in Peking, the Asians, one way or another, resisted.

The Vietnamese began their war of liberation the moment the first French troops landed on their territory; that war lasted more than a hundred years, and only ended with the fall of Saigon in 1975. The Chinese fought in the Opium Wars, and in the end trusted to time to free themselves from the foreigners who ruled with the force of their more efficient weapons. (The last two pieces of Chinese territory still in foreign hands, Hong Kong and Macao, are returning to Peking's sovereignty in 1997 and 1999 respectively.)

Japan, on the other hand, reacted like a chameleon. It made itself externally Western, copied everything it could from the West – from students' uniforms to cannons, from the architecture of railway stations to the idea of the state – but inwardly strove to become more and more Japanese, inculcating in its people the idea of their uniqueness.

One after another the countries of Asia have managed to free themselves from the colonial yoke and show the West the door. But now the West is climbing back in by the window and conquering Asia at last, no longer taking over its territories, but its soul. It is doing it without any plan, without any specific political will, but by a process of poisoning for which no antidote has yet been discovered: the notion of modernity. We have convinced the Asians that only by being modern can they survive, and that the only way of being modern is ours, the Western way.

Projecting itself as the only true model of human progress, the West has managed to give a massive inferiority complex to those who are not 'modern' in its image – not even Christianity ever accomplished this! And now Asia is dumping all that was its own in order to adopt all that is Western, whether in its original form or in its local imitations, be they Japanese, Thai or Singaporean.

Copying what is 'new' and 'modern' has become an obsession, a fever for which there is no remedy. In Peking they are knocking down the last courtyard houses; in the villages of South-East Asia, in Indonesia as in Laos, at the first sign of prosperity the lovely local materials are rejected in favour of synthetic ones. Thatched roofs are out, corrugated iron is in, and never mind if the houses get as hot as ovens, and if in the rainy season they are like drums inside which the occupants are deafened.

So it is with everyone these days. Even the Chinese. Once so proud to be the heirs of a four-thousand-year-old culture, and convinced of their spiritual superiority to all others, they too have capitulated; significantly, they are beginning to find it embarrassing still to eat with chopsticks. They too feel more presentable with a knife and fork in their hands, more elegant if dressed in jacket and tie. The tie! Originally a Mongol invention for dragging prisoners tied to the pommels of their saddles . . .

By now no Asian culture can hold out against the trend. There are no more principles or ideals capable of challenging this 'modernity'. Development is a dogma; progress at all costs is an order against which there can be no appeal. Merely to question the route taken, its morality, its consequences, has become impossible in Asia.

Here there is not even an equivalent of the hippies who, realizing there was something wrong with 'progress', cried 'Stop the world, I want to get off!' And yet the problem exists, and it is everyone's. We should all ask ourselves – always – if what we are doing improves and enriches our lives. Or have we all, through some monstrous deformation, lost the instinct for what life should be: first and foremost, an opportunity to be happy. Are the inhabitants happier today, gathered in families chatting over supper, or will they be happier when they too spend their evenings mute and stupefied in front of a television screen? I am well aware that if we were to ask them, they would say that in front of a television is better! And that is precisely why I should like to see at least a place like Kengtung ruled by a philosopher-king, by an enlightened monk, by some visionary who would seek a middle way between isolation *cum* stagnation and openness *cum* destruction, rather than by the generals now holding Burma's fate in their hands. The irony is that it was a dictatorship that preserved Burma's identity, and now another dictatorship is destroying it and turning the country, which had so far escaped the epidemic of greed, into an ugly copy of Thailand. Would Aung San Suu Kyi and her democratic followers be any different? Probably not. Probably they too wish only for 'development'. They too, if they ever came to power, could only allow the people that freedom of choice which in the end leaves them with no choice at all. No one, it seems, can protect them from the future.

Night fell in Kengtung, timeless night, a blanket of ancient darkness and silence. All that remained was a quiet tinkling of bells stirred by the wind at the top of the great *stupa* of the Eight Hairs. Led by this sound we climbed the hill by the light of the moon, which, almost full, rimmed the white buildings in silver. We found an open door, and spent hours talking with the monks, sitting on the beautiful floral tiles of the Wat Zom Kam, the Monastery of the Golden Hill. That afternoon several lorries had arrived from the countryside full of very young novices. Accompanied by their families, they were all sleeping on the ground along the walls, at the feet of large Buddhas with their faint, mysterious smiles, that glimmered in the light of little flames. Statues though they were, they were dressed in the orange tunic of the monks, exactly as if they too were alive and had to be shielded from the night breeze that came in at the windows. The novices, small shaven-headed boys of about ten, lay wrapped in new saffron-coloured blankets given them by their relatives for the initiation. For years to come the pagoda would be their school – a school of reading, writing and faith, but also of traditions, customs and ancient principles.

What a difference, I thought, between growing up that way – educated in the spartan order of a temple, beneath those Buddhas, teachers of tolerance, with the sound of the bells in their ears – and growing up in a city like Bangkok where children nowadays go to school with a kerchief over their mouths to protect them from traffic fumes, and with Walkmans plugged in their ears to drown out the traffic noise with rock music. What disparate men must be created by these disparate conditions. Which are better?

The monks were interested in talking about politics. They were all Shan, and hated the Burmese. Two of them were great sympathizers of Khun Sa, the 'drug king', but now also the champion in the struggle for the 'liberation' of this people which feels oppressed.

In 1948, under pressure from the English, the Shan, like all the other minority populations, consented to become part of a new independent state, the Burmese Union, with the guarantee that if they chose they could secede during the first ten years. But the Burmese took advantage of this to wipe out the *sawbaw* and reinforce their control over the Shan States. Secession became impossible, and ever since there has been a state of war between the Shan and the Burmese. Here the Rangoon army is seen as an army of occupation, and often behaves like one. In 1991 some hundreds of Burmese soldiers occupied the centre of Kengtung and razed the palace of the *sawbaws* to the ground, claiming the space was needed for a tourist hotel. The truth is that they wanted to eliminate one of the symbols of Shan independence. In that palace had lived the last direct descendant of the city's founder. His dynasty had lasted seven hundred years. Old photographs of that palace now circulate clandestinely among the people, like those of the Dalai Lama in Lhasa.

When we left the pagoda it was still a couple of hours before dawn, but along the main street of Kengtung a silent procession of extraordinary figures was already under way. Passing in single file, they seemed to have come out of an old anthropology book: women carrying huge baskets on long poles supported by wooden yokes across their shoulders; men carrying bunches of ducks by the feet; more women, moving along with a dancing gait to match the movement of the poles. The groups were dressed in different colours and different styles: Akka women in miniskirts with black leggings and strange headgear covered with coins and little silver balls; Padaung giraffe-women with their long necks propped up on silver rings; Meo women in red and blue embroidered bodices; and men with long rudimentary rifles. These were mountain people who had come to queue for the six o'clock opening of one of Asia's last, fascinating markets.

Sitting on the wooden stools of the Honey Tea House we had breakfast – some very greasy fritters, which a young man deftly plucked with bare hands from a cauldron of boiling oil. We dunked them in condensed milk. Among the soldiers and traders at the other tables on the pavement, Andrew saw a friend of his, the son of a local lordling of the Lua' tribe, and invited him to join us. People continued to file past on their way to the market. We saw some men dressed entirely in black, each with a big machete in a bamboo sheath at his side. 'Those are the Wa, the wild Wa,' Andrew's friend informed us with a certain disgust. 'They never part from their big knives.'

He told us that since he was small his father had taught him to be extremely careful of these Wa. Unlike the 'civilized' Wa, these had remained true to their traditions, and they still really cut people's heads off. Shortly before the harvest, when their fields are full of ripe rice, the wild Wa make forays into their neighbours' lands, capture someone – preferably a child – and with the same scythe that they later use for the harvest, cut off his head. 'They bury it in their fields as an offering to the rice goddess. It's their way of auguring a good harvest,' said the young man. 'They're dangerous only when they go outside their own territory. At home they don't harm anyone. If you go and visit them they are very kind and hospitable. You only have to be careful of what they give you to eat!' At times, he said, someone invited to dinner by the Wa finds a piece of tattooed meat on his plate. In a word, it would seem that the Wa are also cannibals – at least if you take the word of their neighbours, the Lua'.

I asked Andrew and his friend to help me find a fortune-teller. Divination is a widely practised art in Burma. It is said that the Burmese, geographically placed between China and India – the two great sources of this tradition – have been especially skilled in combining the occult wisdom of their two neighbours, and that their practitioners possess great powers. Superstition has played an enormous role in the history of the whole region. It was the Burmese king's hankering after one of the King of Siam's seven white elephants, very rare and therefore magical – that sparked off a war which lasted nearly three hundred years – the upshot being that Auydhya was destroyed and the Siamese had to build a new capital, present-day Bangkok.

Even in recent times, astrology and occult practices have been crucial in the life of Ne Win and the survival of his dictatorship. One of the first things you notice on arriving in Burma is that the local currency, the kyat, is issued in notes of strange denominations: forty-five, seventy-five, ninety. These numbers, all multiples of three, were considered highly auspicious by Ne Win, and the Central Bank had to comply.

Like the Thais, the Burmese believe that fate is not ineluctable, that even if a misfortune is forecast it can be averted: not only by acquiring merits, but also by bringing about an event which is similar in appearance to the predicted calamity, thereby satisfying the requirements of destiny, so to speak. Ne Win was a master of this art. He was once told that the country would soon be struck by a terrible famine. He lost no time: he issued orders that for three days all state officials and their families should eat only a poor soup made of banana-tree sprouts. The idea was that by acting out a famine they would avoid the real one – a calamity which in the event never materialized.

On another occasion, Ne Win was told by one of his trusted astrologers to beware of a grave danger: a sudden right-wing uprising which would lead to his deposition. Ne Win gave orders that everyone in Burma immediately had to drive on the right-hand side of the road rather than on the left, as had been the rule since British times. The whole country was thrown into confusion, but this 'right-wing uprising' fulfilled the prophecy after a fashion, and the real revolt was averted.

In 1988 the same astrologer warned Ne Win that Burma was on the eve of a great catastrophe: the streets of the capital would run with blood and he would be forced to flee the country. Shortly afterwards, thousands of students were massacred and the streets of

Rangoon really did run with blood. Ne Win feared that the second part of the prophecy might also come true. He had to find a way out, and the astrologer suggested it: in Burmese, as in English, the verbs 'to flee' and 'to fly' are similar. The president would not have to flee if, dressed like one of the great kings of the past and mounted on a white horse, he could succeed in flying to the remotest parts of the country. Nothing simpler! He got hold of a wooden horse (a real one would have been too dangerous), had it painted white and loaded it on to a plane. Dressed as an ancient king, he climbed into the saddle and flew to the four corners of Burma. The stratagem succeeded, and Ne Win was not forced to flee. He is still a charismatic figure behind the scenes, the *éminence grise* of the new dictatorship.

The new rulers too have their advisory fortune-tellers. Not long ago one of the generals was warned by an astrologer that he would soon be the victim of an assassination attempt. He immediately ordered a public announcement of his death, and so no one tried to kill him any more.

Obviously the reason why the famine, the right-wing uprising, the expulsion of the president and the assassination attempt did not happen was – how shall I put it? – that they were not going to happen, not that they were averted thanks to prophecies. But that is not the logic by which the Asians – especially the Burmese – look on life. Prescience is in itself creation. An event, once announced, exists. It is fact, and although it is still to come it is more real and more significant than something that has already happened. In Asia, the future is much more important than the past, and much more energy is devoted to prophecy than to history.

I had been told in Bangkok that there used to be an old Catholic mission in Kengtung, and that perhaps there were still some Italian nuns living there. We climbed up the hill to the church at dusk. A night light was burning at the feet of a plaster Madonna, and in the refectory young Burmese nuns were clearing the rows of tables after supper. I told one of them who I was and she rushed off, shouting: 'There are some Italians here! Come . . . come!' Down a wooden stairway came two diminutive old women, pale and excited. They wore voluminous grey habits and veils with a little starched trimming. They were beside themselves with joy. 'It's a miracle!' one of them kept repeating. The other said things I could not understand. One was ninety years old, the other eighty-six. We stayed and chatted for a couple of hours. Their story, and that of the Catholic mission in Kengtung, was of a kind that we have lost the habit of telling. Perhaps it is because the protagonists were extraordinary people, and today's world seems more interested in glorifying the banal and promoting the commonplace types with whom all can identify.

The story begins in the early years of this century. The Papacy, convinced that it would never manage to convert the Shans, highly civilized and devout followers of the Dharma (the way of the Buddha), saw instead a chance of making conversions among the primitive animist tribes of the region, thereby planting a Christian seed in Buddhist soil. The first missionary arrived in Kengtung in 1912. He was Father Bonetta of the Vatican Institute for Foreign Missionaries, a Milanese. He brought little money, but with that he managed to buy the entire peak of one of the two hills overlooking the city. It was there that they hanged brigands on market days, and the land was worthless: too full of *phii*.

Bonetta was soon joined by other missionaries, and in a short time they built a church and a seminary. In 1916 the first nuns arrived, all from Milan or thereabouts, all in the Order of the Child Mary. An orphanage and a school were opened, later a hospital and a leprosarium. As the years went by, Kengtung was caught up in the political upheavals of the region, and troops of several armies passed through it as conquerors: the Japanese, the Siamese, the Chinese of the Kuomintang and then those of Mao. Last came the Burmese; but the Italian mission is still there.

Today nothing has changed on the 'Hill of the Spirits': the buildings are all there, well kept and full of children. Father Bonetta died in 1949, and with other missionaries who never returned to Italy, he lies in the cemetery behind the church. Five Italian nuns remain: three in the hospital, and the two oldest in the convent, together with the local novices.

'When I first came here you couldn't go out at night because there were tigers about,' said the oldest, Giuseppa Manzoni, who has been in Kengtung since 1929 and has never gone back to Italy. Speaking Italian does not come easily to her. She understands my questions, but most of the time she answers in Shan, which a young Karen sister translates into English.

Sister Giuseppa was born in Cernusco. 'A beautiful place, you know, near Milan. I always went there on foot because there was no money at home.' Her parents were peasants. They had had nine children, but the seven sons all died very young and only she and her sister survived.

Sister Vittoria Ongaro arrived in Kengtung in 1935. 'On 22 February,' she says, with the precision of someone remembering the date of her wedding. 'The people had little, but they were better off then, because there were not the differences between rich and poor that there are now.'

The Catholic mission soon became the refuge of all the sad causes in the region. Cripples, epileptics, the mentally disabled, women abandoned by their husbands, newborns with cleft palates (left to die by a society that sees any physical deformity as the sign of a grave sin in a previous life), found food and shelter here. Today it is such people who tend the garden, look after the animals, and work in the kitchens to feed the 250 orphans.

It grew late, and as we got up to leave I asked the two nuns if there was anything I could do for them.

'Yes, say some prayers for us, so that when we die we too can go to Paradise,' said Sister Giuseppa.

'If you don't get there,' I said, 'Paradise must be a deserted place indeed!'

This made them laugh. All the novices joined in.

As we walked to the gate Sister Giuseppa took my hand and whispered in my ear, this time in perfect Italian with a northern accent, 'Give my greetings to the people of Cernusco, all of them.' Then she hesitated for a moment. 'But, Cernusco, it's still there, isn't it, near Milan?'

I was delighted to confirm it.

As I went down the hill I felt as if I had witnessed a sort of miracle. How encouraging it was to see people who had believed so firmly in something, and who believed still; to see these survivors of an Italy of times past, which only distance had preserved intact.

People born into a family of poor peasants at the beginning of the century, in Cernusco or anywhere else in Italy, could not dream of having the moon: their choices were extremely limited, which meant

that they had a 'destiny'. Today almost everyone has many alternatives, and can aspire to anything whatsoever – with the consequence
that no one is any longer 'predestined' to anything. Perhaps this is
why people are more and more disorientated and uncertain about
the meaning of their lives.

Children in Cernusco no longer die like flies, and none of them,
if asked 'What do you want to be when you grow up?' would reply,
'A missionary in Burma.' But does their life today have more meaning
than that of the children who at one time might have answered in
that way? The nuns in Kengtung had no doubts about the meaning
of their lives.

And the meaning of mine? Like everyone else, I often wonder.
Certainly one is not 'born to be' a journalist. When I was little and
my relatives bombarded me with the usual stupid question, which
seemingly must be inflicted on all children in all countries and perhaps
in all ages, I used to annoy them by naming a different trade every
time, and in the end I invented some that did not exist. It is an
aspiration that I continue to nourish.

After three days in Kengtung Andrew and his friend had not yet
found me a fortune-teller. Perhaps Andrew's Protestant upbringing
made him reluctant, or perhaps it was true that the two most famous
fortune-tellers were out of town 'for consultations'. Finally, on our
last evening, we found one playing badminton with his children in
the garden of his house. But, with great kindness, he excused himself:
he received only from 9.30 to 11.30 in the morning, after meditating.
I tried to persuade him to make an exception, but he was adamant.
He had made a vow imposing that limit 'to avoid falling victim to
the lust for gain'. If he broke that commitment he would lose all his
powers, he said. His resistance impressed me more than anything he
might have told me.

On the way back to the border we saw the chained prisoners
again. This time we were prepared, and managed to give them a
couple of shirts, a sweater, some cigarettes and a handful of kyat.

At the border we were given back our passports, without any visa
stamp. Officially we had never left Thailand, never entered Burma.
A fast taxi took us to the city of Chiang Rai. We spent the night in
a sparkling new, ultra-modern hotel, where young Thai waiters

dressed like the court servants of old Siam served Western tourists dressed like explorers in shorts and bush jackets. The next day they would be taken in air-conditioned coaches to Tachileck, where they would be photographed under an arch that says 'Golden Triangle', visit a museum called 'The House of Opium', and buy a few Burmese trinkets of a kind that by now can be found in Europe as well.

A French mime, with a bowler hat and walking stick, who had been hired by the hotel on a six-month contract, did a Charlie Chaplin turn between the tables of the restaurant, in front of the lifts and among the customers at the bar, in an attempt to liven up the atmosphere. I could not have imagined anything more absurd, after the chained prisoners, the monks and men who chopped off heads.

The next morning Angela and Charles caught a plane, and were in Bangkok in two hours. I had ahead of me four hours by bus to Chiang Mai and then a whole night on a train. Inconvenient. Complicated. But the idea of keeping to my plan still amused me. I remembered how as a boy, on my way to school, I tried not to step on the cracks between the paving stones. If I succeeded all the way I would do well in a test or write a good essay. I have seen this done by other children in other parts of the world. Perhaps we all from time to time have a primordial, instinctive need to impose limits, to test ourselves against difficulties, and thereby to feel that we have 'deserved' some desired result.

Thinking about the many such bets one makes with fate in a lifetime, I reached the bus station easily enough, then the railway station, and finally Bangkok.

CHAPTER SIX

Widows and Broken Pots

It was inevitable: I began to have doubts. Along came the old familiar voice of my *alter ego*, true to form, ready to question every certainty. The doubts first surfaced when I began investigating the topic of fortune-tellers and superstition from the point of view of a journalist. Was I not perhaps wasting my time with this business of not flying? Had I not succumbed to the most foolish and irrational of instincts? Was I not behaving like a credulous old woman? As soon as I looked at the subject with the logic I would have applied to anything else, it struck me as absurd.

I began by going to interview General Payroot, the secretary of the International Thai Association of Astrology. He was a distinguished looking gentleman of about sixty, lean and erect, with thick grey hair, cut very short like that of a monk. When I came in he handed me not one but, as happens more and more often in Asia, several visiting cards, each of which gave a different address and different telephone and fax numbers.

'Why the *International* Thai Association of Astrology?' I asked, to start the ball rolling.

'We also hold courses in English, for foreign students; last year we had two Australians.'

It doesn't take much to become international, I thought; and I imagined those two, now in some Australian town, making a living by saying heaven knows what about people's destiny, with the prestige of having studied in Thailand, one of the great centres of the occult.

'Also,' continued General Payroot, 'we maintain contacts with the astrological associations of various countries. The German one in particular.'

'The German one?'

'The Germans are at the cutting edge in this field; they are brilliant. I myself have studied in Hamburg.' He had indeed: years ago this distinguished gentleman – in all truth an infantry general in the Royal Thai Armed Forces – had been a cadet at the famous *Führungsakademie*. In the morning he had attended classes in warfare, and in the evening he had learned about the stars at the local Institute of Astrology.

After retiring from the army he devoted himself full-time to his two pet creations: a school for fortune-tellers, with the specific intention of disseminating the 'German method', and an 'astro-business' company which combines astrology with economic research to predict the behaviour of the stock market. 'The system is already fully computerized,' the general explained to me proudly. Clients paid an enrolment fee plus 5 per cent of all profits from investments recommended by the 'astro-business'.

My meeting with the general-astrologer took place in the headquarters of the Academy of Siamese Astrologers, a handsome, spacious wooden villa built at the beginning of the century. The floors were of polished teak, the open verandas were ventilated by large fans revolving slowly on the ceilings. The setting had much to recommend it, too, being at the centre of one of those neighbourhoods that have best preserved the atmosphere of old Bangkok. Across from the Academy is the Great Temple, which in Thailand is rather like the Vatican, being the residence of the Patriarch, the head of the Buddhist Church.

I had arrived early in the morning. Along the pavements were dozens of stalls displaying religious trinkets. There were lucky charms and amulets against the evil eye, statuettes of divinities and venerable abbots from ages past, and the highly realistic little wooden phalluses which it is believed increase male virility and make women give birth to boys.

The Thais have unbounded faith in the powers of the occult, and these little markets of hope and exorcism are among the most colourful and profitable in the country. No Thai walks out of the door without carrying some amulet or other. Many wear whole collections of them around their necks, hanging from thick gold chains. Thais will spend huge sums to procure a powerful amulet, or to be tattooed with signs that can ward off danger and attract good luck. No part of the body is spared: it is said that a certain lady who recently became the wife of one of the most prominent men in the country achieved her goal thanks to some very special shells tattooed on her mount of Venus.

While I was talking with the astrologer-general in the main hall of the Association, from two adjoining rooms came the voices of teachers giving lessons to classes drawn from all over Thailand. Even astrology has been affected by the process of democratization. Originally it was a court art, studied and practised only by kings or for kings. Knowledge of the stars and their secrets was an instrument of power, and as such had to remain a monopoly of the few. Now astrology, too, has become a consumer good, accessible to all. Rama the First, the founder of the dynasty that currently reigns over Thailand, was an excellent astrologer, and predicted that 150 years after his death there would be a great revolution in the country. And lo and behold, at the time appointed, the revolution occurred: in 1932 the absolute monarchy was forced by an uprising of intellectuals and progressive nobles to become constitutional.

'And the present king, Bumiphol, is he a good astrologer?' I asked.

'I cannot say anything about my king,' replied the general, avoiding a subject which is still very much taboo in Thailand. There are too many unresolved mysteries, too many whispered prophecies – including the one about the dynasty coming to an end with the next king, Rama the Tenth – for a Thai to discuss the royal family with a foreigner. The general even refused to admit what everyone knows: that King Bumiphol, like his predecessors, has astrologers in his service, and it is they who determine the times of his public appearances and fix his appointments.

The Academy has a small garden, unkempt but not unpleasing, with a litter of newborn kittens and a couple of mangy dogs, some shirts hung out to dry, and a cement deer pretending to drink from a waterless fountain. Along the verandas stood a number of small tables, each with a palmist studying the lines of a proffered hand with a big magnifying glass, or an astrologer making calculations and drawings on sheets of squared paper and recounting the past, predicting the future, or just giving advice to intently listening women.

Was I becoming like them, even if with the justification of wanting to explore 'the mystery of Asia'? In accepting the injunction not to fly, was I not perhaps behaving like those little old women who came to receive from the stars some constraint or prohibition in the hope that gain would ensue?

I stopped to watch a woman who had brought not only her daughter but the daughter's fiancé, obviously to have him vetted before considering him as a potential son-in-law. As the fortune-teller performed his calculations they all looked on with intense absorption.

The general told me that that very day, it so happened, one of the most famous seers in the country had come to the Association, a woman who combined various methods of divination, but who was especially expert in the reading of the body. Was I interested in consulting her?

'Of course,' I said instinctively, realizing as I did so how this fortune-telling business could easily become a drug, and how one might spend one's life listening to essentially the same things, asking the same questions, each time waiting for the answer with fresh curiosity. So it is, too, at the casino when you put a handful of chips on the black or the red, on the even or the odd numbers: the more you play the more you want to, and you never get bored waiting for that 'yes' or 'no' of fate. And, just as at the casino one who loses is sure his luck will soon change, so it is with fortune-tellers: after hearing so many of them come out with perhaps one true and interesting point amidst a plethora of errors and banalities, we still hope to come upon the most gifted of all, the one who is never wrong, who sees everything clearly. Could it be the next one?

The woman was about fifty, stocky and broad-shouldered, with short legs, her hair still black, and light skin. She was clearly of Chinese origin, but I didn't mention this – I didn't want to get into a conversation that might give her clues as to who I was and where I came from. I sat opposite her without saying a word, and waited for her questions.

She sat for a few minutes as if in prayer, whispering some formula with her hands joined in front of her chest, her head slightly bowed and her eyes closed. She then peered into my face with great concentration and asked me to smile, saying she wanted to examine the way my mouth creased; she touched my ears and the bones of my forehead. Finally, she had me stand and lift the cuffs of my trousers, to get a good look at my feet and ankles.

This is an old Chinese system of divination, and it interested me because, of all the various systems, this one seemed the least nebulous. A body, closely observed, can say a great deal, and if there is a 'book' in which to read someone's past – and maybe a hint of his future, too – it must surely be that shell of life that people wear from birth, rather than some manual of calculations based on the relation between the stars and the hour when one came into the world. People born at the same hour of the same day of the same year do not share the same fate, and they most certainly do not die at the same time. Nor do they have the same creases in their hands. But people with similar physical characteristics do often have similar attitudes, similar qualities and defects. So it is not impossible that one may be able to read in a person's body the signs of his fate.

The reading of people's destinies in their faces evolved in China from medical practice. Patients, especially women, would not allow anyone to touch them, so the doctors had to diagnose their ailments just by looking at them, especially their faces. By dint of observing vast numbers of patients, century after century, the Chinese have concluded, for example, that a small red spot on a cheek denotes a heart malfunction; a wrinkle under the left eye means a stomach problem. Similarly, all rich people are meant to have a particular curve of the nose, and people with power have a mole on the chin. Hence the idea that destiny is written in the body: one need only know how to observe it.

The Chinese discern the character of a person by his ears; in the forehead they read his fate up to the age of thirty-two, in the eyes up to forty, and in the nose from forty to fifty. The eyebrows show the emotional life, and in the mouth are the signs of good or bad fortune in the last years of life. In the crease of the lips, which changes with time, can be read what a man wished to be and what he has become. Not all that crazy, I thought. The body really can be an excellent indicator. Is it not true that after a certain age one is responsible for one's face? And the hands, don't they reveal things about the past that plastic surgery tries to erase elsewhere?

I was very curious to see what this woman would read in my face, my ankles, and especially in the small mole just over my right eyebrow. But her first words disappointed me.

'*Your ears are indicative of generosity.*' (One of the usual gambits to put the 'patient' in a good mood, I said to myself.) '*Your brothers and sisters all depend on you.*'

'That's not true – I have no brothers or sisters,' I replied aloud. 'I'm an only child.'

She was unperturbed. '*If there are no brothers and sisters, then it's your relatives. Your ears say that many of your relatives depend on you.*' (Yes and no, I said to myself, already resigned to more of these generalities.)

'*As a young man you had great problems over money and health, but since the age of thirty-five everything has gone well from that point of view. You're fortunate, because you have always had beside you someone you trust, someone who helps you.*'

'Yes, indeed. I've been married for over thirty years,' I said.

'*Yes, and you married your second love, not the first.*' (Not true at all – neither the first nor the second – but by now I had already given up hope of hearing anything interesting, and did not want to disappoint the lady.)

'*Your ears indicate that one day you'll come into a great inheritance from your parents.*' (Poor ears, they lie! From my parents – my father died some time ago – nothing of that sort can be expected. Certainly if today I asked my mother – eighty-five years old and affected by senile dementia – 'Mother, where have you hidden the money?' she would raise a hand and, with that splendid smile that is party to the things she no longer knows, would say, 'Over there . . . over there', indicating with absolute confidence some point in the air. Well, that money 'over there' is all I will ever inherit. Or should I reinterpret the word 'inheritance', taking it to mean not only money?)

The woman continued, '*In the house where you live is a place where you worship the gods and your ancestors. It's good that you do this. Never give it up.*' (Ah, now this is interesting. In the home of every Asian, especially the Chinese, there is a place of that sort, usually a little altar, and it takes no great powers of second sight to imagine this. It is like telling a devout Christian: 'There's a crucifix in your house.' But this woman can see that I am a foreigner, in all probability not a Buddhist and certainly not given to ancestor-worship. And yet she says this – and she is right. In my house there is just such a place. It came into being over the years. I had become interested in those gilded camphorwood statuettes that the southern Chinese have on their family altars, and I had bought a few in Macao. After a while, seeing them sitting on my shelves like ornaments, I had a feeling that they were suffering, removed from their altars, that they had lost their meaning. I began putting sticks of incense beside them.

69

Then in Peking, in an old second-hand shop near the Drum Tower where I used to drop in now and then to see what the peasants had brought to sell, I saw a beautiful altar of carved wood, one of those on which families used to keep little votive tablets for their ancestors, and I bought it. The Macao statues now had a home; and when my father died his photograph came to rest in the lap of a fine Buddha who by then occupied the centre of the altar. Since then, every day I light a stick of incense, and with that little rite take a moment to remember him. He is buried in a big cemetery in Florence, one of those where you get lost in the maze of alleys and paths, and where every grave is exactly like all the others. I have never wanted to go there. His place for me is in my home, on that Chinese ancestral altar.)

'*The house you live in, in Thailand, is in a beautiful place that makes you happy. Stay in that house as long as you are in this country.*'

Again she studied my face, pondered, and said that money melts in my hand. (Well, there is a consensus on that, at least.) She said that I tend to be lucky, that I have instinct, that where the road forks I always choose the direction that turns out best, and that I always surround myself with the right people. She said that my mouth does not indicate regrets because in life I have always done what I wanted. '*You will have a long life,*' she proclaimed. Then she focused on my mole. '*Ah, this is a sign of your good luck, but it's also a sign that you'll die abroad.*' She paused a moment and added: '*There is no doubt about it: you'll die in a country which is not your own.*'

She asked if I had any questions. I tried to think of one, and remembered that in the autumn the English and German editions of my latest book, the story of a long journey through the Soviet Union in the months when the empire fell apart and Communism died, would be published.

'What should I do to ensure that this book will be successful and sell lots of copies?' I asked.

She concentrated, then replied with an air of complete certainty: '*The book must come out between 9 September and 10 October; it must be neither too long nor too short; it must have a coloured dustjacket, but the colours must not be too strong; and, above all, in the title there must be the name of a person, but not that of a woman.*'

I burst out laughing, glad that Vladimir Ilyich was born male. The book was called *Goodnight, Mister Lenin*, and the dustjacket, long decided upon, was in pastel colours.

She concluded: '*And don't forget that you must pray to Buddha and make offerings on the altar of your ancestors. Only if you do that will the book enjoy success!*'

She did not ask for payment, only that I make a contribution to the Association.

I spent several days reflecting on my decision not to fly and trying to analyze the real reasons behind it. There could be no denying that I wanted to do something different, to have an excuse for a change in the daily routine. But had I not also thought that by obeying the Hong Kong fortune-teller's injunction I would avoid the possibility of that air accident about which he had been so emphatic? That was obviously so, but I found it hard to admit.

I realized that despite having lived many years in Asia, and having adapted myself to the life there, intellectually I still had my roots in Europe. I had not expunged from my mind the instinctive Western contempt for what we call superstition. Every time I found myself starting to feel that way I had to remember that in Asia 'superstition' is an essential part of life. And anyway, I told myself, many of the practices that seem absurd today may originally have had a certain logic which with time has been forgotten. For example acupuncture: it works, but no one can really explain why. And the art of *feng-shui* was originally based on the careful study of nature: the nature which we moderns understand less and less.

In Chinese *feng* means wind, *shui* means water. *Feng-shui* thus means 'the forces of nature'; the expert in *feng-shui* is one who understands the fundamental elements of which the world is made, and can judge the influence of one on another. He can evaluate the influence that the course of a river, the position of a hill or the shape of a mountain may have on a city or a house to be built, or a grave to be dug. Strange? Not at all. Even we, in planning a house, take account of the sun's direction, and make sure the building is not too exposed to dampness.

For many centuries the principles of *feng-shui* have had a decisive influence on Chinese architecture. The plans of all the ancient settlements of the Celestial Empire, beginning with the one that is now the city of Xian, as well as those of the Chinese diaspora, including Hué, the imperial capital of Vietnam, were based on considerations of *feng-shui*. The same is true for all the imperial tombs, beginning with that of Qin Shi Huang Di, the first emperor, with his famous terracotta army. The position of a tomb is very important. A grave that is well located and exposed to 'cosmic breath' can keep alive the soul of the deceased and bring happiness and well-being to future generations. A badly placed tomb, on the other hand, can bring the descendants misfortune after misfortune.

The art of *feng-shui* was born in China, but today it is a common practice in much of Asia. When something goes wrong – a marriage, a business deal or a factory – the first thought is that something is out of joint with the *feng-shui*, and an expert is consulted. A few years ago in Macao a newly opened casino was failing to attract customers. The cause, according to the *feng-shui* man, lay in the colour of the roof: it was red like the shell of a dead crab, rather than green like the shell of a live one. The roof was repainted and business boomed.

Anecdotes of this kind have cost *feng-shui* some of its ancient respectability. But they have not reduced its popularity, and there is a growing number of people in Asia today who, on the advice of *feng-shui* experts, propitiate fate by changing their furniture arrangement, the colour of their office walls or the shape of their front doors. Even the earnest British directors of the Hongkong and Shanghai Bank, when they decided to build their big new head office in Hong Kong, turned to one of the best-known experts in the colony to avoid trouble with the *feng-shui*. During the planning of that futuristic steel and glass edifice the architect, Norman Foster, was constantly in touch with this 'master of the forces of nature', taking note of what he said and following his recommendations. These determined a great number of architectural details, including the strange diagonal placement of the entrance stairway.

After building the bank, Foster helped to plan the new Hong Kong airport (in the shape of a dragon!). But people in certain areas of his office were continually falling ill. So the *feng-shui* expert was called in. He studied the problem, and concluded that the demolition of some old houses in the area had left a gap through which 'evil spirits' flew in a direct line to strike the building. For the people working there it was like having a knife constantly plunged in their chests. His advice was to move all the desks, to curtain the windows and to place mirrors to deflect the spirits. Absurd? Perhaps, but once all this was done there were no further complaints from the staff.

Obviously, the 'successes' of *feng-shui*, as of any magic practice, are partly explained by an element of autosuggestion: if people firmly believe that something can help them, it may indeed do so. The typical case is that of a couple, childless for years, who manage to conceive after following the advice of the *feng-shui* man to change the position of their marital bed.

What is interesting about *feng-shui*, despite its façade of magic, is its basic principle: the constant re-establishment of harmony with nature. For the Chinese everything has to be in equilibrium. Illnesses, misfortunes, sterility or bad luck result from the rupture of some harmony, and the function of *feng-shui* is to restore it. Ecologists *ante litteram*, the Chinese. They knew nature well. They knew nothing else!

The Chinese have never been metaphysicians, they have never believed in a transcendent god. For them nature is all, and it is from nature that they have drawn their knowledge and their beliefs. Even their writing, made up of images, is based on nature and not on some abstract convention like our alphabet. In any European language it would be possible to agree that from now on the word 'fish' means horse and the word 'horse' means fish. But in Chinese such a thing would be inconceivable, because the character used to write fish *is* a fish, and the character for horse *is* a horse.

Western man sees God as the creator of nature, and for centuries has distinguished between the natural world and the world of the divine. But for the Chinese the two are indistinguishable. God and nature are the same thing. Divination is thus a sort of religion, and the fortune-teller is also a theologian and priest. That is why, until the advent of Communism, superstition was never repressed in China as it was in the West, where it was seen as the antithesis of religion and has always been vigorously suppressed. The Chinese – like almost all Asians – have never worried about this distinction between religion and superstition, just as they have never posed the problem – also typically Western – of defining what is and is not science. For centuries the Chinese have practised astrology, for example, without ever wondering if its bases were 'scientific'. In their eyes it worked, and that was enough.

Chinese astrology is based on the lunar calendar. A year consists of twelve new moons to which, every twelve years, a thirteenth is added. Twelve years make a cycle. Each year is characterized by an animal: the rat, the ox, the tiger, the cat, the dragon, the snake, the horse, the goat, the monkey, the rooster, the dog, the pig. The first day of the year is the day of the first moon and the year always begins in January or February.

The animal of the year of one's birth has an enormous influence on one's personality and destiny: people born in the year of the rat, for example, must take care all their lives not to fall into traps; those born in the year of the cat will always land on their feet; those born under the sign of the rooster must always scratch the earth to feed themselves. Women born in the year of the horse are indomitable and therefore difficult wives. Those born in the combination of the horse with fire – which happens every sixty years – are wild, dangerous and practically impossible to marry. 1966 was one of those years, and in Asia many women who found themselves pregnant resorted to abortions to avoid bringing into the world daughters who would not, in all probability, find husbands. In Taiwan in 1966 the birth rate fell by 25 per cent for this reason.

On the other hand, males born in the year of the dragon are destined to be strong, intelligent and fortunate. As 1988 was such a year, coupled with the fact that the Chinese consider the double 8 to be a symbol of double happiness, many couples tried to have sons then. To render the child even more fortunate, many mothers tried to give birth on the eighth day of the eighth month of that year: all the maternity beds in Singapore, Taiwan and Hong Kong were booked up by women prepared to undergo Caesarean sections to bring their children into the world on that ultra-auspicious day – 8 August 1988.

One of the most important factors determining a person's destiny is the exact hour of his birth. Only by knowing that hour can the astrologer draw his horoscope, identify his character, describe the important stages of his life and even foresee the eventual date of his death. To know the hour of someone's birth is to possess a weapon against him; therefore many politicians in Asia keep their birth-hour secret, or give a false one.

Everyone knows that Deng Xiaoping was born on 22 August 1904 (the year of the dragon!), but the exact hour remains one of China's great secrets. Mao Tse-Tung and Chou Enlai were less successful. In the 1920s both of them, then living in Shanghai, went – as a joke, or because they believed in it, who knows? – to see the most famous astrologer of the city, a certain Yuan Shu Shuan. When the nationalists fled to Taiwan in 1949, among the piles of documents they took with them were the horoscopes that Master Yuan had carefully preserved of all his clients. Those of people who had since become famous were published. In 1962 a Taiwanese astrologer predicted, on the basis of the birth times given to Yuan, that both Mao and Chou would die in the same year, 1976. And indeed they did.

Innumerable political decisions in Asia are based on astrology, and therefore the secret services of various countries employ experts to predict what their adversaries' astrologers may advise in certain situations. It is known that the Vietnamese, the Indians, the South Koreans and the Chinese have astrology sections in their counter-espionage agencies. Even the British have one, based in Hong Kong, to keep track of what the Chinese are doing in the sphere of the occult. Increasingly, it seems, all sorts of old practices, banned during forty years of Communism, have now resurfaced to flourish not only among the people, but among the Communist rulers themselves.

In 1990, a few days before the anniversary of the Tiananmen massacre, a strange thing happened. A group of workers erected a large ring of scaffolding around the flagpole in the centre of the square and started working inside it. When the scaffolding was removed, the height of the pole had been increased by a few yards, and the red flag, symbol of China, flew higher than it had ever done since 1949. Apparently a great *feng-shui* expert had suggested to Deng Xiaoping that this would restore the harmony of the square and thus the good fortune of the People's Republic.

I began collecting stories like these because I planned to write an article on the importance of superstition in Asia, but I also wanted to dispel my doubts and to convince myself that I was right to change my life for a reason that had absolutely nothing rational about it. But was that not true of much of the life around me? Especially in Thailand, I had only to use my eyes.

In Thailand it is common for important political declarations to be made on days considered auspicious, and for politicians to reassure public opinion about the state of the economy or national security by quoting astrologers. In the middle of the Gulf War, when Thailand feared attacks from Islamic terrorists because of its pro-American stance, Prime Minister Chatichai called a press conference and said: 'There is nothing to worry about. Thailand will be spared. My astrologer says so.' Nobody laughed. Everyone knew that he was serious. A couple of months previously he had had a mole removed from under his left eye because his astrologer had told him it would bring him bad luck.

In February 1991 Chatichai was overthrown by one of the usual military coups, but after a few months of peaceful exile in London he came back to live in Bangkok. Even in that coup, the occult seems to have played no small role. The generals who seized power had just returned from a secret trip to Burma. In Rangoon they had made offerings in the temple where their Burmese colleagues had made theirs before their successful coup of 1988. Then, taking care not to 'discharge' their energy – which meant never touching the earth, always walking on a red carpet – they went to the car, to the helicopter, to the plane, and at last to the Bangkok general command post. There, still 'charged', they launched their *putsch*, the success of which many in Bangkok believed was due to the Burmese energy.

A year after the coup, General Suchinda, who had become Prime Minister, gave the army orders to fire on a crowd of demonstrators. There were several hundred victims. The crisis was resolved by the intervention of the king. General Suchinda resigned, but not before declaring a general amnesty, thanks to which he and the others responsible for the massacre were granted immunity from any legal action. The deaths, said Suchinda, could not be laid at his door: it had been the demonstrators' *karma* to die. Most people let it go at that, but a group of implacable democrats found it intolerable that no one should be punished for the deaths of so many people. For justice they turned to black magic.

One Sunday morning, on the great Sanam Luang Square in front of the Royal Palace, a strange ceremony took place. The names and photographs of Suchinda and the other two generals of the junta were placed in an old coffin, and the widows of some of the victims burned peppers and salt in broken begging bowls. Coffins, widows and broken crockery are symbols of great misfortune, and the cere-mony was meant to put the evil eye on the three generals and destroy them.

The generals took the matter very seriously. Suchinda went to a famous monk to have his name changed, so that the evil eye would fall on the one he no longer bore; one of the other generals, also on the advice of a monk, changed his spectacle frames, shaved off his moustache and ate a piece of gold leaf so as to make his speeches more popular; the third had a surgeon remove some wrinkles that were bringing him bad luck, and then, to be on the safe side, took his mistress and went to Paris to run a restaurant.

No history book, especially if written by a foreigner, will ever give that version of the coup and the Bangkok massacre. But that is how most people in Thailand experienced them.

One encounter that greatly encouraged me to hold to my plan was with some researchers at the École Française de l'Extreme Orient. For the first time in its history the school had organized a meeting of all its scholars, in Thailand. I went to hear about their work and discovered, to my great surprise, that some of them were studying the subjects in which I had become interested.

One ethnologist gave a paper investigating the revival of occult Taoist practices in the Chinese province of Fukien. He told how one night, under a full moon, he had witnessed a ceremony in which a man immobilized by ropes had suddenly shot like an arrow across the rice fields, drawing after him the whole population of the village, including the local Communist Party secretary.

The story resembled some of those recounted by Alexandra David-Neel about Tibet in the 1930s. Only this was China in 1993, and the narrator was a scholar who could hardly be suspected of exaggeration.

There was something in the air that told me I had made the right decision.

CHAPTER SEVEN

Dreams of a Monk

Is there such a thing as chance? I was coming to believe that a lot of what seems to happen 'by chance' is in fact our own doing: once we look at the world through different glasses we see things which previously escaped us, and which we therefore believed to be non-existent. Chance, in short, is ourselves.

At the end of February the Dalai Lama came to Bangkok on a lightning visit. During his few hours in the city he held a press conference at the Foreign Correspondents' Club on the twenty-first floor of the Hotel Dusit Thani. Before the largest crowd of journalists ever assembled in that room, he appealed for the liberation of Aung San Suu Kyi, the imprisoned heroine of the Burmese democracy movement. He spoke of goodness, love, purity of heart and peace.

His speech left me very disappointed, and I drew no comfort from the fact that as he was leaving the room, in his kindly, smiling way he stopped when he reached me, as if my face were familiar. His hands met in front of his chest, and when I returned his greeting in like manner, he seized my wrists in a firm grasp and shook them, expressing the warmest good wishes and some sort of blessing.

'Is he always so down-to-earth, so utterly simple? He talked like a country priest,' I said to one of the monks who was hurrying after him. He was dressed like the others in a handsome purple robe trimmed with red and yellow, but his face was that of a Westerner, pale and short-sighted, with small spectacles. I had been watching him the whole time as he stood motionless, with a joyful smile, apparently absorbing the Dalai Lama's words as if they were the truest and most beautiful he had ever heard.

Still smiling serenely, the monk replied, 'Greatness may also be manifested in simplicity. This is the greatness of the Dalai Lama.'

His English was perfect, but I realized from his accent that he was not Anglo-Saxon.

'No, no, no. I'm Italian.'

'Italian? So am I!'

This was no chance meeting – I had been looking for this very man! He was Stefano Brunori, aged fifty, born in Florence, an ex-journalist who for the past twenty years had been a Tibetan monk with the name of Gelong Karma Chang Choub. Too many coincidences to be mere chance! He normally lived in a monastery in Katmandu, but his teachers (this word definitely caught my fancy; to have teachers must be wonderful – I haven't had one for a long time) had allowed him to come to Thailand. He needed treatment for gastritis, caused by the ultra-strict vegetarian monastic diet. Next door to our home was an excellent hospital where he could have all the tests he needed. Thus it was that Karma Chang Choub came to stay in Turtle House.

We spent three days together, talking from morning to night. In our lives there were so many correspondences and parallels that each of us, without saying so (for it was only too obvious), could see in the other what he might have been. In that delicate play of mirrors it was easy to become friends, and perhaps to get to know each other a little.

We had both left Florence and travelled about the world, and in 1971 we both arrived in Asia. I came with Angela, two suitcases and two babies, without a job but determined to become a journalist. He too had brought a foreign wife with him, but no children, and as regards work he was already in a crisis. He was more 'on the road', as they used to say of those who have no clearer aim than to travel from Europe to Asia, taking pot luck when it came to transport. Usually such people would eventually disappear into some Indian ashram, or would finish up on the beaches of Goa, or in Bali, or with hepatitis in a Salvation Army hostel. In Chang Choub's case the road had led to Nepal. In Katmandu, he said, something had happened inside him. He parted from his wife, entered a Tibetan monastery as a novice, and after some time took the vows. He was ordained a monk by the Dalai Lama himself.

From then on it was as if the burden of life had been lifted from his shoulders. He had no more possessions, the rhythm of his days was fixed by the monastic routine, all decisions were made for him by his teachers. It was they who decided if he could study another meditation method, if his mother could come and see him. A year previously, they had given him permission and money to spend the winter in a Buddhist monastery in Penang.

We soon got round to talking about my Hong Kong fortune-teller. The fact that I had decided to heed the warning and spend a year without flying did something to narrow the gap between Chang Choub's existence and my own. Like him, I had entered an order of ideas that was anything but Florentine. I too had let myself follow the paths of Asia, and so he felt I understood him a bit better.

Of course, he said, monks with great meditative powers can see the future, but that is not their aim in meditating. They are reluctant to say what they know because they do not want to become like fairground freaks. The truly enlightened ones, like Buddha and Christ, did not like to perform miracles just to convince unbelievers. The ability was there, obviously enough, but they used it only when it was absolutely necessary.

I have always liked the story of Buddha arriving at a river and the people asking him to cross it by walking over it. He pointed to a boat and said: 'That's the simpler way.'

Many Tibetan monks have developed special powers. The Dalai Lama himself has a personal oracle who helps him predict the future and make decisions. It was his previous reincarnation, back in 1959 when Mao's troops were entering Lhasa, who told the Dalai Lama exactly when to leave and in what direction to go. The flight was successful. That same oracle, it is said, is now convinced that the Chinese will soon lose control of Tibet, and that the country will regain its independence.

It amused Chang Choub to speak of his life as a monk. He gave the impression that he saw the whole story from the outside, with the irony with which a Florentine would look on a man like him, a Westerner who becomes a Tibetan monk: an anomaly, a contradiction in terms. The first years, he told me, were very hard. Weakened by the diet and the cold, he was often ill. One thing that he never got used to, and indeed found more and more unbearable as time went by, was the sound of the long horns that woke the monks at three in the morning. 'If it had been Beethoven, Bach, you'd have got up gladly, but that booooo . . . booooo – on a single note that never changes, day after day, booooo . . . booooo – puts a strain on all my hard-won detachment from the things of the world.' He said this almost with anger.

Even in speaking about the religious aspect of his choice, his tone was detached. 'Buddha said we were to question everything, question the teachers and Buddha himself.' He seemed to be justifying a deep uncertainty which, even after so many years, had stayed with him. What sounded strange to me was his way of speaking about the teachers he had studied under. Of one of them he remarked, 'Of course, he is very advanced, he has more than two hundred years of meditation behind him.' Of another whom he wanted to meet he said, 'He is only nine years old, but in his last life he was one of the greatest, and this could well be his last reincarnation.'

I have lived much of my life among the Chinese, Buddhists, for the most part, who find it natural to believe that a man passes through a long series of lives, each time occupying the body of some living being; but that idea had never really engaged me personally. Talking with Chang Choub, who took reincarnation for granted, I at least understood the underlying concept of the belief. Our existence is merely a link in a long chain of many lives and many deaths. Each new birth brings, along with the body, a sum of tendencies and potentialities which result from the spiritual path followed in former lives; this is our *karma*. With this baggage we resume the journey where it had been left off, sometimes moving forwards, at other times backwards. The baggage of wisdom, as it were, has nothing to do with the everyday knowledge of the world which everyone must accumulate from scratch for himself. Even the reincarnation of a great guru must learn again that fire burns, that one can drown in water, and so on.

Some very advanced teachers can remember details of their previous lives with great precision. A classic anecdote tells of a child, the son of peasants, who said, 'It's mine, it's mine,' when he saw the rosary of the late Dalai Lama in the hands of a monk who was travelling Tibet dressed as a beggar in search of the Dalai Lama's reincarnation. He found it in that child. The little boy was taken to the Potala, where he stopped outside the wall, wanting to enter at the exact spot where there had been a door during his previous life – a door that had since been walled up.

Believers also tell the story of a child who saw some Tibetan exiles in India perform an ancient ritual dance. Suddenly he cried: 'No,

no! Not that way!' He ran among the monks and in a trance began
to move like an experienced dancer. They all prostrated themselves,
recognizing in him the reincarnation of a great teacher, the Karmapa.
Then he became a child again, and returned to his mother's arms.

Talking about these things with Chang Choub – I called him by
that name, to emphasize my acceptance of him as he wished to be
– felt like going on a long journey, while remaining seated on the
veranda of Turtle House. It was like taking a holiday from normal
life.

'But surely you can't believe in reincarnation in the strict sense,'
I said. 'The population of the world is constantly increasing, millions
more are born every minute. From whom are they all reincarnated?'
The question was banal and prosaic, a bit like asking a saint to prove
the existence of God by performing a miracle. But Chang Choub
did not perform miracles – far from it. He had learned countless
techniques of meditation, he had been a pupil of great teachers, he
had spent months as a hermit in a cave; but he admitted, with some
sadness, that he had not achieved a great deal.

'What is it you are aiming at?' I asked. 'What are the dreams of
a monk like you?'

And for the first time I heard the word: '*Satori.*'

'Meaning what?'

'A moment of great clarity. The moment when you rise above
everything.'

'A moment. And you haven't managed to get there even a
moment?'

No, he said, and it was like admitting a great defeat. I was left to
wonder why twenty years of effort, sacrifice, fidelity to so many
vows, years of silence, cold, rice with nothing but vegetables, and
the horrible sound of the horns at dawn, should have yielded such
a meagre harvest. Chang Choub told me that a monk he knew had
had *satori* one day after barely two years of exercises – suddenly, just
like that, while driving along a freeway in California.

In the morning Chang Choub would sit in our *salà*, the small
wooden pavilion over the pond, meditating with closed eyes,
motionless and withdrawn. Watching him from a distance, I could
not, try as I might, shake off a feeling of unhappiness which his
presence conveyed to me. Between the colour of his skin and that
of his robe there was a deep contradiction; I felt it too in his pose

as he sat cross-legged on the floor. In him, so Western despite his Asian clothes, there seemed to be something discordant, out of kilter. I imagined that one day, surrounded by monks who are his brothers in name only, speaking a language not his own in a place where not one sound or smell was of home, Chang Choub might feel terribly lonely, lonelier than ever. I asked myself if at the end of his life he would find himself wondering – as perhaps he already does at times – whether he had not spent his days pursuing someone else's goal, prey to an illusion that was not even his.

The crisis that Stefano Brunori had undergone twenty years previously was clear enough. It was one that sooner or later affects everyone in some way. As soon as you start asking questions you find that some of them, especially the simplest, have no obvious answers. You have to go out and look for them. But where? He chose the least expected direction, a difficult one. Perhaps he was attracted by the exotic, by the strange. Those alien words, new to his ears, appeared much more meaningful than the old familiar ones of his own language. *Satori* seemed to promise so much more than 'grace'.

And yet, if that young Florentine had chosen a path furnished by his own culture and become a Franciscan or a Jesuit, if he had retired to Camaldoli or La Verna instead of a monastery in Nepal, perhaps he would have found a solution that was more familiar, more suited, less lonely. And at least he would have been spared those terrible horns in the morning! Was he, like me, a victim of exoticism? Of a need to seek the ends of the earth? After all, I could perfectly well have become a journalist in Italy, in a land which is just as exotic as Asia, a land whose real story is yet to be told.

When Chang Choub left, it felt as if we had known each other much longer than three days. He believed that at the Dalai Lama's press conference we had simply found each other again. It cost me an effort to accept that 'again', but I too felt that we were joined by many, many threads which I would have liked to continue disentangling. Talking about his life had made me look again at my own; talking with him, I began for the first time to think seriously about meditation. I had seen the possible connection between the mind, trained through meditation, and powers including that of prescience. For the first time I had heard someone talk about techniques of meditation, and had been encouraged to try them out. It may be strange, but it is so. How many times had I seen advertisements for courses in Transcendental Meditation, or heard of young people going to meditate at a temple in southern Thailand? I paid no attention; it seemed to belong to another world, a world of weird, marginal people in search of salvation. I felt that it had no relevance for me personally.

Chang Choub, with the life he led, brought all this before me again, and made me think that it might have something to do with me. When he left Turtle House, with his half-empty purple sack over his shoulder, it was as if he left behind a trail of little white stones – or breadcrumbs? – to show me the way towards new explorations.

We promised to meet again in India. I have felt for years that India is in my future. In origin the reason was simple. I had grown up politically in the 1950s, when anyone interested in the Third World came up against two great myths, Gandhi and Mao – two different solutions to the same problem, opposing bets on the destinies of the two most populous nations on earth, two hypotheses of social philosophy from which it seemed that we in the West also had something to learn. Having spent years among the Chinese, trying to understand what a disaster the myth of Mao had been for them, it seemed logical to go one day to India to see what had happened to the myth of Gandhi. Living in Peking or Hong Kong, whenever we felt fed up with the prosaic pragmatism of the Chinese, or noticed ourselves reacting in a Chinese way, Angela and I would say to each other: 'India. India.' For us India had become the antidote to the *mal jaune*, that poison concocted of love and disappointment, of endless small irritations and great faith, which afflicts all those who put down roots for a while in the Middle Kingdom and then find that they cannot tear themselves away.

I would have liked to move to India in 1984, when the Chinese took a decision for me that I would never have been able to take on my own, and thus did me an enormous favour: they arrested me and expelled me from their country. But at the time I did not manage it, and more years went by. To my original reason for wanting to go to India a new and more important one has been added: I want to see if India, with its spirituality and its madness, can resist the disheartening wave of materialism which is sweeping the world. I want to see if India can solve the dilemma and preserve its uniqueness. I want to see if in India the seed of a humanity with aspirations beyond the greedy race for Western modernity is still alive.

Living in Asia, I have told myself again and again that there is no culture with the capacity to resist, to express itself with renewed creativity. Chinese culture has been moribund for at least a century, and Mao, in the effort to found a new China, murdered the little that remained of the old. With nothing left to believe in, the Chinese now dream only of becoming Americans. Students marched in Tiananmen Square behind a copy of the Statue of Liberty, and the old Marxist-Leninist rulers erase the memory of their crimes and their lust for power by letting the people run after illusions of Western wealth.

Which Asian culture has preserved its own springs of creativity? Which is still able to regenerate itself, to develop its own models, its own alternatives? The Khmer culture, which died with Angkor eight centuries ago and was once again killed by Pol Pot and the Khmer Rouge in their absurd attempt to revive it? The Vietnamese culture, which can define itself solely in terms of political independence? Or the Balinese, now packaged for tourist consumption?

India, India! I said to myself, nursing the hope – or perhaps the illusion – of a last enclave of spirituality. India, where there is still plenty of madness. India, which gives hospitality to the Dalai Lama. India, where the dollar is not yet the sole measure of greatness. That is why I made plans to go to India, and meet there my fellow Florentine escapee, Chang Choub.

A rich woman from Hong Kong came to see me. She was in Bangkok to meet her guru, a Tibetan monk and follower of the Dalai Lama, 'a very advanced teacher'. He belongs to the international jet set, at home in New York, Paris and London, and he has a following of such women, usually rich and beautiful, in constant attendance. He plays the guru and the women pay the bills, buy his air tickets, organize his life. 'He's the reincarnation of a great teacher. He can't be bothered with such things,' said the understanding lady, a consenting victim – perhaps like Chang Choub? – of Tibet's great, subtle, historic vengeance.

Quite extraordinary, Tibet! For centuries it remained closed and inaccessible, removed from the world; for centuries, in isolation, cutting itself off from any other field of study, it practised the 'inner science'. Then came the first explorers. At the beginning of the twentieth century the British entered Lhasa; fifty years later the Chinese occupied the country and made it a sort of colony. A hundred thousand Tibetans fled, but that diaspora lit the fuse for the time bomb of revenge.

Tibetan Buddhism, first practised exclusively in the Himalayas and Mongolia, has been spreading throughout the world. Tibetan gurus have settled everywhere, from Switzerland to California, displacing the yogis who had formerly conquered the soul of Europe in its quest for the exotic. Their dogmas, once secret, have become best-sellers. Young gurus claiming to be reincarnations of old Tibetan teachers have become the mouthpieces of this ancient wisdom. With thousands of followers all over the world, they are looked after by little circles of rich lay nuns. Bernardo Bertolucci's advisor on his film *Little Buddha* was one of these young gurus, born and raised outside Tibet, but a reincarnation of a great teacher. The capital of the Dalai Lama in exile, in Dharamsala, north of Delhi, has become a place of pilgrimage for thousands of young Westerners, and he has acquired the stature of a sort of second Pope, not only a spiritual leader, but also the head of the Tibetan government in exile.

By occupying Tibet, the Chinese have indirectly sown the seeds of Tibetan Buddhism throughout the world, thus practically planting a bomb in their own house. Sympathy for the Tibetan cause is growing, and interest in the spiritual aspect has become political. The Dalai Lama is welcomed as a guest in the centres of world power. He has become the symbol of the struggle against Peking's totalitarian regime.

The other side of the coin is that the gurus, with their mythical roots amid the Himalayan peaks and their role as representatives of an oppressed people and bearers of spirituality, provide a perfect alibi for people who pursue redemption while remaining completely enmeshed in materialism. Because of the widespread disorientation from which our culture suffers, people have lost their natural scepticism. Today any charlatan can sell his spiritual potions if he gives them an exotic name.

Am I too a victim of this phenomenon? Is that why I spend days listening to Chang Choub, why I obey the prophetic warning not to fly, and say 'yes' when invited to see a new fortune-teller?

The woman who had served as my interpreter with the blind fortune-teller made an appointment for me with her own astrologer-monk. So, one afternoon, again pretending that I was passing through Bangkok, I arranged to meet her and her friend in the lobby of the Oriental Hotel.

Her friend drove a Volvo. She was of Chinese origin, an importer of medical equipment for Thai hospitals. She was in her late forties, a once-beautiful woman who had allowed herself to put on weight. For want of love? So I concluded while scrutinizing her. I reflected with amusement that, starting with that observation, I too could set up as a fortune-teller and talk to her of her past and her future.

We crossed the Chao Paya by one of Bangkok's many bridges. In the Bang Khun Non quarter we turned off the squalid, depressing cement road, lined with rubbish heaps and shapeless little houses, into a narrow lane. After about two hundred yards we arrived at the hushed, tranquil compound of a Buddhist temple. It was simple and austere, constructed entirely of wood, with long dormitories, beautiful inlaid panels under the eaves, and large windows where the monks' orange robes were hung out to dry. The heat was stifling, but two large trees gave the complex of buildings an air of freshness.

The monk we had come to see was sitting on the teak floor of a wide, shady terrace, surrounded by coffee jars, teapots, small cups and trays, rolls of toilet paper, packets of cigarettes and two fans. He was served by a young couple, his relatives, who handed him things from time to time with gestures of devout submission. Now and then they fanned their baby, a few months old, who slept peacefully with his bottle between two fat astrology books and a geomancer's quadrant.

The monk was about fifty, with a handsome head, and tattoos on his chest and arms. He drank tea non-stop and chain-smoked. Thai Buddhism is extremely tolerant and permissive. Monks are forbidden the use of intoxicants, and most Buddhists include tobacco in that category. But not the Thais, who find cigarettes and tea the best means of combating hunger during the long daily fast. Reading the future is also supposed to be against the rules; in fact Buddha himself forbade it. But in this the Thais follow the tradition of one of his disciples, Mogellana, who began telling fortunes immediately after Buddha's death, using powers acquired thanks to the master's teachings and through meditation.

The monk welcomed us with a big smile and a fine burp. It was noon; he had just finished his big meal of the day, and would eat no more solid food until breakfast at dawn the next morning. My interpreter's friend dropped to her knees and shuffled towards him. She had been there once before, but without giving her name. Her husband was one of the monk's faithful disciples and frequent visitors, and she wanted, without letting him know, to have her future read by the same person who did it for him.

The sitting lasted about an hour, but the surprising part came at once. 'Your husband has many other women, and you should sue for divorce,' said the monk. The woman laughed. My interpreter explained to me that it was absolutely true about these lovers, and her friend had already secretly made arrangements for a divorce. She was only afraid that her husband would refuse to sign the documents, or that he would demand a mint of money for doing so.

'You must leave the house you share with your husband, and go and live elsewhere. If you move during the month of October all will be well with you,' the monk said. My interpreter whispered to me that her friend had bought an apartment of her own already.

'Once you are in the new house,' continued the monk, 'you must make a choice: a new husband or a great deal of money. Take care: if you have even one boyfriend, you'll never become rich.'

'Venerable one,' said the woman, 'help me to make a hundred million baht and I'll buy you a Mercedes!' As if to show that she was in earnest, she took a fine electric thermos out of her bag and proffered it to him very ceremoniously with both hands, bowing her forehead to the floor.

The rest of the session was banal and of little interest; in the end I fell asleep on the beautiful wooden boards. I was woken once my interpreter had had her session and had been advised. It was my turn.

On a piece of paper I wrote the day and hour of my birth. Not the time in Florence, eight in the evening, but the equivalent in Bangkok, two in the afternoon. To tell the truth I have never known exactly at what time I was born. I remember only that my mother said it was 'before supper'.

The monk made some complicated calculations, consulted the quadrant and a thick book, and with a biro on a piece of white paper he drew some circles inside a square – my horoscope, apparently – then some signs. He asked me some more questions, saying he had to check whether the time of birth I had given him was the correct one. He needed certain information about my past if he was to read the right future. It was as if there were different pages for different types of destiny, and before proceeding he had to make sure he was reading the correct one.

'*Are you rich?*'

'No,' I replied, once again struck by the fact that money seems to be an obsession with all fortune-tellers, be they monks or blind men.

'*But the numbers say you are,*' he insisted. I told him that when I was a child my family was so poor that during the war we really did not have enough to eat, and my mother sometimes made strange 'cakes' with sawdust in them.

Grimacing, the monk consulted the signs on the horoscope and said, '*But in the past you've made big business deals, and once you lost many millions in one fell swoop.*'

'No, I've never made any deals, and at no point in my life do I remember buying a single thing in order to sell it,' I said.

He looked perplexed, and a bit lost. '*Perhaps the time when you said you were born isn't the right one. Could it possibly have been half an hour earlier?*' He hesitated for a moment: '*Or three quarters of an hour?*' he said in an apologetic tone.

'Quite possibly,' I said. 'Perhaps in 1938 in Italy they put the clocks back in September, so the difference between Florence and Bangkok would be one hour more.' This cheered him.

'*Tell me if what I am about to say is true, and we'll be sure we have the right time. You have been married for many years.*' (True. Now we're getting somewhere.) '*Your wife is a stronger character than you.*' (Hard to admit, but it's true.) '*You are something like a writer or a journalist.*' (This too?) '*You have a good brain, and you are a sincere, straightforward person.*' (Well . . .)

I told him all this was more or less true, and he was delighted. '*Remember, then,*' he said, '*whenever you see an astrologer: not eight in the evening, but seven, or a quarter past.*' And then he began his readings.

'*You have a sort of shell around you. Your enemies can't harm you. As*'

for money . . . ' (Here we go again!) *' . . . you'll always have some —
now more, now less, but you'll never be poor. You are intelligent and your
lucky number is five. You have a life of highs and lows. Sometimes you are
on top of the world, sometimes depressed. If you have a plan to do something
special this year, be strong, carry it out! This is a good year.'* (I do indeed
have a plan, the plan not to fly.) *'1990 and 1991 were not particularly
good years.'* (Wrong, 1991 in particular was wonderful: I travelled
throughout the Soviet Union, wrote a book . . .) *'But the years to
come will be excellent.'*

'Venerable one, do you see no dangers in my life?' I asked.

'An excellent question,' he said. *'No. I don't see any.'*

'Years ago I was told that 1993 would be a dangerous year for
me, and that I must not take any planes.'

The monk looked at his papers, looked again, and said with great
conviction, *'No, absolutely not. In the past, yes, your life was in danger
several times, but not now. Have you any other questions?'*

'Where is it best for me to live: in Asia or in Europe?' I asked.

He was quite relaxed by now, and spoke without hesitation, *'You
should live here and there, but not where you were born.'* (You are right,
my dear monk. Florence is a safe harbour, but not a place I could
live in, at least not now.) *'The ideal for you is to be always on the move.
If you stay in the same place for long your brain will stop working.'* (Very
true. I am at my best when I am dumped in a place I know nothing
about; curiosity is my best motivation.)

More women arrived, and came up the wooden stairs, timorous
and respectful, bearing gifts. My time was up, but I asked one more
question: 'If I want to improve my life, should I change something?
Should I change my wife? My job? Should I stop always wearing
white?'

The monk laughed cheerfully, and told me with great conviction
to leave everything as it was. I would have done that anyway, but I
was glad we agreed.

End of sitting. Bows, money discreetly placed under the outsize
book, and general exodus, backwards on our knees to the stairs.

As soon as we were out of the monk's sight, the two women
hugged each other and began a chirpy conversation, only part of
which was translated for me. They were enthusiastic about the man's
powers and his advice about divorcing and making money. I realized
that in fact he had talked of little else. All alike, these seers – monks

or no! For all of them the important questions concern the material side of life – in tune with their clients, for whom money is the great obsession, the sole aim of existence.

We drove back to Bangkok through Chinatown, with its thousands of little shops. In each one, behind the counter or the cash register, is a Chinese whose only desire is to be rich. It struck me that not one of the fortune-tellers I had seen had ever used the word 'happiness' – as if that were something non-existent, or irrelevant. Or perhaps unattainable? Strange that it means so little to so many people.

I looked at the woman at the wheel of the Volvo, and thought of the readiness with which she was willing to forswear love in order to become a millionaire, and of her promise to give the monk a portion of her wealth, in the form of a Mercedes. She too was Chinese.

Chinese, all Chinese, were the shopkeepers I saw from the car window. Chinese the ferrymen on the river. Chinese the heads of the food industries. Chinese the builders of skyscrapers. Chinese the bankers, insurers and speculators. Chinese all those who were destroying Bangkok. Yes, they were the ones who were responsible! This was what passed through my mind as the car was again held up in traffic. Coming from southern China as emigrants fleeing the wars and famines in their homeland, they have done better in Thailand than anywhere else in South-East Asia. Here, thanks to the tolerance of the people and to Buddhism, they have found work, married, and become citizens with full rights. Expert artisans and clever traders, the Chinese soon amassed huge wealth. The Thais have little aptitude for war and business; they are playful, always keener on fun than on work. Strike a gong in Bangkok and you will see a Thai sketching a dance step; blow on a pipe and a whole group will lift their hands in the air, sway their hips and begin to dance. '*Mai ping rai*' is their favourite expression. It means 'Never mind,' 'It doesn't matter,' 'Why worry?' Has the wind blown the roof off your house? *Mai ping rai*. Do the streets of Bangkok flood at the first sign of rain? *Mai ping rai*. Has the city become unlivable? *Mai ping rai*.

The Chinese, with their innate practicality, have profited enormously from this Thai attitude, and have become masters of the city. The biggest Chinese festival is the beginning of the lunar New Year.

In Thailand those three days are not officially recognized as holidays, but Bangkok comes to a standstill. The streets are empty and the banks are closed because the Chinese, who control the biggest slice of the city's economic activity, take those days off.

By now the same is true, in varying degree, of the other countries of South-East Asia. If one day all the Chinese of the region took it into their heads to stay at home, close up shop and not go to work, the Indonesians would have no cars to drive, or cigarettes to smoke, or paper to write on; the Filipinos would have no ships to ferry them between their thousands of islands; the Japanese would have no prawns in their pots. Most of the skyscrapers under construction would remain unfinished. The whole continent would shake in its boots, because it is the Chinese of the diaspora who are the fuel that drives the engine of the South-East Asian economic miracle. And who are they exactly? Descendants of coolies and merchants, of the poor devils who for decades have emigrated to seek their fortune in the *nan yang*, the south seas.

As the two women chatted between themselves in Thai I went on thinking about these remarkable, devastating Chinese, missionaries of practicality and materialism. With their energy they are covering the whole world in cement – from Asia to Canada, where tens of thousands of them are arriving from Hong Kong in anticipation of its return to Peking's rule in 1997. I recalled that one of the first big reports I wrote for *Der Spiegel* twenty years ago was about these same overseas Chinese. Then they were seen as a possible Maoist fifth column, always under suspicion and often victims of racial pogroms. How the world has changed in twenty years!

It struck me as a good idea to return to the subject for a new story, one that would take me from Thailand to Malaysia, Singapore, Indonesia. They were all places to which, with a bit of patience, I could travel without using planes.

CHAPTER EIGHT

Against AIDS? Raw Garlic and Red Peppers

At night Turtle House came into its own. The skyscrapers rising all around us were taking away more of our sunshine every day, but in the evening, when the gardener Kamsing lit the lights concealed in the trees, the torches around the pond and the little oil lamps in front of the statues of Ganesh and Buddha in the garden, the house again took on that warm, quiet, tropical magic which had induced us to come to Thailand after five years in the chill and depressing austerity of Japan.

When we arrived Angela and I worked like mad for two weeks to find the right place for every piece of Chinese furniture, every statue, every vase, every god, every scroll, every lampshade of pale yellow silk – the things that give a room atmosphere. We then called a halt, but the house felt better and better with time. It was like us: old and lived-in, full of all that so many Asian years had made of us. The story behind every object was what would remain with us. As for the objects themselves, we saw ourselves as no more than their temporary custodians.

The house had been described by the *Architectural Digest* as 'an oasis of tropical splendour in the concrete jungle'. What the article did not say was that termites were eating the beams, and the wooden floors were getting shakier and shakier. Rats, displaced by the bulldozers, dredgers and cement mixers that filled the whole neighbourhood, found their last refuge with us, and in the night they often woke us with their shrill, riotous cavalcades in our attics, where they joyously reproduced. Luckily we also had a great number of squirrels, so if a guest became nervous about the strange shadows scampering along the branches of the mango tree over our dinner table, or the rustling in the straw roof of the tree house we had had built among the branches of two coconut trees, we would say: 'Don't worry, it's only the squirrels.' Well, the only difference is that squirrels have nice fluffy tails and rats have long pointed ones.

But the rats were deadly. Attracted by the bird food, they got into the aviary and murdered some of the most beautiful specimens I had collected, including a hoopoe that we called Mrs Punk, and the 'fairy-tale bird', a bright green pitta that might have come straight out of the illustrations to Grimm's fairy tales. Nor can we forget poor Callas, a nightingale: whenever I whistled, no matter at what hour of the day, she would launch into the most glorious arias I had ever heard.

Then there was Totò, an Indian myna which we bought when he was tiny. I had patiently taught him – at dawn, both of us in the dark under a big towel – to utter a few words in Italian. He would imitate the ring of the telephone, the barking of dogs and the calls of other birds, but he spoke mainly in Thai, saying things like: 'If you love me, why don't you tell me?' He drowned in his cage when it fell in the pond one stormy night.

Baolì, our beloved family dog, born on the Peak in Hong Kong, had lived with us for five years in Peking and another five in Tokyo. By the time we moved to Bangkok he was so old that he could hardly move, and he seldom barked any more. We needed a guard dog, so we adopted a newborn puppy someone had left in a cardboard box under our car in a parking lot.

Angela used to spend hours reading and writing behind the mosquito netting on the veranda over the water. At first the deaths of the animals at Turtle House caused her a great deal of anger and grief. She wanted justice, or order at least, but in the end she accepted 'the natural cruelty of our ecological system'. 'This is no rose-water pond,' she would say, consoling herself for the fact that the big turtle ate the ducklings as soon as they hatched, the rats ate the birds, and the birds ate the little sparrows that came to peck the crumbs in their cages.

The events of the pond, the garden and the animals were a constant reminder of how important it is for people to have nature around them, to observe it and learn its logic and enjoy it. How can children grow up mentally healthy in the middle of a city, without feeling the rhythm of plant and animal life along with their own? Never in his history has man drifted so far from nature as now, and this has been perhaps the worst of our mistakes.

★   ★   ★

The traffic in Bangkok made it hopeless to attempt any social life. To lunch with someone in town meant arriving home around five in the afternoon; an invitation to dine at some embassy meant setting out at least two hours before. Having built myself a workroom on the other side of the pond, I was one of the few people in Bangkok who could commute between home and office in a matter of seconds. Hence we resisted all inducements to go out, and used Turtle House to tempt people we wanted to see to come to us instead.

The story of my flightless year soon made the rounds of the journalists in the area, and the commonest reaction was good-hearted envy. When the subject came up at dinner, many of them had their own stories to tell. One came from Claudia Rossett of the *Wall Street Journal*, who was living in Hong Kong at the time.

Claudia's family lived in Baltimore. In the 1930s her grandmother had been left a widow, wretchedly poor, with three children to bring up. In those days lottery tickets were on sale in the drugstores, and once she dreamed she had won with the number sixteen. She told her dream to her next-door neighbour, who urged her to put everything on that number. She did, and sixteen won, bringing her a tidy sum of money that changed her life overnight. From then on she never ceased talking about her amazing premonition. Many years later one of her three children, Claudia's father, went back to the neighbourhood where he had grown up. He met up with the woman next door, who told him that her suggestion to play the lottery had been used by his mother's friends to give her money which otherwise, being a very proud woman, she would never have accepted. When they heard of the dream, they had made a collection, and gave the money to the drugstore owner. He then gave it to her, telling her the winning number was sixteen – the very one she had dreamt! The last guest at Turtle House before I took the train for Malaysia and Singapore was Joachim Holzgen, a colleague from *Der Spiegel*.

In early March the United Nations Transition Authority in Cambodia (UNTAC) invited each of the main European journals to send a reporter there. The aim was to interest European public opinion in the UN peace mission preparing for the Cambodian elections to be held at the end of May. The programme included a visit by helicopter to the military installations, and to avoid confronting me with a dilemma *Der Spiegel*'s editors in Hamburg decided to send Joachim Holzgen. It was his first trip to Indochina, and I invited him to dinner with a couple of colleagues who had just returned from Cambodia. The next morning he got on the plane for Phnom Penh, and I went to the Hua Lampun railway station, with my rucksack on my back, and in my head the plan to write about the overseas Chinese.

I have long had a passion for railway stations. I could spend whole days in one, sitting in a corner and observing the life around me. The spirit of a country, the state of mind of the people and their problems are reflected better in a station than anywhere else. In half an hour of watching the sea of humanity as it ebbs and flows beneath the canopies of Hua Lampun station, you can learn more about today's Thailand than by reading any academic treatise. Trains coming from the north disgorge people by the thousand, mostly young, many of them girls, all full of hope. They have left their villages with a bundle of clothes and a one-way ticket, to look for work in the capital.

Recruiters from the construction industry wait on the platform as each train draws up. They offer about 100 baht (£2.50) per day, plus a camp bed on the site. The prettiest girls are invited to work in the brothels. It all happens in a few minutes: offers, wary hesitations, verbal contracts, and then away in the back of one of the many pickup trucks parked outside the station. In the crowd, looking more lost than the others, quite tiny children can be seen. They too find work, right under the noses of the police, who parade up and down with badges all over them and dashing pistols at their sides. Theoretically even in Thailand there are laws against the exploitation of minors, but in practice, as in so much of Asia, nothing is really illegal.

My southbound train was due to depart at 10.20, and it left on the dot. The Thai railways are an example of that efficient public administration which has fostered the rapid development of the country, and which, along with Buddhism and the monarchy, is still one of its cohesive elements. The further the train went from Bangkok, the more people in the stations gave the impression of a militarized society. Everyone had a uniform: students, postmen, taxi-motorcyclists, ticket collectors. The train-conductor, with his chestful of ribbons from heaven knows what campaign, could have passed for an air marshal. The journey was an ongoing banquet.

Dozens of vendors with basketfuls of local specialities got on at one station and off at the next.

I travelled for a day and a night, lulled by the rattling of the wheels. At 5.30 sharp I was woken by the air marshal–conductor. The carriage had a stale smell. I was unshaven and my tongue was like sandpaper from the bottle of Mekong (Thai whisky) I had drunk the night before with the railway police. I began to think that perhaps a year of such trips was madness. But I had only to get off the train and inhale a lungful of that pungent dawn air, full of promises, to feel inspired once more. I was in Yala! How many more times in my life would I arrive in Yala?

I thought of Chang Choub and his advice to meditate. Perhaps this travelling, all alone, was my meditation. Free from the daily routine, accountable to nobody but my own conscience, my mind grew calm. Frivolous thoughts rose to the surface, pleasant thoughts, fleeting impressions. Deep down I felt a great joy. I ate some soup at a stall outside the station and went for a stroll.

Yala is a town like many others, with no character to speak of. The main street is lined on both sides with shop–houses, all exactly alike: the ground floor is for selling, the upper for living. The owners are all Chinese – my tough, practical Chinese, penniless on arrival, who set up as small shopkeepers. They redeem themselves by spending their lives in pursuit of a goal largely despised by their own culture. The China from which these emigrants came was Confucian, and trade commanded scant respect. Merchants were on the lowest rank of the social hierarchy, just below soldiers, and far below peasants and artisans.

My first destination was Betong, a town in the short mountain range that divides the peninsula and marks the border between Thailand and Malaysia. I shared a taxi with five other passengers and we covered the eighty-six miles from Yala in just over two hours. We passed through highly fertile red terrain, covered in rubber and pine-apple plantations, then climbed a tarred road among splendid rocky peaks which appeared and disappeared between dense banks of mist.

In the time when both Bangkok and Kuala Lumpur were fighting an armed Communist insurrection, these mountains were the natural refuge for the guerrillas, and Betong was known as a danger spot chock-full of spies. All that has changed. The first impression is highly pleasing. A handsome municipal signboard at the entrance to the town announces that 'Betong is renowned for its scenic beauty'. Other signs, all in English, point tourists in the direction of the park, the stadium and, for some mysterious reason, the prison. The chief monument they are urged to see is an enormous red letter-box on the main square. A sign proclaims it to be the largest in the world.

Despite this façade of touristic innocence, there is something that immediately strikes one about Betong: the number of barber shops. There are dozens of them, one every few yards, and the fact that they concern themselves with more than beards is clear from their strange names – 'Funny Barber', or 'Sexy Barber'.

Profiting from the proximity of Malaysia, with its immense market of men sexually repressed by Islamic puritanism, Betong has developed one of the most profitable of all industries: prostitution. The services are provided by Thais; the clientele is exclusively Malay. Without requiring a passport, thousands of Muslims cross the border every day on a twenty-four hour visa to indulge in pleasures forbidden at home. Betong is a brothel city.

I had come to Betong to see a man who was said to have been in the Communist guerrillas. I had no idea how to find him, but the task proved easier than I had expected. The porter of my hotel sent me to a photographer, who sent me to a seller of electrical appliances, who telephoned a friend of his, who came to fetch me with a scooter and dropped me off in front of a small pharmacy of traditional medicine with its window full of dried mushrooms for long life and bottles of green ointment. In the space of an hour, passing from one Chinese to another, I had reached Mr Wu, a middle-aged man, small, thin and distinguished-looking.

For close on twenty years Wu had been the guerrillas' doctor. Following their surrender in 1987 he had become the best-known pharmacist in Betong. Thanks to his experience in the jungle, he was the only one with a thorough knowledge of the therapeutic virtues of the plants, roots and barks in the nearby mountains.

Mr Wu offered me tea and produced the family albums. There were photographs of him and his wife as guerrillas, in Maoist uniforms with their feet wrapped in strips of cloth and old rifles over their shoulders. He said we should visit the guerrilla camp, which was only five miles from the city. He shut up shop and off we went.

The Communist guerrilla war in Malaysia began just after the Second World War. The leader was Chin Peng, a hero of the anti-Japanese resistance. Most of the fighters, like him, were Chinese. Inspired by Mao's revolution, they too dreamed of creating a people's republic in what was then still part of the British Empire. The British resisted, declared a state of emergency, and in a fierce military campaign, using tactics later copied with less success by the Americans in Vietnam, they managed to isolate the guerrillas.

In 1957 the British granted independence to a state called the Malay Federation. It was composed of Malaysia and Singapore, plus the territories of Sabah and Sarawak on Borneo (included expressly to prevent the Chinese from forming the majority of the population). Thereafter the Communist guerrilla campaign was no longer a real threat, although a few groups of a strict Maoist persuasion remained active along the Thai border. These groups, however, were torn by internal strife and purges, and in the end they gave up.

In a solemn ceremony on 28 April 1987, the last Communist guerrillas surrendered their arms to the Thai authorities. They were unable to return to Malaysia, so with the permission of Bangkok they stayed where they were, in their camp on Thai territory. They had to make a living, and being clever, practical Chinese, they profitably recycled their past as failed revolutionaries. I had only to set foot in the forest camp to realize this. The old, feared general headquarters, now called 'The Village of Friendship', had become a sort of guerrilla Disneyland with restaurants, video halls, souvenir stalls and tours of the tunnels guided by ex-combatants.

A group of young Malays, each with the Thai 'wife' he had rented for the day, had just finished the obligatory tour when Mr Wu and I arrived. They were trying on green berets with red stars, having their photographs taken holding old rifles, and buying a potent 'guerrilla ointment'. The old Communists had become, like the prostitutes, one of the tourist attractions that made Betong's fortune.

I spent the evening walking around the centre of Betong. At sunset huge flocks of small birds fly in and blacken the sky. Their chirping makes a deafening noise that drowns out the music of the karaoke bars. They settle for the night on the electric and telephone wires along the streets – tens, hundreds of thousands of them.

Equally impressive was the coming and going of Malay men from brothel to brothel. On the dark windows of each is a notice in writing so small as to be barely legible: 'Risk of AIDS without a condom.' I went into a couple of them. Their furnishings were more or less identical: a counter, as in a bar, plastic armchairs with girls in plenty, and some smal cubicles to which the couples could retire. The price varied from 120 to 200 baht (£3–£5) for an hour. The rent for a girl for a whole day was between 1000 and 1500 baht (£25–£35).

'With a condom?' I asked.

'If you don't want to, you just have to pay a bit extra.'

Thus it is that AIDS has been spreading like a prairie fire. A twenty-five-year-old Chinese madam, with a little boy of three playing at her feet, explained to me that there were about three thousand girls in Betong's barber shops, many of them from the north ('They have light skin and the Malays like them better'), and that recently several hundred had been removed because they were under sixteen. But if I was interested in one of these, they were only a telephone call away, in nearby dormitories.

Outside, I was struck by the sight of a Caucasian, who stood out in the crowd, the only Westerner in town apart from me. He seemed quite at home. I asked him what he was doing in Betong.

Scott, aged sixteen, was a Canadian high school student who had come on an exchange programme sponsored by the Rotary Clubs of Betong and his city in Ontario. He was amused to think that in Canada they had absolutely no clue about the place where he had ended up. He was living with one of the most prominent people in town, who was one of the biggest brothel-owners, too.

We went to eat in a small Chinese restaurant, where Scott met his teacher. She was from Bangkok, a cultivated woman in her mid-thirties who had been sent to work in the south as a punishment for her left-wing views. At the end of the meal I asked if she knew of a good fortune-teller in Betong. Yes; she had never been to him herself, but she had heard of an excellent one living a little outside the city. He was an expert in black magic. She offered to take me there, and we agreed to meet the next day at the school entrance.

* * *

The teacher arrived on a motorbike and I climbed on behind her. After about five miles we reached the fortune-teller's house, which was behind a rusting old petrol station. He received us in a big downstairs room with a concrete floor, at the far end of which his wife and two beautiful daughters were preparing a meal. He was a thin, sharp-eyed man of fifty or so, and was sitting on a mat with an image of Mecca — he was a Muslim. In a semicircle in front of him were four women.

One of them looked well-to-do, with a ring on each finger and several gold chains around her neck and wrists; the other three were more subdued. The woman complained that business was not going well, and the girls were short of customers. She was sure someone had put the evil eye on her barber shop, and had brought the three girls for the magician to check. 'They've all run away from their husbands,' the teacher whispered in my ear.

Looking at them, poor little things, it was easy to see why they were unsuccessful: the evil eye was manifest in their appearance. One was small, fat and dirty, another was tall, pale and thin as a rake, and the third was simply dull, with nothing that might have attracted even the most desperate Malay.

The fortune-teller asked the woman if she had brought all the necessary supplies. Yes: from her bag she extracted a chick, some eggs, and some hard green fruits like wild lemons. Turning to me, the magician said it would be half an hour before he was finished with them, and apologized for keeping me waiting. I was happy to stay and watch.

A handsome black cat paced back and forth over the threshold, rubbing voluptuously against the shoes which the women had removed before presenting themselves to the fortune-teller. In such an atmosphere of black magic, this cat with its Satanic eyes brought to my mind the evil eye and images of bad luck; but no one else, so far as I could tell, gave it a thought — which further goes to show that the perception of misfortune and its symbols varies according to the local culture and point of view. For example, we Westerners see snakes as hateful and dangerous. Face to face with one, our instinctive reaction is to kill it. For Asians, however, the snake is a supernatural being. The snake dominates all the elements, it is the lord of all levels of the universe; in heaven it dances, flashing through the clouds; on earth it can live in and out of water, and in the underworld, whose every door is known to it, it feels completely at home. For an Asian the snake is not a symbol of danger and death, but of protection. It is under the shade of the *naga*, the seven-headed snake, that Buddha meditates.

The eggs were put on to boil, the green lemons were arranged on a fine silver plate in front of the fortune-teller, and the madam held the chick in her hands, which she joined in front of her bosom. She stayed like that, eyes closed, utterly absorbed. The magician recited formulae which even my teacher could not translate. All she could tell me was that at the close of the ceremony the eggs would be eaten, the lemons would go into the water that was to wash away the evil eye, and the chick would be set free.

There was a rumbling of distant thunder, and then came one of those magnificent storms, explosive and liberating, which provide temporary respite from the tropical heat. The rain came down in sheets, and the trees behind the magician's house were scarcely visible.

The teacher talked to me about how hard it was to do her job in a town like Betong, full of prostitutes no older than her students. She said that the presence of the barber shops poisoned every aspect of existence, that corruption dominated every social relationship, that the police themselves took part in rape and extortion. In such a climate of violence, sex and money it was impossible to bring up normal young people. She said that in the city's schools it was forbidden to mention AIDS because the local authorities, who shared in the profits, wanted nothing to interfere with the work of the brothels.

The magician concluded his rites. The poor chick was thrown out of the window to run free into the woods, but it remained motionless, peeping feebly in the heavy rain. Its owner paid the fee and left with her three girls.

I still had AIDS in mind, and when I sat down with the magician I asked him what he thought about it. A terrible disease, of course, but he, by studying the girls in the barber shops, had learned to recognize those who had it. 'I feel it as soon as they come near me. Inside they're on fire, as it were, they're burning, but outside they're cold and pale. Their skin's colourless.' However, he said, there was not much cause for concern. He knew for sure that contagion occurred only between people of the same blood group, and that anyway AIDS could easily be avoided.

'By using condoms?'

'No, by eating raw garlic and red peppers.' He was absolutely convinced of this.

He began looking intently at me, and without asking me any questions, without wanting to know where and when I was born or where I came from, without reading my hand, without doing calculations, he slowly began to speak. The teacher translated.

'You're one who travels a great deal, but what you like best is to live in a place in the country.' (Clever fellow! If there is one image that comes to my mind whenever I think of escaping from the world, it is that of our house in the Apennines, with the meadow in front and the chestnut woods behind. That is peace.) *'You're one who attaches no importance to money, and you can't ever hang on to it.'* (Right, but do I have it written all over my face?) *'What you earn you spend. You're attractive to women. Women love you, but you're not all that interested in them.'* (Brilliant!) *'You're made for being faithful, faithful to your wife, and you're lying when you tell her you want a second wife. You don't really want one at all.'* (Well, it takes all sorts of fortune-tellers, and each one reflects the local culture and values. This, for example, is a Muslim area where men can have several wives. So my fortune-teller treats me like a Muslim, just as the blind man in Bangkok treated me like a Chinese, for whom the failure to make money was the worst possible news.)

He continued with a piece of advice that only made sense in terms of the local ethic. *'If you do decide to take a second wife, then take a widow.'* (In that context it was like telling me to perform an act of charity.) *'In any case you won't stay with her all that long. You don't smoke, but you like spicy foods.'* (True.) *'You're acutely aware of smells.'* (True.) *'Wherever you go, you don't run risks. If you have an amulet with you, that's good. It would be best if it were a Buddha. That will protect you.'* (Perhaps his eye had been caught by the one I wear around my neck.) *'You're someone who's sincere with his friends, who always comes out lucky. If you buy a lottery ticket it's a winning one. The problem is that you never buy any.'* (Quite true. I have never bought a ticket in my life, but maybe it's time to start!) *'Your lucky numbers are eighty-eight, one and nineteen. Play and you'll win.'* (Had there been a betting shop in Betong I would definitely have tried my luck!) *'You're forever interested in what you don't know. Before long someone will offer you an important job, but you'll turn it down because what you like is a* simple life.' (Well, I certainly care nothing about having an important job, but nobody is going to offer me one. Anyone who did would be mad!) '*You often have a cough.*' (No.) '*You must eat more rice noodles. You should also wear something green on your right hand, preferably on the ring finger. Yes, a ring with a small jade like those the Chinese wear.*' (I have always hated rings, and even my wedding ring, made with recycled gold from my great-grandparents' rings and with 'Angela' engraved inside, I wore for only a few months.)

I had just had that thought, and in my mind's eye seen the ring with the name on it, when he continued: '*Your wife is very large. She has large breasts and a large bottom.*' (Poor Angela, who practises yoga every morning!) '*You can indulge in sport because your health's good. If you want to keep a cat it must be of three colours: white, black and brown.*' (A bit hard to find, I thought.) '*If you can't find one like that, then it must be all grey. Your car absolutely must be red or mango colour. At the moment you live in a house that's on the right, at the end of a lane.*' (Correct: Turtle House is situated just so.) '*If you really want something, you always manage to get it, but your mind is like a child's: you like to say what you think, you like to say things for the pleasure of saying them. You have an unstable character, all ups and downs. You like to sleep on your side, especially the right.*'

I had the feeling he could go on like this for hours, and I was starting to get bored, so I told him about the Hong Kong fortune-teller. Quick as a flash came the reply: '*No, no, you can take all the planes you like, but only in the afternoon, not in the morning. This year's a difficult one because the winds are in conflict with your age, but you don't run any great risks.*' In a singsong rhythm, he continued: '*Several times in your life you've been accused, and twice you have landed up in prison.*' (Ah . . . that's interesting!) '*The first time when you were thirty-five years old.*' (In Vietnam? I was not exactly arrested, but I was expelled and accused of being a Vietcong agent.) '*The second when you were forty-six.*' (Exactly right! The famous episode in China!)

I was amused to find him so exact, and took a strange pleasure in finding the facts that corresponded to his words. As in a rhyming game, where a line ending with 'moon' has to be answered with one ending in 'June' or 'spoon', sometimes the rhyme has to be dragged in by the scruff of the neck, at others it fits perfectly.

I realized that this is exactly what we tend to do with a fortune-teller. He has no sooner spoken than we are racking our brains to find something in our experience to match his words. And in this there is pleasure, as there is in writing poetry. Suddenly life itself seems to become poetry because of some rhyme that makes sense of the facts, and bestows an order upon them. Rhyme is consoling.

But was it the magician who guessed certain facts about my life, or was it I who made them fit together – like the pieces of a puzzle, which I knew backwards and which he only pretended to know?

He went on: '*The next time you're arrested will be at the age of sixty-one. Problems arise in connection with your work, but you can't manage to keep away from them, and basically you enjoy being arrested.*' (Not far wrong.)

I asked my fortune-teller if he really believed he could see someone's past. He said yes, but that he could see into the future with even greater accuracy. The night before, for example, he had seen that I would come, a foreigner. How? By looking at his hands.

I enquired if he knew Italy, and what he thought about the state of the world. '*I only understand things that happen around me,*' he replied.

I liked the man. His work was not based on any method. He followed no astrological charts, he did no sums nor claim to interpret signs in the hand. He 'felt' the person he had before him, and obviously after seeing thousands he had developed an unusual ability to read them. In this society, where little girls begin selling themselves at thirteen, where teachers may not speak of AIDS and where the policemen are the bandits, he struck me as doing something of service. Part priest, part social worker, doctor and psychoanalyst, he did no one any harm. Quite the contrary. He was there to give advice, to comfort people, to impose taboos that gave the unfortunates of Betong a sense of being able to escape from their troubles and grasp something a bit better. All for the modest sum of 30 baht (75p) per consultation.

I asked the teacher if she would like to have her future told. Absolutely not! She was quite firm. A friend of hers had been engaged to a man she loved very much. Before marrying him she went with her mother to a fortune-teller who told her the marriage would be a mistake. She left her fiancé and has been unhappy ever since.

The rain had stopped and the sky was dramatically beautiful, with big clouds, golden sunbeams, and still some dense black pockets of rain in the distance. The chick released by the woman with the evil eye had climbed up on a coconut, and a big toad had advanced to the doorway. The papaya and banana trees were heavy with well-washed fruit.

I left Betong at dawn. The national anthem was booming from all the loudspeakers in the town, and dozens of big Thai flags were being hoisted in front of schools and police stations. The traffic stopped, and the population stood stiffly to attention.

As soon as I was outside Betong I began to feel I was no longer in Thailand. The villages are dominated by mosques, the men wear sarongs and Muslim skullcaps. Goats graze along the roadside, and lie down on the asphalt itself, so that taxi drivers have to take care not to run them over. Thailand is dissolving slowly, tolerantly, with no border posts, police or controls, with no precise confines except where Malaysia looms up, first with a barbed-wire fence, then another, then some gates and a hundred yards of unobstructed ground, like no-man's-land. At long last you see the blue and white buildings of the border police and customs.

I walked between barriers till I reached a cabin window through which a woman glared at me. She was covered in a blue veil on which a pair of thick spectacles rested. Polite but cold, she asked where I was going and how long I intended to stay. She gave me a visa for two weeks. The atmosphere was disquieting. 'Death penalty for carrying drugs,' said a big notice surmounted by a skull and crossbones.

Where was the Malaysia of twenty years ago? The women in sarongs, wearing brassières that always seemed a size too small, and skin-tight lace blouses? Where were the rich colours and bodies whose joy seemed to reflect nature's? Swept away by Islamic austerity? In the Malaysia I knew in the seventies, religion was marginal. The Malays had their mosques and the Chinese their temples. The Malays ate their goats, the Chinese their pigs. But then, to defend themselves against the overwhelming economic power and materialist culture of the Chinese, the Malays began slavishly following Islam. They took away their women's sarongs and gave them veils and loose two-piece gowns, and shut themselves up in the citadels of their mosques.

At the border post all the policemen and customs officials were

Malays. The taxi drivers who offered to take me to the next town, Kroh, were all Chinese. '*Hua-ren*' – flower men, sons of the empire of flowers – they relished calling themselves, using an expression that is no longer heard elsewhere.

It was less than ten miles to Kroh, and my flower man lost no time in telling me about the problems of the country in which I had barely set foot. 'They have the power and we're second-class citizens. Just think! If I want to buy a flat I pay 100,000 ringit, and if one of them buys it he pays 90,000. For the same flat! Does that seem fair to you? They've all the privileges, we have nothing. They call themselves *bumiputra*, sons of the soil, but what soil? We too were born here, just like them. And anyway, the real *bumiputra* are the *orang asli*, the pygmies in the jungle! What counts is being a Muslim. And we're not.'

I had just arrived, but he took it for granted I knew that 'they' were the Malays, and that the great, unsolved problem of Malaysia was race. Race is everything. Race determines who your friends are, who your enemies are, what job you do, which doctor you see, which vet tends your animals. Race determines where you live, where you go to school, whom you marry and where you are buried. The Malays have the political power, the Chinese have the money. This form of apartheid is not written in any law, but it is rooted in the practice of the past twenty years. To the Chinese the situation seems unfair. But the Malays see it as the only guarantee of social equilibrium.

Originally, Malaysia was really inhabited by the jungle people, the *orang asli*. Then, a few centuries ago, the Malays came and took over. The Chinese have for the most part been here only a hundred years – the British needed manpower to exploit the country's great natural resources, so they gave free rein to immigration. Together with the Chinese came the Indians, also encouraged by the British.

When the British granted independence to these territories, they took care that one race would not be numerically too superior to the other. The Malay Federation, born in 1957 with a population that was 40 per cent Chinese and 50 per cent Malay, was a land of great wealth in which the different races, it seemed, could live in harmony. The only real enemies then were the Communists. Now there are no more Communists, but the races are mutually hostile. The Chinese have become richer and the Malays more numerous.

The Chinese now comprise only 32 per cent of the population, the Malays 62 per cent.

We had to pass several checkpoints. As at the border, the soldiers and policemen were all Malay. 'They're looking for weapons,' said the taxi driver. 'In Thailand you can find all kinds, and the bandits go to Betong to buy them.'

'Like AIDS? That too comes from Betong.'

The driver was astonished. 'There's no AIDS in Betong. It's a small, clean place and the girls are all fresh. AIDS is in the big cities, in Bangkok, in Pattaya.' So the march of AIDS continues.

Soon we were in Kroh. When I went to change money and find out how to get to Penang, I noticed that everyone was speaking Mandarin. Kroh too was practically a Chinese town. I spent a few hours there, just strolling around. As this was the first and last time I would set foot in Kroh, I felt I might as well stay there a while. Kroh! I looked on the map. It was barely a dot.

With the decision not to fly I had regained possession of time: time to stop, to look around, to reflect. No one was waiting for me, and with great pleasure I let the bus for Penang leave without me in order to stay and chat with an old Chinese. He told me about his father who, when opium was a state monopoly, would go and purchase his dose in the building that is now the post office, and spend the rest of the day smoking. He told me about himself, how during the Japanese invasion he was taken prisoner and sent to the River Kwai to build the 'death railway'. He was one of the few to return.

It was a joy to let time go by unconcernedly. I took notes, chatted, let my thoughts wander. Slowly I realized that I was rediscovering the pleasure of travel, of getting to know a place and its people. As a journalist one often has to arrive in a city, interview a couple of people, write something up and leave. But to understand a situation it is not enough to speak to a minister, a general, an expert; and anyway, they always say what they have to say. The important thing is to spend time with them, get them talking about other things, and wait for their afterthoughts, in which they slip in what they really think, answering questions that have not been asked. That is the key to everything. I was tired of running here and there looking for quotations with which to pad out an article.

I travelled slowly and with enjoyment. Once again I had time to look, to get the feel of places. Crossing the border on foot from

Thailand to Malaysia had enabled me to sense many things about the differences and tensions between the two countries. Naturally I could have read about it somewhere, but without experiencing anything, without seeing the colours, the people's faces, without hearing their voices.

I adore travelling like that. Travel is an art, and one must practise it in a relaxed way, with passion, with love. I realized that after years of going about in aeroplanes I had unlearned that art – the only one I care about!

There is a story in Angela's family about her paternal grandmother. A German, born in Haiti, well educated, she knew the classics, had read the great novels, could play the piano and was at ease in society. Before dying in Florence at the age of eighty-six, she said: 'What have I done in my life? A bit of conversation!' If I have time for reflection at the end, I would like to be able to say: 'I have travelled.' And if I have a grave, I would like a stone with a hollow from which birds can drink, inscribed with my name, the two obligatory dates, and the word 'Traveller'.

The distance from Baling to Butterworth is fifty-seven miles. Our shared taxi passed large plantations of rubber and palm oil. The landscape was beautiful, green and orderly. Amid the vegetation at times we could see the white houses of the planters. Everything was natural, luxuriant . . . except the women in their veils. The children were coming out of school, and I looked with dismay at all the little Malay girls in the hot sun, draped in their half-chadors – ankle-length light blue tunics – among their carefree Chinese classmates in short skirts and white blouses. Two peoples now distinct and separate. All in the name of Islamic spirituality versus the materialism of the Chinese? I too dislike materialism, but how can I consider these bigots allies, if they dress their daughters in that way?

The Chinese taxi driver looked at me and laughed. 'When they dress in black, that's when they're really scary! Look,' he said, pointing to a row of deserted stalls in a market. 'For them it's a festival . . . and for a month they fast!' He laughed: the only way a good Chinese can celebrate a festival is by eating.

As I watched from the car window, it seemed to me that Malaysia could not continue living in peace much longer. I had the feeling that one day, when the cake to be shared is not large enough any more, there will be another explosion, another pogrom, whose victims will be Chinese. The last was in 1969, with a death-toll of several hundred *hua-ren*.

The short crossing from Butterworth to the island of Penang on board the windswept ferry was a pleasure as always, and I arrived at the old E&O Hotel in proper style, in a rickshaw pedalled by a Chinese. I had not been there for years, but it was like coming home. When I opened the door of room 147 I was assailed by a whiff of familiar smells, of mouldy carpet, disinfectant in the bathroom. The sounds too were those of yore: the crashing of waves against the stone sea wall at the end of the lawn, the cawing of crows in the palms and on the black barrels of old cannon pointing towards the horizon.

The E&O was like a sleeping beauty, and was pleasantly inefficient. Numerous servants, almost all Indian, walked around the open verandas with worn-out brooms in their hands, but the ants continued their march unperturbed and the termites gnawed away at the old wood. I ordered a lemon tea and was brought coffee.

I spent the afternoon committing my notes to the computer, reading the love letters (never sent) of an early British Governor here, and listening to the sea and the crows. I was happy. I was alone, and I found the solitude a magnificent companion.

CHAPTER NINE

The Rainbow Gone Mad

The news I had unconsciously been waiting for came the next morning. There it was, in the newspaper which was hanging in a plastic bag on my hotel room's doorknob, the *New Sunday Times*. Only a few lines long, on an inside page, dated 20 March, Phnom Penh:

> One of the helicopters of the United Nations in Cambodia precipitated to the ground wounding all the twenty-three people on board. The helicopter was carrying fifteen European journalists invited to Cambodia by the UN mission, three international officials and five Russian crew members. The accident occurred when the helicopter, landing at the city of Siem Reap near the ancient temples of Angkor, lost altitude, turned over several times and fell onto the runway from a height of about fifty feet. There were no deaths, but some of the wounded are in serious condition with lesions to the spinal column. The UN mission ordered that all the other MI-17 helicopters of Soviet manufacture remain grounded until the completion of an inquiry into the accident.

In that first moment I felt absolutely nothing. Then I had a sudden wild sensation of joy. I felt as if I had read the announcement of my own death, and I rejoiced at being alive. I had an impulse to share this pleasure with someone, to buttonhole the first passer-by and say, 'Have you seen this? Have you seen it?' But there was nobody around. It was barely dawn, the hotel was deserted. Everyone I might have telephoned – Angela in Bangkok, my children in Europe – was asleep at this hour. My head exploded with a thousand questions, fragmentary thoughts that popped into my mind unbidden. I thought about the fortune-teller in Hong Kong, about who might have been on that helicopter – Joachim Holzgen, for one, the colleague who had taken my place. I thought how lucky I had been. I thought of going to the airport and boarding the first flight for Phnom Penh. Now that the prophecy had been fulfilled, there was nothing more to fear. No? Was not the accident a further warning? The year was not over.

I read and reread those printed words, fascinated, as if there were something magical about them. In the end, however, they began to seem just a news item like any other, a few lines about something bygone, a world far away, something that had no more to do with me than a crash on the New Zealand stock market or a typhoon in Bangladesh or a ferry that had gone down in the Philippines. All that now concerned me was what I had to do, how to get in touch with *Der Spiegel*, how to help Holzgen. That is how it has to be: when you have obligations, when you have to organize something, your emotions are mastered, set aside. The need to be practical prevents you from being overwhelmed by your feelings. That is why death is attended by so many rites. The sorrow of losing a loved one would be unbearable if one did not have to think about the funeral, how to dress, what music to have. Every people has evolved its own forms of distraction. The Chinese, always so practical and materialistic, have gone to extremes in banishing sentimentality from the pain: their funerals always end in great banquets.

It was Sunday, and my office in Bangkok was closed. But my computer had in its memory the number of the portable phone of the German doctor who was head of the UN hospital in Phnom Penh. That would unquestionably be where the injured had been taken.

'Holzgen of *Der Spiegel*? Yes, he's here . . . hang on, I'm going to his bed.' In a few seconds I had Joachim on the line. As soon as he recognized my voice, he yelled: 'To hell with you and your fortune-teller! You see? He was right, damn it!' He had a broken leg and his spinal cord was compressed, but he would be all right. He told me that the helicopter's rear rotor had stalled, and the pilot had lost control. When they hit the ground the fuel tanks opened, and several colleagues found themselves drenched in petrol. By a miracle there was no spark.

I made a few more phone calls and then went out for a long walk.

Passing the big Chinese temple in Pitt Street, I had an impulse to thank the gods. I bought a handful of incense sticks and offered them at several altars, and with that I considered the episode closed.

It was not to be. The story of the helicopter kept whirling around in my head. I could not see it as the realization of the prophecy; nor as a simple coincidence either. I went on repeating to myself that in the light of reason every prediction is half-true and half-false, that the helicopter might or might not have crashed; but I found it difficult to set my mind at rest and accept that the event had been a simple matter of statistical probability.

Up till that moment, the whole business of the fortune-teller and his prophecy had been partly a game, and the resolution not to fly a sort of bet between me and me to put myself to the test. Well, the game was over. It was no longer a matter of something being theoretically possible. That something was staring me in the face, and in a way that left me horrified. Suggestion did not come into it this time. Subjective projections of fantasies or my fears were irrelevant, for the news was an objective fact: the helicopter had well and truly crashed.

Was this proof that the fortune-teller had been right? What had he 'seen'? 'Seen?' In my heart of hearts I most assuredly did not want it to be thus. I liked to think of the occult as a possibility, not a certainty. I wanted to hang on to my doubt, not to become a believer. All my life I have avoided faiths, and I certainly did not want to talk myself into adopting this one. In accepting the fortune-teller's prophecy and deciding not to fly I had wanted to add a bit of poetry to my life, not another reason for despair. Because if this episode proved that everything was written, then life had no meaning any more. There was no point in living.

Since the beginning of the year I had paid particular attention to reports of planes that had crashed or made emergency landings. Each time I asked myself if I might have been on them. The answer was always no. But this one? In Cambodia! This was *mine*. The helicopter that crashed was one I should have been on. There was no doubt about it. Then was it my fault it had crashed? Suddenly I felt guilty. Guilty before my friend Jean Claude Pomonti of *Le Monde*, and Ira Chaplain, the photographer from *Der Spiegel*, both of whom had been injured, and poor Holzgen, who had taken my place. It seemed an act of disloyalty on my part not to have been with them on that helicopter, just because of a prophecy. Yes, but if I had been on it, might I not have been the spark to have made a bonfire of them all? My mind kept somersaulting uncontrollably.

Being in Penang reminded me of an old friend who lived in the city. He was from a Chinese family, had been educated all over the world, and had become a well-known figure who had played an important role in the development of several Asian countries. We had been students together in the States, on the same scholarship, and had kept in touch over the years. I telephoned, and by chance he was in, resting after an expedition in to the jungle to look for a rare species of palm.

He sent a driver to fetch me in an old blue Mercedes. Crossing Penang, I could see that some people were trying to save and preserve the city, while others were gnawing away at its quiet, provincial elegance and trying to modernize it. In the old residential quarter a few colonial villas, intensely white amid the lush greenery of their gardens, had been restored to their former splendour; others had, as they say, been 'converted' – as if it were a matter of changing religion. One had become a semi-automated distributor of Kentucky Fried Chicken, another a high-class night club. A third was being demolished, and on a large signboard was an artist's impression of the block of flats that would take its place.

My friend's childhood home was in poor condition, but still imposing. The walls were in need of paint, sheets had been thrown over the armchairs, the paper lanterns under the portico were torn, there was dust on the shelves, and the scattered relics of many lives; but that did not spoil its character as a solid, almost grandiose residence. It was built in the 1920s. My friend's father had ordered the tiles from England, and as he was a doctor he had had the symbol of Aesculapius, two serpents entwined around a staff, carved in the fine wood of the stairs and the balustrade that dominated the drawing-room. In one room there were dozens of Balinese paintings, in another a host of wooden statues from Borneo; the first floor was filled with models of boats from the Sunda Straits and stacks of beautiful dried palm leaves, each in its own transparent envelope. In a sitting-room were a grand piano, two cellos, and a spinet on which my friend played Bach 'as it was played in Bach's day'. In the garden were large aviaries with many colourful and vociferous tropical birds, about which he knew everything.

Built for a large, well-to-do family, the house was now empty except for a couple of caretakers. Altogether there was something ghostly about the place, and the ghost was my friend, Lim Cheong Keat. Architect, botanist, musicologist, musician, patron of the arts, essayist and ornithologist, he had made that house his retreat from the world. It was a repository for all the things he loved, and he went there from time to time to enjoy them.

After years of professional success, he had left most of his work to younger colleagues. He was an intelligent and cultured man, and he was in deep despair. He saw the 'development' he had worked for going in the wrong direction, destroying the environment and making people more miserable. He saw his own country increasingly divided by race. He was disillusioned with public life, in which all decisions were dictated by considerations of money, in which no one had the courage to pursue an idea any more, except that of lining their pockets.

Cities all over the world, he said, are decaying because they are no longer populated by their original citizens, but are more and more invaded by transients and people who come to make money. Even the conservation of Penang was being promoted for the wrong reason: to attract tourists.

It was as if Cheong Keat had long been waiting for someone on whom to unburden himself, without reserve, and without fear of being taken for a madman. How I understood him! His despair was mine. Is it not dispiriting to see ancient cultures being eroded and overwhelmed by alien fashions, notions and banalities?

For years Cheong Keat had had a house on Bali, and used to go there regularly. He no longer does so. Now, he said, even there, people perform rites whose meaning they no longer know; they participate in ceremonies without understanding why. 'They're acting a role they've learned by heart. The rainbow has gone mad.'

Recently, his research on palm trees had often taken him in to the jungle, and he had begun to take an interest in the *orang asli*, the true original inhabitants of Malaysia, of whom only a few groups now survive. Living for centuries in the forest, they acquired a remarkable knowledge of nature, and their shamans became great experts on the different plants and their properties. But now they too are attracted by modernity. They are leaving the jungle and becoming urbanized, and all that knowledge, accumulated over generations, is disappearing. The shamans are dying off without handing down their secrets, and none of the younger generation are interested in learning them. After all, what use is jungle lore when everything you could wish for is in the city? For Cheong Keat it was a torment.

I too have seen that old wisdom disappear in my own world. When I was a child, there was someone in every family who knew the medicinal herbs and where to find them in the woods. My maternal grandmother used to prepare bitter cough mixtures, and applied hot plasters to my chest for bronchitis. For my mother that knowledge was already lost: she preferred going to the chemist. Today, who looks at the moon to see if it is the right time to transplant a tree so that it will root well, or to cut it down without having worms eat the wood?

Science having been put on a pedestal, everything non-scientific seems ridiculous and contemptible. Thus we have discarded innumerable practices that could have been of service to us. In Orsigna, when someone cut himself with an axe or a scythe he went to Alighiero, who made the sign of the cross and muttered a secret formula which his father had taught him. He then ran his hand over the wound, and the bleeding stopped. For shingles there was Ubaldo who, having caught it twice, could now 'mark it' and thus cure others of it. He would prick his finger with a pin and trace a circle around the affected area with his blood, while murmuring some kind of prayer. And the 'fire' passed. I have seen it done. Now even in Orsigna everyone goes to the hospital, and those who know how to perform the 'markings' grow rarer and rarer.

St Francis, they say, used to talk to the birds. In his day this was exceptional, but a few hundred thousand years ago it may not have been. Then, perhaps, everyone could understand animals. And perhaps they could also feel the approach of certain events. The Australian Aborigines must have retained some of these primitive skills: how otherwise could they arrive punctually at the funeral of a chief by setting out days before his death?

My thoughts reverted to the helicopter, and I asked Cheong Keat, 'Do you believe in fate?'

I expected him to burst out laughing, but instead he said, 'Let's have a look.' He examined the hand I held out to him.

'*You are destined to have a life out of the ordinary. In this we are similar. Look.*' He showed me his own hand. '*Both of us, in the middle of the palm, have a big "A". Yes, two men with a destiny.*' Then he stopped, as if embarrassed.

'Go on,' I said.

'*I'm trying to find the strength to tell you something I see without ruining our friendship.*'

'Go on.'

'*Your hand plainly shows that you're not an intellectual. You're a man of great feeling, but not of great intellect.*'

'Of course. I'm quite well aware of that.'

'*Anyone looking at your house, your library, would take you for someone devoted to thought alone. On the contrary, you're a man of action, a doer. Never by logic, though, always by instinct. You have great highs and lows in your emotional life.*'

'Where did you learn to read palms?'

'*Not from books, that's for sure. They're all second-hand knowledge. In chiromancy, as in* feng-shui, *there's something of the magical, the divine – you have to feel it, you can't learn it from books.*'

I had known Cheong Keat for many years, but I knew nothing about this interest of his. With his collections, his plants, his birds, the palm trees he studied, I had always thought of him as a man of scientific bent. But here he was talking to me of magic! As with so many people, there was an unsuspected side to him.

Every day I had at least three appointments with people from the university or the business world, and at the end of each interview I would ask if there were any really good fortune-tellers in Penang.

'Fortune-tellers? I detest them!' was the reaction of a history professor who had just given me an excellent lesson on Malaysia prior to the arrival of the British. He told me a story. When he was small, an Indian passed his house and persuaded his mother to let him read her palm. 'You have an illness for which there is no cure,' he pronounced. 'You'll be dead within the year.' The mother was shattered. She said nothing to the family, but from that day on she was no longer herself. She had been a strong, loyal Chinese woman, completely devoted to her husband and children. Now she began to go out, play cards and live it up. Nobody understood why. When she confessed to her husband and told him about the prophecy, he was extremely understanding and let her do as she pleased. Time passed: a year, two years, three. She did not fall ill, let alone die. In the meantime, however, she had grown so used to her new lifestyle that she carried on with it. Twenty-five years later she died of a heart attack. 'Lucky woman!' I said, but the professor did not agree. His childhood was blighted by that story, his mother never at home and his father always struggling to pay her debts.

I had better luck with the wife of an economist. 'Yes, indeed, there's an outstanding one in Bishop Street. He's in the room behind Vogue, the tailor's,' she said. 'He's an Indian. His name's Kaka.'

Bishop Street is in the heart of old Penang. In the shade of low white porticoes is a row of shops – haberdashers, perfumers, tailors and barbers. Their names are all smartly painted in red or black characters on the columns that give on to the street, and I had no difficulty in finding the Vogue tailor shop. But Kaka was no longer there. He had moved, though not far away, and the tailor – also an Indian – offered to take me there. It was a way of doing me a courtesy, but also of ingratiating fate. He told me as we went that he too consulted Kaka from time to time.

I climbed a narrow stairway to the first floor. Behind a glass door was a clean, tidy waiting room. Two stout Indian ladies and a tall, elegant gentleman, broad-chested and perfumed, were sitting in blue imitation-leather armchairs eating dried beans. I realized that it was lunchtime, and the shady room offered a pleasant refuge from the boiling asphalt in the streets.

'I've been waiting for you,' said the man, getting up. I had not uttered a word, but what a perfect way for a fortune-teller to introduce himself! He showed me in to his office and sat down in a big managerial armchair, with me on the other side of the desk.

Date of birth, country of birth, calculations on a piece of paper, and the diagnosis: '*Your lucky number is eight. This is a very important number in your life. Make sure that your house number, your telephone number and the number-plate of your car always contain an eight, or that the numbers add up to eight. That way you will be 100 per cent lucky. The other number is five. Your lucky stone is the emerald.*'

Then he took my left hand and studied it. '*In your family everyone reaches old age, and you too will die old, because you don't have one life line, but two. It's this second line that protects you. If you're involved in a car accident, for example, the car will be wrecked but you'll come out unscathed. When you were forty years old you had problems caused by some friends who betrayed you; but after fifty-five you'll have seven splendid years. You'll soon do something you've never done before, and you'll be successful. If you play the lottery, you'll win.'* (I shall end up believing this!) *'When you were young you had an illness you nearly died from.'* (The year I spent in a sanatorium when I was eighteen?) *'You should now begin to meditate.'* (That is what Chang Choub said.) *'If you do, then you will become able to see the future, and will have the power to cure people.'* (I wouldn't mind.) *'You already have these abilities within yourself, you need only learn to exercise them. If you happen to go to a place where you've never been, and have the sensation of recognizing it, that's because you were there in your past lives. You've already had many lives, some extremely interesting.'*

'What lives? Where?'

Kaka said there were experts who could see these lives in detail, but he could only speak in general terms. *'You've already had many lives, and you're on the point of reaching the higher state, that of . . . '*

'Of a guru?' I said irreverently.

'Yes, it's possible. The problem is that you have a lot of heat in you; you must be always very active sexually, and this saps your energy. You're irascible, at times downright unbearable. You'll be like that into old age,' he said, as if to punish me for my levity.

'At sixteen you had two love affairs: both ended badly. If you were married before the age of twenty-four your marriage failed; if at twenty-eight, you have an excellent marriage.' (Wrong, but I said nothing.) *'Money comes your way in abundance, but it goes just as fast.'* (The same old story.) *'If you want to keep it you must put a gold ring on the middle finger of your right hand. Just a small gold ring. The signs on your palm say that you should have three children. If you don't, it's because one of the mothers aborted, perhaps without your knowledge; otherwise you still have time to have three.'* (That's all I need!)

Taking both my hands, Kaka examined the fingers and nails. *'You are particularly healthy,'* he said, *'and you've no problems with constipation. But if you should ever have it, don't take medicine — eat only fruit and vegetables.'* (Excellent advice.) *'In any case, the vitally important thing for you is to begin meditating.'*

Kaka was clever. By introducing most of his remarks with 'if', he left himself a way out. That was his trick, and once I understood it I lost interest in what he had to say.

'*Your hand shows you've been left a fortune by someone. If not, then you'll win the lottery . . .*'

'Kaka,' I interrupted, 'do you believe in fate?'

'*Yes, but only as a tendency. The lines in the hand are just a warning, they indicate what may happen. Look at my hand. Any palmist can see that I suffer from heart trouble, and one colleague, a famous one in Kuala Lumpur, told me years ago that I'd die at fifty-two. I'm sixty-five now, and even when I do die it won't be of heart failure.*'

Kaka had studied all the medical books he could get hold of. He had learned what causes heart disease, and for years had dieted, exercised, eaten huge amounts of raw garlic, and lived a very regular life: up at half past six, in the office from eight in the morning until seven in the evening, 365 days a year. '*I won't die of heart failure!*' he said, and thumped his chest resoundingly with his fist. '*I won't die of heart failure because the signs in my palm have put me on guard.*'

I told him I had been warned by a fortune-teller not to fly, and that the very helicopter I should have been on had crashed. What did my hand say? Was I really meant to die in that helicopter?

'*Of course not!*' replied confident Kaka. '*You've two life lines in your hand, and if you'd been on that helicopter you'd have got off without a scratch. In fact, if there had been three or four people with hands like yours on that helicopter it would never have crashed. Always remember, in moments of danger it's that second line that saves you.*'

I wish I had known that years ago in Vietnam. There were days when I was obsessed by the idea that in somebody's rifle, somewhere in a paddy field, was the bullet that would kill me. I could see that bullet. I could smell it. I never told anyone, but the thought tortured me. At times, to go where my job, my curiosity or just my spirit of competition with colleagues took me, I really had to pluck up courage. Yes, courage: what is it? I have always thought of it as being the strength to overcome one's own inexpressible fear.

In those years one of my colleagues was an extraordinary Australian cameraman, Neal Davis. Every time I got to where I was told the front was, I would always see Neal, with his white towel around his neck and his old Bolex, ahead of me. He was a man who had no fear of war. Once, in the last days of Saigon, a plane tried to bomb the presidential palace and the anti-aircraft guns started firing wildly. Thousands of bullets rained on the roofs and the square around the cathedral, and we all dashed for cover. But Neal just stood there in that inferno and carried on filming. Ten years later, in Bangkok, during a failed coup, a tank crew mistook his Bolex for a gun and fired at him. Neal put the camera on automatic and threw it down in front of him, thus producing his last dramatic film: that of his own death.

I asked Kaka if he believed the hand was the best guide to a person's fate. He said yes, then added, '*But you must pay attention, and try to understand what the palmist says.*'

He told me the story of a Chinese client of his, a well-to-do businessman. Kaka read his palm and told him: 'Your hand shows that you've two wives. If you don't, you may one day.' The man wasted no time. He went home, gathered the family together and announced that he was marrying his secretary because the palmist had told him to. The family were terribly upset, and went to Kaka. He had to call the man back and explain to him that 'you may have' does not mean 'you *must* have'. He said, 'If I told you that in your hand it's written that you'll die by fire, what would you do? Get a petrol tank and throw yourself in, or prepare a water tank to put out any possible fire?' He convinced the man to remain monogamous.

Kaka said that the signs in the hand do not remain the same all one's life; they change as time goes by, and your fate changes with them. If I began to meditate I would see for myself how my hand would change. I failed to see how this would be possible, but I said nothing.

I walked back to the hotel in the broiling sun. It was the hour when in the tropics everyone takes a siesta. The rickshaw drivers sleep on the passenger's seat with their feet up, shaded by the hood, the Indian tailors sleep on their counters, the Chinese in the dim interiors of their shops.

My visits to fortune-tellers were growing more and more disappointing. What they told me about my fate was a string of banalities. Were there really any among them with special powers? Was the old man in Hong Kong one of them? I brushed away the thought.

Of all the things Kaka said, the only one that stuck in my mind was his advice to meditate. I was most definitely not going to wear a ring on my middle finger. And getting rich did not interest me in the slightest. If you are rich you end up having to be with other rich people, and the rich, as I discovered some time ago, are boring. Also, rich people have to worry about not losing their wealth, and that is a worry I can do without.

And yet there was something enjoyable in my encounters with these characters. As they reviewed the topics of family, health, love and money I was led to think about myself in a way I had not done for some time. Who at my age really thinks about himself any more? Who stops to ask himself seriously if he wants a second wife, a third child, or even a ring on the middle finger of his right hand? Preoccupied with the problems of daily life, we scarcely ever stand back and take a good look at ourselves. How many happily married people take a conscious pleasure in their state? We have fewer and fewer moments in which to reflect on what we have. And who thinks about death any more? For us Westerners it has become a taboo. We live in societies that have been moulded by the optimism of the advertising industry, in which death has no place. It has been banished, exiled from our midst. By contrast, every fortune-teller I saw held it up to my gaze once more.

What changes there have been in death during the course of my life! When I was a boy and someone died, it was a choral event. All the neighbours came to lend a hand. Death was displayed. The house was opened, the deceased was visible, and so everyone became acquainted with death. Today death is an embarrassment, it is hidden. No one knows how to manage it, what to do with the deceased. The experience of death is becoming more and more rare, and one may well arrive at one's own without ever having witnessed another's.

If the Bangkok woman who looked at my mole was right, I shall end my days in a foreign land. What a pity, for there is something reassuring in the idea of dying where one was born, in a room where one knows the smell, the creak of the door, the view from the window. Dying where one's parents and grandparents died, where one's grandchildren will be born, one somehow dies less.

The Chinese have always understood this, and ancestor worship has been their only real religion. In ancient times they would reserve a place at the far end of the cave in which the dead were buried and the women gave birth. Thus a cycle was created, as if the new took life from the old. Reincarnation, in fact. There can be no doubt that remaining for generations in the same place, repeating the same gestures and the same rites, tends to favour the concept of a great continuity of life in which an individual's body is something purely accidental, a convenient shell that just happens to belong to the person inside it.

While meditating, one of the Eight Chinese Immortals once departed so far from his body that when he 'returned' he found someone else had taken it over. Not in the least distressed, he helped himself to the first free body he found: that of a one-legged beggar who had just died. Which is why that particular god of the Taoist Olympus is called Iron Leg Li.

From Penang I had to go to Kuala Lumpur. I could have taken the express train from Butterworth, but that seemed too precipitate, so I decided to work my way slowly down the peninsula. A shared taxi took me as far as Ipoh, a city from which – so they say – come the most beautiful women and the richest Chinese in Malaysia.

Little more than a hundred years ago Ipoh was just a big village. Its name comes from a tree whose wood the Malays used for making poisoned arrows. Then came the British, who discovered that the soil was full of tin. What happened next explains the history of Malaysia and its problems today.

Extracting tin required manpower. The Malays did not greatly care for working in the mines, so the British decided to welcome any immigrants who could manage to get there. In 1879 there were 4623 Malays in Ipoh, 982 Chinese and one Englishman. By 1889 there were 10,291 Malays, sixty-nine Englishmen, and 44,790 Chinese. That was how Ipoh became an almost exclusively Chinese city. A few of these immigrant families, enriched by tin, are today an economic power with which the political power (controlled by the Malays) has to reckon.

'Only 10 per cent of the Chinese here are really rich, but the other 90 per cent work like mad in the hope that they may become so,' I was told by one of the Chinese people I spoke to in Ipoh. None of them dream of going back to their homeland. 'In Malaysia I'm a second-class citizen, but I still have a better life than I would as a first-class citizen in China,' a teacher told me. 'So I stay put.' Nothing if not practical, the Chinese!

On New Year's Day 1993 I imposed on myself a second ban, besides the one on planes: not to stay in any of the usual modern hotels, all indistinguishable one from another, no matter what country you are in.

In Ipoh I found one for $5 a night, very Chinese, dirty, littered with cigarette butts, and with an ancestral altar on each floor. The fire escape was inaccessible, being used for storage, and all the rooms had several beds. But even Ipoh was undergoing modernization. I went to visit the oldest Chinese temple in the city, and found that it had just been completely rebuilt in concrete. I went to see the grottoes in the limestone mountain, where the first Buddhists in the area had lived, only to find that these too had been plastered with cement and lit with neon. The statues in the gorges were new and shiny. The old ones, blackened by incense and age, had been removed.

I arrived in Kuala Lumpur by bus as night was falling. I had not been there for years, and was surprised to find that the city had acquired a Muslim character of its own. The Malays had managed to give a new face to the capital and erase its Chinese look.

I landed up in one of those hotels with dirty carpets, plates left in the corridors after meals, and curtainless showers; but at least I was spared having to view the world as if through the glass of an aquarium. I opened the windows, letting in all the noises and smells of Kuala Lumpur.

The hotel's owners and all the employees were Chinese. The only Malay was the doorman who carried the luggage of the guests, who were also Chinese. After about two words of conversation he too started telling me about the problem that divides Malaysia: race.

'Look,' he said with a sweeping wave of the hand. 'The skyscrapers are Chinese, the market stalls are Chinese, the shops are Chinese, the supermarkets are Chinese . . . So tell me: is this Malaysia?'

Just then a motorcycle with a sidecar pulled up in front of the hotel. The rider took off his helmet and set to work. In the space of a few minutes he had turned the sidecar into a miniature restaurant, with two gas rings and a table spread with tempting specialities on little trays. People stopped and selected skewers with meatballs on them, pieces of octopus, slices of liver, sausages and chicken wings. He would boil them in a pot, then dip them in red, yellow or orange sauces lined up in little dishes. The customers ate standing, and paid by the number of empty skewers they had in their hands. It was all clean, attractive and well organized. The man was Chinese. Chinese were all the people I saw in the streets, busily running here and there on all sorts of errands.

With such competition the poor Malay felt he would never get anywhere.

CHAPTER TEN

Sores Under the Veil

I had been in Kuala Lumpur for barely twelve hours when I was invited to the home of the prime minister . . . along with millions of others. I had read in the paper that on Hari Raja, the holiday when traditionally every Malay opens his home to all, even the head of government's official residence would be open to anyone who wished to visit, with him there to receive them. And this was the day in question.

A taxi set me down at the residence's wide-open gates, and I entered. An enormous crowd milled around the platters heaped with rice, meatballs and pancake rolls. Guests were filling their plates and going to eat on the lawn. Others were queuing to shake the hand of Mr Mahatir, who stood with his wife in the middle of an air-conditioned salon with signs on the walls requesting guests not to smoke.

The overwhelming majority of the prime minister's guests were Malay, all dressed for the occasion in lustrous, brightly coloured silks. The men, even the little boys, wore blouses and trousers with mini-sarongs over them like little skirts, and the Muslim black cap on their heads. The women wore the two-piece garment which has become the national costume: a floor-length skirt with a modest tunic down to the knees. They all looked as if they had stepped out of a fairy tale that began: 'Once upon a time there was a rich land in which the Malay people lived happily and peacefully . . .' They all appeared well-fed, slow-moving, a bit vain, trying to look severe, but really quite mild. I grasped the gist of their fairy tale: 'One day some colonialists came from a faraway land, but the country was rich and the Malays continued to live serenely. But when the colonialists went away, the Chinese remained in Malaysia, and there was no more peace for the Malays.'

For centuries they had lived in villages, *kampongs*, under their sultans, who were both spiritual and political leaders. It was the need to compete with the Chinese that forced them to give up their pleasant life in the *kampongs* and move to the cities. The man who stood in the air-conditioned salon, shaking one hand after another, was the great strategist of this operation. His intention was to ensure that Malaysia would remain Malay and at the same time become a modern country.

The previous governments had likewise tried to protect the interests of the *bumiputras* – the sons of the soil – and to keep the Chinese at bay, but the results had been debatable. They had ruled that Malays must be involved in every Chinese company, and the Chinese had brought in some compliant Malays to act as dummies; they had imposed Malay as the national language, lowering the cultural level all round; they had limited the number of places for Chinese at the universities, so the Chinese had gone abroad to study, returning better educated and more aggressive than the Malays who had remained at home.

Mahatir, on coming to power in 1981, realized that further measures would be required to get to the root of the problem. His aim was to remodel the Malays, reinforcing their identity, and to marginalize the Chinese, while taking every care not to drive them out of the country: 70 per cent of the private economy was in their hands, and their sudden departure might be fatal. Mahatir's idea was to dilute the Chinese presence through a huge increase in the population. Malaysia has only twenty million inhabitants; Mahatir wants seventy million by the year 2020. The fact that as Muslims the Malays can have four wives, and their rate of increase is double that of the Chinese, should produce the desired results. The strategy is a reversal of the process of ethnic cleansing.

When it came to remodelling the Malays to give them a stronger identity, no longer influenced by a century of life alongside the Chinese, Mahatir turned to religion, pushing the country towards a Muslim orthodoxy it had never known before. For someone like me, who had been away from Malaysia for years, the changes wrought by this mass 'reconversion' to Islam were surprising. Apart from the abandonment of traditional female clothing and the introduction of the veil, there were Muslim innovations in every aspect of life. Every hotel room throughout Malaysia is required by law to have an arrow on the ceiling to indicate the direction of Mecca; every restaurant has a special section reserved for Muslim food; each community has a 'Muslim public eye', a sort of religious spy to check on people's behaviour; the newspapers discuss what is 'decent' according to Islam; and the bookshops sell manuals prescribing how a good Malay should behave.

I eyed the crowd of Malays in Mahatir's garden, the house, the city's skyscrapers, shopping centres and luxury hotels. Despite the Muslim patina, Malaysia struck me as not all that different from Buddhist Thailand, or from what the Chinese would have made of it had the country been in their hands. Despite its claim to be different and its anti-Western rhetoric, Mahatir's model of modernity was like all the others: a copy of the West.

I joined the long queue to pay my respects to the prime minister, and eventually my turn came. 'Just imagine how many more hands you'll have to shake when there are seventy million Malays!' I said as he shook mine. 'By then I won't be around any more,' Mahatir instantly replied.

There were not many foreigners in the queue, and my having reached that point led to other invitations. By the end of the day I had been in the homes of some high government officials and three ministers. That too was an experience: their houses were more or less identical, modern and *kitsch*, with no character, no style or tradition, stuffed with electronic gadgets and ornaments bought by credit card in London and New York.

The culture of the *kampongs* was finished, even if certain festivals like Hari Raja were still being observed.

In the days that followed I got down to my article on the Chinese, but another topic had begun to simmer in my mind: the long-term consequences of the Muslim 'reconversion' of Malaysia. With the help of an old Malay colleague of Indian origin, M.G.G. Pillai, I interviewed some academics, a couple of ex-politicians, and a possible future prime minister. The picture that emerged was disturbing. Using Islam as a political tool to strengthen Malay identity had been like letting the genie out of the lamp. This genie was now at large, growing with a logic of its own that was not necessarily what the government leaders had in mind. Young Malays who had been sent

to study in Islamic universities abroad returned influenced by fundamentalism, and were highly critical of the way the country and the
religion were being run. The Malay armed forces, once steeped in
British tradition, were starting to change their character under the
influence of young officers who were more disposed to obeying the
Koran than their superiors. I noticed that the women around Mahatir
and in the ministries wore no veil, unlike almost all the girls at the
university. The government left them free to choose, but the young
Islamic radicals imposed it on female students. Using Islam as a tool
to unravel and divide the Malays from the Chinese now threatened
to divide the Malays from the Malays. Mahatir was particularly concerned at the increase in Islamic sects, one especially, Al Arqam,
which was popular among the young.

My journalist friend M.G.G. Pillai telephoned to arrange a visit
to their headquarters. M.G.G. was invaluable to me. He knew everyone and remembered everything, which did not always make him
popular. Shortly before my arrival, he had found himself once again
on Singapore's list of 'undesirables'. To the diplomat who informed
him of this fact, M.G.G. had replied: 'Never mind. I've already done
my shopping.'

The famous fortune-teller whom Kaka had mentioned in Penang
and who held court in one of the city's big hotels was booked for
every hour of every day for the next three months. This made me
all the keener to see him, and I asked his secretary to let me know
if someone should cancel an appointment. As I did so, I couldn't
help wondering if my eagerness to see the man was related to my
research, or if I were not becoming addicted to 'witchcraft'.

Really, I reflected, if one were not careful one might gradually
poison one's life with this uncertainty, requiring a regular 'fix' in the
form of vague pronouncements from one of those characters. Has
so-and-so said something positive? Something negative? Then a
second opinion is called for. And then a third. Dissatisfied with a
palmist? Well, try an astrologer, and then someone who does tarot
cards . . . It never ends, and as a last resort, to justify one's own
credulity, one may get to the point of bringing about what one of
the humbugs has 'foreseen'.

You have to look at the world from the fortune-teller's point of view, too. The power he has! He shuts his eyes and says: 'I see that you're a person of such-and such a character. Within a year, this, that or the other will happen to you, within two years something else.'

Someone with no respect for other people's humanity might amuse himself by experimenting with this power. He could go up to someone at a bus stop and say: 'Excuse me, sir, but you must be ultra-careful. I see in your face that on the twenty-third of next month you'll have a nasty accident. I see it, take care!' Until the twenty-third of the next month the poor dupe will have no peace! And if he is told that to avoid the misfortune he must run around the kitchen table three times every night, he may actually do it – eventually, half-jokingly, when no one is looking. 'You never know,' he will say.

The mere fact of having formulated the threat is enough to make it seem real, and sets the mind reeling – much more than a prediction of winning the lottery! The positive goes in one ear and out the other, but the negative leaves a creeping doubt, a nagging uneasiness; because fear is at the very root of the human condition.

Something of the sort once happened to Saskia. She had come to Bangkok, and went to visit a Thai neighbour of ours. There she met an odd woman, frustrated and a mass of problems, who wanted to read her palm. Saskia did not know how to refuse. The woman told her that no one would ever truly love her, that she would not marry and would have no children. For a beautiful girl of twenty it was like a curse; for that unhappy woman perhaps it was just a way of taking indirect revenge on life.

Saskia said she did not take it seriously, but I knew that the witch's words would weigh on her mind, and I was afraid she might unconsciously try to make the facts tally with the 'prophecy'. I certainly had not forgotten Saskia's experience when I decided to investigate fortune-tellers and try to understand a little more of how their world works.

I telephoned the Malay wife of a high official, a woman I had known for years and who had offered to help me during my stay, and told her I wanted to see a fortune-teller.

'A fortune-teller? Of course,' she said. 'I sometimes go to an Indian woman . . .' Another surprise: she too, I would have thought, was 'above suspicion'.

The Indian woman lived in a working-class district of Kuala Lumpur. After passing the shops of blacksmiths, glaziers and iron-mongers, we came to a very modest house. Down we went to the floor below, and stepped in to a small room with a cement floor. One wall was dominated by a statue of the Indian god Shiva. At its feet were some small trays of flower petals, an oil lamp, and packets of money left by previous client-patients. The room was filled with the sweetish odour of Indian incense.

The woman was dressed in a cyclamen-coloured sari. She had grey hair, a broad smile, and very intense black eyes. Originally from Madras, she had obviously been a beautiful woman, and still had an air of self-confidence and a majestic bearing. In 1969 her only son had been killed in a road accident, and since that time she had had the gift of sight. 'God gives and God takes away,' she said, turning towards the statue with joined hands and a slight inclination of the head.

There followed the usual procedure: date and time of birth. But she made no calculations. She looked at my hands, my face, then went into a sort of trance, and began: *'You're a sincere person; if you give your word you keep it. You have already made your life. You have gambled, and it has gone well. Now you are thinking of retiring from the world. In your previous life you lived on the island of Sri Lanka. You were of very high caste. This time you were born in a very humble house, but you still behave as if you were of royal blood, and you are at ease with whites and British people.'* (She spoke to me as if I were an Indian from the days of the Raj.) *'For years you've been moving about from country to country, but soon you'll go to a particular one and stay put; but it won't be the one where you were born.'*

India, I thought. Since telling her my date of birth I had not opened my mouth. The woman continued, holding my hands tightly in hers. *'You should go and live in Sri Lanka again, or in India, but not in a village; preferably in a big city in the north. Delhi would be right for you. If you find a place to settle in, then settle. You've wasted a great deal of money, you've given it away to anyone who asked for it. That's why you aren't rich, though the beggars who see you on the street think you are. You have a family . . .'*

She went on in that way for a while, saying nothing particularly wrong or particularly remarkable. She said that in 1997 I must be very careful about my travel documents (perhaps some problem about going to Hong Kong to see the Chinese take the colony back, I thought), and that I must always wear white (as I always did).

The woman had no particular method. She was simply 'psychic', and by going into a trance managed to 'feel', partly through touch, the person whose hand she was holding. In my case she may have felt that I was there from mere curiosity, that I had no problems requiring her help. Once she put herself on my wavelength, so to speak, she found that I had no anxieties that she could get hold of. I failed to inspire her. Only when she asked me if I had any questions, and I asked what would be the fate of my daughter, did she become animated.

'*What's her name?*'

'Saskia,' I said, and the woman began to smile. She stood up as if to touch her, and produced a physical description of Saskia as if she were actually there in front of her. And perhaps in a way she was. At the moment when I pronounced her name, my mind had filled with images, conjuring up a Saskia that she saw and described. Possible? I think so. The existence of a 'language of the mind' may explain such cases. People who know each other well, who live together for a long time, develop this kind of language. How else can one explain something that keeps happening to Angela and me? For example, we are driving on a motorway; neither of us says anything for miles and miles, and then suddenly one of us says: 'Do you remember that time in Australia . . . ?' And just at that moment the other was opening his or her mouth to say exactly the same thing. It has happened to us too many times to be pure chance.

With regard to Saskia, the woman answered in an 'Indian' way. She said that the right age for her to marry would be after her twenty-third birthday, and that it was up to me to choose a good husband for her – best of all some sort of technician, so that if they wished they could emigrate to America, Canada or Singapore.

After we had paid and left, my friend told me she was disappointed; the woman had been much better on other occasions. She told me about someone else whom she had brought to this fortune-teller, a high government official who had lost his job because of a scandal. He was too old to embark on a new career, but too young to retire. He could not find work, and was terribly depressed. The Indian woman told him that he was passing through a period of great misfortune, and it was absolutely useless trying to do anything about it. He was to wait until a certain date. In the meantime he was to pray and put lotus flowers in front of the statue of Shiva every day. Around the stated date he would meet a person who would offer him a good job. Relieved, the man prayed and offered the flowers, and when around the appointed time he went to meet the head of a big industrial complex, he had regained so much self-confidence that he was offered an excellent job. If things had not worked out that time, the fortune-teller would have found a justification and suggested other things for the man to do until his next interview. Sooner or later, luck always changes. It is just a matter of waiting, and of having someone – a friend, a psychoanalyst, or a fortune-teller – with whom to share the anxiety.

A story which has intrigued me in recent years is how modern pirates, with very fast boats and sophisticated weapons, attack supertankers and container ships in the waters of South-East Asia and the China Sea. Many of the incidents had taken place in the Straits of Malacca, and I thought it would be interesting to sail down their entire length. The port serving Kuala Lumpur is the nearby town of Klang, and one morning I went there to explore the possibility of taking a ship for my next destination – Singapore.

The only positive thing I learned from the trip to Klang was that the local sultan was unable to live in his residence by the sea. The old palace was bewitched, and had had to be demolished; the new one was just finished, but ghosts had moved in even before the sultan. As for ships plying the Straits of Malacca, nothing doing. There was no passenger service to Singapore; cargo ships were plentiful enough, but to get on to one I would need a special permit. The Foreign Ministry put me in touch with the Transport Ministry, which asked me to write a letter and enclose my curriculum vitae. It was the first time I had ever had to put in writing where I was born, where I had studied and how many children I had, in order to travel from A to B. But even that was not enough. Every time I telephoned to ask about the permit, they told me to wait.

★   ★   ★

While I was waiting, I went with M.G.G. Pillai in a shuddering red Volkswagen to visit the headquarters of the Islamic Al Arqam sect. Sungai Panchala, a village about six miles outside Kuala Lumpur, had once been the administrative centre of a large rubber plantation. As we approached, the first impression was that it was still just that, with its white masonry buildings and corrugated-iron roofs amid orchards of banana and papaya trees. But the impression was short-lived. We passed groups of children along the road, all in green and white uniforms, and then, like lugubrious triangles in motion, some women wrapped in black robes from head to foot, with black gloves and black veils over their faces and shoulders.

M.G.G., at the steering wheel, had been telling me that one consequence of imposing veils on Malay women was that the dermatologists were making a great deal of money. Given the hot and humid tropical climate, the poor creatures, who had previously washed frequently, oiled their hair and left it exposed to the air, were now developing eczema and sores on their heads. Many went bald.

We came across some extremely elegant men, comfortable in their long light-coloured tunics and handsome turbans. Men! Always the privileged ones, I thought. I noticed too that they wore make-up, a very fine black line around the eyes that gave their expression an added note of intensity. I felt as if I had wandered into a madhouse, and had better be careful not to irritate the inmates.

M.G.G. had telephoned to announce our visit, so we were greeted with the liturgy common to all totalitarian states, parties and movements: a welcoming speech by a reception committee, a souvenir photo for their propaganda publications and a request to write our names, addresses and comments in the Golden Book.

The formula that makes these groups tick is always the same: a simple ideology, a charismatic leader, a uniform, rigid rules of behaviour. In return they promise some sort of salvation; first of all from the boredom and routine of daily life. The idea of Al Arqam is that the world, more and more decadent and corrupted by materialism, is heading for a catastrophe. Salvation will come from Uzbekistan with a new messiah, who under a black banner will lead the regeneration of Islam and the entire human race.

Al Arqam was founded in 1967 by Ustadz Ashaari, a young radical who, having got nowhere in traditional politics, had found his true vocation: that of a guru. For the members of the sect Ashaari is a demigod. Married to four wives and father of thirty-seven children, he has written more than fifty books and has travelled all over the world, meeting heads of state and presidents . . . All this was explained to us by one of his devotees, who in pronouncing Ashaari's name reverently dropped his voice, as the Chinese used to do when they said 'Chairman Mao'.

Between the ages of twenty and forty the members of Al Arqam live in the community in Sungai Panchala, then they re-enter normal life. While they are living within the community they receive food and lodging, plus pocket money for small personal expenses. Those who live outside contribute to the group's finances by handing over 50 per cent of all they earn. The sect has followers in every area of society, from the public administration to the courts, from economics to politics.

The headquarters was bought by the community in 1972. It is mainly a centre of propaganda, producing books, cassettes and videos to spread the ideas of the movement. The audio-visual studio was run by a former technician from Radio Malaysia. He seemed calm and happy.

'We certainly aren't anti-modern as such,' explained the sect's chief ideologist. 'We're only against the Western type of modernity, which is exclusively materialistic and non-spiritual. We favour a development that won't damage nature or exploit other peoples.'

Al Arqam rejects consumerism, and has set up its own alternative economic system, with factories, farms and shops to meet its needs. The members want an Islamic economy, by which they mean an economy not based on the concept of profit. They want to be Muslims in every aspect of life, and not, like the majority, 'only at the hour of prayer'.

With their rejection of the consumerism and materialism of modern society, combined with Muslim integralism, these totalitarian hippies struck me as less mad than I had initially assumed. The pace of life in their community was pleasantly slow, and they seemed serene and calm. But there was still the disturbing idea of Islam with ever-drawn sword, to which was now added the vision of those black banners leading the regeneration of the world.

Al Arqam was an example of how the rejection of materialism leads many young people to search for a new spirituality, for something that will impose discipline and rules in exchange for a sense of belonging.

Islam is well suited to meet this need, and in various ways is trying to fill the empty spaces left by the failure of ideologies like Communism or of economic experiments tainted by capitalism. But Islam is surely too antiquated and too repressive – especially as regards women – to be the hope for the future. Will the twenty-first century see the birth of a great new world religion?

Seeing the 'famous' fortune-teller proved impossible. None of his clients cancelled their appointment. 'Never mind. When you get to Singapore, go and see Rajamanikam,' said M.G.G. Pillai. 'He's really superb.' As usual, the exceptional fortune-teller is always elsewhere.

M.G.G. said that Rajamanikam was truly special, and that some of Singapore's most eminent political figures discreetly sought his advice. M.G.G. had known him for years, and had consulted him when his father was very ill. Rajamanikam was basically an astrologer, but after asking what symptoms M.G.G.'s father had, and the time and date of his birth, he added another question: 'Is your house above ground level?'

'Yes,' M.G.G. replied.

'Then go and dig in the earth right under where your father's bed is, and bring me all you find there.'

They found a paper packet containing some dried herbs and an amulet of the Bugis, the inhabitants of the eastern islands of Indonesia who are the most dreaded masters of black magic. Rajamanikam took the packet, and delicately, as if it were a bomb, defused it. M.G.G.'s father recovered. But not for long. He had a relapse and died. When they cleared out the room his family discovered another amulet hidden under the mattress, identical to the first. Years later M.G.G. was called to the bedside of one of his father's colleagues, who confessed that it was he who had had the amulets put there, because of some old jealousy. Before dying he wanted to get this weight off his conscience.

My request to travel by boat down the Straits of Malacca was utterly unsuccessful. Every time I phoned the Foreign Ministry they said the matter was in the hands of the Transport Ministry, who in turn said it was up to the security services. In other words Malaysia's counter-espionage was still wondering why on earth a European journalist should want to go to Singapore by boat when it was so much more convenient to fly. I resigned myself to continuing over-land. That way, at least, I could stop in Malacca, the most bewitched city on earth.

CHAPTER ELEVEN

The Murmurs of Malacca

If you wait until evening, and then walk silently along the walls, or go up one of the hills and sit quietly on the old stones, you will hear it. It is almost a whisper, like the breeze, but you hear it all the same: the voice of history. Malacca is one of those places. Full of the dead. And the dead whisper. They whisper in Chinese, in Portuguese, in Dutch, in Malay, in English, some even in Italian, others in languages no one speaks any more. But it hardly matters: the stories told by the dead of Malacca no longer interest anyone.

Malacca, on the west coast of Malaysia, is a city freighted with the past, soaked in blood and sown with bones. It is an extraordinary city where half the world's races have met, fought, loved and reproduced; where different religions have come together, tolerated each other and integrated; where the interests of great empires have struggled for primacy; and where today modernity and progress are pitilessly suffocating all diversity, all conflict, in torrents of cement, to create that bland uniformity in which the majority seem to feel at home.

Nine years ago a *feng-shui* expert said that Bukit China – the Hill of the Chinese – was the lung of the city, and that without it Malacca would suffocate. But for that warning, one of the city's most historic and romantic places would have been handed over to speculative builders and their bulldozers. For over five centuries the *hua-ren* of Malacca have buried their dead on the gentle slopes of that sunny height with its sea view. The tombs vary in size and splendour, but all are of the same whiteness, and of the same rotundity, like maternal wombs, all perfectly exposed to that 'cosmic breath' which gives life to those who depart for the other world and brings good fortune to those who remain.

The day I arrived in Malacca was Ching Ming, the Festival of

Souls, and the hill swarmed with Chinese paying homage to their ancestors. Families crouched around the burial mounds, pulling up weeds, laying bunches of flowers, lighting candles and sticks of incense, and neatly arranging bowlfuls of rice, piles of oranges and tangerines and wads of gold-edged banknotes, so that the deceased could help themselves.

Malacca was founded by a young Malay prince who had stopped there on a hunting trip. He named it after the large melaka tree that presided over the mouth of the river. The Chinese landed there in 1409, led by a eunuch, a great Muslim admiral by the name of Chen Ho. China was then at the peak of its power. It built ships that could carry up to seven hundred people, it had invented gunpowder (but only used it to make fireworks), and it sought diplomatic and trade relations with the rest of Asia. The small port of Malacca was an ideal base, but the Chinese did not want to conquer it, only the right to live there, to moor their boats and load and unload their goods. To obtain these privileges they gave the local rulers five hundred marriageable girls, including a daughter of the emperor.

By the end of the fifteenth century Malacca was the largest emporium in the Orient. The products of several continents were traded there, and people came from all corners of the earth. Apart from the Malays and Chinese there were Persians, Arabs, Indians from Gujarat and from the southern empire of Kalinga, there were Africans and the mysterious Lequios, who sailed as far as Japan and who, to thank their gods for surviving a storm, would sacrifice a virgin by beheading her at the stern of a junk. Someone has counted the languages that were spoken in Malacca at that time: eighty-four.

In 1511 the Portuguese arrived. They, unlike the Chinese, came as conquerors. Alfonso de Albuquerque had sailed from Goa with a fleet of eighteen ships and eight hundred men to attack the city and put it to fire and sword. The sultan managed to escape, but his palace was razed to the ground and his treasury sacked. Three ships, laden with booty which Albuquerque intended to send to Lisbon, were caught by a sudden storm shortly after setting sail from Malacca. They are still lying undisturbed on the seabed. Whether, as is claimed, they contain gold which the sultan had hidden in the secret tunnel under the city remains a mystery. It is not even certain that the tunnel ever existed, but for centuries the children of Malacca have been told that if they ever find the entrance they must on no account set foot inside it: no one has ever returned alive to reveal its whereabouts.

The Portuguese remained masters of Malacca for 130 years, and that was the city's period of glory. It was not only an important trading centre, but the launching pad for the Christian conquest of the soul of the Orient. Missionaries from Europe would stay at the Franciscan seminary in Malacca to recover their strength after their long voyage and to prepare themselves spiritually. From there they sailed for Macao and Nagasaki, hoping by hook or by crook to enter and establish themselves in the closed and strictly forbidden universes of China and Japan.

The most famous among these men of God was Francis Xavier, a Spanish Jesuit who arrived in Malacca in 1545. It was here that he performed his first miracles – including reviving a baby girl who had been dead for three days – and demonstrated his gifts as a seer by forecasting the victory of the Portuguese in a naval battle hundreds of miles away. On various occasions, moreover, he warned sailors against boarding ships which then sank. By his death in 1552, probably of malaria, on the small island of Sanqian in the mouth of the Pearl River near Canton, Francis Xavier had laid the foundations for Christian missions in several parts of Asia, from the Molucca Islands to the Philippines and Japan.

The account of what happened to Xavier's corpse can hold its own among the tales of the mysterious East. In Sanqian there were no ships to take the body back to Christian soil, so it was placed in a simple coffin with some lime and buried. Two and a half months later a Portuguese vessel dropped by. Xavier was exhumed, and to everyone's astonishment the cadaver was found to be intact. The sailors hailed it as a miracle. One of them took a knife and cut a piece of flesh from the thigh as a relic, and blood flowed as from a living body. When the corpse reached Malacca the plague then raging in the city came to a sudden halt. Xavier was buried in the church of St Paul on the hill overlooking the harbour. After nine months, however, he was exhumed again and taken to Goa. The body was still intact, and a Portuguese noblewoman cut off the little toe from one foot as a keepsake. The stories of Francis Xavier's miracles, and of his body that death failed to decompose, soon reached the Vatican with a request for his canonization. The Pope demanded proofs. In

1614 the tomb was reopened, and the right arm was cut off and sent to Rome.

In 1622 Xavier was declared a saint, but the mutilations did not end there. Over the centuries all his toes disappeared except for one big one; in 1951 his left ear was cut off. What remains of the body is now in Goa, where to this day it is exhibited for a month every ten years in the Basilica del Buon Gesù. One arm bone is in Rome, another in Macao, in the church of Coloane.

Until quite recently the priest at this church was an Italian, Father Angelo Acquistapace. He had been a missionary in China until 1949 when the Communists expelled him, and had then gone to Vietnam, where I met him in his orphanage north of Saigon. In 1975 the Communists had again driven him out. He ended up in that last remaining patch of Christian territory, taking care of lepers. Every time he celebrated mass, after blessing the faithful he would raise his arms and face the wide-open door of the church, from which Communist China could be seen across a narrow stretch of sea, and would say: '*Vade retro, Satana!*' – Go back, Satan!

He died in good time: in 1999 China will recover Macao, and Francis Xavier's reliquary.

Almost the only place without a bone of the saint is Malacca itself. For centuries there was not so much as a statue in his honour. In 1953 the bishop ordered one from Italy and had it placed on top of the hill that overlooks the port. Three months went by. Then one night, in the midst of a thunderstorm, a branch of a nearby casuarina tree fell, and cleanly severed (mark the coincidence) the statue's right forearm – precisely where it had been amputated from the corpse itself. And thus the statue remained – mutilated.

Malacca's golden age ended in 1641, when the Portuguese were defeated and driven out by the Dutch. The Dutch were in turn driven out by the British, and the British, expelled temporarily by the Japanese in 1942, departed for good in 1957 after granting independence to what became the Malay Federation. All of them left their legacy of monuments, tombs, memories, legends, and innumerable ghosts. Today Malacca is the most haunted city in the world. There are beautiful houses in which no one will live, and places where one is never alone.

Every evening, among the ruins of the Portuguese fort, people see the forms of two young people embracing. The man was one of Albuquerque's sailors, the woman a nun. They were discovered making love and sentenced to death. He was decapitated and she was immured alive, but their passion is undying.

Some time ago a highly respected judge said there was a woman in his office whom he could not get rid of. In former times the building had been a poorhouse, and it was regarded as quite natural that some wretch, among so many who had died there, should return to seek justice.

Even the German electronics company Siemens, when they came to Malacca to set up a factory, had difficulties with ghosts. From time to time the guards would see strange characters entering and leaving the building without clocking in or out. Whenever someone tried to stop them they melted into thin air, only to reappear shortly afterwards. An expert in black magic, a *bomoh*, explained that in building the factory a small Indian temple had been destroyed, and that the spirits who used to live there were now without a place of their own. Siemens agreed to build a new temple elsewhere, and that solved the problem.

In a shoe factory, a female worker had suddenly started screaming, tearing off her clothes and running about like a maniac. Another woman followed her example, then another, and in no time at all the whole place was in an uproar. It took three days and the sacrifice of a she-goat to appease the spirits and normalize production.

Ghosts did not provide the only explanation for incidents of this kind: the young people who had grown up in their *kampongs* found difficulty in adjusting to city life, the discipline of the production line, and reacted by 'running amok'.

In fact the two explanations were not at all contradictory. I, like the Malays, preferred the one which gave the name of 'ghosts' to the frustrations of so many young people. They had eagerly abandoned their work in the fields to go in to the factories, but soon realized that in doing so they had not bettered their lives or made themselves any happier. Quite the contrary.

Malacca is a city unlike any other. I could not see anyone, or go anywhere, without being told strange stories. One woman, with a university education, told me that the people of Malacca took care not to let their children go on the beach after sunset, because they would be kidnapped by the gnomes.

'The gnomes?'

'Yes. No one has seen them, but everyone knows they're there, because they leave a trail of perfume behind them.' Not long before, a stolen child had been found by a *bomoh* inside a coconut tree. He had his mouth full of chicken droppings which the gnomes, having little idea of what humans ate, had offered him. 'It was even in the newspaper,' she assured me.

I had asked about a restaurant with traditional cuisine, and someone had recommended a place in the old Portuguese quarter. I was eating an excellent boiled cod with potatoes, onions, black olives and raw garlic when the chef-proprietor sat down beside me and asked: 'Sir, are you in need of protection?'

Michael Texiera, aged seventy-six, a Malay-Portuguese and a Catholic, had served in the British army and been captured by the Japanese. After the war he was sent to fight against the Communists. He had married when he was very young. He and his wife Nancy had had seventeen children, of whom fourteen were still alive. Twenty years previously Nancy told him her belly could stand no more: another baby and it would burst. Punctilious in their obedience to the Church's laws, they had decided to have no more sexual relations, and this, Michael told me, had given him the power to cure people and free them from the devil. He did this with a small wooden crucifix that his parish priest had brought him from Rome, where he had been on a pilgrimage.

'Of course,' I replied. 'One always needs protection.'

Michael put the crucifix in a glass of water, whispered some prayers, passed the glass around my head, over my chest and my hands, and concluded that I had no problems, as the devil had never been in my body.

What most interested me was the story of his marriage. 'Was it a love match?' I asked. Not in the least. It was his mother who had chosen Nancy for him. At the time of their wedding he had only ever seen her once. He said that they had had a happy life together and were still very close.

Even in the tradition of arranged marriages – still so widespread in Asia – is there a wisdom that we Westerners, with our cult of free choice, have given up along the way?

Ali, the taxi driver who took me back to town, was a Malay. He and his wife already had four children, but were set on having more. 'The rich make more and more money, the poor more and more children,' he said, 'but the poor are happier because they have time to be with their families. The rich, never: they are always busy.'

'Was it a love match?' I asked. No, Ali's marriage had been arranged, too. His father, a bus driver, had come to an agreement with the girl's father, who had a market stall.

'We took one look and we hated each other. But there was nothing to do. Even at the wedding we couldn't stand each other. Love began only with the first child, but since then it has grown and grown.'

Are the Asians perhaps right in their principle: 'Love the one you marry, don't marry the one you love'?

I asked Ali to take me to an Indian fortune-teller who Michael had said could be found on the street where the haberdashers were.

'Him? He's a fool. He can't foretell a thing,' said Ali with a loud laugh. 'How can he read someone else's fortune if he can't make his own? He's been in that chair for thirty years, and every time the monsoon comes he runs for shelter. If he were any good he'd at least have an umbrella. No, no, I believe in fortune-tellers who have made their fortune, who have grown rich.'

I gave up on the Indian and went instead to find Mr Lee. Here was someone to be reckoned with! Three years ago he had predicted to Ali that one day he would stop driving other people's taxis and would have one of his own. And just look! He now had a cream-coloured Mercedes with red upholstery!

Mr Lee, very Chinese, had been conceived on the island of Hainan, born in Malacca, and orphaned at the age of three. As a child he had worked in a city restaurant, and had soon become a salesman for alcoholic drinks. Wanting to learn how to tell if people were trustworthy, if he should grant them credit or if they would run off without paying, he had bought for fifty cents a little book on how to deduce people's personalities from their physical traits. He had struck it rich and made his name as a magician.

'It's become a habit by now,' said Mr Lee. 'Every time I meet a person I look at their hands without them realizing it. Sometimes a sign is all you need to understand them and have power over them.' He explained that while the hand and the face are giveaways, the real signs of destiny lie in the soles of the feet. There, he said, are to be found the permanent signs of destiny. The lines in the hand change with time.

As soon as I had taken off my shoes, Mr Lee said that my father was dead and my mother was still alive.

'That's true. But how can you tell?'

'*Easy. From the shape of your big toe.*'

'But it was the same shape when my father was alive.'

'*Yes, but the shape tells me that your mother has a very strong life line and will outlive your father by many years, and that has been true from the moment when you were born.*'

Then, in great detail and with the aid of a magnifying glass, he examined the soles of both my feet. He told me I was a simple, straightforward character, that I did not provoke people's aggression, that I refused to listen to other people's opinions, but trusted only my own. He said that I had married at twenty-four and that this had been my great good fortune.

All this was quite true, and the likeable thing was that Mr Lee did not make it sound like some giant discovery. According to him, it was all perfectly written in the soles of my feet. There he read – like all the others – that I would never get rich. What he could not say was how many children I had. Birth control, he said, had introduced an element that upset every prophecy.

I told him what the old Chinese fortune-teller in Hong Kong had said, and asked what he thought. He studied my feet carefully.

'*Yes,*' he said, '*there's danger in your life. At times it's great, especially this year. But you needn't worry, because you have haemorrhoids, and the blood you lose will save you.*'

The facts were undeniable. But the interpretation? If nothing else, it was consoling.

Malacca also had a living ghost: Father Manuel Joaquim Pintado, a Portuguese, formerly a parish priest in the city. An amateur historian, he had spent all his life in Malacca, collecting documents on his fellow-countrymen there. A few years ago, when for reasons of its own Rome decided to take Malacca away from the Portuguese missionaries and give it to the French, Pintado refused to leave. He was living in a cottage on the outskirts. In the sitting-room, with a statue of the Virgin which he had brought from his church, he had made an altar where he said mass. The rest of the house was full of old newspapers, books and maps.

When he heard that I was from Florence, Father Pintado searched among his papers and pulled out a photocopy of a letter. Dated 20 December 1510, it was written on the eve of Albuquerque's expedition against Malacca by a young Florentine, Piero Strozzi. The young man describes the dangers of the undertaking, the enemy's poisoned arrows, the way he lived 'with death constantly at his elbow', and asks his family to pray for him. He concludes: 'If I return safely I hope to get two thousand ducats from this voyage.' Money, always money, even then!

I asked Father Pintado if he could introduce me to someone who would show me around the city. He gave me the telephone number of a lady, a member of an old Malaccan family, who had assisted him in his historical research.

We met by appointment in front of the church of St Peter, and spent a whole day together. She was descended from poor Portuguese settlers who, after the Dutch conquest, were unable to go elsewhere or to return to Portugal. For centuries they remained a race unto themselves, with their own language – a mixture of Portuguese, Malay and Dutch – and their own traditions. They were called 'the Christaon people'. In Malacca there are about two thousand of them.

With her, too, every step taken in Malacca was a story of death and ghosts. The houses and monuments in the centre of the city are all painted red. When the British captured Malacca they destroyed the fort and other large Portuguese monuments, but spared the Dutch buildings on condition that they be painted red, to distinguish them from those that they themselves intended to construct. This tradition has survived, and the centre of Malacca is called the Red Square.

'Yes, blood red,' said the Christaon lady. During the Japanese occupation between 1942 and 1945, a thousand Malaccan citizens were decapitated, bayoneted or burned alive to terrorize the rest of the population. My guide pointed out that in the old clocktower there was now a new Seiko, a gift from Tokyo. But the dead, she said, were far from happy about that Japanese presence. At night you could often hear their moans of protest.

We passed Banda Hill, a tract reclaimed from the sea not far from the fortress. It was occupied by an expanse of wooden shacks, each with a small cage hanging from it. 'Indonesian immigrants,' said my companion. 'They come here to work, but they know there's the evil eye in these parts, so they bring cuckoos to protect themselves.'

While we were eating at the Malacca Club, the woman showed me a ring she was wearing. 'I put it on to meet you,' she said. 'I wear it for protection whenever I go with someone I don't know.' On the ring was a little frog. 'It must be worn with the frog's face looking out, and then at six in the evening you turn it towards the inside,' she explained. 'A frog is ugly and repulsive, but if you care for it, if you are kind to it, it is so grateful that it repays you by protecting you and bringing you money. That is why frogs are a symbol of good luck.'

Clearly this was the moment to ask if she knew a good fortune-teller. Not she, she was a practising Catholic, but her sister, yes: she was a follower of a famous woman magician of Malacca.

The next day I found myself with three women in a small van driving towards the outskirts of the town. The two sisters were accompanied by a Malay friend who was also full of strange tales.

The sorceress lived in a small, single-storeyed house set in an open field without so much as a single tree for shade. It was identical to those that stretched on either side of it. They all had wire netting around their little gardens, blue-tiled roofs and white walls. We entered a sort of waiting room with a grey cement floor, plastic armchairs and plastic flowers. On one wall hung a plush carpet with a view of Mecca. The sorceress was Malay, a devout Muslim. She sat at the head of a table on a slightly raised platform; on her left was an elderly man with a kindly expression. On the table, covered by a floral plastic cloth, was a mobile telephone – a status symbol all over Asia.

She was called Ka (Sister) Non: a very thin woman with sparse, fine hair, deep-set eyes, a drawn face and almost transparent skin. She wore a floor-length green skirt and a green smock down to her knees. She was forty-two years old, had grown up in a *kampong* and had never been to school. When very young she had married a man who hit her constantly. During one of these beatings she struck her head and lost consciousness. When she came to she realized she had powers, that she 'saw'. She had left her husband and married the kindly man, also a magician, who now acted as her assistant.

Other clients, all of them women, sat waiting in the armchairs. Everything was conducted openly, aloud, like a group confession in which everyone took part with questions, comments and exclamations of wonder.

Ka Non looked at me with very intense, ironic eyes. I felt that she was testing me, and I stared her down without batting an eyelash. She was not interested in knowing where or when I was born; only my name, which she went on practising till finally she managed to pronounce 'Ticciano'. She shut her eyes and repeated it about ten times, rapid-fire. Then she looked very intently at the palms of her own hands, as Muslims do when they pray. ('For her it's like watching television,' explained her husband.)

When, finally, words came, she uttered them in a sort of trance: '*Ticciano, this year you have started something special, very special.*' (I marvelled at her seeming accuracy. Then it struck me that if I had come to Malaysia to run one of those new factories, her words would have seemed equally apt.) '*Yours is a very special mission. When it's over you'll be riding high.*'

My three companions laughed, and the friend of the two sisters could not restrain herself: 'Are you a spy? Who are you?'

Ka Non continued: '*For years you had been seeking something. Now you have found it. You know what I am talking about. You know your mission, you understand me.*' She told me that soon I would meet someone who would show me the way, who would enlighten me, and that I would then have a great success and become famous.

I asked her if she saw any dangers in my 'mission'.

Still in a trance, she looked amused and then tense. She took my hands and examined them (my television, I thought). Then she flew into a passion and began screaming something I could not understand. Eventually the translation followed: '*1993 is the year in which you began to believe in God.*' (One might explain my presence there in front of her in such terms.) '*Since you set foot in my house you have been safe; that step was the first of a new life, a step that will bring you luck.*'

Ka Non gesticulated wildly, one hand shot up towards the sky like a sword, and the other moved crosswise as if cutting someone's throat: '*From now on everything you desire will be yours, because you are protected, because you have found what you were looking for.*' Of course, I thought, I had found a pleasing rhythm of life, more time to look around me. It seemed to me that the woman had hit the mark. I thought of Anatole France's observation that 'all translations make sense for those who have made them.' It was the same with the vague pronouncements of these magicians: they made sense to those who wanted to believe them.

She told me it was all right to fly, but that my life had been in great danger once in the past. (Well, everyone of my age has at some time experienced danger.) She said I would live to be more than eighty years old. Then she asked the names of my two children.

'The boy is called Folco,' I said. The procedure was the same: Ka Non repeated the name a dozen times, looked into her hands, and said that Folco was very intelligent, he was a *pintar*. (My companions were surprised at that word, but could not think of the translation.) '*Pintar, pintar . . .*' repeated Ka Non, and added that Folco would be successful in the arts, but that he must be careful about some friends who were not morally sound. As for Saskia, Ka Non said that she was extremely determined, and would marry a rich man whom I also liked. (What filial love!) She would have an easy life and one child.

Hearing the woman pronounce my children's names, I felt as if I had done something wrong in revealing them to her. I told myself that this was an absurd taboo, and asked what she saw in the life of Angela (who hates fortune-tellers, and never wants to hear of them). I was lucky. Ka Non said that Angela was extremely sensitive, that one had to take care not to hurt her, and that she might explode if she were not respected. '*Treat her as if she were gold,*' she said. '*Handle her with caution, like a bowl of boiling oil, and take care not to splash it on your hands.*' Good advice for anyone.

At this point my companions wanted to satisfy their own curiosity. 'Does Ticciano have another life? Does he have lovers?' one of them asked.

Ka Non looked at her hands and pronounced: '*Ticciano is an extrovert, he likes to mix with people, especially women, and women admire him. Some even fall in love with him. But he doesn't take advantage of this. He finds it difficult to be unfaithful.*'

They all laughed, and I laughed too, stripped bare as I was.

My session had put everyone in a good mood, and the woman who had recommended Ka Non insisted that her sister, my Christaon lady, must now consult her. She was a Catholic, a believer, and she considered that she was committing a sin, but she yielded nonetheless. The procedure remained the same: name, television in the hands, trance; but the answers were quite different from mine.

'You have great problems,' said Ka Non without hesitation. 'Your husband is continually unfaithful, and now he has a lover he is especially fond of. A friend has robbed you of a large sum of money. A while ago someone put the evil eye on you. Much of it you have overcome, but a few traces remain. I feel it. That is the cause of your problems.'

The woman was aghast, and began to weep. It was all true. Her husband had always had other women, and two million Malay dollars had disappeared with a friend to whom she had entrusted them for a joint investment. The cure? A mixture of flowers and perfumes in her bath every day. Ka Non's husband wrote out the recipe.

Ka Non accompanied us to the door. As we took our leave she said to me: '*Soon you will fulfil your mission. Now that you have seen once, you will see again.*' And with that sibylline pronouncement she let us go.

One of the sisters drove the van. The other was in shock. She said that for some time she had known she must do something, but she was afraid. She even feared her own powers. Once, for example, walking past a bar where she knew her husband spent many of his evenings, she had said, 'I hope that place burns down.' The next day she heard it had been destroyed in a fire.

One of the women remembered the translation of *pintar*. It means 'genius'.

The hotel I was staying in was dusty and grimy, but the sort I like, with large rooms, high ceilings and wooden stairs: everything rather threadbare, but with a past. For two nights I had slept very well in the big bed with its kapok mattress and hard pillows stuffed with tea leaves. But the third night I had a terrible nightmare. I dreamt I was in a place full of stairs with people of different colours climbing up and falling down. I tried to catch them all, but didn't have enough arms. At one point all the stairs shuddered as if in an earthquake, then tumbled down on top of each other and on top of me, too. I woke with a start and realized that the bed really was shaking. Day was dawning, and building work had begun next door to the hotel. Workers in yellow helmets swarmed around bulldozers that were digging their rapacious steel teeth into the ground. A giant crane was driving iron piles for a new building in the heart of old Malacca.

CHAPTER TWELVE

An Air-Conditioned Island

Every city has its own way of presenting itself, of putting its best foot forward. Singapore's is the airport. The airport is its made-up face, its shop window, its visiting card. People arrive and depart there, and they really need see nothing else, the airport being the essence of all that Singapore has to show: its efficiency, its cleanliness, its order, its status as Asia's biggest supermarket of consumer goods, futility and respectability.

The charms of the airport were lost on me, earthbound as I was. Like all the other undesirables, penniless backpackers, immigrant Malay day-labourers and poor Russian traders, I arrived in Singapore by the back door: overland from Malaysia. That was how the Japanese arrived in December 1941. In those days Singapore expected everyone, even possible invaders, to come by sea; the sea was its link with the world, the sea was its wealth, and towards the sea pointed all the artillery of its formidable defences. They were utterly useless. The Japanese avoided the big guns by simply taking them from the rear. In the same way I avoided being seduced by Singapore: I saw its rumpled early-morning face, without make-up, unprepared and from an unintended angle.

The Causeway, an artificial umbilical cord linking Singapore with Malaysia, underlines the fact that this vainglorious island city-state is, physically at least, a mere minuscule appendix of the great Malay peninsula. There is nothing special about it, nothing spectacular. I approached it at dawn. Through the train window I saw, against the background of a blood-red sun, four tall chimneys pouring black smoke into the air. Alongside the railway ran three huge iron pipes for the imported water that keeps the city alive, and a superhighway jammed with the cars and motorcycles of commuters who live in Johore Barhu, where the cost of living is lower, and work on the island, where wages are higher. Singapore looked like any other place in Asia, with the shacks, the rubbish heaps, the rusty corrugated iron, the patches of vegetation and weeds – remnants of nature waiting to reclaim any land left to itself.

The first Singaporeans I saw from the train were like those I had known years ago: plastic sandals, black shorts and white T-shirts, exactly like the protagonist of one of the first stories I heard when I came there to live in 1971. A doctor had among his patients an old man in black shorts and singlet, so simple and humble that he squatted in the waiting-room armchair with his shirt rolled up over his stomach. The doctor took him for a pauper and charged him less than the others, sometimes not at all, until one day he looked out of the window and saw him climb into a chauffeur-driven Mercedes. He controlled the city's entire rice trade.

For me that old man has always been the epitome of the Chinese of the diaspora: self-assured but inconspicuous, powerful but reserved and modest for fear of arousing the jealousy of the gods or the rulers. There are very few left like that. The new generations of Chinese are afraid only of not being seen to be rich. They wear all those things that give them security and – they think – respectability. Singapore is like that, too; hence its eagerness to be on display, all shiny and modern, starting at the airport.

The railway station, on the other hand, had a dilapidated air which I liked. When it was built, in the 1920s, it was completely paved and tiled with coloured rubber that muffled the noise. The silent elegance of those days was enhanced by the shabby calm of a place that is no longer fashionable. Few Singaporeans use it; many do not even know it exists. The old station has no part to play in the Singapore of our times: it is an embarrassment, like a poor relation.

We got off the train and had to queue for an hour for passport control. The policemen sat in smelly cubicles, surrounded by huge books, some nearly a foot thick, containing the list of all Singapore's 'enemies'. There were no computers and every passenger was checked, minutely, by hand. The most assiduous in filling out the forms and answering the usual questions were a group of Russians, who tried their best to ingratiate themselves with the impassive customs officials.

In my mind echoed the opening line of the *Romance of the Three*

Kingdoms, the great Chinese classic: 'Empires wax and wane.' How quickly the Soviet Empire had waxed and waned! Only a few years ago the Russians were the proud citizens of a great power, and as such they were feared and respected. Now, poor devils, half ridiculous and half pathetic in blue jeans and trainers, they travel for days and days by train towards the Mecca of consumer goods, hoping to fill their bags with something they can sell back home for a rouble or two: calculators and silk panties, cigarette lighters, video recorders, electronic gadgets and brassières.

It really is a strange animal, the economic system which nowadays is expected to save the world! No one makes anything with their own hands any more, no one works out how to make a cooking pot or a flute or a cart; the best thing they can think of is to go to another part of the world and buy something to resell elsewhere, at a profit.

Shopping, shopping, shopping. In rich countries it has become a way of life, in poor ones a way of surviving. Is there not perhaps something profoundly wrong in all this? And is it not understandable that some of the young, like the 'madmen' of Al Arqam, are trying, with their autarchy, their turbans and their women in black, to have nothing to do with it?

For some people, the sight of the world rushing ever more blindly towards materialism reinforces the belief that only some dreadful event, like a plague or a great famine, can restore order and give men back a sense of life. With the end of the millennium so near, such ideas readily find followers, especially among idealists looking for a cause. The current resurgence of religious fundamentalism, in its different versions, can also be seen in this light.

For me, returning to Singapore was like going to find one's first love again. It was there, in 1965, that I first smelled the tropics, first enjoyed the heat and the colours; it was there that I realized how being far away made me feel at home. I was only there for a few days, but the impression ran deep. In 1971 I came here to live. I had left Olivetti, had studied China and the Chinese language in New York, and as I could not find a way of getting to Peking and did not want to go to Taiwan, I had decided to go and live among the Chinese of 'the third China', the China of the diaspora. We stayed in Singapore four years. There Saskia took her first steps, Folco went to his first school, and I wrote my first book.

I had friends and acquaintances in Singapore, but I had not told anyone I was coming. I wanted to revisit the city alone, to form my own impressions, and above all to be free to write what I wanted without fear of getting my friends into trouble. Because Singapore is like that: behind all its alluring and welcoming shopping malls, shopping arcades and shopping centres, it remains a police state, a society shot through with a subtle fear. Also, I wanted to be like a newcomer, to give myself to what Singapore had now become, and what so many foreigners found extraordinary.

It did not take me long to realize that in the fifteen years I had been away from Singapore, the city had changed beyond recognition. There were new streets, new flyovers, new gardens and squares. Even the people were no longer the same. I saw them at the bus stops, all elegant and well dressed; but nobody spoke. I noticed more and more people with nervous tics, as in Japan. The warmth and kindness of the Indians, the voluptuous naturalness of the Malays, the sarcasm of the Chinese, the leisurely pace, due perhaps to the sluggish heat of the tropics, had disappeared.

The heat itself had disappeared. I remembered Singapore as being torrid, at times scorching. There was an hour after lunch when even in our house among the trees the air was so steamy and immobile, the chirping of the cicadas so deafening, that we used to lie under the fan and wait for the liberating crash of a rainstorm or a breeze from the sea. In the new Singapore, however, it was literally cold. Cold in the hotels, in the shops, in the public buildings, in the offices, icy in the restaurants, in the underground, in the taxis, in the hospitals, houses, cars. Apparently the conditioned type was by now the only air Singapore could breathe. The whole island seemed to be under a huge bell jar, living an artificial, efficient life that had lost contact with the surrounding nature, with the heat of the Equator. Women no longer wore light blouses, floral sarongs or silk trousers; the new national costume had become the jacket and skirt with stockings or tights, just like London or New York.

Once upon a time Singapore was a city full of smells – smells of mould, damp earth, fresh fruits, decaying vegetables, fried garlic, rotting wood. These too had disappeared.

For a visitor like me, the new *homo singaporianus* inevitably first presented himself as a taxi driver, and the initial impression was horrible.

'Take me to Alexandra Park.'

'Are you going to see friends?'

'No.'

'Do you live there?'

'No.'

'Where do you live, then?'

'Far away.'

'Are you in Singapore to do some shopping?'

'No.'

'Business? How many days are you here for?' And on and on until we reached my destination.

Nosy and intrusive as policemen, the taxi drivers struck me as reflecting all the banality of the new Singapore, where seemingly nothing was left to chance or to free individual choice. Just looking at the dashboard of a taxi, with the box of tissues, the bottle of rose-scented deodorizer, the form on which every ride had to be recorded, and a series of notices which the law required to be plainly posted, gave me the creeps. One card, with the driver's photo, gave his name, license number and a telephone number to call if you wanted to report him for some misdemeanour. Another gave the weight of the wheels, the maximum number of passengers, and the speed he could go at. Another said 'Be loyal to Singapore.'

My main worry was how to proceed with my journey. I wanted to go to Jakarta by ship, but once again this proved highly difficult, for the reason I knew all too well by now: the ships carried only cargo. It was incredible. The roadstead of Singapore, the second largest port in the world, was full of ships – ships of all flags, all tonnages, all types – ships waiting to load and unload and then sail off, some undoubtedly for an Indonesian port where I would be glad to go. But none of those ships wanted me as a passenger. Finally I managed to speak with an official of the Singapore Port Authority who promised to help me; and then – this is typically Singaporean – he asked what my real reasons were for wanting to travel by ship.

Singapore is a paradise for tourists, but they must be the kind of tourists that Singapore wants. As long as you're not looking for a ship, you can find everything here, and find it cheaper than anywhere else, because Singapore is a free port and there are no taxes: a suit in twenty-four hours, a precious jade, a fashionable pair of glasses, a swimming costume, the latest record, the smallest camera, the most powerful stereo, the lightest personal computer. There are whole stores stuffed with them. Singapore is the Bethlehem of the great new religion: the religion of consumerism, of material comforts and mass tourism. There is no need for cathedrals or mosques. The new temples are the hotels. By now it is the same almost everywhere in Asia. There are no more beautiful palaces or pagodas to grace the urban panorama: only hotels. Hotels are the centres of life, the places where you meet, reflect, have fun, unwind, enjoy yourself. Hotels are what cafés, churches, squares and theatres once were – all rolled into one. In Kuala Lumpur as in Hong Kong, in Seoul as in Bangkok. In Singapore everything better than anywhere else.

I spent the first eighteen years of my life in Florence, and I do not think I once set foot in a hotel. In Asia you are always in one. You make appointments to meet in them, you eat, you celebrate holidays and birthdays, you get married. In hotels you go swimming, shopping, dancing. The new Asia's affluent youth scarcely know anything else. Taking a walk, for many of them, means going from one hotel to another, often by way of huge shopping malls with their marble pavements and plastic trees. Yes, Singapore is on the Equator and on the verge of the jungle, but the best trees, which by now you see everywhere, are artificial ones. They need no rain, only a little dusting now and then.

I soon realized that I did not know the rules, the etiquette and the taboos of this new society. I had invited to tea the secretary of an important official at the Foreign Ministry – its office is on the thirty-ninth floor of a hotel – to enlist her help in finding a ship, and to discover which in her opinion were the best fortune-tellers in town. We met in the lobby of a big hotel, and I asked for some hot water to add to the pot. 'Sorry, sir, but our tea is un-refillable,' replied one of the very young waitresses, dressed in 'Chinese style' with the skirt slit up to her bottom to appeal to the tourists. What an extraordinary expression! Only the Singaporeans could invent it: un-refillable tea.

One day, in the very centre of town, I passed the office of a firm which, according to the large sign in the window, was a shipping line that ran a service exclusively between Singapore and Indonesia. When I entered and made my usual request for a passage to Jakarta, a vacuum formed around me: the director was at a meeting, the sales manager was out to lunch, and all the other employees, blind and deaf, had their heads buried behind their computers. My friend M.G.G. Pillai had warned me: 'In Singapore you'll be suspect. Nobody trusts anyone who doesn't travel by air, and in business class, who doesn't stay in a first-class hotel and who doesn't pay by credit card.' He was right. The question in the minds of all those clerks who tried not to see or hear me was obvious: a terrorist?

In a society where countless things are forbidden, from long hair on men to the chewing of gum, where there is one correct form of behaviour, a reaction prescribed for any situation, the most unacceptable thing is to deviate from the norm. The social duty of all is to help their neighbour behave properly, not to help him be different. I was only passing through, but even I had the sensation of being constantly guided, either by people ('Take my advice: go by plane!') or by some invisible presence. Everywhere in the new Singapore you hear metallic voices issuing announcements or advice from hidden loudspeakers in hotels, lifts, escalators, in the underground, on lamp posts. Everywhere you see notices remonstrating ('Don't bring AIDS home') or imposing prohibitions ('No fishing from the bridge', 'No spitting'). Others offer fatuous warnings: 'Watch your head! Low branches ahead', you read if you are about to walk under the few old trees remaining along the river. For those who fail to get the message there are little pictures showing how a branch can strike your head.

To mould the citizens into what the system wants, there is a succession of 'campaigns' – to keep gutters clean, to plant trees, to water flowers. When I arrived there was a campaign for 'wellness', and the 1800 employees of a local firm had pledged to keep fit by not using the lift for a month. As I left they were initiating a campaign to starve the city's last free creatures to death: 'Let's not feed the pigeons. They bring diseases and nuisance', said the street signs.

Even so, it was splendid! Seen from the height of Fort Canning, where I went running every morning, Singapore was a dream city, with its transparent skyscrapers like geometric clouds against the sky, its immaculate gardens, and no traffic jams. The university was a delight: perfect avenues, ultra-modern libraries flooded with sunlight, lawns in various shades of green interspersed with playing fields and thick shady trees – a splendid creation. Nothing was left to chance, from the combination of different-coloured grasses on the slopes to the curve of a branch bent back to avoid obstructing cars. But I only had to talk to someone and I was again in despair.

'Our students are of tip-top quality. They're trained up to an international level, and they're politically trustworthy. They know when to speak, and above all when to keep quiet,' the director of a university research institute told me. He saw this as a sign of maturity. All of a sudden I hated the flowerbeds, the trees, the beautiful lawns and the sunshine in the libraries.

I spent my days in a continual seesaw between admiration and disgust, between wonder and horror. 'This is the future, and it works,' I said to myself in moments of depression.

The future is the invention of one individual: Lee Kuan Yew, a man of great intelligence, great arrogance, great ambition and no scruples. Lee assumed the reins of government in 1959, and was holding them when the republic left the Malay Federation in 1965. In 1990 he retired as prime minister, but he remains an 'emeritus member' of the government, and is still the ultimate tribunal for all decisions.

It is he who has transformed this Equatorial port into a centre of modernity. He has remodelled the city, manipulated its climate, remade its inhabitants; he has created the most efficient and least corrupt administration of all the Asian states, paying its officials like captains of industry. It is he who has established one of the most advanced educational systems in Asia, whose teachers receive some of the highest salaries in the world. There is no question that his experiment has been highly successful.

The price? A city without life, a humdrum people, and dictatorship. Despite the appearance of a democratic political system, with parties, a parliament and elections, Lee Kuan Yew has never left anyone in the slightest doubt that the power was his and would remain so. He has used all possible allies, and destroyed them one by one as soon as they threatened to become rivals. As for opposition, no one has had the ghost of a chance to challenge his power. Like every dictator he has throttled at birth every voice of dissent, taken control of all organs of information, tried to rewrite history and blot out the memory of the past.

Archives of Singapore newspapers are extremely hard to find; even Lee Kuan Yew's speeches are a state secret. They would reveal too many contradictions, too many changes of line, too many truths that became heresies and vice versa. For dictators memory is always a terribly dangerous thing. Even mine!

I remembered a multiracial Singapore that tried to persuade Chinese, Indians and Malays to forget their origins and become 'Singaporeans'. Now I saw a city that was almost exclusively Chinese, in which the most widespread language was Mandarin. An exhibition being held in the city celebrated the cultural greatness of China. By now all non-Chinese, still 25 per cent of the population, feel excluded.

One evening I was dining in an open-air restaurant with an Indian who was born and had lived all his life in Singapore. The Chinese customers at the nearby tables treated him as a foreigner and me as a 'fellow-citizen', just because I spoke Chinese and he did not. In spite of his assertion 'I am Singaporean,' in English and Malay – theoretically still official languages on the island – the others jeered. One answered him in Chinese: 'Singaporean? The Singaporeans are all dead. Here there're only Chinese.' The rest of the group laughed and applauded.

Even a few years ago such a display of chauvinism would have been unthinkable. But times have changed. China is Communist only in name; the Chinese of the diaspora are no longer suspected of Maoism, and can reaffirm their identity without restraint. China is a great power, hence they too feel powerful. The step to racial arrogance is a short one.

One need only remember history to understand. The vast majority of the Chinese in today's Asia left China during the past century. They left as boat people, in vessels that did not always arrive. They fled from famines, wars and poverty. The country they left was humiliated by colonialism, weakened by opium, and lacerated by conflicts of one kind or another. They were not mandarins, they were not poets. They were a labour force: coolies. *Ku li* in Chinese means 'bitter strength' – a fine expression, written in two simple characters, which sums up the condition of people who are desperate.

Like all emigrants, these Chinese had only one dream: money.

With money they could buy the protection of the rulers of the countries where they found themselves, with money they could save their lives. People without any culture, they came to the *nan yang*, the south seas, and with them they brought the traditions and the gods of the village, all too soon supplanted by the culture of money and material wealth.

The great merit of Lee Kuan Yew was to have understood all this and to have realized, in his little island city-state populated by coolies, the dream of all Chinese emigrants: to have a safe refuge, a place to bring up their children, a bank to put their savings in. That is how Singapore, skilfully remaining equidistant from Communist China and the Nationalist China of Taiwan, has become the capital of the third China, of the Chinese of the diaspora. That is how Lee – intelligent, able and with great aspirations (at one point he hoped to become Secretary General of the United Nations), but condemned by circumstances to be virtually the mayor of a small Chinese city of barely three million inhabitants – imposed himself as the natural head of this tribe without a country, this population of refugees from an Israel to which none of the twenty-five million expatriate Chinese scattered all over Asia wants to return.

From the historical point of view Lee has done even more: in his little island he has demonstrated that the Chinese, like everyone else, can progress and get rich. With this he has fulfilled the dream of every Chinese intellectual since the end of the nineteenth century – modernization. With a Chinese model? No, copying the West – but nobody blames him for that. Indeed today Singapore, where everything is Western – from the architecture to the educational system, from the underground to the cranes, from the computers to the pencil-sharpeners; Singapore, where even the quintessentially Chinese abacus has been replaced by calculators, where the people dream only of wearing a Pierre Cardin belt and a Rolex, writing with a Mont Blanc and driving a Mercedes – is what China itself would like to become. Singapore is China's new model.

Lee Kuan Yew has done all this with firmness, at times with unnecessary cruelty, without respect for anything or anybody, and above all with no qualms of conscience. He has destroyed people and things that stood in his path, sweeping away the old to build the new. In Orchard Road, the central street in the city, was an Indian temple that some said was the oldest on the island. It was demolished because it got in the way of the underground. An ex-president of the republic, Lee's old collaborator, was noticed courting some dissidents. He was ousted on the charge of being an alcoholic. Whole areas of old Singapore have been razed to the ground. Whole generations of Singaporeans have been whipped into line by a sophisticated system of creeping terror.

The ratio of policemen to population in Singapore is among the highest in the world. But the policemen are nowhere to be seen. Traffic control is automatic. A car goes through a red light? A video camera records its numberplate and in a flash its owner receives a fine. To enter the city centre at peak hours a tax is charged: an electronic eye automatically subtracts the amount from a magnetic card each time the car passes the control points.

The overwhelming majority of the police are engaged as internal spies. They are everywhere, incognito: in working-class housing blocks, in offices and factories, and especially in the university. Under a state security law, anyone can be arrested and detained indefinitely. Dissenters, real or merely suspected, used to be kept in prison for years without trial – the record was twenty-three years. Now the system has changed. A person is arrested, 'broken', and returned to circulation with a government job where he can be constantly blackmailed and kept under control. The 'breaking' takes place in an underground bunker beneath an old Chinese cemetery in Oreat Road, off Thompson Road. It was built in the 1960s with the help of experts from the Israeli police. The prisoners are held in special cells which are ice-cold and without daylight, fed on drugged foods and interrogated half-naked. The psychological tortures end when the prisoner decides to 'confess'. Thus he is 'broken'. In the past twenty years no more than a thousand people have passed through that centre, but the terrorizing effect continues.

Those who know him say that Lee has had the upheavals in Eastern Europe very much in mind, and is worried that once he loses power he himself may be tried for the violations of human rights perpetrated under his regime. His appointed heir is his son Lee Hsien Iong, who before entering politics had a dazzling career in the army and became a general. This dynasticism arouses no particular resentment among Singapore's docile citizenry. In Chinese society everything revolves around the family, and if a man can leave his shop to his son, why not a state? That is how dynasties wax . . . and wane!

And the Singapore dynasty does not in fact seem destined to last long. Even in the history of Lee Kuan Yew's great success, there is something mysterious and disturbing in which Asians cannot but see the hand of fate: the first male grandchild, the general's son, was born an albino; his mother, a doctor, committed suicide. And Lee's son and heir was struck by a serious form of cancer, while his other son suffers from recurrent depressions. The man who has foreseen everything has been unable to programme fate.

'Black magic . . . Black magic,' I was told, with great conviction, by one of the few Malay taxi drivers in the city. 'The hatred of him is so great that someone has managed to focus it.'

The more I looked into Singapore's history, the more I realized that behind the glass and steel façade, behind the screen of super-efficiency and rationality, even in Singapore the world of the occult was still alive and perhaps on the increase. I would return to my hotel and find messages from people to whom I had barely mentioned my new interest, wanting to introduce me to a *bomoh* or to take me to a woman who can diagnose cancer from afar. I had asked a Singapore journalist to collect all the stories of fortune-tellers which had appeared in the press in the past three years. He came up with a list of several hundred.

One or two people told me that Lee Kuan Yew himself had had recourse to fortune-tellers. He had also promulgated a law making the profession of fortune-teller illegal 'if practised with intent to deceive'. Despite this, the yellow pages of the Singapore telephone directory were full of seers, astrologers and magicians of one kind or another.

I had also heard talk of a noted personage in Singapore's high society, a successful businessman, who had the powers and was an excellent palmist.

Finally I received a promising telephone call from a travel agency. There was a passenger ship bound for Jakarta. Was I interested? Most definitely. It was a cruise ship transformed into a great floating casino with roulette and baccarat tables. Splendid! It seemed made for me. The illusion lasted only a couple of days. Another telephone call announced that the cruise had been cancelled.

I felt caged in Singapore, but I wanted to stay. One reason was that on 27 April there would be the first official meeting between the Chinese Communists and Chinese Nationalists since the end of the civil war in 1949. The fact that the meeting was taking place in Singapore, and with the mediation of Lee Kuan Yew, struck me as highly significant in the context of what I saw as the resurgence of Greater China. It was a historic moment that I did not want to miss. Another reason was that I had made contact with Rajamanikam, the fortune-teller mentioned by M.G.G. Pillai. Several people in Singapore had told me he was the best in town. He was heavily booked, but had promised to see me.

Singapore irritated me more and more. I could not bear this society of shopkeepers who had made it, and who could afford everything except to think. I was annoyed by their crassness and arrogance, the way they confused the GNP with the IQ, average income with progress, *kitsch* with beauty, quantity with quality. One university student asked me in a provocative tone how many floors Italy's tallest skyscraper had.

As the days went by I became more and more aggressive.

'Take me to Holland Park,' I said to a taxi driver.

'Are you going to dinner?'

'No.'

'What country are you from?'

'Africa.'

'How? You're white!'

'There are whites in Africa.'

'What do you do for a living?'

'I murder taxi drivers who ask too many questions.'

He looked at me in some surprise. He said he had only been doing his duty: a campaign of courtesy to tourists had just been launched. I noticed that he had two rings: one with a blue stone and one with a brown stone. 'I've been wearing them for twenty years. They protect me from all kinds of evils,' he said. Seeing that I was interested, he showed me a little white ball he had on a chain around his neck. 'A coconut pearl,' he told me. For every ten thousand coconuts, there's one that has a pearl inside. 'It was given me by an *orang asli*, and it's highly potent.' He also had to observe certain taboos if his various protections were to be effective.

Suddenly I felt disgusted with all this talk, these trinkets around the neck and on the hands, and the taboos that went with them. I was disgusted at myself for wasting time on such matters. All that had formerly seemed poetic and interesting struck me as absurd, stupid, humiliating. I felt that I had fallen into a trap, that I was going mad myself. I had a strong impulse to go to the airport, take a plane for Jakarta and make an end of it.

Or did I? Did I really want to get back into line, return to normality? To logic? To the logic that had created Singapore? I held back. Taking a plane would have been like cutting a vacation short.

That evening I was invited to dinner by a famous architect. He had just returned from a trip to Bombay, where he had spent two days at a conference with Indian architects and intellectuals. He was impressed: he had not heard a word about money the whole time, or about contracts assigned or to be assigned. Perhaps I was right to want to move to India.

Over dinner I mentioned my problem with transport, and the fact that at times I had really had enough of following the dictates of a fortune-teller. An elderly lady sitting across the table from me said: 'Tomorrow I'm going to mine. If you would like to come and ask her opinion . . .'

And so the next day I found myself in a car on the way to Rangoon Road, off the great Serangoon Road, the street of the Indians. Beside me was the vivacious, shrewd, elderly Chinese lady. She had just passed her eighty-first birthday, and was born in Shanghai when it was the Asian metropolis. 'Great fortune-tellers were to be found there, oh yes,' she said. When she was still very young one of them had warned her: 'If you stay in Shanghai you won't live beyond the age of twenty-five,' and she had given him heed. She was a stage actress, and when her troupe came to Singapore on tour, she stayed there. She met a well-to-do local youth, married him and had three children. She had never returned to Shanghai.

The problem that was worrying her was her house. She had lived there happily for fifty-five years with her husband, but since becoming a widow she felt that it no longer brought her good fortune. The investments she had made turned out to be mistakes, her business deals were fruitless, and she wanted to move. So it was that we were on our way to a famous card reader, a woman in whom she had great faith. She had advised her not to go back Shanghai even for a short stay: 'If you do, the old prophecy will lose no time in getting its claws back in you.'

We stopped in front of an old Chinese temple dedicated to happiness and longevity. The card reader was in the room next to that of the gods. She was a fat woman with a beautiful serene face, a pleasant smile, and extremely thick hair combed back and cut straight at the neck. She was wearing brown pyjamas with yellow and blue flowers. She must have been about seventy. Sitting at a round table, she had in front of her a well-worn pack of cards in which it was hard to recognize the various figures. My companion wanted me to go first.

The woman told me to choose one card from the pack, and asked me the year and month of my birth.

'*1938. Year of the tiger,*' she said, beginning to lay out the cards on the table. '*Last year was consequently difficult for you. It was the year of the monkey, and the monkey likes to tease the tiger. Last year you were even in danger of your life. Did you know it? But as from next month the dangers will all pass and you'll begin a second life. The best part of your life. Your life has always been good, but after your fifty-fifth birthday it will be outstanding. Really outstanding. The reason is that you, born a tiger, are only now becoming a real one. Up to now you've been a sort of oversized cat. You did everything for others and little for yourself. If there were rats around, people would come to you and you would go and catch them. If there were no rats to catch, nobody called you.*'

The woman spoke beautiful Chinese, and her short, dry phrases were like aphorisms.

'*Everywhere you go you have friends; people take a liking to you, but you're not much interested in people. At most you are interested in your family. You have two children, a boy and a girl.*' (Well done!) '*You're on your first marriage and it'll last all your life. What's your wife's sign?*'

'Rabbit.'

'*Good. The older the rabbit gets, the more beautiful it becomes. Your wife is like that: ye lao ye piaolian, the older the prettier,*' she said, chuckling. '*The marriage will last because the tiger is very accommodating with the rabbit. You're a tiger born of darkness. You, therefore, take great care of your children and go hunting for food for them. You are more of a mother than the rabbit.*' I was amused at how the animals of the zodiac were used to describe a person, to reconstruct character.

The woman kept looking at me and at the cards in front of her. '*Soon you will go to live in a new country, and the people there will help you greatly.'* (Did she mean India?) *'You are alert and intelligent. You have your own opinion on everything and you don't need to wait for the opinions of others to have your own. Your paternal grandfather was a good man and a great help to you as a child.'* (Well . . . he was the only grandfather I really knew, and the memories of particular walks with him are precious to me. Helped? Only in that sense.)

'Have you any questions?'

'I'd like to change my job. To do something completely different from what I'm doing now,' I said.

'If you really want to change, go ahead, but only after the Rice Festival in August. It's not wise to change, however. You know the work you do now. It gives you a salary. You will lose that if you change. Better not to change. Take my advice.' It struck me that, more than the cards, this was her Chinese practicality talking.

She shuffled the deck and arranged the cards in rows of eight. *'This month you must be careful. Try not to swim in the sea, because the dragon will not protect you. You can swim in a pool, but not in the sea. After the end of May, swim where you like. Also, don't go into the mountains. Avoid mountains for the next two months. And mark my words! Last month a Japanese came to see me. I advised him not to swim in the sea, but he said he had to because he was a pearl fisher. I've just learned that he has drowned!'* (Who knows if it is true, but these stories always have a persuasive effect.) *'Take care. April is still a month of dangers for you.'*

'Can I be a politician?' I asked her.

'No. Governments are not made for you. You are against governments by inclination.' (There she hit the mark!) *'And then, with the work you do, you're already half a politician.'* (My job as a journalist had never been mentioned.)

She shuffled the cards again, and laid them out in the form of a cross, then a circle. *'Now listen carefully: never eat turtle meat or snake meat, and you will have a long life. When you are sixty, throw a big party and invite all your friends, and you'll live to the age of eighty-three. If you take a bit of care, you may even reach eighty-eight.'*

All the other customers, who had been listening with great curiosity to my destiny while waiting their own turn, broke into laughter as I gave up my place to my Chinese companion.

The card reader told her to move from her present house as soon as possible: her husband's death had deprived it of a stabilizing element. If she remained there everything would go badly for her, and she would very soon fall gravely ill. My companion was convinced.

It was only as she was accompanying me back to the hotel that it occurred to me that she had the same surname as one of the men closest to Lee Kuan Yew, a pillar of the regime. 'A relative?' I asked, expecting a 'no' and ready to change the subject. Instead: 'Of course, he's my son,' she said. I felt secretly pleased. Lee Kuan Yew and his acolytes had even changed Singapore's climate, but here was something ancient and irrational which they had not managed to uproot, not even in their own families.

CHAPTER THIRTEEN

A Voice from Two Thousand Years Ago

Sir Stamford Raffles was absolutely right to choose Singapore as a base for the East India Company in 1819. Every ship that sailed in the region had to pass through there to avoid the monsoons. Singapore's geographical position was its wealth. It is still so today, and Singapore is one of the great maritime centres of the world. But a very vulnerable one.

All it would take would be a canal across the narrowest part of the Malay peninsula, the isthmus of Kra, and all ships travelling between Europe and Thailand, Indochina, the Philippines, China and Japan would be spared hundreds of nautical miles. Singapore, cut off, would soon become a dead city, like those that sprang up and died in the American goldrush. Lee Kuan Yew and those around him are aware of this, and are already recycling Singapore to prepare it for another role: that of Asia's information-technology capital, the first truly all-in 'intelligent city' on earth.

Singapore has more robots per capita than anywhere else in the world, and the most computer-literate population. Computers, and courses on their use, are everywhere. Thus on this island, where already materialism is rampant and money the sole criterion of success and morality, another element of narrowness is added: the binary logic of machines that are changing not only the way people work, but the way they think.

'This is the future,' I heard again and again in Singapore, and I was terribly depressed to think it might not only be Singapore's future, but also that of millions of other Asians. And perhaps ours as well.

Once upon a time, even in Singapore, schools taught children how to think. Now they mainly teach them how to programme. But what happens to a society that grows up like this, without learning to make distinctions, with only the computer's logic of 'yes' and 'no'? What happens in the heads of children who grow up with the impression that every problem has a solution, and that everything is at most a question of software?

Singapore scared me because to a great extent it already works that way. The state is the computer and society is regulated, like the temperature, by a sort of electronic thermostat. Does the evidence show that the children of intellectuals have a higher IQ than others? University teachers are encouraged to procreate. Does the evidence show that the young are not marrying in sufficient numbers? The state creates a special Social Development Unit to organize cruises and dances to help bring them together. Is this rich, modern city discovered one day to be boring and cultureless? Take an army general and make him a minister: his job will be to give orders so that the arts may flourish.

I was curious to meet this character, and asked for an appointment with him, but I was only permitted to invite one of his secret service agents and a secretary to lunch. I asked them which artists I could meet, but there was not one they could name. Instead they wanted to know what I was doing in Singapore, and reminded me that with my tourist visa I was not entitled to interview anyone.

Did they know that I had met – with all due precautions, including the tricks of taking two taxis and walking the last stretch – a recent victim of their totalitarian state? This was a young university teacher who had believed in the rhetoric of democracy and had laboured under the illusion that he could offer himself as an opposition candidate in the next elections. The regime began digging into his past, and exposed his crime: he had posted a personal letter with university stamps. He was accused of theft, sacked and subjected to a severe campaign of denigration. In protest the poor wretch had gone on a hunger strike, but he got no sympathy. Everyone was against him: the university chancellor, his colleagues, the press and public opinion of this island with no feelings and no soul. He was a fine character, an idealist, and was still determined to make his dissenting voice heard. 'If I don't do it, who will?' he told me. It was precisely this that the computers found unacceptable.

'Ah, you're interested in strange things? Go to the Chee Tong Temple this evening, then, and you'll see some good examples.'

About twenty years previously I had known an architect called
T.K. Soon. I met him again by chance, and we began talking about
what we had done in the meantime. He had been teaching and
building. The Chee Tong Temple was his design. 'A unique experience!' he said.

Originally the temple, an old Taoist sanctuary, was in the northern
part of Singapore. As it was in the way of a modernization scheme,
it had been demolished. In compensation the government gave the
Taoists another piece of land on which to build a new temple. There
was a competition, T.K. Soon's plan was successful, and he was
invited to discuss it with the Master. The Master imposed certain
changes: the roof had to be designed so as not to point at people or
at any other building, and there must be no right angles in the entire
temple. T.K. Soon obeyed: after all, the Master was a Taoist sage
who had died more than two thousand years ago.

The taxi driver who took me there said that by now everyone
called it 'the temple of the Glass Lotus', and when I saw it I realized
why. It stood in the middle of a working-class housing estate – row
on row of houses differing only in the numbers painted on the
front. Wrapped in a bluish light, this unconventional, ultra-modern
structure really did look like a flower miraculously blooming from
the asphalt. The petals were the overlapping roofs curled upwards
to the sky, and the columns on which they rested formed the stem.
The roofs were all of glass. Between the columns there was not a
single wall, and the whole building, standing on an octagonal white
marble platform, appeared transparent. Thus the temple looked like
a vast empty space, open to the breeze. Beautiful! In the centre
was an altar with many oil lamps, whose flames were reflected and
multiplied in the panes of the ceilings. On the altar were statues
of the Monkey God and two Taoist saints. The right-hand saint,
a smiling old man with a very long white beard, was the Master,
Kuan Lao Xiang Xian, who had lived a hundred years before
Christ in China, near Chengdu. It was his spirit which every
Thursday evening, without fail, visited the temple in this anonymous
suburb.

A couple of dozen people were waiting. In front of the altar,
ensconced in a big red chair with arms in the form of dragons, was
a corpulent woman of about fifty dressed in flame-coloured silk
pyjamas. Her eyes were closed, and she sat straight-backed and

motionless. She was the medium. Two other women also dressed in red, her assistants, hovered around her with bowls of tea, sheets of green paper and a calligraphy brush. In the background people carried on with the irreverent to-ing and fro-ing and casual chatter which one finds everywhere in Chinese temples.

The secretary of the Temple Association came up to ask me who I was and what I wanted. From his visiting card it turned out that, among his various functions, he was president of the Singapore Restaurant Association and chairman of the Rotary Club. I told him I had come, like all the others, to speak with the Master. He had no objections, but he warned me not to go too close to the medium – the slightest touch might shake her out of her trance. The two assistants were the only ones who could touch her.

I sat down on one of the marble benches. Time passed. The secretary told me that the temple itself was the fruit of a miracle performed by Kuan Lao Xiang Xian. It was he, the Master, who had designed it, who had decided every detail and done all the engineering calculations. 'Incredible, isn't it? A man who lived two thousand years ago, and so modern!' he exclaimed. I did not tell him that T.K. Soon was an old acquaintance of mine. After all, I thought, the miracle makes a better story, and as the years pass it will be told and retold and will gradually become the only true version.

Suddenly the woman in the chair began to shake, rocking her body backwards and forwards. 'He's come!' cried the secretary, and the temple fell silent. A very strange, shrill old man's voice seemed to come from the bowels of the woman. The secretary said that as I was a guest from far away I had precedence over the others who were waiting, so I found myself kneeling on the right of the chair with my hands joined over my chest, facing the woman. Her agitation subsided, and only her head continued to move convulsively. Her half-closed eyes were fixed on the statue of the Master. One of the assistants put a pipe in her mouth and lit it. She inhaled a great lungful of smoke, and then, as if she really were the old man of the statue, slowly began to caress, from lip to tip, the long white beard which she did not have.

She asked me my name and where I came from. I re-exhumed my old Chinese name, Deng Tiannuo, and introduced myself. I saw her shake herself, nodding her head violently, and then I heard a brief, almost sardonic, laugh. I looked around, because I could not make out where it came from. Then it was heard again. It came from the woman's stomach: she was a ventriloquist. From her half-closed lips issued a beautiful ancient voice, speaking in fine classical Chinese, rhythmical as the language of the Peking Opera:

> '*Kuan Lao Xiang Xian is glad*
> *that you speak Chinese.*
> *China is a great country,*
> *a country of great culture,*
> *an ancient country.*'

I had to smile: even a shaman, if Chinese, could not escape the racial arrogance of all the children of the Yellow Emperor. '*What do you have to ask of Kuan Lao Xiang Xian?*' she enquired.

I would really have liked to ask her what a Taoist sage thought of modern Singapore; what a man who had spent years as a hermit felt on seeing his followers all obsessed with making money. But a little crowd of the Master's faithful had gathered around me, and I thought they might be offended. In the end I settled for: 'A fortune-teller told me . . .'

The woman wanted to know who the fortune-teller was and when he had made that prediction. Then she did some calculations in the Chinese manner, starting with her hand open, bending the fingers in turn, beginning with the thumb, to count to five and then extending them again, beginning with the little finger, to reach ten. She said:

> '*What you are afraid of*
> *is fear, not planes.*
> *If you want to be unafraid,*
> *you must fly.*
> *Sit in a plane*
> *convinced that nothing will happen,*
> *and nothing will happen.*'

Her manner of speaking was extraordinary. Every sentence was like a verse of a classical poem, four characters recited in the rhythm of alternating rhymes.

'But are there no dangers ahead of me?' I asked.

> *'The danger is in life itself:*
> *even you are born only to die.'*

'When?' I asked, inwardly ashamed at such a banal question. The woman gave one of her nervous laughs, caressed her long, imaginary beard and said:

> *'Everything has its time.*
> *Love has its time,*
> *marriage and children.*
> *And death too.*
> *Yours too will come,*
> *but late in life.'*

She swept her right hand outward as if to suggest a very long road.

> *'Kuan Lao Xiang Xian will give you*
> *something,*
> *a precious paper*
> *that will help you.'*

She was sweating, and one of her assistants constantly wiped her brow. The other put a cup of dark tea to her lips, making her sip it slowly as one does with a sick person. The medium never looked at me. Her eyes were fixed on the statue of the Master, who looked down on all of us from above.

One of the assistants gave her the pipe to smoke again, and the other leaned on the base of the altar to lay three strips of green paper in front of her. The shaman shook herself, made some long hissing sounds, and waved her hands as if to drive something away. Then they put a brush in her right hand, and with firm, precise movements, constantly shaking her head backwards and forwards, she began drawing signs on the paper. They looked like characters, but I could not make out which. The three strips were taken away by the secretary, who set them on one side in front of a small altar. One of them, said the shaman, must be burned on that altar, one I had to swallow, and one I had always to keep with me.

Then came the taboo.

> '*You must take care.*
> *All protection*
> *will depend*
> *on your will,*'

said the woman, continuing to speak in an old man's voice, between a mouthful of smoke and a sip of tea.

> '*You must not taste*
> *dog meat,*
> *you must not eat*
> *cow's meat;*
> *do not drug yourself with heroin.*'

'*Is that all right?*' she asked, as if one could somehow bargain over these prohibitions.

'All right about the dog meat and the heroin, but I would have a problem not eating beef.'

She shook herself violently. Again from deep inside her came that strange, sardonic laugh, and then the ancient voice: '*Think of the ox. A strong, handsome animal. He helps man in the fields and on the road. To eat him you must kill him. That meat enters into you and turns you, too, into a murderer. No. You must never again eat beef. Every time you feel tempted, think how the ox is killed. You will lose the desire. You must respect nature, respect animals. One must live in a natural way. If you eat beef Kuan Lao Xiang Xian will no longer protect you.*'

The secretary signalled to me that my time was up. With my hands still joined I thanked the woman, using the Chinese expression *xie xie ni*, 'thanks to you'. She corrected me: '*Not to me. Thanks to Kuang Lao Xiang Xian.*'

The worst was to come. The secretary made me kneel on the Yin and Yang symbol at the centre of a large Taoist octagon in black and white marble. Before my eyes he burned one of the three paper strips, put the ashes into a glass of water and ordered me to drink it. Thus the protection would enter me. I knew it would be of little use, because I fully intended to eat a steak from time to time, but how could I tell him that? I swallowed it. The second strip, while burning, was passed over my body and head, only an inch or so away from me so that it might create a cloud of protection. He put the third into a little green envelope and handed it to me as if it were extremely precious.

A few days later I called T.K. Soon to tell him how much I liked his temple, and he came up with another story about the shaman. Shortly after the temple was completed and the spirit of Kuan Lao Xiang Xian had got into the habit of coming there on Thursdays, the Taoist Association organized a trip to China, under the guidance of the shaman-woman, to see the places where the Master had lived and to look for the original temple erected in his honour. In Chengdu, nobody could help them. No one had ever heard of a Chee Tong temple. The woman ordered everyone on to their buses and told the drivers to go in a certain direction. They travelled for more than two hours, and found themselves in a peasant village. Nobody knew of the temple there either. In a trance the woman began walking across the fields until she came to a plain. She pointed to the ground, and there lay the remains of some old foundations – the site of the temple. Not far away they found the grotto where the Master used to meditate.

I could not bring myself to ask him what I did not want others to ask me: 'Do you believe it, then?' If he had said yes, I would have taken him for a fool. If he had said no, I would have been sorry, because it is, all said and done, more pleasing to live with the thought that such a story might be true.

The wait had been worthwhile. I would not have wanted to miss seeing the Chinese Communists and Nationalists signing their first agreement and clinking champagne glasses in a Singapore skyscraper. This was the beginning of the process of the reunification of China. For me it was further proof that I was not mistaken in thinking that China had renounced its diversity, had stopped looking for Chinese solutions to its problems and was becoming a country like all the others, dominated by the scramble for Western-style modernization, with no ideology except for money and race.

This was obvious after a glance at the Communist and Nationalist Chinese: there was no difference between them any more. Even a few years ago a Peking official would have spoken, dressed, moved and behaved in a very different way from a Taiwanese. No more. Now they were identical: all dressed like Western businessmen, all ready to talk of common economic interests. One Communist official had gone even further: he actually added that the meeting was important 'to safeguard the interests of the whole Chinese race'.

Thus the Chinese of the diaspora in the various continents of the world were again the children of the Yellow Emperor, reunited under a single roof. The sleeping dragon that had worried Napoleon was perhaps about to awaken.

At last I obtained my appointment with Rajamanikam, too. I would have been sorry to leave Singapore without seeing him. Everyone told me he was a genuine astrologer, serious and reliable. He was related to a leading politician of the regime, and was sometimes consulted by members of the government.

On the telephone Rajamanikam's secretary asked if I knew exactly at what time I was born. 'More or less,' I answered. 'No,' she insisted. 'You must know it exactly, to the minute, otherwise there is no point in coming.' I had to call Angela, who happened to be in Florence. In an office at the Palazzo Vecchio, at the Registry of Births and Deaths, a clerk found the time in the original 1938 register: 7.15 p.m. Incredible: the monk in Bangkok who had arrived at it by quizzing me on my past was right! I was not born at eight o'clock, but exactly three quarters of an hour before: an enormous difference for an astrologer.

Rajamanikam lived in an Indian neighbourhood on the road to the airport. His house was modest, with pictures of Hindu divinities on the walls. He received me in a small, clean and pleasantly scented study, sitting at a desk with a shelf of old books behind him. Lean and dark-skinned like all Tamils of southern India, he had an elegant air. He was dressed in a starched *gurta*, whiter than white, with two small gold buttons on the front, and a sarong, also white. He wore ultra-thick-lensed glasses, and had a beautiful smile. He held some sheets of paper and a pen, with which he continually made calculations. His presence was formidable and reassuring. Nothing about him seemed false or designed to curry favour with whoever was confronting him. He spoke with the rolling cadence of the southern dialect, repeatedly nodding his head as punctuation. On the wall was an old German pendulum clock which struck the hours and chimed the quarters.

'*You were born in the fourth phase of the star Parani,*' began Rajamani-kam, '*and so you're under the influence of Jupiter, the king of the planets. Your sign in Western terms is Virgo with the moon in Pisces. A good combination that makes you intelligent, able and independent-minded, a person who likes debating. You could have studied law.*' (Well done! That is exactly what I did.)

He stopped, and examined his notes at length. He knew nothing about me. I had given his secretary the details of birth, and on that basis he had prepared a folder with a beautifully decorated cover of traditional design, containing my horoscope and some notes in red and blue pencil. He looked up. He had begun to suspect something.

'*Are you by any chance an astrologer?*' he asked.

'No.'

'*But you could become one. Otherwise you might be a writer, a journalist or a researcher. People can trust you and believe what you say. One day you'll suddenly acquire a fortune, and as an old man you'll be rich. Your mind never stops, it's always on the go, and you're a good worker. You are straight, you're sincere, and you couldn't succeed in hoodwinking anyone. You're destined to make a name for yourself, perhaps to become very well known. You'll live to the age of ninety-four, but there are two critical periods in your life: one between the ages of fifty-nine and sixty-one, the other at the age of seventy-seven. In those years keep away from water. Have nothing to do with water. Don't go sailing, don't swim. A period when you must be especially careful about water is between 8 August 1997 and 11 August 2000.*' (Just when I want to be in Hong Kong to see how the Chinese retake the colony. I hope I won't have to escape by swimming!)

'*In your life there are still many changes to come, but all for the better, because the best period of your life is still to come.*' (That's the second time I've heard this.) '*The year of the great change will be when you're fifty-seven. There's a very strong light coming towards you. On 2 December 1995 the best part of your life will begin. You'll turn out to be very influential in what you do. You'll be lucky in a matter involving property, and for the first time in your life you'll be rich. Up to now money has come and gone, but this will change after you reach the age of fifty-seven. At the moment you're in a period of transition, of uncertainty.*'

Rajamanikam spoke, my cassette recorder turned, I automatically took notes, and my mind played with his words. I felt that basically he was right. Not that I expected a better life than the one I had had, but the idea that the best part was still to come seemed to have a certain logic. Up to the age that I had reached, you did your duty, you had children, you worked. You played the part you had chosen or been assigned. You behaved as you should, you created your own personality. And then at last you were free. I don't mean free to retire. For me getting older means becoming more outspoken, more unconstrained. It means being able to say what I think, and to spend my time on what I consider important, even if it does not appear so to others. When you are older you can be free in a way that is unacceptable when you are young. You can live outside the usual patterns, outside the rules that preserve society. Have I not already begun, maybe? Here I am consulting a fortune-teller. At thirty I would never have done it! The man inspired me.

'*Your mother has a strong vital sign and will live long. But your father has a weak sign, very weak, he must already be dead.*' (Quite so.) '*You have been married for a long time, but take care of your marriage. If it has lasted this long it is because your wife has a strong sign. If it had been up to you, the marriage would have ended several times. Your problem is that you can't manage to be sexually faithful to one person. Sex for you is very important and dominates your attitudes. Sexually you are an elephant. Sex will interest you until you die, and this will lead you into difficulties of one kind or another. Temperamentally you are someone who can have more than one wife, even at the same time. Whether you remarry or not will depend on your wife's horoscope. But if you manage to stay married to your present wife until your sixty-second year, the marriage will be perfect thereafter. When you were thirty-nine you had a matrimonial problem. The marriage was about to break down.*' (Not really, but if there ever was the beginning of a crisis, it was precisely in 1977.)

'*You should have three children: one weak, two very strong.*' (Yes, now that I have learned to interpret these words: one child was so weak that it was never born.) '*The two strong ones are a boy and a girl. On your name there's a sort of light. It's a name that doesn't come from your family, but one you made for yourself. From time to time you have health problems, and your body will have to undergo an operation between the ages of fifty-nine and sixty-one, and another between sixty-five and sixty-six. You've travelled all your life and you'll continue to travel until you die.*'

Rajamanikam spoke as if he were reading from a book, and the book seemed to have pages similar to those read to me by others. In fact that is the case, and that is why astrology, especially if practised by experts, has a particular attraction. It is presented with an air of certainty which is lacking in other methods of divination. In astrology there are texts, rules, measures. Once the date and time of birth are known you need only know how to apply the method properly, taking account of all the variables, and at the end the message is 'Go to page 232.' And there they all end up reading more or less the same things. With repetition, therefore, the prediction gains more and more credibility.

Rajamanikam took a sheet of handwritten numbers from the folder. This was my detailed horoscope for the years to come. '*Between 18 April 1994 and 14 March 1995 you must move house and go and live in another country.*' (Again this idea that I must leave Bangkok.) '*From 14 March 1995 to 8 August 1997 you'll have to face some expenses, but nothing that will ruin you. But take care . . . from 24 August 1997 to the year 2000 there'll be numerous changes in your life. This is also a period in which the influence of Saturn will begin acting on you, and it's the period of your great power. If you want to enter politics you must do so in that period, and you'll win. It's also the period when you must take care of your health. If you want to stand for election, you must announce your candidacy on 8 August 1997, and you can only rise and rise.*' (At most I might run for the presidency of the Foreign Correspondents' Club in Hong Kong. That is where I want to spend the summer of 1997, seeing the end of the last colony in the world.)

'*You'll have a very happy old age. Your lucky numbers are five, three and nine. In particular five and three are excellent. Your stone is emerald.*' (That's what Kaka said in Penang, too: same page of the same book?) '*And the yellow sapphire. Any questions?*'

I asked him if he thought I should go to India. '*Certainly, but you must go and live in northern India, not in the south.*'

'What's a good time to do it?'

'*Absolutely before your fifty-seventh birthday. Preferably before you turn fifty-six.*' (That means before September 1994: impossible. Our lease for Turtle House runs until May 1995, and it's not certain that *Der Spiegel* will want to send me to India. Anyway, not for two years. I shall have to acquire some merits, I told myself.)

I was struck by what he said about my marriage. 'Should I look for another wife?' I asked jokingly.

'*That's not the problem. Whether you want to or not, there'll be another woman in your life, because you're an elephant and can't have only one. Another weakness of yours is that at times you're not firm in your decisions, you're not capable of carrying out what you've promised yourself. But remember: the best time of your life is still to come.*' That was a consoling thought.

I liked the man. Of all those I had seen, he was the most detached. Never for a moment did he give the impression of wanting to please me or flatter me. He was not saying: 'I see problems, but I can help you solve them.' He offered nothing. It really seemed as if he were reading in a book to which he held the key, and in that reading there would be nothing personal, as if my life had nothing to do with him. His detachment carried conviction.

By now I had learned that these people, who are always talking about the lives of others, are happy deep down to find that someone is interested in theirs. I asked Rajamanikam to tell me about himself. He had no hesitation. It was a Saturday, when normally he was not available. He was seeing me only because I had insisted so much and because he had the time.

He was born in Tamil Nadu, in southern India, and had recently turned seventy-three. His father had been an astrologer, and so had his grandfather. His whole life had been dominated by astrology. 'You foreigners say that Indian astrology is six hundred years old, just because it was only six hundred years ago that you realized it existed; but it has been practised for thousands of years. The Indians themselves give it little thought, they don't boast of it, but in India there are old books, copied from other older books, that describe how horoscopes should be made according to the various epochs. In our own epoch, which began 5995 years ago, the moment to consider is the one when a person is born; in a previous epoch what counted was the moment of the first sexual intercourse. That determined a person's destiny.'

Rajamanikam said that astrology was a science based on mathematical calculations. The problem was that these calculations had to be exact. It was very important, for example, to know at what time the sun rose in the place of a person's birth, because that influences his fate. He said, too, that the various calculations should be interpreted according to the culture and social environment of a person and the times in which he lives.

According to Rajamanikam there are ancient books in which it is predicted that men will travel among all the planets; others forecast floods, earthquakes and other cataclysms in the different regions of the world for a thousand years to come. He said that there was a time when the Indians could determine the sex of a child according to the position of the couple at the moment of conception. He said that in temple-building they knew the nature and influence of the stars so well that they could calculate, for example, the hour when a certain stone could be most easily lifted. Legends, myths. But perhaps there was a grain of truth in them, I thought as I listened.

Rajamanikam had begun taking an interest in astrology at the age of twelve. He read his father's books, but his father did not approve. He said that astrology did not pay, and that to make a career in British India a boy had to go to school. To force him to go, his father beat him. One day a *sanyassin*, one of those holy vagabonds who have renounced worldly goods and go about clad only in a loincloth, living on charity, passed through their village. The *sanyassin* looked at Rajamanikam's palm and told his father that the lad would not study as he wished, but even so would become famous among people of other castes, tribes and races, that he would be carried about on a palanquin, and would marry a woman with a mole on her breast.

'It all came true,' said Rajamanikam. He studied astrology in a nearby village. In 1938 he emigrated to Singapore, where he was known by people of all races and religions. As for the palanquin, he laughed, he now drove a Volvo.

'And the wife with the mole?' I asked.

It happened when the Japanese occupied Singapore. All the unmarried young men were being rounded up and sent to build the Burma railway, known as the 'death railway'. So Rajamanikam had to find a wife quickly. A matchmaker offered him one who was perfect, but she did not have the mole. Time was pressing, the matchmaker continued searching, and finally found a girl who had one. They were married. Just before they celebrated their golden wedding anniversary, the wife suddenly died and Rajamanikam fell ill. 'The only regret I have is that I didn't die with her,' he said. Another of those cases in which love is not the point of departure but of arrival.

I asked Rajamanikam if he had ever cast his wife's or his own horoscope, and if he had been able to foresee the events in his own life.

'An astrologer is like a doctor. If he falls ill, if he needs an operation, he must go to another doctor,' he said. After the *sanyassin* he had never had his fortune told by anyone, because his life was guided and protected by Durga. So saying, he turned his eyes upon a picture of the goddess seated on a tiger.

He told me a number of stories about people he had saved by putting them on their guard against certain dangers, and of others who had not listened to him. The best story, I thought, was Rajamanikam himself – so solid and serene, so sure of what he read in the book of other people's lives.

I thanked him and left an envelope with my 'offering'. I stepped out of the house as if on tiptoe. The man had made an impression on me.

He had also made me very hungry. A few steps away I came across a working-class restaurant, and sat down at one of the tables. In a big room with a cement floor there were several stalls, each with a Chinese cooking his own speciality. The customers looked into the boiling pots and chose what they wanted. I had a good soup of rice noodles with soyabean sprouts and some very thinly sliced chicken liver.

The whole neighbourhood was perfect: clean and tidy, the grass was cut, the trees pruned, the drains cleared, the streets without a scrap of paper or a cigarette butt. The people spoke in low voices as if they did not want to disturb each other. It was pleasant, but stifling at the same time.

My every attempt at reaching Jakarta by boat had failed. The only way to get out of Singapore was to take a ferry to the nearest Indonesian island, Pulau Pinang, and try to find another lift from there. I had no choice. I felt more and more oppressed by claustrophobia, as if Singapore had me by the throat. When I paid my bill and lifted my backpack on to my shoulders, it felt like a real liberation.

Not even the taxi driver who asked why I was taking the ferry, how many days I had been in Singapore and what I had bought could spoil the joy of leaving that air-conditioned island. On the way to Keppel Pier the taxi passed near the house we had lived in for years, but I did not dare go and look at it. I feared I would find it changed, destroyed, remoulded in plastic, or simply 'deleted' like a file in the memory of a computer. I wanted to remember Singapore as it had once been.

CHAPTER FOURTEEN

Never Against the Sun

I had been looking forward to the joy of sailing away from Singapore, to the renewed sense of freedom the sea would give me; but it was not to be. Keppel Pier was not the sort of port I had imagined. It was a space-station, with everything performed electronically, and my ferry was a spaceship – flat, aerodynamic, extremely fast, and hermetically sealed so that we could enjoy the air conditioning. It seemed that in Singapore even the sea had been recycled and sterilized, as if they had added dye to produce that magnificent jade-green colour.

We passed the island of Sentosa, which I remembered as a wild and barren place. Now it was a tropical paradise, or rather a copy of a tropical paradise. Pure white sand had been imported by the shipload from Indonesia, hundreds of palm trees had been planted around the new hotels, and 'old' British blockhouses had been rebuilt from scratch to be admired by unsuspecting tourists as mementoes of the Second World War.

I was the only foreigner on the ferry. Apart from a few Singaporean Chinese, all the other passengers were Chinese from Indonesia – provincials returning from a visit to the capital. Wedged in the middle of a row of seats, I tried to read a complacent article in that morning's *Straits Times*, the Singapore newspaper, about Asia's 'economic miracle' and the inability of even informed Westerners to understand it.

I experienced the effects of that miracle all around me. From the moment the ferry left the pier I was deafened by a cacophony of music, howls and whistles from various television sets, each with its own kung-fu film of incredible violence, with murders, stabbings, stranglings, blood. This was accompanied by songs from a video and beeps from a large number of electronic games in the passengers' laps. My neighbour, a Chinese woman of about thirty, loaded with gold jewellery, was so absorbed in her game that she totally ignored her small son as he repeatedly poked his fingers into my ears. They were all Chinese of the new diaspora generation which I was getting to know: self-confident, vulgar, exhibitionist. The modest uniform of the old days – white singlet and black shorts – had given way to the floral shirt, bleeper and mobile phone, comb and fat wallet in the back pockets of the trousers and lots of gold around wrists, necks and fingers. Everyone carried a 'project' in his head, to develop, to build, or to cover in cement.

The project of the man on my other side was soon on his lips. Together with some of his relatives in Taiwan, a brother in Singapore and a few Japanese investors, he was building the first big hotel on the island to which we were travelling. The long-term plan included eight more. 'We want to turn Pulau Pinang into the Hawaii of South-East Asia,' he said. He gestured towards the horizon, where I saw only a beautiful row of distant palms, but where he could already see the glint of skyscrapers.

I had not tried to imagine Pulau Pinang, and at first sight I found it magnificent, still natural, not yet ruined by modernity. The boat tied up at an old wharf and we disembarked down a long wooden plank. The streets were narrow, the houses all one or two storeys high. Nobody appeared to have air conditioning. I took a room in an old inn across from a mosque, and hired an interpreter and a driver who came to offer their services. We would be spending a couple of days together, and I thought the best way of getting acquainted was for us to go and have lunch. In hiring the driver I had not worried about what sort of car he had, and I was pleasantly surprised: an old-fashioned Chevrolet, held together with wire.

'We're lucky,' said Nordin, the interpreter. 'In the Riau archipelago we have cars that don't exist even in America any more.'

Pulau Pinang (*pulau* means 'island', *pinang* means 'betel nut'), three times the size of Singapore and with a population of only 250,000 people, is the main island of the Riau archipelago, lying between Sumatra and Java. The Riau islands are rich in oil – they supply most of Indonesia's crude petroleum – and other natural resources. Pinang itself has large deposits of bauxite, exploited in the past by the Dutch and now by the Japanese. The capital of the island is

Tanjung Pinang (*tanjung* means 'port'), with a population of about ninety thousand. The overwhelming majority are Chinese, who here, as elsewhere, control all the shops and all commercial activity.

The restaurant we went to, the best in town according to my two companions, was Chinese. We sat on a beautiful wooden deck, overlooking the sea. Everything you might want to eat was in a tank below: different sorts of fish, crabs, lobsters and prawns, all alive. You looked down from above and made your selection, then a boy scooped out the victims and sent them to the cook in a basket. In due course the bones and shells were thrown over the railing back into the sea to be carried away by the tide.

In travellers' tales, even modern ones, one rarely reads about what people eat; yet in Asia food is still one of the great pleasures. The variety is enormous, the methods of preparation are still simple, and the smells and colours are as much a part of the pleasure as the tastes. Every dish has a magic property all its own: one is good for the liver, another for the circulation; one fruit warms, another cools; and many things are good for sex, a common obsession of all peoples in this part of the world.

Sex also dominated our conversation. Nordin began by telling me to be careful in Indonesia when speaking the little Malay that I knew. Indonesian and Malay are virtually identical languages, but several words have quite different meanings. '*Aqua*', for example, means water in Malay but something else in Indonesian. A week before, the Pinang football team were in Kuala Lumpur. They had asked for some *aqua*, and a little later they saw arriving . . . a group of transvestites!

Nordin told me that his name meant 'light of religion'. That religion was obviously Islam, 'But Islam of the Indonesian variety,' he added – that is to say extremely relaxed and permissive. Nordin came from Sumatra; he was a Batak, very proud of his origins. The Batak people are divided into four tribes. Nordin belonged to the Karo tribe. He told me that when a girl dies unmarried the custom is to put a fresh banana in her coffin 'to keep her company on her journey to the underworld'. In the coffin of a celibate boy they put a thick segment of bamboo with a hole in the middle.

Every people seems to have its own myth of the creation and of how men came into the world. Nordin told me the Batak version:

one day the monkeys realized that there was no more room for them in the trees of the forest. They had had so many children that nobody could swing, run or jump from branch to branch any more. So they decided that half of the monkeys should go and live on the ground. A pretty version of Genesis, it seems to me. But where shall we send half the human population when we finally realize that the living conditions on the ground have become like those of the monkeys in the trees?

Still on the subject of sex, the driver of the Chevrolet – a big, tall fellow, who looked like a pirate with long hair down to his shoulders – told me that sex was the reason he had had to leave home. He came from a village in western Sumatra where there is still a very strict matriarchal regime: women rule everything, control everything. If a girl wants a certain boy, she need only go to his house and talk to his mother, and the poor devil cannot refuse. For my driver the only solution was to run away – the girl who wanted him was ghastly, he said. Another rule in his village was that a woman can always get rid of the man she has chosen: all she has to do is put his black Muslim cap outside the front door. She is then a divorced woman, and can marry someone else.

For the driver, escaping to Pulau Pinang had been a liberation. He told me that many young men of his area were doing the same, and the women were growing discontented.

I, for my part, felt perfectly happy. The stories told by Nordin and the driver took me back to a world of people who were different, not homogenized – people who still lived in their own way, with aspirations and concerns other than getting rich. I enjoyed the way my two companions described the women of the various islands, their characteristics, their good and bad sides: faithless were the women of Aceh, who, according to them, were a mixture of Arab, Portuguese and Indian; splendid were the Javanese, who have an extra muscle in their most private parts, and are of a courtesy beyond compare. If a Javanese girl accidentally steps on your toe, she apologizes a thousand times for having to continue using the offending foot.

I asked my companions if anything strange ever happened on the island, if there were any *bomohs*. Of course! Masses of them! But in the Riau archipelago the *bomohs*, experts in magic, were called *dukuns*. In a village on the north coast of the island there was a very powerful one whom the driver had known since he was a child. His voice was enough to make anyone quake. But if I was interested in the occult, they said, I absolutely had to go to Lingga, an island five hours away by boat. It was a mysterious place, once the capital of the sultans, where now the whole population has special powers, and even the fish can speak. On that island are the ruins of an ancient civilization, which no one knows anything about. It seemed the place for me.

Nordin made a few telephone calls and we went and looked for a Chinese who had a boat suitable for the trip, but by the time we found him it was too late to put to sea, especially as a storm was brewing. We would try the next day. All I had to do now was to go and see the *dukun*.

We drove for over an hour along a good asphalt road that ran around the island ('The army built it,' said Nordin. 'They don't have to fight the Communists any more, so they devote themselves to public works'). Then we turned off on a red earth track that took us into a plain dotted with coconut trees. The old Chevrolet shook and creaked, but I was the only one to be worried. 'The *dukun* lives far from any populated area, because he needs peace to concentrate,' said the driver, and I thought how I too would choose a tranquil and solitary spot if I was to set about becoming a guru or founding a new religion. One of the specialities of the *dukun* was to cure madness, and in difficult cases he had to fast for a few days to gather enough strength to drive the disease from a patient's body.

The trees became more dense, and in the middle of a beautiful thicket we saw an old wooden house which had been painted blue many years before. A sign over the door said '*Salamat Datang*', wel-come. An elderly man in a sarong, wearing a dark vest and a greasy old black cap, sat on the veranda. Around his feet some scrawny little cocks were learning to fight; a few children stood watching with puppies in their arms. Dogs are taboo for Muslims, but the man explained to Nordin that they were useful for keeping away the wild boar, which would otherwise destroy their fields. Another example of the relative flexibility of Islam in Indonesia.

The man was blind in his left eye, which was completely white and expressionless, but the incredible vivacity of the right one com-pensated for this. He signalled to us to step inside, into a large room.

We sat on benches around a big wooden table. A pleasant breeze blew in through the open windows. On the walls were images of Javanese women dancers, along with portraits of Sukarno, Suharto and other Indonesians who were unknown to me. On a little altar was an old print of Muslim saints with white beards. An acetylene lamp hung from the ceiling for the night. The *dukun* had no electricity, hence no television.

He had not yet spoken a word to me, and I realized it was up to me to introduce myself. I came from far away, I said, and had heard of his powers. I wanted to know if someone had put the evil eye on me, if I had anything to fear in the time ahead, and if this year he saw any danger for me in planes.

'*Baik!*' good, he said. '*I'll give you all the protection you need.*' His voice did not make me tremble exactly, but it was deep, firm, cavernous. An assistant came and poured out some very sweet tea, and the driver showed me the rooms where patients stayed during prolonged treatment. The *dukun* explained that I must submit to a special examination to see if I had the evil eye. He had a habit of raising his hands in the air while speaking, as the woman magician in Malacca had done. His nails were dirty and long, especially those of the two little fingers.

He led me through a beautiful curtain made of shells, which made a pleasant sound when they moved, into a dark, windowless room. On the floor of trodden earth was a straw mat, on which we sat cross-legged in a circle. The *dukun* lit three small candles, and in the centre of the mat I saw five round mirrors facing in different directions, and a few eggs. There were more eggs in a basket to the right of the *dukun*.

'*What's your name?*'

'Tiziano.' He practised saying it a couple of times, and then in a stentorian voice began reciting a long litany in which I recognized only the name of Allah and, now and then, perfectly mastered, my own. From a paper envelope he took out a magnifying glass, with which he slowly looked into the mirrors one by one while continuing his prayers. Then, with an air of supreme confidence, he said I had no evil eye on me, that I must not worry, and that anyway he would give me a special oil with which to protect myself. From under a cloth he took a tiny bottle which shone like gold in the candlelight. As he opened it a strong, sweetish scent filled the room. He put the bottle to his mouth as if to spit into it, but instead blew as hard as he could, perhaps to instill his soul or that of the spirit he represented. Then he closed it, lifted it towards heaven with new supplications, and handed it to me as he would an object of the utmost preciousness. Whenever I felt in danger I was to anoint my forehead with this oil. With that little bottle on me, no one could do me harm. If someone tried to shoot me − because, yes this was a risk I ran − at the last moment the weapon would jam, the arm of the person holding it would bend and the gun would point at the ground. Everywhere I went, thanks to that oil I would be protected and respected. All who came my way would grasp that they were up against a superior being. Generals and ministers would get the message. There was only one thing I had to be careful about . . . The *dukun* spoke without pausing, but slowly, so Nordin had time to translate word for word: '*Never piss against the sun. Remember: never! You must never do it facing the sun, or the oil will lose its strength. Understand?*'

The *dukun* joined his hands. I observed his long, dirty fingernails and the vacant white eye which suddenly, in the dim light of the candles, appeared to see. He began reciting an extraordinary litany in which my name was intoned with the words Bangkok, Hong Kong, London, Pakistan, Jakarta, India, Europe, America, Australia, New York, Asia, Germany, Rome. Names of cities, countries, continents, repeated at random, backwards and forwards for minutes on end in an obsessive crescendo: all the places where I could go with the assurance of being protected and respected as a superior being.

The ceremony was over. We made our way back to the big table and I asked the *dukun* to tell me his story. How had he discovered his powers? No. He could not answer such questions. If I had come in the morning he would have told me all, but the propitious time of day had passed. Even he had his taboos, and were he to break them he would lose all his power. He said only that his name was Ismail, that he was seventy-seven, that he had come to Pulau Pinang from Java after the war, and that he was descended from those white-bearded sages portrayed in the prints above the altar. Those were extraordinary people, he said: if they wished, they could make themselves invisible. That he could not do, but he was able to stop bullets, and for that reason many young men of the island came to him before going to do their military service. He made them invulnerable.

The *dukun* was good with words – which is perhaps the real power of most of these magicians. At a certain point he said that he and Sukarno, who had led Indonesia to independence and who was president until 1967, had the same great-grandfather. Sukarno had great powers, said the *dukun*, and it was directly from Sukarno that he had received his own. If Sukarno's car or plane ran out of petrol, he had only to urinate into the fuel tank and the engine would start running. His last wife had wanted to remarry, but on the eve of the wedding he had appeared before her and the marriage had not taken place. Did I know that Sukarno was not dead? It was his statue that had been buried. The real Sukarno was still alive, wandering around Indonesia. The *dukun* was absolutely convinced of this, and in a way he was not mistaken. Sukarno died in 1970, but his presence is felt in Indonesia perhaps even more today than when he was at its head. As time goes by the myth grows, and even his successor Suharto, after almost thirty years in power, has to reckon with this ghost that still circulates in the archipelago and in whose name all sorts of miracles are performed. By now Sukarno has become the tutelary divinity of whatever is connected with magic in Indonesia. Which is almost everything.

A computer programmer who loses a disk goes to the *dukun* to find out where to look for it; the police enlist the services of magicians to help trace a thief or identify a murderer; high government officials consult masters of magic before approving important contracts already vetted by economic and financial experts. Recently a group of car mechanics claimed they could iron out dents by using magic. They do it in a few hours and for a fraction of the normal price. Even the representative of the World Bank in Jakarta turned to them to have his Toyota repaired. All of these people come from Biltar, Sukarno's birthplace, and like the *dukun* they claim to have received their power from him.

I asked the *dukun* what he thought about the fact that man had been on the moon. Again he flung up his grimy hands. 'It's not true. Man can't go to the moon because the moon is God's creation. Man's imagination can go to the moon, but not man. Human beings have limits, and these limits must be respected, otherwise terrible things happen.' I could not but agree with him.

On the table in front of us was one of those little plastic envelopes containing coloured medicines one comes across in every market throughout Asia. 'Do you believe in modern medicines?' I asked the *dukun*. Of course he did. He took them himself, and recommended them to his patients for ailments with a physical basis. The problem, he said, was that these medicines were not up to curing any sickness that had been brought on by magic. These would only respond to a magic that was stronger. For example, madness, he said, was caused by magic, and there were no medicines capable of curing it. People would come to him after having tried the city doctors to no avail. The boy who had served us tea intervened to tell us that many women who had been brought in by their relatives with frightful tremors and convulsions would go away calm and tranquil after two or three days' treatment.

'It's not I who do it,' said the *dukun*. 'It's God who does it through me.'

It was time to pay. The driver had said there was no fee; only if the client was satisfied did he leave anything. But when I asked Nordin he suggested the equivalent of twenty dollars. A fortune here, I said to myself, but if the oil worked . . . And then, I could not come and probe in to these people's minds with the excuse about planes, and not leave behind some token of gratitude, some goodwill that might bring me at least as much benefit as the oil.

Discreetly, making sure no one noticed, I fished out a pocketful of rupees and concealed them in my hand. Making a slight farewell bow, I held out my right hand to the *dukun*, supporting the wrist with my left in that courteous gesture which is obligatory in Asia. He did the same; our hands met, and as he felt the money his face brightened into a beautiful, broad smile of satisfaction. He was very happy, and I felt protected and important.

On the way back Nordin told of his own experience with a *dukun*. In 1979, two years after he had come to Pinang and begun taking tourists to the nearby Island of the Bees, he started feeling ill. He was constantly weak, had headaches, and often vomited during the night. The doctors gave him medicines, but he grew even worse and could no longer move. His wife called in a *dukun*, a woman. She gave him some ingredients to drink, some leaves to apply to his body, and after three days Nordin, 'light of religion', was in shape again. The explanation? The people of the Island of the Bees had put the evil eye on him. They were jealous because he spoke English, and by bringing tourists to the island he profited from their existence without sharing anything with them. The woman *dukun* performed some counter-magic and the evil eye disappeared. But she warned Nordin that for the rest of his life he must show more respect for others, must not bother them needlessly and must share what he earned with those who helped him.

Nordin took this advice very seriously. Well, what can one say? There is no denying the fact that all revolutionaries and positivists have seen these magicians, in their different versions, as enemies of modernity and exploiters of the people. They have even tried to eliminate them physically – as Mao did in China – to free the people from the shackles of superstition. But who has taken their place? Who now teaches these important banalities? Who gives lessons in common sense, even if mediated by potions and oils? And besides, even in these there may lurk some sense!

Nordin reached for his wallet and pulled out a paper-thin piece of metal with writing on it, which the woman *dukun* had given him. That was his protection, and he always had to have it on him. But was it not merely a reminder? Did it not recall, every time he saw it, his promise not to 'bother people'? A knot in his handkerchief would have served the same purpose, but it would have had less of the sacral, the magical. Nordin also had a taboo of his own in connection with this little piece of metal: he had to remove it every time he went to the toilet, and he must never eat meat that was not *halal*, slaughtered in the Muslim way. Everything had to remind him of his duty towards others.

I thought again of my *dukun*: he was the first fortune-teller who had not mentioned money, getting rich or not getting rich, coming into an inheritance. Nor was there anything materialistic in the other stories I had heard about *dukuns*. I welcomed this departure from the Chinese.

We drove back along the coastal road. The storm which had threatened did not materialize, but the sky was low and grey. The sea, so smooth and clean, was a joy to behold: very pale green near the shore and very dark, almost black, at the horizon. The beach was narrow and fringed with coconut trees. About a hundred yards from the water's edge we saw fishermen building huts on piles. These would be swept away by the monsoon in September, and rebuilt the following April. Every year the same, for generations: they build houses to live in, to fish from with big nets hung from the porch, and to be carried away by the sea.

'The fishermen are Malays. Their customers are Chinese. It's the same all along the coast,' said Nordin. 'If the fishermen don't fish, the Chinese lend them money to live on, and get it back with interest from the future catch. Now and then the Malays run amok and attack Chinese shops, and we have a bit of a massacre.' He said this in the same tone he used to describe how the sea destroys the houses every year. Even massacres seemed to be a seasonal matter.

The great pogrom of 1965, launched by the military who later brought Suharto to power, was aimed at the Communists; but the people, especially in the small islands, took advantage of it to settle their own accounts with the Chinese. More than half a million people were slaughtered in a matter of days. Some of the most atrocious crimes occurred on the peaceful and paradisal island of Bali.

That evening we ate at the local market amid dozens of stalls, each with its own speciality. Seafoods, meats, vegetables and an endless variety of fish were displayed in the light of acetylene lamps: a fascinating mosaic of colours and forms, with strong odours wafting about. Oil flared in the big cauldrons, which the Chinese cooks handled like conjurers. Packs of dogs and beggars circulated in the darkness behind the stalls. From under a table appeared a little boy who offered to shine my shoes. 'One at a time,' Nordin warned me. 'If you give him both together he'll run off and sell them, and you'll be left barefoot. He won't know what to do with one on its own, so he'll polish it for you.'

In the crowd Nordin saw the only other white man who seemed to be on the island, and beckoned him over to our table. 'He knows everything about the island of Lingga,' said Nordin by way of introduction. Michael was Australian, a former philosophy student, he said. He was about forty, had come to Indonesia a few years ago, and had ended up in Lingga. Since then the island had become his obsession.

'Why Lingga?' I asked.

'Lingga's the capital of the Bunyan people. You know who they are, don't you?'

'No.'

'The Bunyan are the soft people. Do you follow? We're the hard people,' said Michael, touching my skin to show that it was solid, hard. 'They, you see, are soft. Do you follow? In Lingga there are lots of them, but no one can see them. They live their own lives. We live ours, and only occasionally do we mix with them. One of the hard people, like you and me, has been known to marry a Bunyan. It happens. But only seldom. I know a man on Lingga who married a beautiful Bunyan girl. He had to go to bed with her once a week, on Thursdays, otherwise he was free, and could even marry another woman.'

I listened, fascinated. People continued to cook, eat and beg all around us; the little boy polished my second shoe. Michael talked very seriously about the Bunyans, in the way that others might talk about the stock market. I found his stories quite magnificent. In the Chinese tradition too there are marriages between dead souls, arranged by the parents of the deceased; this is done, for example, to prevent an unmarried girl from returning as an evil spirit to disturb the young men of the village.

'One Thursday this fellow forgot his appointment,' continued Michael, 'and the Bunyan girl took offence and was no more to be seen. In the past, when people got married on Lingga the Bunyans would go to the wedding, and they would lend their golden plates for the guests to eat off. Once, however, a guest hid one of these plates with a view to stealing it, and after that the Bunyans stopped going to weddings. Around the same time one of the three mysterious peaks of the mountain on Lingga split. The mountain's sacred; it's only four thousand feet high, but nobody can climb it.'

Michael said that there are people who claim to have reached the top, but they only have the vaguest memories of how they did it. He knew a woman who had fallen ill, and the doctors had said she was done for. Then, on the point of death, she vomited up some strange herbs and recovered. She said she had been seized by seven Bunyan girls, carried to the top of the mountain to eat in a meadow, and then taken back to her bed. This had saved her.

'The Bunyans,' Michael went on, 'always have everything clean around them. If a house is dirty they're no more to be seen. They're friendly, they want to help the "hard" people, but they also want you to respect what's theirs. If you go in to the forest and cut down a tree that belongs to the Bunyans, you get lost and can't find your way home. The *gharau*, for example, the tree used in making the world's best incense, which the Chinese have come here to buy for centuries, belongs to the Bunyans. All the *gharau* trees are theirs, and woe to anyone who cuts them down without asking permission. They give it to those who treat the forest as they should, who cut the undergrowth and keep the clearings tidy, who respect their dwellings.'

'But how do you recognize them, these Bunyans?' I asked.

'Easy!' intervened Nordin, who had followed the whole conversation and seemed to find it all quite normal. 'You only have to look at their upper lip, here.' He pointed to his own mouth. 'The Bunyans don't have this division that we have, here under the nose. Their upper lips are flat right across.'

At midnight the market was still bustling with people. On my way back to the inn, I was struck by something I had not previously noticed. Amidst the crowds there was an extraordinary number of madmen: peculiar, grubby types with copious beards and tufts of long tangled hair. One of them paced back and forth, a sack in his hand, constantly turning to stare at the ground as if he had lost something; another rushed about intoning litanies; others dragged plastic bags full of useless rubbish. One stood leaning against a lamp post as if expecting someone.

'Who are you?' he asked me in perfect English as I brushed past.

'Who are *you*?' I found myself instinctively replying. It was dark and I could not make his face out. When I tried to approach him and see if his upper lip was flat, he ran off.

CHAPTER FIFTEEN

The Missionary and the Magician

Every place is a goldmine. You have only to give yourself time, sit in a teahouse watching the passers-by, stand in a corner of the market, go for a haircut. You pick up a thread – a word, a meeting, a friend of a friend of someone you have just met – and soon the most insipid, most insignificant place becomes a mirror of the world, a window on life, a theatre of humanity.

I was in Tanjung Pinang simply because it was the one destination possible for those wanting to leave Singapore by sea. I meant to stay there just a couple of days, long enough to find a ship bound for Jakarta. But little by little I became involved in the daily life of the town, and I could have spent weeks there, following up something or someone that had caught my interest. Tanjung Pinang: another of those places, hard to find on the map, where I landed up through that infinite chain of chances which had begun with the Hong Kong fortune-teller.

One morning I had got up very early, run for half an hour and then gone looking for somewhere to have breakfast. And that was how I came to meet Old Yang. He had just finished removing, one by one, the numbered wooden boards that formed the door of his restaurant, had lit a cigarette and begun sweeping. First he pretended he had not noticed me, as is the way with Asians, convinced as they are that there can be no communication with a foreigner. I addressed him in Chinese, which reassured and surprised him.

'I am Chinese too,' I said.

'Chinese?'

'Yes. I belong to an ethnic minority: the Italians.' The joke never fails. China is a great empire, populated mainly by the Han – the 'flower men' – but also by a great many 'people in small numbers',

198

minorities: the Mongols, the Tibetans, the Uighurs, the Kazaks, the Dai, the Hui, the Miao, and – why not? – the Italians. From the Chinese point of view it is quite plausible; in fact, every now and then there is someone who does not realize it is a joke.

Old Yang was a classic Chinese of the diaspora. His father was from the province of Canton. He arrived on Pulau Pinang at the end of the last century with nothing but the singlet and shorts he had on, and worked in the bauxite mines as a coolie. When he had saved enough, he had a wife sent over from his village in China, and produced five children with her. Old Yang was the first-born, so he had remained in Tanjung Pinang to look after his father and then to run the restaurant his father had opened. His two brothers and two sisters, by contrast, were sent to study in China in the early 1950s. In those years tens of thousands of young Chinese, children of poor emigrants, returned to the mother country from the various countries of South-East Asia. China was liberated, the universities, once the preserve of the rich, were open to all, and to study was free. To the Chinese of the diaspora it seemed the ideal chance to give their children a Chinese education. Many never returned. They got caught up in the drama of that long-suffering land, and became victims of the Cultural Revolution. The fact that they came from abroad, from families who lived in capitalist countries, made them suspect. They were denounced as spies and counter-revolutionaries and sent to labour camps, to be re-educated or to die.

It was only in 1972, thanks to Chou Enlai, who took a personal interest in these 'seeds of the dragon' scattered around the world, that the survivors were able to leave China discreetly. But where could they go? The countries they originated from, all engaged in fighting against Communist guerrillas, suspected those who came back from China of being Maoist agents and would not permit them to return. A few thousand remained for years and years in the limbo of Macao. Old Yang never saw his siblings again. One brother was beaten to death, the other was unable to leave China and is still living in Dailian. His two sisters, after years in Macao, finally got to Hong Kong and thence to Canada, in that ceaseless migration that has taken the Chinese to every corner of the earth.

While we were talking, Yang's son walked in. A businessman, one of the new generation. He had formed a company with some in-laws in Singapore, and bought and sold land on the island. He too had the beeper and the Ray-Ban case attached to his belt. His dream? To emigrate. Where? 'To any country where the average per capita income is higher than here,' he replied. Typical!

Old Yang and Young Yang were born and had lived all their lives in Tanjung Pinang, but they had no affection for the place, no real contact with its original inhabitants. They found the Indonesians rude and uncultured, and boasted of belonging to 'the great Chinese civilization', of which, however, they bore precious little. They felt themselves to be Chinese: their ancestors were Chinese and their descendants would be Chinese. China was their mother country. Where that China lay was far from clear. It was not the China of Mao and Deng Xiaoping – too poor; not Taiwan – too small and insignificant. It lay in the idea of China, an undefinable Chineseness with which the great multitude of the diaspora identify themselves.

Of Pulau Pinang, Old Yang said: 'It's an excellent spot, there's freedom to do business here, and if things go badly, we can always turn to our relatives in Malaysia, or ask for help from those in Singapore.' That is how the Chinese reason wherever they have emigrated: for them the countries they live in are rather like chessboards on which they play out a game.

Indonesia has a population of 190 million. The Chinese constitute barely 2 per cent, but 70 per cent of the country's trade is in their hands, and the top five industrial groups and the major banks are theirs. Everything is the product of Chinese companies: from soap to cement, from cigarettes to coconut oil. Even Tanjung Pinang is largely in Chinese hands: they control most of the shops and the boats that shuttle between there and the nearby islands, and they are involved in all the new development projects. The city's first karaoke bar belongs to a Chinese, and so do the brothels, disguised here too behind the innocent signboards of barber shops.

There I had the whole story of the diaspora Chinese – strong, tough, hard-working, always ready to move on and adopt the passport of any state that would guarantee them security and protection. One of their new ways of making money is to build, to cover everything in cement – and in this activity the Chinese are in the forefront. By now their influence extends all over Asia. They are destroying Bangkok. Soon they will do the same with Rangoon, Hanoi and every other city to which they have access. It is the diaspora Chinese who, with their massive investments, are now remaking the coastal cities of China in their own image. They are the new models of success, heroes of the Chinese youth disoriented by the failure of Maoism. The Chinese of the diaspora seemed to me more and more like missionaries of that materialism from which I was trying to escape.

During my morning run I had seen a Catholic church on a hilltop, and Nordin told me the priest was a Frenchman who had been there at least ten years. Certainly this must be a man to talk to.

That afternoon I went there on foot. Churches are always oases of peace, order and cleanliness, with their ranks of pews and the noticeboards listing the times of masses and prayers. I enjoyed the contrast with the smelly chaos of the city, but, to my disappointment, the priest was not there. He had gone to another island on a retreat, and would be back in two weeks. I had already turned away when a cleric came after me, saying: 'If you like, there's a Dutch father here.' I waited a while in a beautiful airy room. The sun was streaming in. A tall, elegant man of about fifty appeared. He had long blond hair and was dressed in brown trousers and a white shirt, with leather sandals on his feet. Father Willem was in Tanjung Pinang for a few days' visit, like me. He came from Bangka, an island further south, towards Java. The Dutch, being interested in the tin mines, had given Singapore to the British in exchange for Bangka. Not a good bargain!

Father Willem had travelled all over the archipelago, and in his opinion the situation was practically the same on every island: the Chinese are a minority everywhere, and everywhere the most enterprising, the most active, the wealthiest. The difference between them and the local people, he said, was simple: 'An Indonesian goes fishing and has a good catch. He's happy, he goes home and for days he enjoys his earnings and feels he can put his feet up. A Chinese goes fishing and has a good catch; he thinks, "This is the good season, and I've found the best waters." He unloads his boat, goes fishing again and catches a lot more fish.' Father Willem believed it was a question of race, and there was nothing to be done about it.

I mentioned that someone had spoken to me of the Bunyans. Of course, he said, they were famous even on his island, but Lingga was their capital.

And magic?

'Here magic is the real world,' he said, as if wishing to make his position clear in case I was the usual dismissive sceptic. 'If you don't understand that, you don't understand anything about Indonesia. Magic is everywhere; magic determines people's lives more than anything else.'

Father Willem was born in Holland before the war, and had come to Indonesia as a missionary in 1960. He had remained there, becoming an Indonesian citizen so as to avoid problems of visa and residence. 'When I arrived, as a good European, I thought that magic was superstition, and I wouldn't accept any part of it. But with time I've learned to respect it. It's something I now bear in mind. At the risk of your misunderstanding me, I might go so far as to say I believe in it. In magic there's something profoundly real, and true. Here the people say they are Muslims, or Christians in the case of my parishioners, but that's all on the surface. Underneath there's that other world, with these beliefs which are so much stronger, hence so much more genuine.'

There are two kinds of magic, he explained. White magic, practised mainly by the Chinese, who make use of it to get on in business or to arrange good marriages; and black magic, practised exclusively by the Malays, to control the will of other people, to do harm, to carry out vendettas. He said that in Java a friend and colleague of his, Father Lokman, had spent more than thirty years studying black magic, and had himself acquired some powers as a medium. His conclusion was that magic has to do with brain waves.

'Why is it,' he asked, 'that when you meet one person you'll say he's nice, while of another you'll say you can't bear him? There is some process of invisible communication. How do you explain love? We've lost the habit of asking these questions, but the problem remains. Why does one see a woman and fall in love with her? This is something we haven't explained yet.'

Here was a priest who asked questions about love. There was something splendid in that. I have noticed on other occasions that the clergy talk about love as if they know more about it than ordinary mortals. And perhaps they do: they have given it more thought, more reflection.

'In the thirty years I've spent on the islands I've seen things that, were I to talk about them in Europe, I'd be taken for a madman. I've seen nails removed from people's bodies. I've seen the bottom

of a bottle extracted from a woman's breast. A man in my parish
had terrible back pains. He went to the doctor. They X-rayed him
and found he had three nails inside him. They operated, but only
succeeded in removing two of them. They couldn't get the third
out. They X-rayed him again and found seven more. These things
happened before my very eyes. In Bangka I saw a man who, by
thought alone, sent a nail to his enemy which was so hot that when
it hit the wooden boards of his house they burst into flame. Along
came a lay Dutch brother who had studied magic for years, and he
said: "I could send the nail back where it came from, but I can do
even better." He put the nail in the freezer and the man who had
sent it nearly died of cold. I too wonder how it's possible, how it
works, but I would never say that it didn't happen, or that it was
ridiculous.'

'Could it be,' I asked, 'that all this belongs to a wisdom whose
origins we no longer know, but whose techniques some people still
know how to use? A bit like acupuncture: it works, but no one
really knows how.'

It was possible, he thought. 'My grandfather knew three prayers
and he used to say them, when we were small, to take away our
toothache until we could get to the dentist. Believe me, it worked.
Well, I'm a priest, I know those prayers, but if I say them they have
no effect. Why? Perhaps because I don't believe in them. On my
island, when someone breaks an arm and can't go to the hospital
because it's too far away, the family find a black chicken and pound
it to a pulp in a tub. Then they put this poultice on the arm, and
in four days it's cured. Sometimes the bone isn't set correctly and
the arm remains a bit twisted, but the bone's knit. How to explain
it? Why a black chicken and not a white one? I don't know, I don't
know, but it works; I've seen it with my own eyes.'

The missionary spoke impetuously, with passion, not to convince
me, but as if he had to convince himself anew. The stories he told
were the sort one always hears sooner or later in Asia. You listen
and you forget because you cannot believe them. But here they were
coming from a man of the cloth, a man who had spent his life with
the problems of the spirit, and who spoke from an experience of
over thirty years.

'And love?' he said, returning to a subject that seemed close to
his heart. 'When a man desires a woman he tries to get hold of a

hair, a piece of clothing, anything that belongs to her. He takes it
to the *dukun*, who makes a little packet and has him put it under his
pillow . . . and one night the woman comes to him. She can't help
coming. She does it in a sort of trance, but she comes. It's incredible.'

Father Willem told me that, not long after he had first set foot on
the island he once said jokingly to a *dukun*: 'Try with me! Send me
a pretty girl!' The older priests, none too pleased, gave him a word
of warning: one should never challenge these people. Faith, they
said, is a great defence against magic, but even faith has its ups and
downs, and a powerful *dukun* might be able to overcome it.

To understand the practices of black magic, said Father Willem,
one had to understand that in the eyes of an Indonesian there was
no clear dividing line between inanimate objects and living beings,
whether men or animals. For an Indonesian many objects have life.
The *kris* for example, the ceremonial knife, has a spirit of its own,
just as a body that loses life, a corpse, still has a spirit in it. The
power of the *dukun* consists in knowing how to use this spirit,
whether that of a *kris*, a nail, or someone who is dead. What remains
in the corpse of someone who has died a violent death, especially if
he has been hanged or stabbed or has committed suicide, is a very
powerful force in black magic.

Just as amulets can be 'charged' with a positive energy that protects
the person carrying them, so an object – a knife, for example – can
be charged by the *dukun* with a negative force that turns it against
the person using it, making it the weapon of an involuntary suicide.
Father Willem had heard of a *dukun* who could do this by concentrating for at least a month on the object he wished to animate. The
principle is that a charge of energy is transferred from the mind of
the *dukun* into the object by a process of meditation.

It is also, said Father Willem, important to understand the way
people express themselves on the subject of magic. On his island,
for example, they say the *dukun* is capable of talking to plants. What
they mean is that he knows all qualities of the roots, the leaves and
the flowers. They mean he can use plants to concoct poisons that
kill or potions that apparently bring the dead back to life.

I found Father Willem's interpretation of magic particularly interesting, because it was similar to what I thought I understood about
feng-shui. In his opinion, behind the practices of the *dukun* lay the
natural human aspiration for harmony, the need to re-establish a

marred equilibrium. A man suffers because a woman does not love him? Magic is used to restore harmony by making her fall in love. Someone has committed a crime for which he has not paid the penalty in accordance with justice? Let him pay by magic.

'I can't understand how it works,' said Father Willem, 'and that's the truth. But take the case of Belitung Island, quite near here. In the middle of the island there's a mountain. On the top of the mountain they erected a transmitter for the Jakarta television station. To get there they built a road right up to the summit. You can reach it by jeep, but first you must get permission from the guardian-spirit of the mountain, the *penjaga*, a strange being that lives at its foot and controls access to it. Try going up there without its permission! The jeep stalls, it seems to have run out of petrol or to have broken down. I don't know how to explain it, but believe me, that's what happens.'

It came naturally to Father Willem, as by now it does to me, to complain of the way the world is losing the diversity that first inspired his – and my – fascination with Asia. 'It's sad, but even magic is dying out,' he said. 'People turn more and more to Western medicine. Television opens up the world and everyone wants to become like everyone else. Sad, but that's how it is.'

He stopped, as if looking for the words to say something he had had in mind for some time, but found difficult to express. 'And now I find myself involved in a strange phenomenon: they're moving more and more towards my civilization, and I'm moving more and more towards theirs. This has turned into a real problem of conscience for me. I am a priest, I came here to bring my faith, but somehow I'm more and more interested in theirs; I'm fascinated by their world, the real world, the one that lies beneath the world of appearances, the one created by Islam, by Buddhism, even by my Christianity.'

How I understood him!

This conversation with Father Willem hung about me like a lingering scent, and when next morning I went jogging and saw that church on the hill with its white bell-tower, I felt a keen pleasure, a kinship deep down inside me at the thought that it held a missionary who was in some way under the spell of magic.

*   *   *

Nordin had gone to see the Chinese who had the boat that was to take us to Lingga, and Michael had found us a guide for the island. But at the last minute, when everything had been arranged, I decided not to go. I preferred to keep hold of the image of the Bunyans which I had formed from Michael's stories on the first evening. Anything further I saw or heard could only count as a disappointment.

I did not even want to see any more of Michael. Nordin told me he was setting things up for taking groups of Australians to the island. He had already prepared leaflets advertising 'Adventures in the Lost Empire'. So even Lingga was on its way to becoming a tourist attraction; and the Bunyans – I was certain about this – would make themselves more and more scarce.

I decided to leave. At six the next morning the weekly passenger ship for Jakarta was scheduled to call at Kijiang, the main port of the island, about nineteen miles from Tanjung Pinang. Buying a ticket wasn't easy, but by tipping an agent Nordin managed it. Meanwhile, however, everything I heard about these voyages between the islands made my hair stand on end. Many of the ferries had light hulls made of fibreglass that could never withstand a rough sea. Nobody obeyed even the most basic safety rules. Boats licensed to carry a certain number of passengers crammed two or three times as many on board. There were never enough lifejackets or lifeboats. The fire-extinguishers were not in working order, the safety exits were always blocked by people and baggage . . . I had no choice: I was lucky to have found a ticket. Anyway, the fortune-tellers all told me I wouldn't die before I was eighty.

Nevertheless, I had a very bad night. The bath tap refused to turn off properly, and the water dripped non-stop. As I lay half asleep I had the impression that a terrible storm had struck the city, and that the ship would not sail. I was obviously looking for an excuse not to go. I wrapped a towel around the tap and fell asleep, but only to dream: I had come to our country retreat, but nowhere could I find my hiking boots. I was supposed to go camping, but without the boots I was unable to leave the house. I was acutely disappointed. I looked everywhere for the boots, but could not find them.

I woke, and the dream seemed to me a very clear message from my subconscious: don't sail, the ship will sink! I turned over all the stories I had heard about premonitions. What, though, is a premonition? Pure chance. How many of us, at least once in our lives, have had a premonition and changed our plans: we decide against taking a plane, against getting into a car – and then nothing happens: the plane doesn't crash, the car doesn't have an accident. But then it happens that someone misses a train on which a bomb explodes. A premonition, people say.

Insomnia feeds obsessions, and my mind went through more twists and turns than my body as I tried to sleep. I won't die until after I am eighty? Of course, because it is written that tomorrow I shall not get on that ship! That's why I had the warning dream. My mind was reeling with this nonsense. The fact is that there is no solution to this problem of fate, I told myself. Either you can see life as being written somewhere in advance, or you can see it as being written by you every minute as you go along. Both versions are true. Every decision can be seen as either a free choice or a product of predestination.

Is that not perhaps the meaning of Oedipus's prophecy, which lies at the very roots of our culture? A fortune-teller tells his father, Laius: 'Your son will kill you and become his mother's lover.' To avoid this, Laius gets rid of Oedipus by sending him far away. And just because of that act the returning Oedipus can kill Laius without knowing he is his father, and, without knowing that she is his mother, he can become Jocasta's lover. If Laius had ignored the fortune-teller, nothing would have happened; the prophecy is fulfilled precisely because he takes it seriously and does his best to avoid the consequences. So fate is ineluctable, and the prophecy is part of it: it precipitates events which men, left to themselves, would never choose to bring about. The Greeks understood and said everything five centuries before Christ, and today we have to reinvent and rediscover it all!

I imagined a stormy sea, and how the ship would roll over and sink like a stone in a matter of seconds. I remembered another story which I had heard that day from Nordin, who in his youth had been a fisherman. His grandmother had taught him that when the sea gets rough and frightens you, you must take two fresh eggs, one in each hand, say some prayers, shut your eyes, concentrate intensely on your own survival, and then throw the eggs into the waves, one fore and the other aft. The sea subsides. Nordin said he had done this on a number of occasions and it always worked. But where would I find two fresh eggs in the middle of the night?

Through the window I saw the ugly neon star of the mosque, and my mind took a leap: star, stars. What a fantastic combination of stars there must have been in the fifth century before Christ! So many great spirits, all born at the same time: Sophocles, Pericles, Plato and Aristotle in Greece; Zoroaster in Persia; Buddha in India; Lao Tse and Confucius in China. All, more or less, in the space of a hundred years. Today many, many more people are born, but not a single one who can measure up to those. Why? Is the reason in the stars?

Someone knocked at my door. It was four o'clock. The taxi I had ordered was ready to leave. There was no escape. Premonition or not, I was on my way to Jakarta. We drove off towards the park in impenetrable darkness. The car was an ancient relic, the product of several cannibalizations held together with wire. As we passed through the open country a group of armed men with pocket torches blocked the road and signalled to us to stop: police or bandits? 'Police *and* bandits,' replied the driver. He gave them a pack of cigarettes and on we went.

We put a few more miles behind us, then the car spluttered, wheezed, had a coughing fit, and stopped. It had died on us. The driver opened the bonnet and fiddled with some wires, but whatever he did to try and bring it back to life got nowhere. He was worried, but when he saw me laughing merrily, he relaxed. He lit a cigarette and sat on the bonnet.

By now the sky was astir with huge grey clouds outlined in red. A little solitary star gradually lost its brightness. I was as happy as could be. Here was proof of my powers, it seemed. I had blocked the engine of the car. I would not go to Jakarta, and if that ship did sink indeed, then most decidedly I should switch jobs! Sorcerer!

I went back to the city on a motorbike. In the afternoon the sister ship of the one bound for Jakarta was due to call at Kijiang en route to Medan on the island of Sumatra. That was fine with me. I would finally be sailing the Straits of Malacca, and it would be easier to get back on the homeward road from there.

For good measure I still had time to go and visit the oldest *dukun* in Tanjung Pinang.

★   ★   ★

The *dukun* lived in a village about nineteen miles from Kijiang, on the beach at Trikora. His wooden house was built on piles. He was sitting on an old mattress laid on the ground. He was very thin, and breathed with difficulty. Leaning against the wall was his wife, much younger than he was. His second. Two children were playing with a cat on the fine wooden floorboards. The elder had already read the whole of the Koran, said the old man with pride.

The old *dukun* did not know exactly when he was born. He did know, however, that his granddaughters were already having children of their own, and so with all those generations coming after him he figured he was at least a hundred years old. And then there were the coconut trees in front of the house: he had seen his father plant them, and now they were gigantic.

The family had always lived there, and all the surrounding land belonged to them. Moreover, they had always been the *dukuns* of those parts. Landowners and magicians, a perfect combination for achieving complete mastery, I thought. And so it was. 'Whenever two people marry,' said the centenarian, 'they have to come to me for a blessing, otherwise the marriage won't last, they won't get on, their rice will rot and have stones in it always.'

It was his father who had passed on the powers to him, on his wedding day. 'The powers must be given to a member of the family, someone trustworthy who won't use them to do harm or for purely selfish ends,' said the old man. His father had given them to all his children, both sons and daughters.

The *dukun* was weak, and it was a strain for him to sit upright, but he liked talking. Throughout his life he had used his powers to help people find lost possessions and to recover stolen goods hidden by thieves, but mainly he had used them to cure the victims of ghosts. 'The really bad ones are the ghosts of those who have died violently, who have been put to death, and this island is full of those,' he said. 'First the Dutch . . . They murdered large numbers; then the Japanese. This is a strange island, full of evil spirits.'

I asked him why, if the *dukuns* were so powerful, they had not used their powers to resist colonization by the Dutch and fight the Japanese.

'There's a saying of ours: "Magic doesn't cross oceans,"' replied the *dukun*. 'That means that from here we cannot influence events on another continent. It also means that foreigners have spirits unbeknown to us and over which we've no control. With the Europeans in particular it's very difficult to use our powers.'

During the war, however, he had been present at a number of impressive feats. There were certain *dukuns* who could make people vanish when the Japanese were about to shoot them. The old man swore he had seen this with his own eyes, and the two children were obviously impressed. The story will continue for at least another generation.

I asked the old man what he knew about the Bunyans. He knew them. They lived in the mountains. They were people, not ghosts.

The storm I had been so afraid of finally broke out. A cool, dense rain began to fall, and a pleasant moist breeze entered the wooden house by the open windows and doors. The old man started coughing. He said that since falling ill he had no more power. The last case he had cured was that of a boy of twenty whose head and arms had suddenly begun to get bigger and bigger. He had given the boy a herbal potion to take three times a day after saying some prayers. In the course of a month he had returned to normal. What caused the illness? The boy had been stealing, said the *dukun*. Similar cases had occurred in the past. People who had taken pineapples from their neighbours' fields suddenly found their bellies swelling as if they were pregnant. Their bellies were full of pineapples! The same thing happened to people who stole coconuts.

This, to be sure, was a clever way for the *dukun*-landowners to terrorize potential thieves. But could it not also have been a response to people's natural desire for justice and harmony?

I would probably never again have a chance of seeing a *dukun* close to death, so I ventured to ask the question that had been on my mind since I stepped inside the house: 'Are you afraid of death?'

'I don't know . . . I know only that in the course of my life I've seen spirits of all types. I've seen spirits of old women with long white hair, I've seen the ghosts of animals, I've seen the ghosts of the sea that sometimes invade the bodies of fishermen when they are out on their boats. I've seen many strange things, and I expect to see more . . . even after,' he replied.

His wife was getting worried, afraid I might be another expert on black magic who had come to steal some secrets from her husband. In her way she was right, and I apologized to her. The old man was sorry I had to go, and wanted to give me his blessing. One more would do me no harm.

The driver had parked the car in front of the district infirmary, and the head doctor, responsible for the whole area, happened to be there. What did he think of the *dukuns*? People believed in them, he said, and that was enough. With normal medicines he could cure a fever in a few days, but a *dukun* could sometimes do it in minutes, and people preferred going to a *dukun* rather than the infirmary. He himself, when he took up this post, went to pay his respects to the *dukun*. 'He owns the land, so he has control over the ghosts. Here everything works by a different logic from the one I learned at university, but it's a logic all the same. So where does that leave me? I work here, and I have to believe what the people believe.'

When I reached the port the ship for Jakarta had just pulled away from the quay, ten hours behind schedule. A woman stood at one of the kiosks that sold drink, weeping desperately. Taking advantage of the long stopover, she had gone to Tanjung Pinang to do some shopping, and when she returned the gangplanks had already been taken up. All her baggage, documents and money were on the ship. The director of the Pelni Lines in Kijian scolded her severely and talked about discipline. He said his firm was not responsible and she would have to deal with the problem herself. Then he suddenly became very kind and offered to lend her the price of an air ticket to Jakarta: she would arrive before the ship, and would recover her things. She could send him the money by post. 'This is not a problem of the Pelni Lines, but it is a human problem and I am responsible for everything here, even human problems,' he said ironically and kindly, turning to me and giving me a wink of complicity.

Black-rimmed spectacles, a felt peaked cap and gold braid like that of an American admiral, a thin drooping moustache and a wide mouth full of big white teeth, Evert Bintang had sailed to all the corners of the earth. He spoke Dutch, the language of the colonizers, but he had no respect for them. 'They were here for three hundred years, and what did they leave? Palm trees!' he said, pointing to a row of their beautiful crowns against the sky. He also spoke excellent English, and had clear-cut ideas about the women of different countries. The Italians? Splendid. The Spanish? Seductive. The French? Professional. As for Nordic women, however, they were horrible, the lot of them. 'It's the skin . . . that white skin gives me the creeps,' he said.

Given that he helped everyone, could he help me, too? I had a ticket for Jakarta, but I wanted to go in the opposite direction, to Medan. 'No problem,' he said. Turning to the crowd that had gathered to watch the woman's trouble and then my own – dockworkers, passengers, motorcycle-taxi drivers, soldiers and fat policemen with rusty pistols at their hips – he announced: 'This man is not only a guest of the Pelni Lines, he is a guest of our country. So: red carpet!' He mimed unrolling a very long one in front of my feet. Everybody laughed. He took my ticket, called a young assistant, whispered something in his ear and off he went.

I adore these characters – braggarts and ham actors and even scoundrels, but basically warm-hearted. I adore the theatrical aura they create around themselves, the intrigue, the words whispered in the ear of someone who comes and immediately goes, wads of cash passing from hand to hand like stolen goods, and finally the slap on the shoulder, the grin after the booming voice, the rolling eyes and menacing gestures.

Evert Bintang was born in 1939 in north Celebes. He joined the anti-Communist youth and in 1957, with a group of extreme right-wing guerrillas, went into the jungle to fight against the left-wing regime of President Sukarno. In 1962 he was granted amnesty, enrolled in the commandos and was sent first to Irian Jaya to fight the separatists, and then to Celebes 'to root out the Communists', this time by order of the government. 'I was at home there,' he told me. 'I knew the area, I knew every path because I had myself been a guerrilla, and we didn't let a single Communist escape. We caught them, we tied them up and threw them into the sea. We loved our country and we were ready for anything to keep it from falling into the hands of the Communists,' he explained. He had married a woman from Sumatra and this 'mixture', as he called his marriage, had produced 'eight true Indonesians'.

The problem with Indonesia, he said, was that if the central government allowed the people even a little freedom the country would immediately split into ten different republics, because they all want to be independent: the Bataks, the inhabitants of Acheh and of the Moluccas . . . 'And so we'd end up like the Soviet Union or Yugoslavia.'

He was not mistaken. Today's Indonesia is an empire held together and dominated by the Javanese, who hold the key positions in the army and the civil administration. They realize that the strength of Indonesia depends on its remaining united. Hence the military dictatorship, hence the instant brutal use of violence against any dissent or any demand for greater autonomy. Hence the occupation of Timor, the Portuguese territory in the middle of the archipelago, and the repression of the local independence movement. For the Indonesians of the other islands the problem of national cohesion has little importance – they do not see far beyond their own village. But the Javanese are determined to hold the country together, and are relying on time to create a stronger feeling of unity among the people.

Evert Bintang told me he was a Protestant. He came close to my ear and whispered: 'We're a minority, but we've a future! Now that we've saved this country of ours from the Communists we certainly don't want it to fall into the hands of the Islamic fundamentalists!' He seemed ready to pick up his rifle again, to tie up all the fundamentalists and throw them into the sea. 'As Indonesians we believe in the five principles of Pancha Sila, and that is enough for us. The first principle is: 'All Indonesians must believe in God. The second . . .' and here he got stuck. Luckily, in the huddle of people around us there was a boy fresh out of school who mechanically reeled off the rest of the principles: 'Humanism, unity of the Indonesians, democracy and socialism.'

'Right,' said my director, 'even socialism. Yes, because we don't want unrestrained liberalism of the American kind. But the important thing is that the first principle says to believe in God – without saying which God, however. It means that Indonesia is a country with different religions, not only Islam. Not only Islam, do you follow?' he said, with a sinister gleam in his eye. 'We're an archipelago of 13,677 islands, large and small, with 186 million Indonesians who believe in the five principles of Pancha Sila. No way do we want to make Indonesia into an Islamic country, but it must be a great country – a great, very great country indeed!' He reached a peak of fervour. 'And don't forget, foreigner, that the sun rises on our side, that east is east and west is west and never the twain shall meet. You Westerners work a lot with your heads, but you often forget the heart. But we ... well, never mind. The sun rises here and one day we'll rule the world, because we've all we need to do it. We've land, we've people, we've resources.' Then he added, 'Even if we're lazy and stupid!' He laughed. 'Foreigner, look at the sun and you'll understand. In Norway for six months of the year you don't see the sun, not once. We have it twelve hours a day. We have splendid views of the sun: the sun rising, the sun setting. In Norway, nothing, none of all this! The sun will never rise in the west. Never. So remember, foreigner: the future is here!'

The sun, his sun, was preparing one of its splendid picture-postcard sunsets, a flaming sky behind the black silhouettes of the palms. A melancholy Indonesian song, blaring at full volume from speakers on board, announced my ship's arrival: a big, beautiful yellow and white vessel filled to overflowing with people who trundled down the gangplanks in a never-ending stream – beautiful, slim women in brightly coloured sarongs, men in batik shirts and black caps. 'Pinang ... Pinang ... Pinang,' yelled the taxi drivers, motorcyclists and minibus drivers, tugging people by the arm, trying to grab baggage or children out of their hands to get them as customers. Oh, yes, this was the East, all right!

I thought of Singapore, which I had left barely a few days before and which already seemed so far away, as if on another planet. To me this world was beautiful – a world of cardboard boxes tied with string, bundles, embraces, pushing and shoving, problems solved between people and not between computers, with lots of superfluous words and gestures, but with more feelings, fewer laws, fewer rules; a world where a director-patriot-philosopher-murderer at a kiosk on the harbourfront generously offers drinks to all his friends, to his assistants, to a woman who has missed her ship for Jakarta, and to me, a foreigner.

With a fresh ticket in my hand I boarded the ship. I was bound for Medan.

CHAPTER SIXTEEN

Hurray for Ships!

The ship was a real joy: built about thirty years previously in a Hamburg shipyard, it had wooden decks, cabins with portholes, a restaurant, a ballroom, a bar, a mosque and a church. In sum it was a ship the way they used to be, a ship like a little city to explore, to walk from one end to the other, to climb from deck to deck, to stand at the rail watching the horizon, to scan the passengers for an interesting face, for someone to talk to.

We sailed among small deserted islands covered in palm trees. The sky and sea glowed like copper as the last rays of light grazed the earth. The spectacle had something religious about it. Passengers stood on the decks enjoying the beauty of nature gliding past, and with them stood the sailors in blue uniforms, the officers in white, the stewards in black trousers and red jackets with brass buttons, all silent.

Soon it was the hour of prayer. Then dinner-time.

What a wonderful invention, ships! Of course, I am told, they are bound to disappear for 'market reasons', because they no longer pay. That is how our world works, and so we deprive ourselves of one more pleasure. In the end we shall even get rid of women! Inventions of God! Of course, we shall do without them the day we find a way to make children more cheaply in test tubes without waiting nine months, the day we find there is no longer a 'market' for love, and men can stick their willies in a machine electronically programmed to satisfy all desires with no risk of diseases – a machine that will ask nothing for itself, except money.

Hurray for ships! With their puffing and sighing and shuddering as they meet the caress of the waves, the embrace of the sea, ships have a human feel. Let us keep them alive as a token of love, to make the last romantics happy. Let us use them to cure the depressed.

Let us prescribe sea journeys for those who can no longer bear the burden of life, who feel suffocated and see no reason to carry on. Think what we shall save on pills – no more Valium and Prozac!

After dinner I went out on the stern and lay down on the wooden deck looking up at the sky. My gaze lost in infinity, I felt as if thanks to that Hong Kong fortune-teller I was rediscovering not only the pleasure of travel but that of life itself. Gone was the anxiety; no longer did I feel the passing of the days to be fraught with drama. I listened to those who spoke to me and enjoyed what was happening around me; I had leisure to put my impressions in order, to reflect. Time and silence – so necessary, so natural – have by now become luxuries which only a few can afford. That is why depression is on the increase.

In my case it started in Japan, where life was a constant rush, packed with obligations, every relationship difficult and strained. I never had – or thought I never had – a moment to catch my breath; never a moment when I did not feel guilty because of something else I should have been doing. When I got up in the morning I felt the weight of the world on my shoulders; there were days when just seeing the pile of newspapers under my door was enough to make my gorge rise.

In Japan the whole society is in a straitjacket, the people are always playing a part and can never behave naturally. Just being there was oppressive, but I was also paying the price of my bizarre trade, journalism. A foreign correspondent always has to be where there is some drama taking place, and one cannot spend years observing failed revolutions, unsolved crimes, disappointed hopes and intractable problems, and emerge unscathed. Vietnam, Cambodia, Tiananmen – always dead bodies, always people fleeing. Slowly one comes to feel that nothing is of any use, that the time for justice will never come. In the end it seemed to me that words – words used over and over, always describing the same situations, the same massacres, the faces of the dead, the tears of the survivors – had utterly lost their meaning. They had come to sound, every syllable of them, like the rattle of broken crocks.

It was natural to feel depressed in such circumstances, natural for anyone who still has an idea of what life could be and is not. Depression becomes a right when we look around us and see nothing and no one to offer us a spark of inspiration, when the world seems to be sliding into a morass of imbecility and cheap materialism, with no more ideals, no more faiths, no more dreams. One has nothing great to believe in any longer, no mentor to emulate.

Rarely has humanity, as in these times, been without true leaders, guiding lights. Where today do we find a great philosopher, a great painter, writer, sculptor? The few who spring to mind are merely the products of publicity and marketing.

Politics more than any other sphere, especially in the West, is in the hands of mediocrities – thanks precisely to democracy, which by now has become an aberration from the original idea. Once it was a question of voting whether or not to go to war with Sparta, and then going there in person, perhaps to die. For most people today democracy means showing up every four or five years to put a cross on a piece of paper to elect someone who, precisely because he needs to please such numbers, must perforce be average, mediocre and banal – as majorities always are. If a truly exceptional person ever came along – someone with ideas out of the ordinary, with a perspective beyond pleasing everyone with promises of happiness – he or she would never be elected, would never win the vote of the majority.

And art, that short cut to the perception of greatness? Even art no longer helps people to understand the essence of things. Music now seems to be made for the ears, not the soul; painting is often an offence to the eyes; literature, even literature, is increasingly ruled by the laws of the market. Who reads poetry any more? Its exalting power has been clean forgotten! And yet a poem can light a fire in the breast as strong as the fire of love. Better than whisky, better than Valium or Prozac, a poem can lift the spirit, because it raises the vantage point from which we see the world. If you feel lonely you can find more company by reading poetry than by switching on the television.

Angela says that if she could eliminate one of this century's inventions, even before the atomic bomb she would choose television. She is not entirely wrong. Television lowers our capacity for concentration, blunts the passions and impedes reflection, imposing itself as the main – almost the only – vehicle of knowledge. And yet no truth is more illusory than that of television, which transforms every event and every emotion into a spectacle, with the result that no one can be moved any more, or indignant about what is going on. Television has loaded us with huge masses of information, but left us morally ignorant. It distracts us, helps the time pass – but is that what we really want?

The more one looks around, the more one sees that our way of living is becoming more and more senseless. Everyone is running, but where to? And why? Many believe that in this race for material things we are losing our old pleasures. But who has the courage to say: 'Stop! Let's look for another way'? If anyone did, most people – themselves depressed – would take him for a madman. If we were lost in a forest or a desert we would surely start looking for a way out. Why not do the same with this blessed progress, that lengthens our lives, makes us richer, healthier and better-looking, but deep down less and less happy?

It is not surprising that depression has become such a common illness. In a way it is almost heartening – it shows that inside people there is still a yearning for humanity.

At the end of five years in Tokyo, with its incessant noise and crowds, I felt as if I were poisoned, and decided I had to heal myself. After closing up the house and sending the furniture and books to Thailand, I shaved my head and went like a pilgrim to climb Mount Fuji. I wrote my last article on the disquieting character of Japan from the height of that ever less sacred mountain, and then withdrew to a forest refuge in the province of Ibaragi. For a month I had no one to talk to except my dog Baolì, whom I had taken with me. I spent hours reading, listening to the wind in the trees, watching butterflies, enjoying the silence. After years of constantly thinking about the fate of the Vietnamese, the Cambodians, Communism, the Chinese, the threat of Japan, my children's future, problems of family, friends and the world, at last I had time to have time. Nature, marvellous nature, reached out a hand to me and put me back together.

On my return to Europe I went and saw a famous doctor. 'If from time to time the weight of the world should seem too much to bear, take one of these,' he said, and gave me some Prozac. From then on, that packet always travelled with me, along with my passport, chequebook and driving licence. I never once opened it, and with time it became a sort of good-luck charm, like the oil of the *dukun*, or the strip of green paper given me by the shaman in Singapore. Little did I imagine how useful it would be to me one day.

* * *

The ship continued its throbbing, confident course through the dark. As I gazed at the sky and inhaled great lungfuls of fresh night air, I felt as if I were filling myself with stars. If that monster we call depression, which is always there in the background, lying in ambush, had put in an appearance there, it would find no room to enter. Hurray for ships!

Towards midnight we passed Singapore. From afar even that city, so perfect, so proud and so oppressive, was only a vague luminescence on the horizon.

I was the only Westerner on board, and my presence attracted the attention of other passengers. One was an old Chinese man who, on discovering that I spoke his language, took me around to show me off to other amused *hua-ren*. Another was a tall, thin, extroverted Indonesian young man. When he approached me with the usual 'Where are you from?' I quickly countered by asking, 'Tell me, do you believe in the power of the *dukuns*?' Embarrassment, as often happens with Asians, threw him into an almost hysterical burst of laughter.

It took no time to get him to tell me about his experiences. He was the eldest of fifteen brothers and sisters, of whom five had already died of illnesses – 'stomach trouble, fever, asthma'. One day a large sum of money disappeared from the house. The parents suspected a poor boy whom they had recently taken in as an adopted son–cum–servant. The mother and my young friend went to the *dukun*, who set a bowl of water before them. (Like my bowl in Florence when I was a child!) In it, as on a television screen, they saw the youth enter the room and take the money. They confronted him, he confessed and returned the money.

'Couldn't it be that you and your mother projected the image of your suspicions on to the water?' I asked the young man. 'If it had been a stranger, would you have seen him in the water just the same? How does one imagine a stranger?' He was surprised that I did not understand.

At long last I was sailing through the Straits of Malacca, as I had wanted so much to do when I was in Kuala Lumpur. Yet they never looked like real straits: when you saw one shore you did not see the other, and most of the time both were invisible, giving the impression that you were on the open sea.

By the third meal on board I began to hate religious tolerance: as the Muslims eat no pork and the Hindus are vegetarians and the Bataks I know not what, we always had to fill our stomachs with a tasteless cabbage-and-potato soup, big plates of white rice and some small fried fish. The fact that all Indonesians are required to believe in a god, and the many different gods must all be respected, was certainly not conducive to good cuisine on board.

We called on schedule at Belawan on the east coast of Sumatra, the ship's loudspeakers blaring forth at full blast the same melancholy tune they played at every port of call. Moored along the quay were rusty old ships, flying the washed-out flags of unheard-of countries, all there to load the great, stinking wealth of the island: rubber.

From Belawan to the city of Medan is a good twenty miles, which I travelled in a cart pulled by a motorcycle. This time I think my first impressions were right: Sumatra is a rich island, but full of poor people. We passed fertile palm plantations, but alongside them, amid dirt and heaps of plastic bags, were the fetid hovels of the poor devils who worked them. Wherever these people settled, churches sprang up. It intrigued me to find out how many there were, but I soon lost count. There were churches of all denominations. Again, it was a question of market forces: as every Indonesian was now required more or less by law to have a god, merchants had moved in to exploit this new market in souls. There were Baptists, Charismatics, Evangelicals, Seventh-Day Adventists and lots more. As far as the government was concerned, the more missionaries the better: they all do their bit in the fight against Communism.

I stayed in Medan for four days. I wanted to see a few prominent Chinese who, here as elsewhere, held the strings of the economy, but before getting to work I called at the office of the Pelni Lines. I asked the director what had happened to the weekly ship from Medan to Jakarta, the one I had not taken. He looked at me, understandably worried. 'Nothing, sir. Why?'

So the ship had not sunk, and my premonition was wrong. Better so: otherwise fear for the future would have entered my every thought. And yet one still suspects that there might be such a thing as premonition, and when it turns out to be right, once in a thousand times, or ten thousand, or a million, that suspicion is reinforced. To prove the contrary with facts is much simpler, but also less interesting. Is it not the same with prophecy?

While I was travelling, the Sri Lankan president, Ranasinghe Premadasa, was killed by a bomb, probably planted by the Tamil Tigers – the same guerrillas who assassinated the Indian prime minister, Rajiv Gandhi, in 1991. Premadasa was known to have in his retinue some famous astrologers and experts on the occult; the opposition had even accused him in Parliament of relying on their advice to run the affairs of state. Had no one warned him? Had no one put him on his guard? Yes. In a Medan newspaper I read that an astrologer from the countryside – not one of the president's usual crew – had gone to see him and warned him to be very careful between 14 April and the beginning of June. In that period, he said, the president must avoid travelling and appearing in public. The man was right. But what about all the others, the ones Premadasa consulted regularly? And those who at the beginning of the year had forecast health, wealth and happiness for the president? As in roulette: there is always some player who places his bet on the lucky number. But for each round the winner changes.

Medan too was a goldmine – a goldmine for me, that is – a place where I could follow threads leading to many worthwhile stories. In Medan, a Chinese showed me an old photo of the family of Tjong Ah-fei, the man who to all intents and purposes had founded the city. He had arrived, penniless, from China at the end of the last century, and in a short time he owned eight hundred properties, fifteen plantations, a bank, the opium monopoly, and the house which today, though abandoned, is still the most fascinating of the city. In 1908 Tjong Ah-fei married a beautiful Chinese girl of sixteen, and in 1921, after doing great charitable works, building hospitals, schools and a temple, he died. The photo, with the widow in the centre, the children and about twenty relatives in order of seniority, was taken in 1927. In the front row, towering over the Chinese and with a devil-may-care look in his eye, was a young white man.

'And this one, who's he?' I asked.

'An Italian. It's a long story,' said the Chinese. It took me two hours to unravel it. Pietro Maurizio Lungo, born in 1899, was a tennis player, cyclist and racing-car driver who worked as a dancer in a nightclub in Geneva. There he met Tjong Ah-fei's young widow, who took her tubercular children to Switzerland every year for the air, and in 1927 he came to Medan as her 'secretary'. An elegant man of the world, Lungo set the fashion for this provincial city. He introduced cycling to Sumatra and organized the first bicycle races on the island. In 1959 he met a beautiful Javanese woman forty years his junior and married her. To do so he had converted to Islam.

By the time I arrived, Lungo had been dead for some years, but I managed to find his Javanese wife and their two daughters – the eighteen-year-old had just won the title of Miss Medan. They got out old photograph albums, letters and newspaper clippings. I could happily have got lost on the trail of another of those adventurous, footloose Italians who have left their traces all over the world.

The same Chinese who had shown me the photo of Tjong Ah-fei's family told me about a most unusual temple. It is run by a sect of vegetarian virgins, each of whom, to carry on the tradition, adopts two young girls. These virgins read the future – one of them by using the petals of a flower picked in their garden. How could I not go there?

From the road I could not tell that it was a temple. The Chinese in Indonesia have no right to their own identity: they are not allowed to speak their language in public or teach it to their children, they have to take Indonesian names and give up their own, and they are not allowed to display signs with Chinese writing on them. So the gold characters on a large black panel in the Temple of Celestial Fortune were hidden, like everything else, behind a high peripheral wall. Once I was inside, however, it was like being in a corner of old China – clouds of incense, statues of various deities on the altars, courtyards with pots and plants, a papier-mâché tiger with dozens of little candles at its feet, and a sort of oven in which the faithful burn wads of money to show the gods how little they care for material blessings. The money is obviously counterfeit – the gilt-edged banknotes are issued by the 'Bank of Hell' – but the gods are unaware of this. Always practical, my Chinese!

Even the virgins were in the old style, dressed in pink silk pyjamas, with their long hair tied in a bun at the back of the neck. The one who told my fortune sat at a high square table, pale and beautiful. She sent me in to the garden to pick a flower – a sort of large daisy with a yellow centre and white petals – then asked me when and where I was born, and looked at my face and hands. Pulling off the petals one by one and laying them out before her like cards, she announced that if I had not had an operation before I was thirty-eight, I would have one at sixty; that I would live to be over seventy; that I was destined to marry a second time and have a third child, a boy. Perhaps I looked worried, because she added that the second marriage need not be official. I would be able to keep the second woman as a *xiao lao può* – a 'little wife', a concubine. I did not yet know the woman, but I would meet her the following month, in June. There was no doubt about this: the petals said I must have two wives and a second son besides the one I already had and my daughter. (There she hit the mark.)

As for my professional life, I had made a mistaken start. (Quite right – dealing in typewriters at Olivetti certainly suited me less than banging on one.) Only at thirty had I begun really doing what I wanted. (Right again.) And only after thirty-eight had I been success-ful. (Well, yes and no.)

The virgin told me I must be very careful during my fifty-ninth year, because then there would be a great obstacle. (Always that year, when I want to be in Hong Kong to see the end of the colony.) Between sixty-four and sixty-six years of age I must avoid going to dangerous places or war zones. (What the devil made her think that this was a possibility?) In that period, too, there is an obstacle.

On the question of money she repeated what all the others had told me: money slips through my fingers. Her advice was to put a gold ring on my left middle finger. In any case I need not worry, because in my old age I would be rich and would leave plenty of capital and property to my three children. She may have been reading in the petals, but she seemed to be looking at the same pages of the same book which others had read to me already.

She said that for me this was a very lucky year, with many novelties including the 'little wife' I was soon to meet. I was tickled by this beautiful nun who so insisted on my having a second wife, and found myself asking her, 'But couldn't it be you?' She gave a little laugh and ended the interview by apologizing if she had said things that had not pleased me, or anything that was not true. She blessed the petals with a few words and a gesture of the hand, packed them tightly into a piece of fine pink paper and gave it to me as an amulet. I was to go nowhere without it. The taboo? I must be vegetarian. But I could eat fish now and then if I liked.

The next morning as I was having breakfast at the Hotel Dharma Deli, a legacy of the Dutch colonial period, a distinguished-looking Indonesian gentleman sat down next to me. He had come from Jakarta on business. He was an official of the Ministry of Forests – a low-ranking official, he explained. Married? he asked me. For a change I said no, and in this I seemed to him very fortunate. His second wife did nothing but quarrel with the first, and he had had to put her out of the house together with their two children. He had remained with his first wife and three children, but now he missed the others. Who had sent him to me to tell these stories? Was it Heaven, to put me on guard against the 'little wife' I was to meet the following month?

In Medan some countries of the world are represented not by professional diplomats but by honorary consuls, usually old-time residents with a long experience of the place. I was sure I could learn something from them, so I went to see the German consul. He was away, but his secretary suggested some people to see, and made a couple of appointments for me. Finally we got on to the usual subject.

'*Dukuns*? My grandfather was a famous *dukun* in the region of Lake Toba,' said the secretary. 'He was a rajah, a prince. When the revolution against the sultanate reached even here, many other rajahs were slaughtered and their homes burned, but my grandfather was spared because he had used his powers for everyone's good. The people of the village hid him underground and kept him there for days on end. When he died he was 118 years old. He was an expert in black magic, but first and foremost he had a thorough knowledge of forest herbs. My grandmother helped him a lot; she mixed medicines for his patients, and most important she raised ducks . . . but only red ones.'

'Ducks?'

'Yes, because my grandfather's powers came from red ducks. He had to eat at least one a week, and it had to be cooked without anyone tasting it. When he received patients Grandfather always held a wooden stick carved with many figures. We still have that stick in the house. It was the symbol of his powers.'

The secretary's grandfather had had seven wives and eighteen children. Her own father was the eldest son of the first wife, and as such should have inherited the powers of the *dukun*. 'Grandfather, on his death bed, called my father to him and whispered something in his ear, but my father said he was very sorry, he couldn't do it: he had studied, he had converted to Christianity and become a Protestant pastor, he couldn't have anything to do with magic,' she said. 'Grandfather died a very disappointed man at not being able to pass on his secrets.'

The young woman remembered her grandfather's house as a place of great peace and serenity. This was a formula I knew of old – as if there really were a relation between harmony, equilibrium with nature, and the exercise of occult powers. For that, if for nothing else, I felt it was a shame that her father had not wanted to maintain the old tradition on the shores of Lake Toba. Another page ripped out from the book of human knowledge?

From Medan I took a ferry that crossed the Straits of Malacca and set me down in Butterworth, a city on the Malaysian coast across from Penang, and from there I took my beloved old train for Bangkok. It was full of backpackers and those seasoned foreigners – American ex-soldiers, German petty crooks and an assortment of dropouts who survive by running bars with girls for rent – who have to go to the Thai consulate in Penang every three months to renew their 'tourist' visas.

At the end of my compartment – second class, because there is air conditioning in first and you could die of cold – I noticed a monk. He was tall, with the usual orange tunic and shaved head, and a yellow canvas bag over his shoulder. He had dark skin, and from a distance I took him for an Indian. I went and sat next to him, and found that he was in fact a tanned Dutchman. He was thirty-five years old, and had been born in Surinam, where his father was a judge. At sixteen he was sent to Holland to study. He had scarcely arrived when he went through a crisis. 'I came from a world that was poor, with no modern conveniences, where people were relatively happy, and I found myself in a world of wealth and comfort where everyone was unhappy.' This had set him 'on the search path', as he put it: six years meditating in India as a yoga with a 'great teacher', never cutting his hair or beard, wearing nothing but a rag around his waist; then as a Buddhist monk in Sri Lanka with various teachers.

'Buddhism is very well suited to our Western mind,' said Bikku – he chose to be called thus, by the simple name of all monks in Thailand. 'It meets our need for rationality. A principle of Buddhism is: "Don't believe anything you can't prove, don't believe in anything you can't experience yourself." The teachers are important, all of them. The great difference is that the Thai Buddhists only show you the way, you must make it on your own, while the Indian teachers tell you: "Believe, have faith in me and I'll take you to paradise!" And in the end you follow the path sitting on their shoulders.'

Only in a train, with so many hours of travel ahead, with the countryside gliding pleasantly past the windows and a fine sudden tropical storm with bucketing rain you catch by the handful to splash your sweaty face, can you let yourself go like that, and talk without worrying about the time or the apparent absurdity of the conversation.

'Bikku, do you believe in the powers?' I asked him.

'Of course. It's through meditation that one acquires them.' Of this he had no doubts. Through meditation he had managed to cure himself of a throat tumour, he said. From his bag he fished out a small purple book, which in a few pages told the story of a Burmese nurse who was given up for lost by the doctors. She began meditating, and she was cured of cancer. You need only believe, the power of faith does the rest.

Bikku said there is no cure for all illnesses, and that every healer is able to cure only certain diseases. It is the same with the powers. There are masters who can materialize another person's thoughts (you are thirsty, and the master creates a glass of water in your hand), others who know how to talk to plants or to postpone their own death. The teacher of his teacher in Sri Lanka had lived several hundred years, and his own teacher, Ananda Maitreya, was now ninety-seven and could go on living as many years as he cared to, through meditation.

Speaking of powers, Bikku said one must be ultra-careful in developing them. An important role of the teacher is that of guide, because the powers can be used for evil as well as good: they can cure, but also kill. The *bomoh* and the *dukun* use, for black magic, the same powers the monks use on the path of enlightenment.

Bikku, despite his declared need for Western rationality, had become an absolute believer in the way of Oriental mysticism. It seemed to me that he needed to believe it. He, like Chang Choub, had felt the need for a teacher, and had gone a long way to find him. I had the impression that along the way he had somehow lost himself, but that the road home had by now become impossible for him.

Bikku was returning to the small monastery near Hua Hin where he lived. He had been in Malaysia for kidney treatment. Since entering the monastic life he had been constantly ill. I venture to say this was due to the food and the rhythm of life, but he disagreed. His ailments, he said, were a form of purification from the bad *karma* that he had accumulated in his previous lives. Meditation also helped him to draw those evils out and rid himself of them.

Like Chang Choub, despite years of effort, self-denial and hard spiritual exercises, Bikku too seemed to me an unhappy person deep down. I was struck by his story of an experience in the mountains of Nepal, when he had the sensation that his body was dissolving and he was becoming part of everything around him – plants, mountains, grass, air. Then he heard a voice saying to him, 'No. Not yet. Your time has not come.' The memory of that sensation had never left him, he said, and the thought that one day his body would dissolve in that way gave him a great sense of well-being, 'Because the body is like a shoe that's too tight. You can't walk properly and you want to throw it away.'

While Bikku, thin and ailing, was speaking to me in that poetically veiled way of his desire for death, in the corridor two strapping Americans who ran a bar in Pattaya were discussing the problems they had with the girls, and the methods they used to get them to come to work every evening and hand over the right percentage of the money they made from the customers. I joined them, and after two hours I knew enough about the subject to open a bar of my own if need be. I learned that one must hire at least eight girls (they do not all turn up every night, and there is always some client who rents a couple of them for a week); I learned to avoid making mistakes, above all not to pay the girls more than the other bars. I could earn at least two thousand dollars a month. Net! Even after paying off the local police! Where, if not on such a train, would I have had such a lesson in survival?

At dinner-time Bikku only drank some fruit juice, and then went to sleep. I spent the evening in the restaurant car, where the police, the train attendants and my bar owners went on swapping stories about Thai girls. We all drank that lethal mixture of local whisky and soda with ice and lemon which they say eventually makes you go blind, especially the fake one made with methyl alcohol. But how can one tell? One must trust to luck. When I returned to my couchette I left the curtain open to enjoy the breeze. A large moon looked as if it were hung on a nail in the square of the window, as the train rumbled on through the warm night.

I woke early to say goodbye to Bikku, who got off at Hua Hin, 130 miles before Bangkok. Through the pale dawn light I could see the pinnacles of temples, like golden cut-outs against the dark foliage of the palms. High up on a hill I made out the silhouette of the small monastery where Bikku lived.

Another couple of hours, then the train slowed down and began that pleasant clattering over the switches, the weaving and straightening-out that announces the arrival at a main station. Bangkok at long last! Two months had gone by. Two months travelling without planes because of a fortune-teller. Sheer madness, many people already thought. But being taken for a madman amused me more and more.

CHAPTER SEVENTEEN

The *Nagarose*

I have never been able to feel for Somerset Maugham the affection that he inspires in most of his readers. He has always struck me as an excessively English writer, not the slightest bit interested in Asia for its own sake but only as an exotic backdrop to his stories of whites.

It happened by chance — by chance? — that when the car was waiting for me at the gate of Turtle House, my eyes, as I searched in a last-minute dash for a book to read at sea, fell on *The Gentleman in the Parlour*, which was lying on the round Chinese table in the library. It was a first edition which I had bought in Singapore twenty years previously. The book had been attacked by the Bangkok termites, and had just come back after being rebound. I shoved it into the last empty corner of my rucksack and left.

So it was with great emotion, compounded not only of pleasure but also of that uneasiness one always experiences when confronted by a mystery to which one has no key, that when I came to open this book, sitting on a pile of ropes on the afterdeck of a small cargo ship en route from Bangkok to Cambodia, I realized that Maugham was describing the identical voyage, made on a similar ship in 1929.

The book began: 'I have never been able to feel for Charles Lamb the affection that he inspires in most of his readers.' Maugham tells how, on the point of departure, he looks for a book to take along; his eye happens to fall on one with a green cover, and subsequently he begins reading it on board ship . . .

What a bizarre year this was turning out to be for me! And life so splendid once again, so unusual, so full of surprises. Of coincidences?

Maugham had begun his journey in Rangoon, and was bound for Hanoi. And I, where had I begun mine? What was my destination?

And who was there pulling the strings of what happened to me? Because I had a feeling there was someone.

The chain of cause and effect that links human affairs is endless, and that means they remain without a real explanation. I was on that ship as the result of an infinite series of 'becauses', of which it was impossible to establish the first. That is the maddening thing about destiny – and the wonderful thing.

There is always an inexplicable bridge of San Luis Rey, where different people with different stories, coming from different places, meet by chance at the moment when the bridge collapses, to die together in the abyss. But the first step of each of the journeys which end in that assignation cannot be retraced.

In my case, any starting point that I might fix – the fortune-teller in Hong Kong, the escape from death in Cambodia, the decision in Laos, even my own birth – was not it. Perhaps because, when you come down to it, there really is no beginning.

I called out to Leopold, an old friend who had offered to join me in this adventure, and the three of us – Somerset Maugham was by now a powerful presence – celebrated the fact that we were there, enjoying the calm progress of a ship called the *Nagarose*.

I had to be in Cambodia for the elections organized by the United Nations, and luck was on my side. The overland route was difficult and dangerous. The frontier with Thailand was officially closed, and the Khmer Rouge, having decided to boycott the elections, were threatening the road between Poipet and Battambang. The foreigner's only point of entry was the Phnom Penh airport.

One day, however, I had seen a small notice in a Thai newspaper announcing that a ship bound for the Cambodian port of Kompong Som was taking on cargo in Bangkok. I had telephoned: the ship belonged to a young American, a fledgling ship-owner. I invited him to dinner at Turtle House and persuaded him to take me on board. Leopold had joined me enthusiastically.

A fine character, Leopold. Born into an old patrician family, many of whom had given their lives for France, he had been a law student in Paris in 1968, and had 'made revolution'. Frustrated at the way it turned out, he had gone on the road: India, Nepal, Thailand, and then Indochina. I met him in Saigon in 1975, in the garden of the

Hotel Continental, after the city had been taken by the Communists. Of good bearing, elegant, always in a beautifully ironed silk shirt, Leopold was not in Vietnam for the same reasons as the rest of us journalists, businessmen or adventurers. He was an observer of life, and Saigon in 1975 was an ideal place to indulge that passion. Later, after years of wandering, he wanted to prove to himself that he too was capable of doing something. He went to Bangkok, where through a series of coincidences he started a jewellery factory. He gave it a high-sounding French name taken at random from the Paris telephone directory, and it made him a fortune.

'But one can't spend one's life making useless things like jewellery,' he said fifteen years later when we met again. He had decided to make the factory over to the workers as a co-operative, and to devote himself to something else. 'Giving is better than selling,' he said. 'In future if I need anything they'll help me. In Asia gratitude is more binding than any contract.'

Our departure was postponed from day to day. It was raining and the ship could not load its cargo of sugar. Then at last we were told to come to Quay 5 at Tomburi, across the Chao Paya, the great river of Bangkok.

An appointment with a ship is like one with a woman you have spoken to only on the telephone. You go to meet her, all curiosity and with an image in your mind, the product of fantasy, and regularly it fails to match the reality. Small, rusty, haphazardly repainted in light blue and white, her decks filthy and littered with cigarette butts, her Maltese flag blackened by smoke from the funnel and her main mast bent from some encounter with a crane, the *Nagarose* was not as I had imagined her.

Accompanied by a tall and distinguished young sailor who seemed utterly out of place on that old tin can, I stowed my sack in the cabin that had been allocated to us. It was minute, baking hot and with no ventilation. On the door I was surprised to see a portrait of Aung San Suu Kyi, the heroine of the Burmese resistance to the military dictatorship. 'I was one of her bodyguards,' said the young man in excellent English. 'I was in my third year of physics, but when she was arrested I had to flee.' All the crew were Burmese. Many, like him, were former students who had fled to Thailand to escape the repression.

We slipped our moorings at six in the evening. The *Nagarose* had made barely a hundred yards when a glorious girl, wrapped in a beautiful close-fitting sarong, appeared on deck. Making her way to the stern she arranged a garland of jasmine flowers, some strips of coloured silk, sticks of incense and a bunch of orchids. 'It brings luck. It's our protection,' said the captain, also a Burmese. He was a man of forty to fifty years intensely lived, to judge by his face.

The ship glided away, hugging the left bank of the Chao Paya, passing the Naval Academy, several pagodas and a Chinese temple surmounted by a large yellow sculpture in the shape of a coin. Here and there rows of old wooden houses on piles could be seen, each with a ladder from which children were diving in to the water. In the old days, when the river was the main avenue of access to Siam, these were the first sights that greeted travellers before they saw the sparkling roofs of the Royal Palace in the distance.

At nine o'clock we reached the mouth of the river. We dropped our Thai pilot and made for the open sea. Ahead of us lay hundreds of fishing boats with lamps hung on long poles over the dark water. We seemed to be moving towards a city full of lights and life.

Our dining-room consisted of a rough table bolted to the floor and two benches, but the dinner would not have disgraced any restaurant. It was magnificent, like she who had prepared it, the girl we had seen before. She was twenty years old, dark-skinned, with high strong hips, and unusually full-breasted by Thai standards. On her wrist she wore several bracelets, one of which had a little gold bell that supplied a musical accompaniment to all her movements.

The captain had seen her selling T-shirts in a Bangkok market. She had just arrived from the provinces and this was her first job. He asked how much she earned, and offered her a thousand baht (£25) more per month to perform the office of his wife. Done! Then he managed to hire her as the *Nagarose*'s cook. Both seemed happy enough with the arrangement. The 'hired wife' is an old tradition in Thailand, and Leopold and I readily agreed that it was a most civilized one.

We sailed all night among the fishermen's lights. Sleeping below decks was impossible. The ship had been made in Norway, for northern seas, not the tropics. Big pipes belched heat from the engine-room into the cabins, turning them into ovens. You couldn't walk barefoot on the steel-plated floor of the corridor, it was so hot.

Only the big cockroaches scurried happily back and forth. The crew had their bunks below, but the captain slept in a comfortable hammock, hugging our cook and enjoying the cool breeze from the only fan on board.

Leopold and I abandoned our cabin and lay down on the upper deck at the foot of the funnel, but neither of us could sleep straight away. The night, the atmosphere of the ship, and once again the sense of being completely outside the everyday world, had dealt me that exhilarating feeling of freedom which is my drug. To Leopold it dealt a great desire to talk and laugh.

'Just think of that American who says: "I am the owner of the *Nagarose*." He's maybe never set foot on it, and spends all his time in an air-conditioned office sorting out problems of insurance and sugar-loading. And you and me? Here we are enjoying his ship!' said Leopold. The idea that the American had only a piece of paper declaring him to be the ship's owner, while we, without even a ticket, had the run of it, made me laugh too.

'In life one should always be as on this ship: passengers. There is no need to own anything!' he went on, as if to justify his decision to get rid of the factory.

I think it was then that Leopold first spoke to me of John Coleman. 'He's an exceptional man. You must meet him. He's really a great master, and he can teach you to meditate.'

We fell asleep where we were. Now and then, with a change of wind, I felt puffs of smoke blowing over me, but I was too tired to move. I was awakened by the sun.

I spent most of the day on deck. At the stern the ropes were coiled in big rings, forming nests in which a prehistoric bird might have laid its eggs. I stayed there sunbathing and reading Somerset Maugham, sometimes aloud so that Leopold could join in the 'conversation'. I did not spare him the story of how Maugham, when he arrived in Bangkok, went to stay at the Oriental Hotel and had an attack of malaria. The German manageress, rather than have him die there, tried to persuade a doctor to take him away. Poor Maugham! He would be turning in his grave if he could see how today the Oriental boasts of him as one of its illustrious guests, with a suite named after him, all his books, specially bound, in a showcase on the Bamboo

Veranda, and his photograph on the menu with suggestions as to what he might have eaten for breakfast and drunk at sunset.

In the afternoon the heat became unbearable, but it was the rainy season, and at three o'clock the daily storm punctually brought its cool relief. Afterwards the sky was like a vast fresco of blues and blacks and greys, with a few very white clouds, motionless like grandiose monuments.

The ship made slow progress – in fact sometimes it seemed to be motionless. Once the fire alarm suddenly went off, but nobody seemed to get excited. It was caused by an overheated accumulator, and the captain gave orders to reduce the speed even more: three knots at the maximum. We would reach Kompong a day late.

The sea was a desert. The only ship we saw for hours on end was another old freighter with a Burmese crew. Our sailors knew them, and tried to make contact by radio, but no one replied.

'Travel makes sense only if you come back with an answer in your baggage,' said Leopold. 'You've travelled a lot; have you found it?'

For him too the ship was a break, a release from routine. He spent the long empty hours reflecting on matters close to his heart, and I was like the sandbag at which a boxer practises punching. This time the fist hit me hard, because I knew I had not found the answer. Quite the reverse: along the way I had lost even those two or three certainties that I used to think I possessed. Perhaps that was the answer, but I refrained from telling Leopold so. Trying to lighten the tone of the conversation, I said that I travelled because my nature is that of a fugitive: sooner or later I always have to escape from where I am. Leopold was not satisfied.

'We've both spent half our lives in Asia, and we've had some pretty strange experiences,' he said. 'We must have got at least a clue from it all. We can't go home with nothing in our bags but a few yarns to spin, like old sailors.'

I have never thought about that baggage; still less about what to put in to it on the way home. If I ever want to return.

The ship was wheezing painfully, and every breath sounded like her last. Suddenly we heard a loud clashing sound, like stones in a grinder. The long-haired youth in charge of the engine scratched his head and disappeared into the hot belly of the ship. This time it was a pump that had broken down. Fault put right. On we went.

For dinner the beautiful cook had prepared a stew of pigs' trotters, fried fish and vegetables with ginger, and rice. We all ate together except for the two lads who stayed on guard above, scanning the pitch-black sea where not a single light was to be seen. As if the food were not already spicy enough, the Burmese constantly helped themselves to red peppers from an old glass jar. After dinner the youngest sailor prepared little packets of betel for everyone.

The captain realized that betel was not our favourite dessert, so he sent for a bottle of gin and another of lemonade, and we spent the small hours together. For him we were the break, the respite from routine, and he wanted to unburden himself. He was forty-four years old, and had been sailing for twenty. He had been everywhere and had done a bit of everything, from smuggling cigarettes to smuggling electronics. His family were in Rangoon, but he could not go back there: he had taken a stand against the dictatorship and would be arrested. He had chosen the members of the crew one by one, and they were utterly loyal to him. The man looking after the ship's machinery was an engineer, two of the ship-boys were architectural students. Because of the military dictatorship Burma had remained backward and was now treated with contempt, especially by the Thais, he added.

The Thais, he said, think of nothing but money. Even their Buddhism is mercenary. In Burma, on the other hand . . . he put his hand in his shirt to show me his Buddha. Then he noticed that I too had one at my neck and, as is done in these cases, each of us took off his chain and in cupped hands offered it to the other for admiration.

His Buddha had saved him on a number of occasions, and I said the same of mine. Perhaps it was true, but I had never thought about it before. I had it around my neck that time in Poipet when the Khmer Rouge were about to shoot me, but neither then nor afterwards did I make the connection. For me that Buddha was not an amulet, it was a matter of habit, like the watch you automatically put on your wrist every morning. I had had it since 1972. When I first came to Cambodia I had noticed that in battle the soldiers would put the Buddhas they usually wore round their necks in their mouths.

They told me it helped to repel the bullets, and I decided that I needed one too.

I bought a little ivory Buddha and had it mounted by a Chinese goldsmith. It had to be blessed by a monk, and Pran, my interpreter – who later became famous when the story of his life under Pol Pot and his flight into Thailand became the subject of the film *The Killing Fields* – suggested that I go to the head of the most sacred pagoda of Phnom Penh, at the top of the mysterious hill in the middle of the city. He organized the ceremony and fixed the price: I would pay to have a scene from the life of the Enlightened One frescoed on the coffered ceiling which the monks were restoring.

And so one afternoon I found myself sitting on the ground in front of a dozen or so monks who intoned strange litanies designed to protect me.

'From what?' the head of the pagoda asked Pran, between one chant and another.

'They ought to know,' I whispered. Pran translated back and forth, but the monk still did not understand what I wanted to be protected from.

'Well, just tell me, what work does your foreigner do?'

'He's a journalist.'

'Ah. Very good,' exclaimed the monk, as if this finally clarified everything. 'Then he must be protected from fire, water and syphilis.' And he returned energetically to his chanting with the others. The little Buddha was handed back to me, I made the agreed offering, and since then none of those three dangers has troubled me.

But my Buddha also has its taboo: I must take it off when making love. Pran explained to me, however, that 'in urgent cases' it was enough to swing it round to my back by a simple tug of the chain. The important thing was that it should not see!

The beautiful cook began reading some comics in the hammock under the fan. Then, realizing it was hopeless waiting for the captain, she fell asleep. We carried on chatting. After the first bottle of gin the captain wanted to start a revolution to free Burma from the dictators, Leopold wanted to free the world through meditation, and I wanted to take everyone back in history to find the point where we had taken the wrong path.

At last I went to my sleeping place under the funnel. With a rustling sound the ship continued to cleave the phosphorescent waves. The night was extraordinarily dark, and the sky, with millions of stars, seemed to have a depth that I had never seen before. I slept very well until a wonderful smell of incense and fried eggs reached me from the kitchen. The beautiful cook had been the first to get up; she had tidied everything, made her offerings at the little altar, and was now preparing breakfast.

'One day she too will free herself from her slavery to the captain, and we'll find her as a hostess on a Thai International Airlines plane, serving frozen omelettes,' said Leopold. She undoubtedly dreamed of such a future, but I could not wish it for her.

We entered the harbour of Kompong Som one day late. Somerset Maugham, more than half a century before, had taken a fraction of the time to cover the same distance. The beaches were whiter than white. Behind the crests of the palm trees there were no buildings to be seen, and from a distance Cambodia looked like a desert island. The sailors were ready to disembark, having showered and put on clean trousers and shirts. As we came closer we could see the port nestling in a bay, but the motorboat that should have delivered the pilot didn't leave the shore. '*Nagarose* here . . . *Nagarose*, do you read me?' the captain called repeatedly on the radio. Nobody answered. An hour. Two hours. Nothing. The crew got back into their work clothes and returned to their various jobs around the ship.

Stretched out on one of the benches in the dining-room, I read Maugham. On disembarking, he too had gone to Phnom Penh and from there to Angkor. Like so many other visitors he had been especially struck by Ta Prom, the temple that had been left to the jungle. There, in the nature that was reconquering the stones laid by man, he had felt 'the most powerful of all divinities'.

Personally, I have always been more impressed by the temples in which the work of man seems in itself to touch the divine. There are a few places in the world in which one feels proud to be a member of the human race, and one of these is certainly Angkor. Behind its sophisticated, intellectual beauty there is something profoundly simple, something archetypal and natural that reaches the heart without needing to pass through the head. In every stone there is an inherent greatness whose measure remains firmly in the mind.

There is no need to know that for the builders every detail had a particular meaning. One does not need to be a Buddhist or a Hindu in order to understand. You have only to let yourself go, and you feel that somehow Angkor is a place you have been before. 'The ruins of Angkor had already appeared to me in the visions of child-hood, they were already part of my museum,' wrote Pierre Loti in 1901, remembering how, as a child, he had looked out of the window of his home and tried to see those mythical towers.

In 1972, from a window in the Grand Hotel of Siem Reap, I too saw those towers, the towers of Angkor Wat; but I could not reach them. The Khmer Rouge had occupied the whole temple complex, and those grey pinnacles, rising above the green of the forest, were for me an unattainable mirage. The road that runs from the hotel to the temple was cut by a ditch after five miles. That was the front, and to go near it meant to put one's life in the hands of some sniper hidden in a tree.

Eight years later, when I managed to go the last four miles of that road, Angkor seemed to me even more moving, more tragic, more mysterious than I had imagined it. The Pol Pot regime and the Khmer Rouge had just been overthrown by the Vietnamese intervention, and the Cambodians I met, ill and starving, seemed like survivors of a lost and disoriented race that no longer had any connection with the greatness declared by its monuments.

Over the centuries the Khmer people had forgotten Angkor, the great capital built between the ninth and eleventh centuries and abandoned in 1431 after the Siamese devastated it with fire and sword. If it were not for Henri Mouhot, who 'rediscovered' Angkor for the world, and for the Cambodians themselves, the Khmer would not have a history to look back on.

And yet, in that immense complex there was everything. There was life: past and future. Yes, because Angkor was, among many other things, a sort of prophecy in stone left for posterity. Or at least so it seemed to me when I first stood there amid the screeching of monkeys and the chirping of cicadas. That impression has never left me.

I was the only visitor at the time. Accompanying me was Pich Keo, one of the old guides, who had survived the massacres of Pol Pot. Cambodia was a vast field of death, and in a strange way the grandeur of Angkor seemed to reflect the greatness of that tragedy. In one of the great bas-reliefs I saw the same scenes of torture –

people quartered, cut to pieces, impaled, beaten to death, or fed to the crocodiles – as those I had heard of while travelling through the country. The stories told to me by survivors of the death camps were there, carved in stone ten centuries before. A prophecy? A warning? Or simply the recognition of the immutability of life, which is always joy and violence, pleasure and torture? In the bas-reliefs it was so. Next to the scenes of frightful suffering were others of great serenity; beside the terrible executioners were sinuous dancing girls. Orgies of pain and orgies of happiness, all under the great stone smiles, under the half-closed eyes of those mysterious faces in the jungle. I had no doubts: the message of Angkor remained what it had been for centuries. On the lintel of a door, an ancient hand had chiselled a message that Pich Keo translated: 'The wise man knows that life is nothing but a small flame shaken by a violent wind.'

The hours passed. Night fell. From the radio room I heard the voice of one of the crew constantly calling: '*Nagarose* here . . . *Nagarose*, do you read me?' No reply. Not until ten the next morning did the ship's radio pick up an answer. The pilot would come, but not immediately. We must wait. He came on board in the early afternoon, and at four o'clock Leopold and I said goodbye to everyone and disembarked. We were in Cambodia, free to go where we liked . . . but without an entry visa. That would be a problem when we left, I thought. The most urgent problem now was to get to Phnom Penh.

From Kompong Som to the capital is 185 miles. The asphalt road is one of the best in the country, but because most of the supplies pass over it, also the most hazardous. Government soldiers disguised as Khmer Rouge, real Khmer Rouge, and plain bandits lay tree-trunks across the road, sack the trucks and rob the cars. Once in a while, to make sure of being respected, they murder a couple of people.

We went to a hotel in Kompong Som. It had been opened not long before to accommodate officials of the United Nations and all the other organizations involved in the international effort to bring democracy to Cambodia. Our first impression was that democracy, marching to the tune of dollars, was definitely on the advance. Kompong Som, which only a year before had had only a few feeble lamps alight after eight in the evening, was now a *ville lumière*, with several restaurants and bars open until all hours, and a big discotheque where scores of girls flocked from the nearby villages, dressed like dolls and made up like kabuki masks. Prostitution, I have come to learn, is the first sign of liberalization and economic recovery.

My room was right under the dance hall, and I did not fall asleep until one in the morning, when the pounding beat of the music stopped and a cheery crowd – girls for rent or already rented, experts in humanitarian aid, soldiers and international police, businessmen and election observers, all tired and sweaty – filed between two rows of Khmer beggars in old military uniforms, who appealed to their distracted charity with empty hats, amputated legs, arms without hands, and pathetic smiles. The international community, which had come to Cambodia to bring democracy, was finally going to bed.

In Kompong Som the most important United Nations unit was a battalion of the French Foreign Legion. A colonel received us: tall and elegant, with blue eyes and two scars on his cheek that might have been made to measure, self-assured and most civil. On hearing Leopold's unusual surname, he gave him a fixed stare: 'Like the lieutenant of Dien Bien Phu?'

'Yes. My cousin,' replied Leopold. The colonel stood to attention and gave him a smart salute, as if my friend had himself been one of the glorious dead in that battle and one of the Legion's heroes.

He invited us to breakfast, and after a little while he asked us the obvious question: why had we arrived by ship? I told my story, and the colonel observed: 'Too bad you weren't on that helicopter in Siem Reap. The fortune-teller told you: "If you survive an air accident in 1993" . . . Well, then! You should have been in that accident and survived. That way you'd be sure now of living to the age of eighty-four.' He found it very amusing that I had not thought of it before.

He advised us to leave soon for Phnom Penh, as the ambushes usually occurred in the early afternoon. He let us take an interpreter with us, an old Vietnamese whom we had already met at the market and who spoke Chinese, Khmer, English and French. He was a survivor, and had plied his trade as an informer for all the past regimes (except perhaps that of Pol Pot). The Legion gave him $50 a month to make a daily report on the rumours circulating in town. Often, he told us, the report consisted of just three letters: R.A.S., *rien à signaler* (nothing to report).

The old spy was a great help. He found a car with a driver willing to take us to Phnom Penh. For miles and miles the road was deserted, without a single car coming the other way. We sped past the carcasses of cars that had been ambushed. The heat created mirages in the distance, and at times it really seemed that tree-trunks had been laid across the road a few hundred yards ahead, and that armed men were moving about. Our silence was a sign of the fear that each of us kept to himself.

On reaching the outskirts of Phnom Penh we all drew a sigh of relief. 'Mission accomplished: R.A.S.,' said the Vietnamese spy. We burst out laughing.

As we drove past the airport I saw the Thai Airlines plane that flies daily between Bangkok and Phnom Penh coming in to land. I had an idea. Telling the driver to park the car, I took my passport and Leopold's, and went in to the airport. With an air of some importance, waving a UN pass that had expired months before, I mixed with the passengers queuing up at the counter where entry visas were being handed out for $20 a time. I filled in the forms, signed for myself and for Leopold, paid the fee and presented myself at the immigration window.

'And this one?' asked the policeman.

'It's my friend's passport. There he is over there, looking after the luggage,' I said, pointing at the crowd. Thump . . . thump. Two stamps, and in no time I was outside.

And that was how, on 20 May 1993, I arrived in Phnom Penh from Bangkok — officially by plane.

CHAPTER EIGHTEEN

Buddha's Eyelash

In Cambodia I never slept well. There was something in the air, something that haunted me in the silence of night, that hovered around me, that made me stay on guard, and never let me sink into a deep slumber. When I did drop off, it was for a brief, light nap, from which I kept waking to feel that presence again. During the war this had never happened to me. It began when I returned there shortly after the fall of Pol Pot.

What had happened in Cambodia between 1975 and 1979 under the Khmer Rouge regime defies any fantasy of horror – it was more frightful than anything a man could imagine. The whole society was turned upside down, cities were abandoned, pagodas destroyed, religion abolished, and people regularly massacred in a continuous purificatory orgy. A million and a half, perhaps two million Cambodians, a third of the population, were eliminated. I looked for those I had known and found no one. They had all ended up as 'manure for the fields' – because, as the Khmer Rouge said, even the 'counter-revolutionaries', or at least their corpses, must serve some purpose.

I travelled for a month through a tortured land, collecting eyewitness accounts of that folly. The people were so terrorized, so stunned by horror, that often they could not tell me about it, or did not want to. In the countryside I was shown the 'collection centres for the elimination of enemies' – usually former schools – where the traces of torture could still be seen. I saw wells from which you could no longer drink because they were filled with the dead, rice fields where you could not walk without treading on the bones of those who had been clubbed to death on the spot in order to save bullets.

Everywhere new mass graves were being found. There were

survivors who could not bring themselves to get on a boat since they had seen their relatives taken to the middle of a lake and fed to the crocodiles. Others could not climb a tree, because the Khmer Rouge had used trees to test their victims and decide who should live and who should die. Those who could reach the top were considered peasants, who could be employed; the others were intellectuals, to be eliminated.

Since that time Cambodia has never been the same again; the marks of that suffering were everywhere, and the invisible weight of pain which had built up during the four years of Pol Pot filled the air, made every silence oppressive and every night sleepless. Even I could no longer hear the voice of the gecko, the speaking lizard, without counting its cries and asking, as with the petals of a daisy, 'Will I die? . . . I won't die . . . Will I die?' I could no longer see a row of palm trees without thinking that the tallest were those most fertilized with corpses. In Cambodia even nature had lost its comforting innocence.

Leopold and I stayed at the Monorom Hotel in the centre of Phnom Penh. It was hard to find a room. The city was invaded by foreigners: soldiers, bureaucrats, experts in this or that, journalists. After years of ignoring the tragedy of Cambodia, at last the international community had intervened on a massive scale. Not, of course, to punish the murderers or to restore order and a minimum of decency in life. To do that was 'politically impossible': China, which had always supported Pol Pot and the Khmer Rouge, was not willing to abandon its protégés. And so, for little Cambodia, the 'Great Powers' had found one of those solutions that serve to justify any immorality: a compromise. With the Paris Agreements, signed with great pomp in 1991, the massacres were forgotten, executioners and victims were put on the same level, the combatants on both sides were asked to lay down their arms, and their chiefs to stand for election. May the best man win! As if Cambodia in 1993 were the Athens of Pericles.

By the time I had been in Phnom Penh for a few days, I had the impression I was watching a colossal show of folly. In a palace of the 1930s, once the residence of the French governor, the United Nations Transitory Authority in Cambodia (UNTAC) had set up its general headquarters. Every day, standing on a beautiful terrace, a young Frenchman issued information and instructions to the five hundred journalists who had come from all over the world to witness 'the first democratic elections in the history of Cambodia'. An American explained that it was forbidden to photograph voters at the ballot boxes or to ask them who they had voted for as they left the polling station.

On the upper floors, in small offices carved out of the large halls of former times, were other international officials, lawyers and judges borrowed from various countries, and university professors on contract to the UN. They sat at their computers and drew plans for the development and modernization of the country. They drafted a new constitution, wrote laws for the reorganization of the customs services and prepared regulations for the restructuring of the school system and the efficient functioning of hospitals. To hear them talk, one would believe that this was a unique opportunity for Cambodia to get back on its feet, to become a normal country again. The whole world was there to help it.

And on paper that was true. The United Nations had been in Cambodia for more than a year, with a force of twenty-two thousand military and civilian personnel and with $2.5 billion to spend. The trouble was that with all those people and all that money, the UN had not managed to accomplish what the Paris Agreements had defined as the first step in the peace process: to disarm the combatants. The Khmer Rouge had categorically refused to lay down their arms. They carried on ambushing and killing, while their formal chief, Khieu Samphan, Pol Pot's number two, the man who had rationalized genocide, went on living in Phnom Penh and meeting UN representatives and Western ambassadors who all shook his hand and called him 'Your Excellency'.

But the international community could not accept defeat. The object of the whole exercise was the elections. Let there be elections then! Even if all the premises were lacking. The important thing, said the diplomats, was to get the economy started again, to begin the peace process. Surely the Khmer Rouge would join in sooner or later.

The 'international community' – a motley crowd of people of all colours, sizes and languages – seemed to have only one common interest: to receive their daily expenses of $150, what an average Cambodian earned in a year. My impression was that they all wanted

Buddha's Eyelash

to stay in Cambodia at the cost of any compromise. The fate of the Cambodians was not the great priority. For the UN it was to bring their intervention in Cambodia to a satisfactory conclusion so they could go and repeat the operation somewhere else.

But the United Nations, who were they? To judge by the news on the portable radio which I always have with me, the whole world was now in the hands of this omnipresent, wise and just government. The United Nations were in Cambodia, the United Nations had something to say about Iraq, they were going to intervene in the former Yugoslavia and in Africa. They were the first item in every news bulletin.

Then I went outside, on to the streets of Phnom Penh, and the United Nations were Indonesian soldiers (those responsible for the massacre of Dili on the island of Timor) and Thai soldiers (those who had shot at unarmed crowds in the centre of Bangkok) and policemen from various African dictatorships. All of them with blue berets on their heads, bearers of democracy and respect for human rights.

There was one thing the United Nations had achieved: their presence had restored business confidence. House prices in Phnom Penh were as high as in New York, and everywhere new hotels, restaurants, nightclubs and brothels were opening. The peace process had reintroduced that logic of the market economy which knows no principle but that of profit. In the course of a few months Cambodia had become a centre for speculators, mostly Chinese from Bangkok, Kuala Lumpur and Singapore. Thanks to the widespread corruption in the local administrative apparatus, they had laid hands on the country's natural resources and its shadiest traffic, from expired medicines to smuggled cars and precious stones. One businessman – an American this time – was trying to bury in Cambodia the nuclear waste that no other country would touch.

Everywhere big new billboards had appeared: 'Angkor: The Pride of the Nation.' An invitation to visit the temples? Not at all! A new beer. The brewery that made it was financed by the only foreign investment in the industrial sector. Perhaps beer was not what the Cambodians needed most at that juncture, but the economy had its own logic. Like nature. After years and years of wars and massacres, life was returning to triumph over death, but it was doing so in the cruellest and most primitive way: the law of the jungle.

On the pavements of Phnom Penh bands of dirty, famished women and children went about begging. On the increase, too, were the numbers of shiny brand-new Mercedes, with smoked-glass windows at which those wretches vainly tapped with their bony fingers. Peace was rapidly recreating two Cambodias: that of the rich few and that of the poor many; that of the cities and that of the countryside. The situation of the past, the situation that Pol Pot had exploited, was repeating itself. His theory was that the city is corrupt, rotten, and cannot be saved. The only solution is to abandon it and start again from scratch, to return, as he said, to 'the purity of the grain of rice'. According to Pol Pot everything that had come from abroad had bastardized and weakened the Khmers, the true Cambodians. To return to the greatness of Angkor meant cutting all links with the outside world and expunging any foreign presence. Hence the decision to blow up the central bank, leaving wads of dollars fluttering about in the wind; hence the demolition, stone by stone, of the Catholic cathedral; hence the evacuation of cities, symbols of the modernity so detested by the Khmer Rouge.

And now just look at Phnom Penh! Alive and corrupt, risen from the ashes. Seen from the peasants' huts, still infested with mosquitoes and malaria, the city again seemed something to be eliminated, purged; and there were already those, especially among the young, who wanted Pol Pot to return. What was this but madness?

But was it not equally mad of the United Nations to think they could solve the whole Cambodian problem at a stroke with some elections? And were not these officials mad who imagined that with their computers, with new laws and new programmes and plenty of good will, they could, almost like Pol Pot, remake Cambodia?

If the international community had wanted to do something for the Cambodian people, it should have put them under a bell jar for a generation and protected them from their hostile neighbours, the Thais and the Vietnamese, and from the rapacious businessmen who had descended on the country like locusts. It should have helped them first and foremost to live in peace, to rediscover themselves. And then, perhaps, it might have asked them if they preferred a monarchy or a republic, if they preferred the Party of the Cow or the Party of the Snake. Instead of sending experts in constitutional law, economics and communications, the UN should have sent a team of psychoanalysts and psychologists to deal with the ghastly trauma which this people has suffered.

There was a psychiatrist-anthropologist in Phnom Penh, but he was there in a private capacity, with a grant from his university and a video recorder. Maurice Eisenbruch, Australian, forty-three years of age, was convinced, as I was, that the UN, with their massive foreign presence and their logic, were sweeping away what little Khmer culture had miraculously survived the American carpet-bombing and Pol Pot's massacres.

The task that Maurice had set himself was to gather the last remaining traces of that world on its way to extinction. One of the ways of handing down the Khmer tradition was through the *kru*, or wizards, the village healers, and for months he had been travelling around Cambodia, seeking out the few survivors and putting together a sort of manual of their wisdom.

'According to the *krus*,' said Maurice, 'most illnesses are the work of spirits. A newborn infant thrashes around in its cradle? That's because its mother in its previous life is trying to enter its body and carry it away. For the Cambodians spirits are real in the way viruses are for us. Which of us has ever seen the AIDS virus? And yet we believe in it. The truth is that neither we nor they can determine our lives. They call it fate, we call it genetics. But what difference does it make?'

Maurice, speaking as a psychiatrist, would say the Cambodians were victims of a mass trauma. They were still frightened, and they did not know what of. 'Since time doesn't exist for them, they fear the death of years gone by when they saw so many people disappear, and they fear the life of today in which they see themselves as dead people.' According to Maurice not one UN official asked himself what might be the deep-down consequences of the policies being adopted. What would all the election propaganda mean to the Khmers? 'The Khmers are sick,' he said. 'But what doctor has ever prescribed democracy as a cure for the ills of the soul?'

According to Maurice, the tragedy of the UN intervention was that the Khmers would never become modern democratic capitalists: the only ones to profit from the situation would be the Cambodians of Chinese origin. In the countryside, populated by the pure Cambodians, progress would come only in the form of greater exploitation. 'With every new hotel, with every new supermarket that's opened, the Khmers are being pushed another step further from their own civilization.'

I felt that instead of all those blue berets, all those development technicians, the UN would have done better to have sent Cambodia a few experts on ghosts in order to exorcize the ones that made the air so heavy and the nights so sleepless.

The only way of finding Hoc was to go and see him early in the morning. He had a house near the Olympic Market, where his wife ran a little rice shop.

Hoc was a journalist. He had a motorbike, and whenever I went to Phnom Penh he was my taxi driver and interpreter – not only of the language, but also of the politics. Especially the politics. I had a great affection for him: to survive he had had to perform all the somersaults of recent Cambodian history, but in his heart he had remained undefiled.

He was born under Prince Sihanouk, when it was obligatory to be a monarchist; he had studied law at the time when one had to declare oneself republican; he had escaped the killing fields of Pol Pot by pretending to be a Marxist-Leninist peasant. In 1979, when the Vietnamese intervened to put an end to Pol Pot's regime, Hoc had become a pro-Soviet Communist, and had been sent to study in Hanoi and in various Eastern European countries. With the fall of the Berlin Wall and the arrival of the United Nations and all those other international bodies, Hoc, like so many of his colleagues, could have made another tack, could have changed his spots again and found a well-paid job. But no. He remained a member of the party, but free of mind. He kept away from the ever-widening circles of corruption, and for a small salary ran a political weekly.

I found him in his spacious cement room that opened on to the street, and asked him to help me with the story of the election and to find me the best fortune-teller in town. This time I was interested not so much in my own fate – I had already collected enough versions of that – as in the answer to a question that had been spinning in my head since the start of the year: if it is really possible to predict the future, if man does in fact carry inside him the seeds of what lies in wait for him, then Cambodia was the place to prove it. In the course of four years, one person in three had died in this country, most of them violently. Had the fortune-tellers predicted it? Had there been someone somewhere to warn Cambodia of the coming bloodbath? If the palm of one's hand bears a sign that denotes an illness at the age of eighteen and the possibility of a heart attack at fifty-two, what must there have been in the hands of the millions of Cambodians who filled the country's mass graves? If no one had known how to read their future, it meant that whoever claimed to do so was an imposter, that the future was not written in anyone's hand, it was not in the stars. It meant that fate did not exist.

Hoc knew of a fortune-teller behind the Doeun Thkol market whom his wife consulted regularly. We went there in the late afternoon. His house was raised on wooden piles, in a street that was all potholes and mud. We climbed some steep stairs, took off our shoes and sat down to wait on a wide table-bed on the porch.

The fortune-teller was in a dark room lit only by one oil lamp. Written in chalk over the door was: 'Carnal passion, jealousy, violence, drunkenness, intransigence, ambition: if you cannot rid yourself of even one of these ills, you will never be at peace.' It struck me once again that here, as almost always around such people, there was a magnificent peace.

The man was attending to a whole family, and I was intrigued by the respectful way in which Hoc behaved in that house, making the appropriate gestures to the woman who brought us water to drink. He was a Communist, but he was still a Khmer, and to him the fortune-teller was a priest. Like all the Khmers, Hoc believed in the power of amulets. He had a very powerful one himself: a Buddha his mother had given him in 1979, which had protected him in the years of the war against the remains of Pol Pot's army. The taboo this amulet carried was that Hoc must not eat dog meat. Once, out of courtesy towards the Vietnamese military advisers, he had had to taste a bit of their dog stew, and at that very moment the Khmer Rouge attacked the village he was in. It was a miracle that he survived.

I showed him my Buddha, and he asked me how long it was since it had been recharged. Recharged? Yes, amulets lose their force with time and must be recharged. My Buddha had gone without being recharged for over twenty years. According to Hoc it must have 'expired' by now. He knew of a monk in a pagoda not far from the airport who was very good at restoring the force to amulets. 'He's an odd monk. Sometimes he appears as an old man, at other times as a young one.'

The family that had been consulting the fortune-teller came out. It was now the turn of a woman who had come with her daughter, and we sat on the floor behind them. The woman wanted to sell a plot of land, and asked advice on how to proceed. The fortune-teller told her that within five days two women would come and ask her the price, but that it would be hard to conclude the deal because the property had no easy access. That was true enough, the woman said. Most properties have problems of access, I thought.

The woman wanted to know what to expect for the very young daughter kneeling at her side. The man said that for this they would have to return the following week: it is not easy to predict the fate of so young a girl. That struck me as fair: the less past one has, the harder it is to predict one's future. There are no signs; the face is without any history, and the fortune-teller, who is often nothing more than an instinctive psychologist, has little to go by.

Hoc whispered his translation in that delightful Indochinese-French *patois* of his, full of verbs in the infinitive and with much *monsieur* and *madame* instead of 'he' and 'she'. I noticed how interested he was in the whole process. It was the first time he had been there, and the fact that the fortune-teller was the one his wife consulted did much to arouse his curiosity.

The fortune-teller was about sixty. He had managed to escape death by leading the Khmer Rouge to believe he was a rickshaw driver. Sitting in the lotus position against a wall, he asked the date of my birth and which day of the week that was. He wrote down some numbers on a sheet of paper, arranging them in the form of a pyramid, and then, referring to them continually, he began:

'*In the march of your life you should already have died several times. Until the age of twenty-one you had great difficulties both with money and with your health . . .* ' and so on, all the things I knew so well by now, partly true and partly false. Nothing interesting, nothing new, except that this year I would be the victim of a theft: I would lose something very dear to me. Not wanting to offend him, I let him continue.

Then I interrupted to ask him the question I had on my mind: had he ever predicted that Pol Pot would come to power and that so many people would be murdered?

The fortune-teller was surprised. He thought he had misunderstood my question, and Hoc had to translate it for him a second time.

'*No. But nobody back then asked me about anything of the kind.*' That struck me as ridiculous. '*Anyway, it was already all written in the prophecy of Buddha. The Khmers knew it. And it all came true,*' he added.

As we were leaving, the fortune-teller asked Hoc how his wife was. Hoc was stunned. He had given him no more than a couple of snippets of information about himself, if that, and the man had immediately realized who he was. Easy, I said to myself, in a small community, for someone with an eye for detail and the talents of a psychologist to identify various local characters. The rub comes with someone like me, an outsider of a different culture, with different ways of expressing myself and different questions.

'What is this prophecy of Buddha?' I asked Hoc as we put our shoes back on.

'A thing everyone knows, in verses. I can't recall it all that well,' he said. I insisted, and Hoc began to recite with some difficulty, as if he had to dig deep into his memory:

'There are houses,
but none live there.
There are roads,
but no travellers.
There are stairs,
but no one climbs them.
The black crows seem unarmed,
but within the fruit
the worms are there.
Only at Angkor there is feasting,
but of humanity none remain,
save those who stand where lies
the shade of a rain tree.'

Extraordinary! There it all was: the evacuation of Phnom Penh, with the houses and roads left deserted; the Khmer Rouge in their black pyjamas, ostensibly bearing the fruits of peace, but in fact unleashing the massacre; Angkor, the only place not touched by the revolution; and at the end so few survivors that they could all stand in the shade of a large tree.

How far did these verses date back? Hoc had no idea. Before Pol

Pot? He did not remember, and I had a nagging suspicion that they were quite recent, composed *a posteriori* to explain the past.

It was already dark. In nearby houses we could see small fires on which people were preparing supper. We saw some joggers, sweating profusely as they jumped over the puddles: UNTAC officials out for their evening exercise, they passed right under the house of the Khmer fortune-teller. Two worlds, I thought, that will never meet, however they may run.

There was only one person who could give me an authoritative answer to the question of Buddha's prophecy: Olivier de Vernon, a scholar from the École Française de l'Extreme Orient, an expert on the Khmer language and on Buddhism. Olivier had been living in Cambodia for a number of years, and had taken a mission upon himself: to reconstruct the religious memory of the Khmers, which Pol Pot had tried to destroy. He travelled around the country, especially to the pagodas, collecting every banana leaf with writing on it, every old manuscript that had survived the bonfires of the Khmer Rouge. He photographed them and transcribed them on a computer. On the strength of these scraps found here and there, he was reassembling the classics of the tradition. He distributed copies to libraries, pagodas and the Buddhist schools that were reopening.

I found Olivier in his tiny office between the outer wall of the Royal Palace and the Silver Pagoda. The prophecy of Buddha? Of course he knew it! It existed in several versions, he said, and he had found traces of it in different parts of the country. The oldest manuscripts went back about two hundred years, but that did not mean that the prophecy itself could not be far older. Banana leaves do not last long, and one of the traditional tasks of young monks was to make new copies of old texts that were becoming illegible. He had never heard Hoc's rhyme before, but in his opinion it was possibly an updated popular version of the old prophecy, which, he said, ran more or less like this:

'Around the middle of the Buddhist era,' (the five-thousand-year era beginning with the birth of Buddha in 543 BC, so the exact middle would be in 1957) 'a palace of gold and silver will rise at the confluence of the four rivers.' (Where the Mekong and the Bassac rivers meet, forming four branches, Sihanouk had had a casino built.

Subsequently, however, the vicissitudes of politics got in the way and the casino never opened. It has now been turned into the Hotel Cambodiana.) 'After that there will be a devastating war in the land, and the blood of the victims will run as high as the elephant's belly.' (The American war and then the massacres of Pol Pot.) 'Religion will be eliminated.' (Pol Pot banned all Buddhist activities, destroyed the pagodas and killed most of the monks.) 'Then will come a man disguised as a Chinese,' (Sihanouk returned from Peking) 'accompanied by a white elephant with blue tusks.' (The white UN vehicles with the blue berets of the soldiers on board.) 'There will be another brief war, until a monk brings back the sacred scriptures from the Kulen Mountains,' (today one of the bases of the Khmer Rouge) 'and changes the name of the country from Kampuchea' (the Khmer name for Cambodia, meaning '*karma* of pain') 'to Nagar Bankat Puri. Only then will happiness reign, all illnesses disappear, every man have fifty wives and live to the age of 220 years.'

Sure enough, this prophecy seemed exact . . . with hindsight. But even so it was impressive.

The day of the elections began with a heavy and most beautiful downpour. It was Sunday. The Cambodians put on their best clothes and showed up enthusiastically at the polling stations. The atmosphere was festive indeed. Everywhere there were UN soldiers in their blue berets and the uniforms of their different countries; everywhere foreigners directing operations, observing, photographing; everywhere journalists, TV cameras, microphones. The act of voting itself was a novel and entertaining spectacle for the Cambodians. To prevent people from exercising their democratic right more than once, as soon as they had voted they had to dip their right index fingers in an invisible ink which made them glow under a special lamp. This was a piece of magic that left the Cambodians dumbfounded.

Who to vote for? The parties were legion. Each one was represented by a symbol on the voting slip: there was a snake, a cow, the face of Prince Sihanouk, the towers of Angkor.

The Communist Party, still in power, was the first on the list, and it had ordered people to make a good firm cross in the first square. But which was the first? You had only to turn the sheet upside down, and the first became the last. Many were those who stood perplexed in the voting booths, turning the ballot this way and that, unable to make up their minds.

In the end everything turned out for the best, and the world's conscience, especially that of the West, could congratulate itself on another 'triumph of democracy'.

On Prince Sihanouk's return from Peking to become once again the head of state, the Royal Palace had been repainted and refurnished. It was passed off as the seat of Sihanouk's ancestors, though in reality, like all the finest buildings in Phnom Penh, the palace had been built by the French during the colonial period specifically to give the local monarchy a touch of regal pomp.

The famous Silver Pagoda was also of recent date, while the so-called 'crown jewels' consisted of a modest collection of small gifts presented to Cambodia by visitors at the end of the last century. The all-steel Napoleon III Pavilion had been built by the French to celebrate the opening of the Suez Canal. Having served its purpose in Egypt it was sent as a gift to the King of Cambodia, who had had it erected in front of the Throne Hall.

Only the three sacred jewels, symbol of the monarchy's power, were said to be antique; but these had mysteriously disappeared with the departure of the last head of the pro–American republic, General Lon Nol, shortly before the arrival of the Khmer Rouge. One of these jewels was a sword used in divination: whenever the king had to take an important decision, the court fortune-tellers would read heaven's answers to the problems of state in the patterns of rust on the blade.

Thus it was that Sihanouk, on his return to the palace which had seen him first as king, then prime minister and finally prisoner of the Khmer Rouge, found himself without any of the traditional emblems of power. But he did not need them. He had been on the political scene for more than half a century; most Cambodians revered him as the father-god of the nation, and that was enough for him. He reigned with a kingliness that was his own, over this palace furnished with hideous armchairs in fake Empire style, cheap carpets, and a few old portraits of him and his wife Monique which had been foraged from the cellars. Sihanouk had no need of trappings. He felt himself to be the direct heir of all the greatness of Cambodia.

'You're sitting at the table of the kings of Angkor,' I was told while lunching at the palace a day after the elections. The table was a long affair of polished wood, bought in Thailand; but it was true, as Sihanouk observed with pointed irony, that I had been preceded at this table, or another very like it, by such figures as Mitterrand, Tito and General de Gaulle – 'my hero', as Sihanouk called him.

As we ate we were constantly under the eyes of North Korean guards whom Kim Il Sung – 'my great friend' – had loaned him. The conversation was about politics, but I soon managed to introduce the subject of ghosts by telling Sihanouk I had gone to look for André Malraux's in the old Hotel Manolis. In that building on Post Office Square, now rotten and crumbling, the French writer had stayed with his wife at the time of his famous expedition to Angkor, from which he had stolen one of the great carved slabs of stone from the temple of Bantei Serei. He was caught and sentenced to three years' imprisonment, although he never served them.

'Malraux wasn't a thief, he was an art lover,' Sihanouk interrupted me. 'What he did wasn't stealing. It was an amorous abduction!' Sihanouk said his aunt had always refused to shake Malraux's hand on that account, but for him he was a great man.

I asked Sihanouk if any of the court fortune-tellers whom his aunt and his mother used to consult were still alive. I was interested in this tradition, I explained. Sihanouk referred the question to one of the ladies present and she, like all those addressed by him, joined her hands on her breast, bowed her head and whispered the reverential formula '*Pom Cha . . . Pom Cha*'; and my question was lost.

Not that Sihanouk was uninterested in the subject. From the moment he returned to the palace – entering through the 'Gate of Victory' and as first priority going to thank the spirits of his ancestors – he had had to concern himself with the world of the occult as much as that of politics. He had not been back long when there were rumours of a prophecy according to which he would die within a year. To avoid that fate – or so it was said in the markets of Phnom Penh – he had made a pact with the King of the Dead: his life in exchange for those of five thousand young Cambodians, many of whom were to offer themselves voluntarily. The palace had to issue an official communiqué denying both the prophecy and all the rumours that surrounded it. The story had been taken seriously to the point that many young people had begun tying white threads around their wrists to let the King of the Dead know that they did not wish to be among the victims.

Another crisis had been provoked by Buddha's eyebrow. Forty years previously, Sihanouk had brought this precious relic back from his travels in India, where it had been given him by Nehru. The astrologers ruled that the most propitious place to preserve the eyebrow was in front of Phnom Penh's railway station, so Sihanouk had erected a *stupa*, a reliquary, in the middle of the forecourt. But he had a niece, a dancer and magician, who thanks to various premonitory dreams had escaped the Khmer Rouge massacres in which Sihanouk lost fourteen of his children and close relatives. In 1992 this princess 'discovered' that the *stupa* was in the wrong location, that all Cambodia's problems stemmed from the fact that the relic was disrespectfully housed near a dirty and chaotic place like the station, and, worst of all, that it was constantly exposed to the sun. 'As long as Buddha is in the heat the country will burn,' the princess said.

Sihanouk took heed. He had the eyebrow removed and placed in the shade of a great tree at the foot of the hill in the centre of Phnom Penh. He then began work on a great new *stupa*, 150 feet in height, which will change the skyline of the capital. The mysterious hill built by Cambodia's enemies to weigh down the head of the *naga*, symbol of the country's strength, will no longer be the highest point in the city. Sihanouk's new *stupa* will dominate it – thus changing Cambodia's destiny, according to legend.

After lunch, while Sihanouk gave me a tour of the palace and introduced me to Micki, his dog, one of the court ladies asked if I would like to meet the woman who had been the queen mother's fortune-teller. She would come to the palace at five that afternoon. I took my leave of Sihanouk and the Princess Monique, and with much discretion I was taken to wait in a building used by the secretariat.

The fortune-teller was a thin woman with very short hair, a long black silk skirt and white blouse. We sat on the floor around a towel on which she laid out her cards.

'*You're the son of a very rich and powerful family,*' she began, making me think that I might as well leave there and then. She went on for the best part of an hour: at the age of ten years and ten months I had been very ill; a couple of influential people had stolen an idea from me; in October I must beware of two individuals who would try to ruin my reputation, one of them eight years younger than me, the other of my own age. She said that never in my life would I make money, and that if someone offered me a business deal I should stay clear or I would lose everything.

I wanted to thank her and leave, but I could not. From the window I could see Sihanouk walking in the garden with Micki. It would have been terribly embarrassing if he had seen me there after I had formally taken leave of him. In the end I asked the woman if she saw any dangers lying ahead. Yes: between 20 July and 1 August. *'That's the time when you shouldn't cross any borders. But if you really must, then take great care of your travel documents,'* she urged. That was precisely the time when I was planning to leave, overland, for Europe.

Not much remained with me from that fortune-teller, except the fun of sitting at the feet of the woman who in her time, with her chitchat, had influenced the destinies of a court, not to mention the fun of hiding from the king as he walked in the garden with his dog. When I finally managed to escape without being seen through a side door of the palace, I felt as if I had just stepped out of a fairy tale.

One of the haunts where the representatives of the international community met in the evening was 'No Problem', a sort of club-café-restaurant which had opened in an old colonial villa. One evening, sitting next to a table of strangers, all UN officials, I heard someone talking about a German journalist who had been told by a Cambodian fortune-teller not to fly, and who had saved himself at the last minute by not boarding the Russian helicopter that had crashed in Siem Reap. By now the story had a life of its own; it would be told and retold, each time with new details and new additions, and thus would become more and more true.

I spent my last evening in Phnom Penh at the palace. Sihanouk was showing the diplomatic corps the latest product of one of his old hobbies: film-making. The film was a love story between a young man dying of cancer and a nurse. The title seemed designed to exorcize one of the many prophecies that concerned our host: *See Angkor . . . and Die.*

The palace, faintly illuminated by the warm glow of a few torches against the ochre-coloured walls, seemed more and more beautiful and unreal. Sihanouk, on great form, was clutching a microphone and translating the Khmer dialogue into French and English. We were in the small open-air pavilion in front of the Throne Hall. A fresh breeze drifted lightly among the columns. Under the star-studded sky reigned a magnificent, surrealistic peace.

At dawn, Hoc and I left by taxi for Battambang, expecting to reach the Thai border by nightfall. The Khmer Rouge had been relatively quiet and the traffic was running smoothly as far as Poipet. The frontier post was theoretically closed, but we had heard that the UNTAC officials could go to Aranyaprathet in Thailand for shopping or dinner.

In Poipet the taxi set us down in the market square. I instinctively went to see the wall against which the Khmer Rouge had put me in April 1975. I stood there a few minutes in silence, as if it really were somebody's tomb. I thought of the many things that had happened to me since, of the many places I had been, the people I had known, the countless words I had written. I thought of all the things I would not have done had my life ended there – so much, and after all, nothing.

I saw a white car with the UN logo heading towards the border. At the wheel was a young Japanese woman on her way to Aranyaprathet to meet her fiancé. Both she and the military frontier guards thought that I too was from UNTAC, and in a flash I found myself outside Cambodia. I found a car, and during the last couple of hundred miles to Bangkok I slept, without nightmares and without dreams.

CHAPTER NINETEEN

The Destiny of Dogs

The month of June had passed without the prophecy of the virgin of Medan coming true. I had not met my *xiao lao può* – the second 'little wife' she had promised me – or if I had met her I was not aware of it. I had used that month to prepare for my annual trip to Europe. Above all, I had been trying to obtain visas for the different countries whose borders I would have to cross by train. This was no easy task, because some of them, including Vietnam, would like all visitors to arrive at an airport. Only after long explanations and arguments would they concede an overland visa, valid only for the particular frontier post named in the passport.

I spent the last evening choosing what to take with me, knowing that where I was going there would be no trolleys, escalators or porters to make things easier. I had said goodbye to everyone and was already feeling the familiar thrill of beginning a journey, the sense of relief that always fills me when I know that I cannot be reached, that I am not booked or expected anywhere, that I have no commitments except those created by chance. How wonderful it is to mix with a crowd as an ordinary traveller, free from one's own role, from one's self-image, which at times can be a cage as tight as that of the body; to be sure you won't meet anyone with whom you will have to make conversation, and to feel free to send to the devil the first person who tries to start one.

In this mood, with only the weight of a backpack on my shoulders and one piece of hand luggage, I left Turtle House one morning to begin a great journey, one of the longest of my life and one of the slowest: Bangkok to Florence. Though I was heading west, I had to begin by going east. As it was impossible to cross Burma towards India, I had to enter Cambodia and then pass through Vietnam, China, Mongolia, Siberia, and on and on until I reached home.

'Even a journey of ten thousand leagues begins with the first step,' say the Chinese, who have a proverb for every situation. My journey would be about 12,500 miles, but that very first step seemed the most difficult: how could I get to the station in time? Sukhumvit Road was completely choked with traffic; in half an hour my car had moved barely a dozen yards, and there was no hope that the situation would change. I thanked the driver and jumped on the back of a motorcycle-taxi which, by zig-zagging between cars, cutting through narrow side lanes, going the wrong way down one-way streets and often mounting the pavement, got me to the station on time.

The train took five hours to reach Aranyaprathet, speeding through the 'kingdom of smiles' that smiles no more. The Cambodian border was crowded with people pursuing an extremely profitable activity: smuggling. Loaded with bags and bundles, hundreds of Thais and Cambodians went back and forth undisturbed from one country to the other, under the eyes of the soldiers of both sides. I tried to slip through by mixing with the crowd, but my white clothes betrayed me and I was stopped at once: 'No, no, foreigners cannot cross. It is forbidden,' said the soldiers. 'Foreigners must go by plane.' I knew the old refrain, but did not lose heart. In Asia no prohibition is absolute, no rule inflexible; and soon, for a very reasonable price, I was 'smuggled' into Cambodia on the back seat of an 'authorized' car.

Before the war the Cambodian railway line went all the way to Thailand; but with the country in ruins and all its resources up for auction, the tracks from the border have been sold as scrap iron. The train to Phnom Penh now starts from the city of Sisophon. The train? Well, not exactly. Two or three times a week a string of broken-down cattle cars, loaded with contraband and passengers, many sitting on the roof, braves the 206 miles to Phnom Penh. The time of departure is erratic and is never announced in advance, so as to confuse the bandits who regularly attack and loot the train. All it takes is a mine or a tree-trunk on the track; the bandits – or soldiers of the regular army? – open fire, kill one or two luckless passengers to scare the others, grab everything and leave. The news is given at most two lines in the local newspaper. Sometimes not even that.

I settled down among the baskets, bundles and passengers. They were all Khmers with very dark skin, the Khmer of the countryside and the forest, people of another age.

The simple, orderly beauty of the rice fields helped me to shake off the thought of the bandits, but when the train finally entered Phnom Penh I drew a sigh of relief, even though the station presented a disheartening scene, occupied as it was by an army of beggars, homeless people, desperate characters of every kind – those produced in the past by war and those produced now, with equal cruelty, by the free-market economy.

In Phnom Penh I remembered the monk that Hoc had told me about, the one who appeared sometimes as a young man and sometimes as an old one. With the journey I had before me, I thought it would not be a bad idea to 'recharge' the Buddha I wore on my neck. Hoc was not sure if the monk was still alive. His wife had heard that he had been killed by bandits who had robbed his monastery. We decided to try anyway the next morning, very early so that I could go on to Saigon.

It was the sort of dawn that leaves you with an eternal sense of nostalgia: the dark tops of sugar palms against the immaculate pastel sky, the water motionless in the rice fields reflecting the gold of the pagodas. We went on Hoc's motorbike. For the last three miles the road was full of holes, and we laughed at the idea that before 'recharging' the Buddha we were unprotected, and might get stuck out there in the middle of nowhere.

The monk had not been murdered, or at least not his youthful incarnation. More than a magician or guru, he looked to me like a paratroop commander. A strong, muscular man, he ruled his 120 monks with an iron fist.

Hoc explained my case to him: the danger of flying and my Buddha which had not been recharged since 1972. The monk said that for a proper job I should go to seven pagodas and have it recharged by seven monks, but since I did not have time, I should at least offer seven white lotus flowers to the great image of the Enlightened One enthroned in his temple. I did so, reflecting that the number seven has been magic in all cultures and all times: the seven days of the week, the seven dwarfs, the seven fat years and seven lean years, the seven-league boots, and the seven lotus flowers. Even in Cambodia!

The monk told me to lay out not only the Buddha on its chain but all the other objects that I usually carried with me, especially when travelling. These too had to be 'charged' so they would protect me. Meanwhile he went to look after some other patients.

A group of young men, mentally disturbed or epileptic, were waiting for him. Brought from various parts of the country, they stood in a corner of the garden under a big tree, naked except for a *krama* around the waist. Beside them was a goatskin full of water. Some of them were too agitated to stand still, others were trembling. They all knelt down. With both hands the monk picked up a bucket, plunged it into the water, and with all his strength, reciting aloud some prayers or magic formulae, poured it over those wretches: one bucketful after another until the goatskin was empty and the madmen, whether by magic or just from the cold shower, had all quieted down.

Hoc told me the monk was expert in curing the traumas of war, and that all these men were ex-soldiers. Luckily my case was different: a 'half bath' would do, said the monk, but if I preferred I could strip naked like the others. I preferred not. He took the Buddha and the objects I had selected: my old Rolex, my old Leica, and a clip I use to hold money in my pocket. He put them in a silver bowl, scattered some jasmine flowers over them, laid his hands on top, said some prayers and sprinkled them – just as well! – with a few drops of water. But as for me, while I sat on a chair with a crown of flowers in my joined hands, he slowly poured a whole basin of water on my head. It ran in to my collar and down my back. And then another basinful, and another. Chanting the whole time. Instead of concentrating on the blessing, I was thinking the madmen had been much wiser to take their clothes off. By the end of it I was soaking wet.

When the ceremony was over the monk gave me a small image of Buddha on laminated paper. Whenever I felt in danger, he said, I must immediately press it against the centre of my forehead and strike it with the palm of my hand as if to drive it into my head. He demonstrated with a couple of whacks that set my whole brain spinning.

We made our offering and left. As we went out, Hoc translated an inscription I had noticed on one wall of the temple: 'Life is not yours, and it can be taken from you at any moment. Reflect on this.'

* * *

The Cambodian railway, even in colonial times, had never been linked directly with that of Vietnam. The fastest way of getting from Phnom Penh to Ho Chi Minh City, as Saigon is now called, is by car. Dozens of broken-down vehicles, their doors held together by wire, run back and forth between the two cities carrying thousands of carpenters, builders, painters and Vietnamese prostitutes in search of fortune.

For the people of Vietnam, Cambodia has become a sort of El-dorado: the country is underpopulated, the rice fields are fertile, the rivers full of fish, and the cities full of people who have got rich quickly with the traffics of war and then of peace and the United Nations.

At Neak Leung all the cars, lorries and carts had to board a ferry to cross the Mekong. That powerful river, dense with mud and history, cuts Cambodia in two from north to south, and no bridge links the two shores. For centuries the great danger of this country has been that of being torn apart along this natural border: the west bank in the orbit of Thailand, the east in that of Vietnam. Today the demographic pressure of its two neighbours (Thailand with sixty million inhabitants and Vietnam with seventy-one) still threatens Cambodia with its present population of eight million.

The Cambodian border is marked by a great triumphal arch in pink stone, surmounted by a reproduction of the towers of Angkor. From there I had to walk about a hundred yards to reach an unadorned grey cement portal that demarcates the entrance to Viet-nam. Foreigners are very rarely seen there, and my arrival aroused great curiosity, a detailed search of my bags, and an interrogation in which the recurring question was: 'Why didn't you take a plane?'

The difference from Cambodia is immediately striking. After the semi-deserted Khmer plains, Vietnam seems absolutely crammed with people. Everywhere you look you see nothing but people, people, people. People sawing, hammering, welding, sewing, cook-ing, in what looks like an obsessive preoccupation with survival.

The distance from the border to Saigon is forty-six miles – the last, until Europe, that I was to travel by car: another rickety, shud-dering old banger.

On entering Saigon I realized that I was not prepared for the shock. I had thought about all the practicalities, but not about what the return would mean for me. The Saigon that came to meet me was a bedlam of humanity. I felt lost and almost frightened. In that city I had spent some of the most intense moments of my life; but now I felt that the past was something from which I must keep my distance. I began by avoiding the hotels where I had stayed before: the Continental, whose lovely terrace overlooking the square had been modernized with an ugly glass enclosure, and the Majestic, whose view of the river now took in several huge advertising bill-boards. I took a room in a cheap hostel for backpackers. Some of my former friends were dead; Cao Giao, my old interpreter and teacher, had died of cancer after years in the prisons of the Communist regime he had supported. I was unsure whether to look up the others.

I walked for hours and hours at random through the city I had known, without recognizing anything or anyone. It was like walking in hell. At every turn someone tried to attract my attention, holding out a cap, or offering a ride in a rickshaw, a bowl of soup, a girl. Though it had changed its name, Saigon was again the old Saigon: a thoroughly Oriental city full of decadence, corruption and vitality – extremely materialistic, but even dirtier, more chaotic, more indecent and more lascivious than it had been during the war.

Memory can be a wonderful refuge, and if I ever live to be old, as the fortune-tellers predict, I shall enjoy rummaging around in it as in an old family chest forgotten in the attic; but it can also be a terrible burden, especially for others. As I walked, constantly haunted by one recollection or another, I realized how obnoxious I was with this memory of mine: obnoxious to people of my own age, because my memories of the past made it hard for them to lie about promises that were made and not kept; obnoxious to the young, who live in the present and do not want to hear about the world of yesterday. I was obnoxious, but at least harmless. In that war I had lost only some illusions – a loss that was not even visible. But what about those who in that revolution – a failed revolution, like all the others – had lost legs, arms, eyes, or even just their youth, and who now dragged themselves around the streets, begging? They were really obnoxious, with their memories so physical, so visible, such a burden for everyone.

On the morning of 30 April 1975 I had wept with joy to see the tanks of the Liberation Army rolling in to Saigon: the war was over, and the Vietnamese would now be masters of their own country.

When I returned ten years later I had wept with despair when I saw how the Communists had wasted their chance to make Vietnam a truly free country. Now I was even more heartsick. The failure was everywhere, in the life of every one of those who had won the war.

During the war years I had been greatly impressed by the revolutionaries I met: they were poor, tough, dedicated to a cause they believed in. Some of them reminded me of modern saints. In twenty years they too had lost their haloes and had become banal, commonplace figures. One had gone into business with some French Communists in the import–export trade. Another, in his own words (at least he still had some irony), was in the 'yellow slave-trade', recruiting Vietnamese workers for Korean building companies. A man who had been a mythical figure in the Vietcong told me the tragedy was that they had won the war: losers are forced to adapt, to change, and thus to improve; but winners think they have nothing to learn.

The S-10 train for Hanoi is called 'The Reunification Express', but by the looks of it, armoured as it was, it still seemed to belong to the time when the pro-American south and the Communist north were at war. All the windows were fitted with steel grilles to be lowered 'in case of need'.

'What need?' I asked.

'Bandits,' explained one of my fellow travellers, an ex-soldier. With a small tip to the conductress he had managed to smuggle in his young wife to share his bench-bed, so instead of six passengers in the compartment there were seven of us stretched out on those wooden boards, barely padded with soiled straw mats. Above me were another soldier and an old woman who talked all the time; on the opposite side were two strange young men with several days' growth of beard and no baggage.

The train was poor, dirty and primitive, as if it had been hastily cobbled together by a blacksmith. When we left Saigon there was already no water in the toilets. I tried to sleep, but it was not easy. Whenever the train stopped it was besieged by a howling mob of women, children and beggars trying to get on, to sell something or to cadge a handout. Many passengers got off to crowd around the women who carried pots of soup on shoulder-poles to serve on the platform. In the darkness of the stations the flames of their oil lamps flickered like fireflies: a medieval scene. Poor Vietnam! The only modernity this country seems to have known is that of war: weapons, planes and missiles are products of this century; all the rest still belongs to the past.

The night sky was moonless and crowded with stars. Below the black silhouettes of the hills the presence of villages could be guessed from the light of the small fires on which people were cooking their meals. At every station the assault of peddlers and the uproar of bargaining was repeated. In the middle of the night the conductress entered our compartment, made us all get up, and began probing under our straw beds. A passenger had reported the disappearance of his baggage, and they were trying to identify the thief. They did not find him.

Dawn came, fresh and pure as if this were the world's first day, with not a cloud in the sky, the palms and hills mirrored in the still water of the rice paddies. For two days and two nights the train panted northwards up the coast: a long, rattling train of poverty. But for the villages we passed through, the train was a symbol of wealth and abundance. At every station a forest of skinny arms reached up towards the windows. Some of them offered things for sale: ragged youngsters sold hot water from battered aluminium teapots covered with straw, little girls offered pieces of sugarcane. Most offered empty hands. Amputees boarded the train to display their stumps, the blind to chant their singsong tales of woe. The police drove them all out again. They were undoubtedly victims of the war, but nowadays in Vietnam only the dead are honoured as heroes. For them there is a monument in every town and every village. For the lame there is nothing but contempt: they are a burden.

The conductresses and inspectors were also ex-soldiers. They were paid starvation wages (15,000 dong, about $15 a month), but they got by thanks to various dealings which the train made possible. In Saigon they would buy a television set imported from Thailand, and resell it in Hanoi for a $10 profit. The great problem was to have the $700 to buy the first television.

The talkative old woman and the ex-soldier's wife were also doing big business. Both had bankrolls hidden in their blouses, and our compartment slowly filled up with baskets of grapes, skewers of dried fish, and medicinal plants bought at stations along the way. The old woman would haggle over the price until the train started moving, and then, with the goods already in her hand and the vendor running frantically alongside, at the very last moment she would throw out whatever she chose to pay. Take it or leave it! In Hanoi she would resell everything at a handsome profit. The two unshaven young men without baggage had not a penny to invest, and thus no way of making any money.

The landscape outside the windows was movingly beautiful. Equally moving was the human landscape. At mealtimes, when the conductress came with a big pot to ladle soup in to greasy aluminium bowls, a few skinny and grubby children would creep along the corridor waiting for scraps, which they furtively stowed in plastic bags. They would climb in through the windows, and as soon as the train began slowing down they would jump out again, gambling constantly with death.

All through the second night the train ran alongside the sea. From my window, whenever the track curved it looked like a long, luminous snake. At dawn we arrived at Kim Lu. The population was already waiting with bowls of water on which cut-off beer cans floated to serve as cups. This water was for our washing. Dozens of women, children and old people with basins on their heads had been waiting for hours for the train to pass. So had the dogs who dived under the carriages, hoping to snatch a few crumbs of our wealth.

My ex-soldier companion and his wife saw how horrified I was, and explained that we were in the province most heavily bombed by the Americans. Gesturing with their hands, they mimed the B-52s which had dropped their loads of death on the people. The story was twenty years old, but it still seemed to justify the poverty of the present.

When we passed the city of Vinh the loudspeakers announced something I could not understand. My fellow-travellers rushed to lower the grilles over the windows. Why? We were crossing the region where Ho Chi Minh was born, and I wanted to photograph the people in the rice fields. Annoyed, I pushed up the shutter again . . . and was hit in the face by a handful of mud and manure thrown by the peasants. A hail of stones clattered against the train's iron sides and barred windows.

For the heirs of 'Uncle Ho' the train was the symbol of all the promises which the revolution had not kept. Loaded with party bureaucrats, city dwellers and sharp traders, that train of luxury and comfort – as they saw it – passed by, as it had always passed, without a thought for them. The peasants felt betrayed and brushed aside, and now they took out their rage on the train, pelting it with anything they could lay hands on every time it passed.

I realized that for the past two days the Vietnam we saw from the windows had consisted of nothing but huts; that its cafés, its dentists', its bicycle-repair workshops, its tailors' and hairdressers' were all miserable straw roofs supported by four bamboo poles, that the people were all dressed in patched rags and the children were all barefoot.

The train rolled through that misery, whistling all the time. It ran parallel with the main road, crossing it now and then. Often there was not even a level crossing and the whistle was the only warning. A man on a bicycle failed to get off in time and was knocked down. It happened on every trip, they told me. At last the loudspeakers broadcast some patriotic music, and the mellifluous voice of a woman announced that we were arriving at Hanoi. The train slowed as if it had to break a path through the vegetable gardens and houses, bicycles and children, almost grazing shops and street stalls, and entered the city.

The station, built by the French when Vietnam was a colony, looked like a miniature Versailles – a pathetic contrast with the mass of scrawny, dusty people who slept along the tracks and on the stairways.

'Do you know where to find an opium den?' I asked a rickshaw driver in front of the modest hotel for Vietnamese travellers where I was staying. The man shook himself out of his weary lethargy, smiled toothlessly, motioned to me to climb in, and pedalled away through the Hanoi night.

Along the broken pavements, lined with old houses whose yellow paint was now peeling, under beautiful French trees strangled by electric wires and signboards, swarmed the usual poor, pale, sickly humanity in shorts and singlets. Sweaty, tired, angry. Every entry hall was a little shop, every stall sold cigarettes or newspapers or petrol. Two stools at a little table made a café, a pump and a bucket of water was a tyre repair shop. Every conversation looked like a quarrel, and often it was. Everything seemed to be rotting: the roofs, the doors, the walls, the people themselves. The city smelled of mould. I have always liked walking around cemeteries, but the vast graveyard that was Hanoi offered no inspiration. The austere, silent, heroic Hanoi of the war was now just a city of poverty in which everything was for sale. A symbolic journey into the political illusions of my generation would begin from here, where the night again concealed a thousand secrets.

The rickshaw man had his own. He set me down in the city centre, at the end of a dark passage between two large buildings. A young man beckoned to me and led me into the ancient belly of Asia, which the fire of the revolution had wanted to destroy for ever, but which had come back to life. We crossed a court and went up the elegant wooden stairs of an old colonial house, past a row of huts built on what had been its balconies, around the edge of a terrace, along a gallery and up another small wooden stairway. Finally a little door brought us into the shadows of a beautiful room, its walls lined with bamboo, where the air was heavy with the sweet, familiar odour. On a little stove opium was being refined, boiling in an iron bowl. On the floor, covered with straw mats, lay some young people, each with his head against a wooden support. A beautiful, slim woman with very white skin moved from one to the other with the small oil lamp on which the pipe rested. By the light of that little flame I saw the shadows of other bodies stretched out along the wall, the outline of an inlaid frog on the pipe that passed from hand to hand, the tattoo of a butterfly on the naked shoulder of a girl lying beside me.

I spent about an hour enjoying that padded torpor, without memory, without weight, without disappointments. When I left I felt reconciled with the world, and when I saw that the opium den was only a few steps from the head office of the *Party Daily*, I had to smile.

The rickshaw was waiting for me, and I asked the driver to give me a complete tour of the city before returning to the hotel. No other form of transport gives the passenger that majestic ease, that sense of freedom, that cool air in the face. My rickshaw glided along the avenue skirting the Lake of the Found-Again Sword, in front of the Opera Palace and the Old Residence of the French governor, then back towards the river and the narrow lanes of the old city. I felt as if I were on a spaceship floating between past and present, but with no more need to make comparisons or to judge. History and politics had nothing to do with me. I was fascinated only by the life that continued to flower, tenacious, greedy and lascivious, amid that decay. The rickshaw raced through streets that buzzed with vices and temptations, and I took in only some disjointed images: naked bodies in a cone of light, women talking together, laughter and obscene gestures from girls by a door, an occasional rat scurrying along those walls unpainted for decades.

That night – I do not know if I dreamed it, or imagined it with open eyes – I saw myself throw away a dictionary which I had been using until then, and get a new one that contained only positive words. Later, half asleep, for no reason I remembered the words: 'Take great care of your travel documents.' The fortune-teller of Phnom Penh! I went to check my passport and . . . lo and behold, my exit visa from Vietnam was not marked 'surface travel'. The clerks in the Bangkok embassy had forgotten to write 'Friendship Pass', the Chinese frontier post. If I had turned up there I would undoubtedly have been sent back.

Though I was in Hanoi, it was not easy to obtain that visa. It took letters and recommendations, and two more days of waiting.

First the man cut away a little skin just behind the ear, then he plunged in the knife and slowly began probing for the jugular vein. When the blood began to gush out he collected it in a pot. The dog, its jaws tied, hung upside down by its feet from the door frame; it could not even moan. A crowd of children watched, most of them indifferent. The man skinned the dog and cut it up: the breast for stew; the legs, perhaps, to be roasted.

I had gone out for my morning run in the streets near my ramshackle hotel. The sight of that domestic butchering made me very angry. How could death – even a dog's death – be so casual? I remembered a news item I had recently read: in Tokyo they had opened the first astrology shops for domestic animals, especially cats and dogs. In Hanoi they would have no problems of prediction: the destiny of dogs is to end up in the pot! Then I started blaming the dogs. They are supposed to have such a keen sense of smell: why do they not realize that these Vietnamese stink of the dog meat they have eaten for centuries? Why do they not realize that man, whom they think is such a great friend, has no scruples at all?

But the life of dogs went on, in the same absurd way as all other lives. As I ran I saw many other dogs, exactly like the one I had just seen quartered, playing with children, scuffling together and digging in garbage heaps from which the beggars had already helped themselves.

I tried to get the address of a fortune-teller in Hanoi, but it seemed that it would not be easy. I was told that nobody believed in them and that they no longer existed. Then, through the usual chain of chance encounters, I met a woman who knew of one. She herself had consulted her a few weeks before: her son, a drug addict, had taken the family television and gone to sell it at the port of Haiphong to buy heroin. She did not know what to do. 'Wait three days and the boy will return,' the fortune-teller had told her. And he did.

My informant was the quintessence of everything that filled me with despair about Vietnam. She came from a family of great revolutionaries, she had been a guerrilla and had married a fighter. But when the war was over her husband had gone off with a younger woman and left her alone with her son and all his problems.

The fortune-teller lived not far from the Temple of Literature, and we went there by rickshaw. Her house was very modest, little more than a cube of cement. She was a thin woman of about fifty, with an unusual head of curly hair and a warm, friendly manner. She had begun to 'see' after a grave illness. She had been cured by a ray of light that fell on her one day.

We sat on tiny stools around a low table. She did not want to know anything about me. She took both my hands and caressed them, looked into my face, and began speaking in a very sweet, affectionate voice. She asked me in what years my wife and I were born.

'That's bad,' she said. 'For one of the tiger like you it is absolutely not advisable, indeed dangerous, to marry a rabbit.' (The exact opposite of what the Singapore fortune-teller told me.) 'It is your wife who has prevented you from making a good career and being successful. You should leave her, or at least stay far away from her for long periods, otherwise you will have grave problems of health.'

This was interesting. Using the system of interpreting each pronouncement with its own key, I could see some truth in this description of my relationship with Angela: if we had been together for over thirty years, it was partly because we had alternated long periods together with long periods of separation. When the children were small, if I was at home for more than two or three weeks Angela would say, 'Isn't there anything happening in the world? Isn't there an offensive in Vietnam?' And something would happen, and I would leave. I would be away a couple of weeks, and the return would be magnificent for all. Many marriages die simply of boredom. That is certainly not what the fortune-teller meant, but it was what came into my mind.

'*From now to the end of your life you will have no problems. There is only one, linked with the place where you live. Under your house there is a young dead man who prevents you from becoming rich.*' (So that's the reason!) '*Every time you make some money he destroys it. You need to appease his soul with an altar, or to open a new door in the south-west corner of the house, facing India.*'

A beautiful woman of about fifty had come in. She had listened to my 'destiny' and was preparing to present her own case. She said she often came to the fortune-teller, who had become her best friend. A railway engineer, she had studied in China, had been a member of the Party and had married a high official. Her husband had had a lover, and the fortune-teller had helped her with advice. What advice? To have patience, talk with her husband, understand him, confront the problem together. The advice which any friend would give, but which neither her colleagues at work nor those in the Party had offered her. Is this not also one of the functions of fortune-tellers?

Again I found myself sitting among fifty-year-old women with marital problems, before a simple charlatan. But I found the women much more agreeable and interesting than my saintly revolutionaries-turned-businessmen.

I asked the fortune-teller if she saw any risks for me in aeroplanes. No, absolutely none, she said, but I should be very careful about trains. Those were more dangerous for me.

'Too bad. Tomorrow I'm taking the train for Lam Son and the Chinese border,' I said.

'*Not that one! Don't take it. It's a train full of bandits and thieves.*

Often the police themselves pretend to be bandits and rob the passengers.
Change your plans! Go by air! That train is dangerous for you!'

At that point I no longer knew if she was speaking as a fortune-teller or as a passenger of the Vietnamese railways. Either way, I was not going to take her advice.

CHAPTER TWENTY

A Ship in the Desert

There was a big storm during the night, but even that did not relieve the suffocating latrine stench of Hanoi station. Like a defeated army in retreat, hundreds of passengers bivouacked on the stairs, in the corridors and along the platforms, waiting for trains. It was still dark, and every time I asked a policeman or a railway employee where I could find my train he waved his hand in a different direction. Finally a woman led me past rows of parked carriages, in front of trains about to leave, and handed me over to the man in charge of the express for Lam Son.

This train for the Chinese border was even more modest than the one on which I had come from Saigon; the straw mats on the wooden seats were even dirtier and more tattered. My presence created a great problem for the authorities: how should they protect me and my baggage? They decided to evict all the passengers from two rows of seats near the ones reserved for the police, so I would never be out of their sight. Anyone who tried to come near my seat was sent packing. Perhaps the fortune-teller was right after all, and the train was beset by bandits. Or was the danger in the policemen themselves? The court fortune-teller in Phnom Penh had also said that travelling at the end of July would be risky.

The train pulled out of the station at 5.30. It was just dawn, and from my window I saw Hanoi waking up, a desolate panorama of shanties, pigsties, garrets, hovels and patched huts – a vast rabbit warren. Every shack was ringed with barbed wire and walls topped with broken glass, to protect each pauper's miserable patch from the pauper next door.

We crossed the Red River – red with silt that turned the water to mud. Old men were doing exercises on the bridge, in the lanes reserved for bicycles. It was there that the guerrilla fighters entered

274

Hanoi in 1954, and that the defeated French departed. It was on that bridge that a Vietminh soldier gave a French officer a contemptuous kick in the backside.

The train was extremely slow. For hours we chugged through rice fields, and after the greyness of Hanoi I was comforted by their orderly calm and their age-old green beauty. At one station a man with a bamboo water-pipe boarded the train. He had a basket containing an oil lamp, a teapot and two small glasses. You put a pinch of tobacco in the pipe, you inhale, you hear the water gurgling as the smoke passes through it, you breathe deeply and you remain in a daze. It is a bit like fainting, but the little glass of tea, strong and bitter, restores you.

Two boys caught riding without tickets were brought to sit next to me, handcuffed to the seat, and slapped by the policemen. One of them cried, but the other was stonily defiant as if he meant to get his own back some other time.

At the Dong Mo station the train stopped for half an hour to give everyone time to eat at stalls on the platform. When it started again the track led up a mountain. The train climbed so slowly that some youngsters were able to get off, drink from a fountain and jump on again. The mountains were wooded and damp. This was the strip of land that the Chinese occupied in 1979 to punish Vietnam for invading Cambodia and overthrowing Pol Pot. When they withdrew they destroyed everything in their path. In former times the line crossed the border and linked up with the Chinese railway system, but during the incursions the Chinese ripped up and carted away the last few miles of track, so when the train reached Dong Dan it could go no further. It had taken us exactly eight hours to travel the hundred miles from Hanoi.

I covered the last miles to the border on the back of a moped. The Vietnamese officials gave me a thorough going-over. The customs officers insisted on searching my rucksack, and the police, arrogant and rude, examined my overland visa with a magnifying glass.

The border posts of Vietnam and China are a little over half a mile apart. The road runs uphill through a dense wood, and I walked alone towards China, sweating, with the trepidation one feels when going to meet a beloved that one has not seen for a long time. Again the excitement of crossing a frontier that I could see and feel physically; again the joy of arriving in a different country, a joy I felt I had earned with the effort of walking slowly towards one of its passes. I rounded a curve, looked up, and there was China – its history, its culture, its greatness – in the shape of a grand old fortress whose high, studded wooden door bore three elegant characters: 'Friendship Pass'. All around was a sober, ancient stillness. I felt a strong emotion, like coming home. The contrast could not be more explicit. I had left behind a poor, hard-bitten, stubborn little country, and was now entering a majestic empire, confident and full of itself.

This old, gigantic empire still called itself socialist, but by now even China seemed to know only one god. '*Qian*' was the first word that greeted me; *qian*, money, was the word I heard in every conversation during the five days I spent crossing China from south to north. The customs officers at Friendship Pass quarrelled with the Liberation Army men for the privilege of changing my dollars on the black market. Passengers on the minibus that took me to the first railway station offered me, in exchange for *qian*, tiny monkeys, fat snakes and other rare jungle animals, most of them no doubt in the Red Book of endangered species. I didn't buy any and they all travelled on, in their bamboo cages, towards the cooking pots of the great restaurants of southern China.

A small local train took me to Nanning. From there the tracks apparently continued without interruption to Europe, to Florence. One had only to buy a ticket.

Until a few years ago foreigners in China were privileged, treated as guests of honour. Their tickets were sold at special windows. Today it is no longer so. 'Foreigners? In the queue like everyone else!' I was ordered by the first railway employee I turned to at Nanning station. A few thousand people crowded before tiny hatches protected by steel gratings. Hefty policemen armed with electric batons kept the surging, sweaty, quarrelsome crowd at bay. Everyone was trying to find a way to jump the queue, to claim some privilege. When an army officer pushed in front of me I told him off in Maoist style, reminding him that the meaning of his uniform was to serve the people. Everybody laughed, as if that famous phrase of Mao's, with which generations of Chinese had been brought up, had become a joke. But it worked, and the poor fellow beat a retreat.

It took me three hours to buy my ticket – time to experience a
hostility which I had never before felt in China. The impatience
between foreigners and Chinese is mutual, and in the Chinese it is
now mixed with envy, anger, and an ever less concealed racial aspiration to settle old scores with outsiders.

Nanning is a southern Chinese city in full expansion. Its skyscrapers
mimic those of Hong Kong. Luxurious new hotels, sparkling restaurants, nightclubs and massage parlours are the oases of a new
privileged class who move about in Mercedes, escorted by bodyguards and with portable phones glued to their ears.

From Nanning to Xian is 1500 miles, and the train journey took
two days and two nights. The ticket I had managed to get was valid
only for the 'hard seats', but the head conductor was a self-styled
'collector of foreign banknotes', and by contributing a few dollars
to his collection I managed to get a couchette.

The train was chock-full, but at every station more masses of thin,
dirty people, loaded with baggage, threw themselves at the doors
and tried to get on. In Mao's day a Chinese who wanted to travel
needed a special permit from the Party Secretary of his work unit.
Today anyone is free to go where he likes, but with that freedom
goes an absence of protection. The pressure of ideology has disappeared, and no other system of values or social norms has taken
its place. Everywhere one sees a progressive lapse into anarchy. People
with *qian* are increasingly powerful and aggressive, while those without it are more and more defenceless.

The train itself was a perfect illustration of this change. Gone are
the days when the teapots, even those of the 'hard' compartments,
were constantly refilled with boiling water, when the corridors were
swept regularly and women employees with pigtails jumped off at
each stop to wipe the door handles. On my train nobody took care
of anything. As the hours and days went by, the smell from the
kitchens grew more and more similar to that of the toilets, outside
which there was always an impatient, noisy queue of people banging
on the doors.

As we passed through the Guilin region I saw the famous mountains, but what struck me most, as in Vietnam, were the rice fields
and the accumulated labour embodied in them. Everywhere I go,
agriculture gives me a sense of strength; I have the impression that
these countries hold together because the peasants hold out. Mao

regimented them and involved them in politics; his successors will have quite a task to keep them at bay.

Xian announced itself with a yellowish cloud of dust and smog. On the walls of the houses along the tracks, where once you could read the latest political slogans, were big posters urging you to buy cigarettes, wine, motorcycles and beauty creams. The city appeared to be seething with activity. The minute I stepped out of the station I was accosted by a young girl in a mini-skirt.

'My name is Milly,' she said in English. 'Do you want sex?'

'Sex? Where?'

'Over there, in the Liberation Hotel.'

Smiling women, plastered with make-up, touted for business in dark corners. Young men with megaphones invited passers-by into their 'video halls'. Never in the five years I lived in China had I felt so much like an outsider, so insecure, so in danger of being attacked and robbed, as I did then.

To get from Xian to Lanzhou I took train No. 44, famous for the mafia that controls it. The 'Chief of Chiefs' was sitting in the restaurant car. I introduced myself and explained my problem: 'I have a ticket for the hard seats, but as you see I am tall, and I would like to stretch out to sleep.' No problem: for fifty yuan I obtained a place in the 'soft' carriage. As he also controlled the kitchen, for a couple of extra dollars I also enjoyed a good dinner, served most exceptionally on a white tablecloth rather than the usual plastic ones, sticky with the remains of previous meals. However, shortly afterwards, one of my cameras disappeared. Part of the tip? No use talking to the police. They might have been the ones who took it.

Or was this the robbery I had been told to expect? 'This year you will be the victim of a theft. You will lose something very dear to you,' the fortune-teller of Phnom Penh had said. He had not predicted the massacre of one or two million people in his country, but he had predicted the theft of one of my cameras on a Chinese train! Still, if I wanted to rhyme fact with prophecy, this was made to order. After all, I do not remember having suffered another theft in my whole life.

Gradually, as the train rattled along northwards, I slowly forgot the new, vulgar, aggressive chaos of the cities and rediscovered the ancient, soul-restoring order of nature, worked for thousands of years by man. We crossed Gansu, one of the most backward regions of the country. The earth was yellow, the fields small, the donkeys thin, and the peasants, as always, bent to work. This was still the old, poor China which does not make news, which does not have impressive rates of development and where no one goes to invest. On the walls of the mud houses you could still read revolutionary slogans, and red flags still fluttered on the roofs. Seen from the train window, this was a China in which Mao might still have been alive: men and women still wore blue trousers and jackets, and the streets were swarming with bicycles. It was as if Deng Xiaoping's reforms had never reached these parts.

How long can it all last? My two travelling companions were sure that soon the contradictions would explode. One of them, a major in the Liberation Army, spoke of a possible civil war: province against province, the coastal regions against the interior, peasants against city dwellers. He was not the only one in the army to think that way, he said. The other man was an old Party cadre, now retired. In his opinion the whole system established by the Communists after 1949 was about to collapse. 'The teachers go to the market instead of to school because they earn more by petty trading than teaching. The policemen no longer catch thieves because they themselves have become gangsters. How can a country go on like this?' He spoke loudly enough for all to hear. Such freedom of speech would have been unimaginable just a few years ago. 'The only way of preventing anarchy,' he concluded, 'is for the army and the security forces to take the country in hand and reimpose order by force.' China, he believed, would soon become a fascist country. The major seemed to agree.

For a whole afternoon the train ran through the Gobi desert, and then for a whole day alongside the Yellow River. The natural environment was very poor and wild, but man had tamed it and made it bear fruit. An endless line of electricity poles stretched to the horizon; for hundreds of miles the railway was protected by wide borders of tenacious grass planted to keep the sand from burying the tracks. Everywhere I saw dikes, bridges, irrigation canals, and incredibly long palisades of green poplars, planted to defend distant Peking from the murderous dust storms. All these works were realized with the collective labour of the last forty years. Who will carry out such projects in the future?

At Huhehot, where my train turned east towards Peking, I got off to take the north-bound express train to Mongolia.

I stayed in Huhehot for a day and a night: time to wash my clothes, grimy from the journey, and to sleep in a real bed. Time to walk, not in a narrow corridor but in the streets of a city full of people, bicycles, cars, old carts pulled by donkeys and others pulled by men. I listened attentively to the sounds, comparing them with those I remembered from the past. I still constantly heard that word 'qian' which had greeted me on my arrival in China. A man at a market stall kept shouting it as he displayed a pair of women's underpants. I did not understand why, and went to look: they were special panties with a secret pocket in the front in which to hide money.

When the station windows opened at six in the morning the tickets were already sold out. I paid double price for one on the black market, and climbed aboard the express for Ulan Bator.

At last a train where one could walk in the corridors, and use the toilets without people constantly banging on the door. The few passengers were mostly Mongolian, and I enjoyed watching their manoeuvres. One took a screwdriver out of his trousers, opened the ceiling of the compartment and shoved in a cardboard carton; another, with a long iron rod, started fishing in the belly of the train through a small trapdoor in the corridor. I had heard of a Mongolian drug route from Yunnan to southern China and Ulan Bator, then across Siberia and Poland to Germany. Was I observing its couriers?

There were very few Chinese on the train. They have no reason to go to Mongolia, where they are still feared and viewed with hostility. Mongolia is vast, but with only 2.5 million inhabitants it naturally feels threatened by the gross overpopulation of China. As the descendants of Genghis Khan see it, the Chinese have already seized a big slice of what was once their country – the province of Inner Mongolia, whose capital is Huhehot. It was as a defence against Peking that the Mongolian Republic chose to become a satellite state of the Soviet Union.

Until a few decades ago the Mongols were a nomadic people, and anything modern they have today is copied from the Soviet Union. Even the gauge of their railway tracks is a metre and a half, like that in the USSR. For that reason my whole train was taken to a shed at Erliang, the last Chinese station, and the Chinese wheel trucks were replaced with wider ones of the Soviet type. The operation took five hours, which the Chinese turned to account by selling mountains of merchandise to the Mongolians. In the centre of Erliang they had set up a big market where all the main Chinese consumer goods were on display. The Mongolians filled their sacks with clothes and food. Bottles of beer were sold in clusters of ten, tied together with plastic cord. When the train started again it was more a goods train than a passenger train.

China ended symbolically with an imposing triumphal arch and a turret with a big red star. The low barbed-wire fence that marked the border was lost in the green, deserted plain. As soon as we crossed the border the Mongolian passengers began making merry. They were home, and celebrated with one bottle of beer after another. When a bottle was empty they threw it out the window, and the night crackled with the continuous sound of glass breaking on the tracks. In the silver light of the moon, the infinite expanse of the prairie was like a quiet sea, and the train like a ship. Now and then we stopped at places that seemed to consist of just a couple of houses. I seldom saw a human figure, but in the night we passed great herds of horses and oxen, and hundreds of camels.

The sun rose on a monotonous green plain that stretched as far as the eye could see. It began to play with the train, casting shadows that grew longer and shorter, as if in a distorting mirror, as they snaked along beside us. That enormous space, without a soul in it, was a great relief after China – always so suffocatingly full of humanity. The horizon was a slender thread of gold in the distance. Nothing else could be seen, absolutely nothing but the immense green surface. It was not the jade green of the rice fields or the dense dark green of a jungle, but a pale, lifeless green. Not a hill, not a river, not even the distant form of a mountain, no point of reference but the track itself and the endless thousands of electricity poles alongside it, all exactly the same. What does this monotony do to the mind? People who live, reproduce and die in this universe which is all the same, what can they dream of if not demons?

Meeting the Mongolians as a group for the first time, I found it hard to recognize in them the progeny of those conquerors who put half the world to fire and sword, and who governed China for over three hundred years. Only in their physical beauty was there still a suggestion of greatness.

Entering Mongolia, the train had lost its identity as a modern machine and become like a caravan, with no timetables and no need for punctuality. Now and then it stopped for no apparent reason but to let a passenger drop in on a relative in a nearby *yurt*. At sunset on the second day we stopped for two hours to wait for a train coming the other way. All the passengers got off to watch the flaming orb of the sun as it sank beneath the horizon, and people and dogs came out of the four houses at the nearby 'station' to see what was going on.

I had been longing to arrive in Ulan Bator of the steppes, but as we approached I saw in the distance not the golden roofs of its famous Lamaist temples but the smoke of its socialist chimneys. Our entry into the station, eight hours behind schedule, was like a party. Relatives and friends helped the passengers unload their enormous sacks and boxes of Chinese goods and the few bottles of beer left over.

At last we were there! Yes, *we* were there, for I had not come to Ulan Bator alone.

CHAPTER TWENTY-ONE

With my Friend the Ghost

He had been with me for years without my realizing it. Then one day, by chance – the chance that seems to rule every moment of existence – I noticed him. I became fascinated by his story, and I promised him that together we would go to Ulan Bator. For me it would be the first time, but he had been there long ago when the city was called Urga; he would be my guide. He had passed through the city while fleeing from his enemies, struggling to reach freedom, with death always lying in ambush, and in Urga he had had the strangest experiences of his life. Afterwards he had continued his journey and finally reached what he thought he desired, then spent years of fame and banality waiting to die. But isn't life always like that? You go running after something with high hopes, and then once you get it you find it is never as good as the running and hoping. Even in my quest for fortune-tellers, it was the search that meant the most to me.

Ferdinand Ossendowski, born in Poland at the end of the nine-teenth century, was an officer in the Russo–Japanese war and pro-fessor of industrial geography at St Petersburg University. He had ended up as a mining engineer in Krasnoyarsk, deep in Siberia. In the winter of 1920 the Bolsheviks were advancing in that region. Knowing himself to be on their blacklist, he fled. At first he headed south, hoping to reach India via Tibet; then he turned east and zig-zagged through Mongolia towards Peking. Throughout Asia it was a time of upheaval, with armies pursuing each other and bandits terrorizing the populace. Ossendowski's flight lasted nearly two years, during which he was constantly involved in battles and ambushes, and his life was always in danger. On one occasion his death was announced, his papers having been found on a corpse half devoured by wolves in a forest. But Ossendowski himself had killed the man, a Bolshevik commissar, and exchanged documents to assume a new identity and thus fool his pursuers.

That epic flight through one of the most mysterious regions on earth, over the mountains and plains of 'the land of demons', as Mongolia was then called, against the background of the Russian civil war and the fighting in the heart of Asia, led to Ossendowski being called 'the Robinson Crusoe of the twentieth century'. The story of his adventures, published in New York in 1922 with the title *Beasts, Men and Gods*, became a best-seller.

I had bought an old copy of that book for £2 during one of my summer visits to London, and for years it had languished unread on the shelves at home. Then one day, at the beginning of my flightless year, I was attracted by the title and began thumbing through the pages. I read how in May 1921 Ossendowski met Baron Ungern von Sternberg and travelled with him to Urga. He was present when Ungern was told by two different fortune-tellers on a single night – a lama in the Temple of the Prophecies using dice, and a woman burning bones in a fire – that he had only 130 days to live. And in fact at the end of September Ungern was betrayed by some of his officers and handed over to the Bolsheviks, who killed him. Exactly how and when he died has never been clear, but it was around the 130th day after the prophecy, and his death must have been horrible, as predicted.

Ungern was a strange, controversial figure. A former officer in the Russian navy, born into an old aristocratic Baltic family whose forebears included knights and crusaders, pirates and brigands, he had converted to Buddhism and become one of the fiercest and most notorious warriors against the Red Army as it moved east. Ungern was sure that the Bolshevik revolution was the 'Great Curse' foretold by certain seers, and that the war between whites and reds was the clash between the forces of Good and Evil forecast by several religions. He saw himself as a man of destiny; obsessed by his mission to save humanity from the 'depravity of the revolution', he threw himself into the fight with a determination and cruelty that made him famous. His troops were a motley horde of Russians and Mongolians, visionary idealists and psychopathic murderers; when they passed through a village or town, anyone suspected of Communist sympathies ended up, at best, hanged from a lamp-post.

In Bolshevik propaganda Ungern was portrayed as a monster, and perhaps he was; but to the old Mongols he was a hero, a new Genghis Khan, the reincarnation of the God of War – because, among other things, he fought to preserve Mongolia as an independent republic, not a satellite of either Peking or Moscow as it later became.

Ossendowski depicts Ungern as a tragic figure who bravely accepted the prophecy of his death, steeped as he was in Mongolian mysteries and legends. For Ossendowski too these were a source of endless fascination. He writes of an old lama who caused his wife, who had remained in Europe, to appear before him; and of another who resuscitated a man who had just been beaten to death. Ossendowski, a scientist and member of the French Academy, explains these phenomena as the products of hypnosis practised on him and his companions, who saw exactly the same things. But how is one to explain the fact that the landlord of a Mongolian inn where he stopped one night, on reading Ossendowski's future in a sheep's bone burnt in the fire, warned him of an ambush from which, thanks to that prophecy, he managed to escape?

And so it was that I promised to go to Ulan Bator with him. I wanted to search for the traces of that story, to find a link with those fortune-tellers of long ago. I travelled light as always, but I had with me my yellowed old copy of *Beasts, Men and Gods*. On the train I read and reread the book, and it was under my arm as I got off at Ulan Bator. I stayed there a week, and we were not apart for a moment. Ossendowski described places he had known long before, and together we revisited them. He spoke of prophetic rites, and together we looked for someone to perform them anew.

It was not easy. Over seventy years had passed, and the revolution against which Ungern had fought in vain had changed the face of the land and the people. Urga, when Ossendowski was there in 1921, was like a vast encampment lying on the banks of the Tola river among densely wooded hills and mountains. It was the seat of Hutuktu Bodgo Khan, the Living Buddha – the third most important reincarnation of Tibetan Buddhism, after the Dalai Lama and the Tashi Lama. The Urga of those days no longer exists. The hills and mountains are bare. Of the hundred or more monasteries, only three survive – and these are officially classified as 'museums'. Of Urga's thirty thousand gold and bronze Buddhas only a few dozen remain, no longer on the altars but locked in glass cases. Even the gigantic gilt bronze Buddha who sat in the lotus position at the centre of the ancient Gandan Temple on the high plateau is gone: he was donated to the Soviet motherland to make cannons in the Second World War. Ossendowski tells us that Ungern never liked that statue: it was of recent origin, and its face had not come to wear those tears of sorrow and joy which only time can bestow. How right he was, that bloodthirsty but cultured baron! New things lack that ballast of history which always adds to the pathos of an object.

The sixty thousand lamas of Ossendowski's day have dwindled to about a hundred. Some of them are old men, recently returned thanks to the new policy of liberalization; the others are young novices. Even trying to find the old places is problematic. The city has been completely rearranged, the names are different and the new generations have no memory of the past. All they have been told is that the past was the cause of Mongolia's underdevelopment and backwardness. The revolution had taught the Mongols to despise their past, to be ashamed of their ancient culture and to dream of becoming 'modern', like the Soviets who had arrived with the revolution. The symbol of modernity was the city, and so even the Mongols – nomads, shepherds, men of the steppe used to living in *yurts* – had to have one. The Soviets prescribed a city of enormously wide streets lined with massive yellow and white buildings, a mausoleum for the national hero – in the same marble, the same shape and orientation as Lenin's tomb in Moscow – a museum, public buildings full of columns supporting nothing, a Palace of Culture like a sort of Parthenon on top of a Colosseum, blocks of flats lined up row upon row, and supermarkets with empty windows and shelves, exactly the same as the Soviet ones.

On my first morning in Ulan Bator, I went out at dawn for my daily run. In the huge Red Square with its grandiose socialist buildings a lone uniformed road-sweeper was scratching away at the vast emptiness. Suddenly from behind one of the numerous columns on the deserted square, a man appeared before me and said in perfect English: 'Please don't laugh, but would you like to buy a wolf?' Before I could tell myself he was mad, he dived back behind the column and brought out a splendid fur coat. I took the opportunity to ask him the way to the old residence of Hutuktu, the Living Buddha. Then it was he who thought he was talking to a madman.

When I got back to the hotel, I began making telephone calls. I had been given a few contacts, but as soon as I asked about the

Temple of the Prophecies or the *dalchin* – the technique of reading the future in fire – there were strange silences at the end of the line. In the end I gave up and decided to rely on my best contact: chance. And so, with Ossendowski always under my arm, I went strolling around the city like a tourist.

One of the first things that struck me was that clearly the practice of telling the future had not died out, or else it had come back into fashion with the recent liberalization. At the central bus station, among the drunks lying on the ground I saw an old Mongolian telling a soldier's fortune. On a red cloth with geometric patterns he dropped a handful of white pebbles. He divided them into pairs and groups of three and four, moved them about and gathered them up again while murmuring formulae that sounded like poems. An old system: one reads the future in the way the stones fall, as with cards, with the advantage that stones can be found everywhere on the plain, and the squares and circles can be drawn on the ground. In front of one of the new department stores I saw another old man calling out to the passers-by, offering to read their future by burning some *arz*, the scented Mongolian herb which is dried and ground to a fine powder.

In Gandan, the old complex of temples and monasteries, all that remains are the empty shells of a few structures. There I saw an old woman sitting at the foot of a pole around which people circled clockwise, praying. She told the future by means of a Buddhist rosary, wrapping it three times around her wrist and then dividing the beads into twos and threes. I asked her to do it for me. Her words were translated by a drunken Mongolian who had approached me and offered in French to be my guide:

'You are a good and generous man,' she said. 'A good future awaits you, and your life line is straight. At the end of this journey a great success awaits you.'

'Is that all?' I asked my interpreter.

'They're all crooks who take advantage of tourists! Now we've got freedom and they're all over the place,' he replied. I asked him if he knew someone who could perform the *dalchin*. He had no idea, but with the help of Ossendowski's description he was able to direct me to a small unadorned tower that had two rows of prayer wheels in front of it. Inside it was empty, but the walls, darkened by time and the shadows of long-gone furnishings and statues, attested to the history of the place. Monks sat on wooden benches, feeding flocks of pigeons, but none of them knew what that history was. This was once the Temple of Prophecies – the place where the lamas, throwing a handful of dice on a low table, had counted the number of Ungern's remaining days: 130. As I stood there rereading Ossendowski's words, with my feet on the same stones, I seemed to see the temple restored to life, with everything in its place. As if in slow-motion I saw the baron walk towards the altar with the small stone statue of the Enlightened One, brought from India, and kneel to pray before it.

After that visit to the temple Ungern, with Ossendowski beside him, went to ask a final blessing from the Living Buddha. I retraced their path, but when I arrived the 'museum' was already closed. A guard saw me peering through a crack in the door and let me in. He wanted to sell me some small Buddhist paintings taken from an old manuscript; I wanted to visit the place alone. In the easy language of gestures and money, we came to an understanding.

A vast, deathly peace reigned within the enclosure. The grass grew tall and uncut, releasing a sweet smell as my feet pushed through it. I picked a few flowering stalks and laid them between the pages of the book to please Ossendowski: the same grass he had known, the same scent. I walked from one pavilion to another, and entered the room where Ossendowski and the baron were admitted to the presence of Hutuktu. Perhaps because the Mongolian Communists wished to show something of their past, especially to foreign guests, this place was preserved intact – a neatly arranged museum, empty of life. From a high window a thin ray of light from the setting sun found its way through the shadows of banners and *tankas* hung from the ceiling to reveal strange figures of painted gods and animals, golden forms of Buddhas, smiles and grimaces of demons lined up along the walls. At the far end, on a raised platform like an altar, the golden throne stood empty. Not a candle was lit, not a stick of incense burned; but the smell of yak butter, used for centuries, had permeated every piece of wood and fabric and still hung in the air to remind me of the past.

On impulse I put Ossendowski on the ground and sat cross-legged before the throne to speak to him. 'I've kept my promise. We're here.' The air was motionless; then a breath of wind, stirring the fillets of coloured silk hung beside a *tanka*, seemed to conjure a vision of other times. I felt the presence of Hutuktu on the throne, the presence of Ungern and Ossendowski, with others, behind. Of course in seeing and hearing these things I was playing a game, but it brought home to me how easily suggestion can work on a receptive mind, and how places and objects have a hidden life that opens before those who know their history.

I would gladly have gone on playing at being in the past, at living for a few moments in that other time, to which I have so often felt I belonged more than to my own. But I remembered the guard, who would soon come to see what I was doing; and suddenly I heard the sounds of today, hooting buses far away on the road, and the vision dissolved.

Only Ossendowski was still with me. With my intense interest, I had redeemed his book from death, made it something more than a mere object. Was that not how the Malaysian *kris* acquired a soul? Was it not also the message of a Tibetan story told by Alexandra David Neel? A merchant goes to India, and his mother asks him to bring her a relic. He forgets. On his next journey he forgets again. The third time, when he is about to return home yet again without the relic his mother desires, he pulls a tooth from a dog's skeleton lying by the roadside and brings it to her, saying it belonged to a great holy man. The mother is delighted, and venerates the tooth; other women come to pray before it, and in the end they all see rays of light emanating from that 'relic'. Hence the Tibetan proverb: 'If there is veneration even a dog's tooth gives forth light.'

I was tired, and decided to make an exception to my usual rule and have dinner at my hotel. But in the large socialist dining room there were no free tables.

'Do you smoke?' I asked a Western gentleman sitting alone.

'No.'

I sat down. He was an American meteorologist.

'Ah,' I said, 'you work at predicting the weather, I work at predicting the future.'

The man was taken aback, and could not see what we had in common. He told me his science had almost reached the limit of its possible development. 'At present we can predict the weather with 99 per cent accuracy for the next three days. The last step will be to master the theory of chaos. With that we'll be able to make exact predictions for two or three years ahead,' he said.

'But if one can predict the weather that way, why can't one predict the future of a person? What's the difference? We too are made of air, solids, clouds, dreams . . . and depressions,' I said.

The meteorologist appeared sure he was dealing with an unbalanced person, and perhaps, from his point of view, he was not entirely wrong.

In the next few days chance came to my aid several times.

I stopped on the street to have my shoes cleaned by a barefoot man who sat on the ground on a piece of newspaper. He turned out to be a veterinarian specializing in the artificial insemination of cows. He had studied in East Germany, and said he had a friend from school – the most brilliant of his class – who had become a monk and might be able to help me in my search for the *dalchin*.

One morning I took a taxi and learned that the driver was the head of the faculty of geology, trying to eke out his salary by driving a friend's car. He took an interest in the history of his country, and had heard of an old temple, just reopened, where novices were again studying the mysteries of prophecy.

And through the hotel manageress I met a woman who for years had been a member of the Communist Party and a government officer. Now she was interested in religion, and could take me to the most famous fortune-teller in the city.

The first to reappear was the vet, who telephoned early one morning before I went out running. Was I willing to pay for a sheep to be slaughtered before me, its scapula removed and burned? Of course!

In a couple of hours we were in a sort of two-storeyed wooden convent on the outskirts of the city, not far from the Gandan Temple. The vet said this was where the government housed all the lamas who returned from the countryside. A strong odour of cooked mutton wafted from the open doors, from which women and children peered to watch the unusual spectacle of a foreigner climbing the dusty, rickety stairs. The lama awaited us in a tidy room where I recognized all the tokens of Central Asian prosperity: a Chinese thermos, an alarm clock, a small radio. The only furniture was a large bed covered with a carpet, on which he sat to receive his guests.

He was a tall, thin man with a handsome open face, a dark red tunic, dirty hands, black fingernails. He said he had learned to perform the *dalchin* from his father, a shepherd, who in turn had learned it from a lama who had also taught it to Hutuktu Bodgo Khan. That may not have been true, but I didn't want to know – this wonderful story formed the last link in the chain of coincidences that connected me with Ossendowski and the baron, the chain that had guided me to that room.

My lama knew the past well. He knew that it was Hutuktu who first forecast von Ungern's death. The two were very close, he said, but not even Hutuktu could alter the baron's fate. 'He was a strange one, Hutuktu,' added the old lama. 'He could make rain. He would take a shirt, hang it on a line, and its shadow would soon become a big cloud full of water.' After the civil war Hutuktu went to the United States, where he lived to a great age. His reincarnation was now living in Russia.

Talking about the past had put the lama at ease. 'When Hutuktu was born, a hunter saw a great fire in the valley – the *yurt* of his friend burning down,' he recounted. 'The hunter was alarmed for his friend's wife, who he knew was pregnant, and ran to help. When he arrived the fire was gone and the *yurt* undamaged. Inside was the mother with the newborn boy. But the fire? Then everyone understood: it was a sign that a special person had been born. Soon afterwards the child was recognized as the reincarnation of the Living Buddha.'

The lama said he was eighty years old. He was born in the year of the rat, 1912. 'I don't have much time left now,' he said, as if he were late for an appointment. I asked him if he was afraid of death. 'I am weary of this life, and long to enter the next. I know it will be better, much better, and without suffering,' he said, laughing. He never once used the word 'death' in all our conversation.

The *dalchin* had been prepared in the courtyard of a house some distance away. We walked for half an hour through a maze of lanes between endless wooden fences, behind which lay the grey sprawl of Mongol dwellings, all identical: a green or brown door with white designs on it led to a yard of trodden earth with a mud-brick shack on one side, and on the other, as a constant reminder of the nomadic past, a felt *yurt* blackened by time.

The sheep was bleating amid a group of curious children who had

come to watch. The old lama entered the *yurt*, sent all the others
out, and began to pray. I saw a ritual knife, curved like a half moon,
pass from his hands to those of a young novice. There was a com-
motion behind the house, and soon the novice returned, carrying a
flat fan-shaped bone the size of a hand. 'This is the shoulderblade,'
said the lama, and with another knife he began to scrape off the
remaining fragments of meat. Then he took a cloth and vigorously
rubbed the bone until it was spotless, almost gleaming with a buttery
whiteness like that of old jade.

'Material purity is reflected in spiritual purity,' said the lama, inter-
rupting his litanies. 'On this purity depends the quality of the prophecy.' The preparation of the bone took at least an hour. The
time passed slowly, punctuated by the murmur of prayers and the
clatter of knives and basins behind the house where the sheep, my
gift to the family whose guests we were, was being skinned and
quartered.

Holding the bone before his eyes like a priest holding up the
ciborium, the lama rose and went into the *yurt*. Only I and my
veterinary interpreter followed him. It was vital for him to concentrate, so no one could be near him who might communicate, even
involuntarily by thought, the answers he was to give.

We sat on the ground by a brazier made of an old petrol can. The
fire burned slowly, fed with small round cakes. 'Excrement of cows,'
said the vet. Into the brazier the lama threw a small handful of *arz*
which filled the *yurt* with grey smoke and a dense, agreeable smell.
He apologized for not being a great fortune-teller: all he could do,
he said, was look in the bone for the answers to my questions.

'How many days do I have to live?' the baron had asked his lama.
I asked mine the same thing. He gazed intensely into my eyes,
brought the bone to his lips, and in a whisper repeated the question.
After some further prayers, he laid the bone in the fire with two
metal chopsticks like those the Mongols use for eating. It slowly
turned black. He took it out, blew off the ashes and studied its surface
for a long time. Finally, in a solemn voice and in what the vet said
was a literary and sibylline language, he said:

'*According to where one is born, one believes in different gods. But you,
though born elsewhere, have your life here. Buddhism will help you more
than any other religion. Your vital sign is very strong, and if you follow the
path of Buddha for which you are made, that sign will become even stronger.*

The paths of the future are open to you.' He threw another handful of *arz* on to the fire.

'Do you see no obstacles in the time ahead of me?' I asked.

Slowly the lama took up the bone again, whispered, prayed, again scrutinized the veinings made by the fire, and said: '*There are no mountains to cross, there are no precipices to conquer, only a level road.*' (What a bore!) '*You must only be careful in travelling by ship, especially if the voyage has to last for some days.*'

I thought of my plan to return from Europe to Asia by sea, and asked what I could do to protect myself.

'*I will give you a mantra which is excellent for you and which you will recite whenever you feel in danger. Here it is. Write:*

> Om Dadid Ada
> Om Dadid Ada
> Om Muni Mujni
> Maha Muni Ye'soha.*'

The session went on for some time longer, with other questions and other answers of little import. The whole ceremony had left me cold and disappointed. Not for a moment had I felt the mystery which had so fascinated Ossendowski, and me too as I read his book. Perhaps it was because his was a time of great events, when people lived and died more dramatically; but whatever the reason, that rite performed for me in a *yurt* in Ulan Bator had lost all the meaning it had had for him in the old city of Urga. The procedure, the gestures, formulae and invocations were probably the same. What I missed was all the rest: the collective consciousness of a people, its fear, its faith in the occult, its hope for some kind of salvation. My *dalchin* lacked the spirit of the time.

The Mongolia of 1921 was a different country from that of 1993, and in the interval the Mongols had become a different race. There, as in Tibet, the previous government was an oligarchy of monks, headed by Hutuktu, who was at once god and king, priest and feudal lord. The lamas had all the power: they were the administrators, the doctors, the fortune-tellers, the generals, the magicians and the judges. Life was pervaded by great uncertainty, death was a constant companion. For the Mongols, legends and myths were as true and real as the rising of the sun. A lama could send hundreds of ill-equipped soldiers into battle simply by conjuring before their eyes, with a wave of his hand, a glorious vision of the future: opulent *yurts*, fields with huge flocks, women dressed in silk and covered with jewels. The soldiers believed it all, and really saw that world for which they went to their death.

Nature was animate. Every mountain was the refuge of a god, every ford the lair of a demon. The whole immense land was a realm of mystery, strewn with the bones of ancestral shepherds and conquerors and the ruins of ancient cities like Karakorum, swallowed up by the sand. From that land salvation would come. The Mongols in 1921 lived in the certainty that even if the whole world were doomed to destruction, beneath their feet the Underworld would survive. It was populated by an ancient tribe which had vanished sixty thousand years before, ruled by the King of the World who had meanwhile penetrated all the secrets of nature. In that Underground Kingdom there was no more evil; there science had developed not to destroy but to create; there men and women were the possessors of all that was knowable; there the destiny of all humanity was written. When Ossendowski arrived in Mongolia he was told that barely thirty years before, the King of the World had made a brief visit to a monastery near Urga. When he arrived all the altar candles had lit spontaneously, all the braziers had begun burning incense; and he, the mythical King of Agharti, described for centuries in the sacred texts, had sat on his throne before an assembly of the most important lamas of the time and forecast the future of the world. He began with the words: 'More and more shall men forget their souls, and care only for their bodies . . .'

The Mongols of 1921 believed all this and lived by it. In Ossendowski's Urga — a place of mystery and horror, but also of great fascination — incredible things could happen. Now, no more. Modernity has swept away that universe of faith. It has 'liberated' the Mongols from the slavery of their legends and their lamas, but at the same time it has emptied their temples, destroyed all the meaning of their ceremonies, and in so doing impoverished their lives. The prophecy of the King of Agharti has been amply borne out: men no longer think of anything but their bellies, and in their world there is no more room for poetry.

Before leaving I asked the lama how he read the answers in the bone. It all depended, he said, on the veining brought out by the fire. The bone has two sides, of which one is held facing the person performing the *dalchin* and the other towards the person enquiring about his future. If the veins appear on the outer face the answer is positive, if inside it is negative. The other criterion is the direction of the veins: the best are those that radiate from the centre of the bone to the edge. Veins that go up are a sign of good changes, those that go down are bad.

'*The answer is always there,*' said the lama. '*The problem is to see it in the bone. That's where the difficulty lies.*' In case of doubt one could take the bone, hide it under one's arm, and approach some people who are talking: the answer will be indicated in the first words one hears. Rather like deciding to do or not do something according to whether the first person you see on leaving the house in the morning is a man or a woman.

I paid for the sheep, distributed some gifts which the vet had advised me to bring, and took the small packets of *arz* which the lama gave me for protection against various ills. The vet was enthusiastic: he felt that he had seen something wonderful. On the way back we passed many beggars: grimy children standing on pieces of plastic in the middle of the pavement, women with cards explaining how they had been widowed, or had been victims of fires or other misfortunes. 'Regress,' said the vet ironically: we had talked so much of the 'progress' which in my view had not yet compensated the Mongols for all that was taken from them.

The scene in which Baron von Ungern hears for the second time that his days are numbered is described dramatically by Ossendowski. The fortune-teller, a sort of small witch, very thin and haggard, goes into a trance. She tears up her headcloth, makes grimaces of fear and pain, twists her body, and at last the words emerge, strained but precise, from her lips: 'I see him . . . I see the God of War . . . His life is ending in a horrible way . . . And then there is the shadow . . . black as night . . . Shadow . . . 130 steps remain . . . Beyond, darkness . . . Nothing . . . I see nothing . . . The God of War has disappeared.'

Ungern bowed his head. 'I shall die, but that is not important. The fight has begun and it will not die. No one can put out the fire in the heart of the Mongols,' he said. Then, rising to his feet, he spoke of his vision of a great Asian Buddhist state that would soon extend from the Pacific to the Indian Ocean and to the banks of the Volga, a state governed by a man more powerful than Genghis Khan and more merciful than the Sultan Baber, who would rule until, from his subterranean capital, the King of the World would come. 'But first Russia must cleanse itself of the insult of the revolution, it must purify itself with blood and death. All those who have accepted Communism must perish, with their families, so that not one seed remains and there are no descendants,' said the bloody baron, departing towards his destiny.

The woman who read Ungern's future in 1921 was a famous seer whose powers were said to have come from her mother, a gypsy. According to the Mongol legends only a few human beings had visited the Underground Kingdom; among these were the gypsies, who returned with the art of reading the future in cards, in grass, and in the palm of the hand.

For me, meeting the most famous seer of Ulan Bator, described to me as 'a sort of witch, of strange origins', was another step in my journey in Ossendowski's footsteps. The appointment was made by the former Communist official who had become religious. She introduced herself by telling me she was the reincarnation of a lama, that on her left shoulder she had three black marks where her predecessor had thrown his tunic, and that in all the religious places she visited she was immediately recognized as a person who had already gone a long way towards enlightenment. Even the Dalai Lama, during a visit to Ulan Bator, had singled her out and had given her some of his very special pills for protection in case of danger.

'In what year were you born?' she asked as we drove to our appointment with the witch.

'1938, the year of the tiger,' I replied.

'The tiger? So was I, but twelve years later. The 1938 tiger is the one with eight white spots. Your element is water. The tiger is generous, it controls its territory. You are always seeking food for your family, and always on guard to protect it.'

The palmist in Singapore had told me similar things.

'In Buddhism', the woman continued, 'the tiger is the great enemy of demons; therefore in the lamaist rites there is always a tiger, and the tiger's tail is often portrayed in the *tankas*. No animal is stronger than the tiger. The tiger can kill everybody, but it has one great enemy: man, because he is more intelligent. Between the tiger and man there is a relation of love and hate, of mutual attraction and fear. I have a difficult marriage because I married a man born in the year of the monkey, and the monkey is the animal closest to man. Like many tiger women, I have trouble having children. Tiger women are greatly feared. Therefore in Asia a woman who is a tiger never mentions it, otherwise she would not find a husband. The tiger always seeks quality, she wants the best, and this can be a great defect when the tiger insists on the best food, the best clothes, the best way of living. Then she must control herself.'

I listened to her with great pleasure, until it struck me that even tigers are an endangered species. How will the people of the future manage to orient themselves towards the character and personality of their neighbours when they no longer have animals to observe, when they no longer have nature from which to learn?

By now we were out of Ulan Bator, heading north. We passed a large cemetery on a hillside. The line of white wooden steles resembled an immense picket fence. 'In the past the dead were left to nature, to feed the birds, but since the revolution we bury them,' said my companion. 'If the body disappeared in three days it meant that the deceased was a good person. If it lasted longer it meant that not even the animals wanted him, and that was a bad omen for his reincarnation.' A remnant of that tradition can be seen in the fact that the Mongols consider ravens and vultures as sacred, and no one kills or eats them.

We passed a recently reopened temple with a beautiful pair of gilded beasts on its roof, and at last we arrived at a large colony of *yurts*, each ringed by the usual crooked wooden fence. Even the green doors, decorated with strange white dots and circles, were all awry. The home of the witch was in a cluttered courtyard with the usual *yurt*, and at the back a small white house. We entered through the kitchen, where women sat on the ground frying doughnuts in a big cauldron of oil.

The witch's room was very tidy: a bed covered by a tapestry of horses, some suitcases, a chest with photos of her family and men in military uniform on top. Under socialism everything is regulated, even the occult: on the wall hung framed documents certifying that she was a member of the Traditional Medicine Association and the Mongolian Association of Persons with Special Powers, as well as various other honours and photographs of her with prominent people.

As soon as I saw this 'witch' I realized that there was no better word to describe her: tiny and thin, with a wrinkled face, long greasy hair, very small eyes and a gold tooth. She wore a green floral dress, and over it a modest smock of a lighter green. She told me she had once worked as a bus driver in Ulan Bator, but her powers had made it impossible to continue. Driving along the street she would constantly feel the good or evil qualities of places and people, and this made her very nervous. If a thief or murderer got on the bus she immediately felt it and could no longer drive. She said she was fifty-eight years old, and was born in a region of the north near the Gobi desert. Of gypsy parents? She did not know. They were very poor, but her birth had brought them good fortune.

The first time she realized that she had powers was when she was nine years old. Her father had sent her to guard some sheep, and she saw that the wolves and dogs were afraid of her and did not approach the flock. Even then she felt that her mission was to help people. If she saw that someone was near death, she had the ability to prolong his life for three or four years. Not more, she added modestly.

She sat on her bed, and indicated that I was to sit on a low stool at her feet. She had a strange way of breathing, continually puffing like someone who feels a hair on his face and tries to blow it away. She picked up a Buddhist rosary and began scrutinizing me very intently, especially behind my ears, as if she were searching for something. Then she looked into a mirror behind me which reflected another mirror on the chest. Gazing into my eyes, she began to speak. My ex-Marxist companion, reincarnation of a lama, translated.

'*Your family consists of four persons. You have two children, the first is a boy, the second a girl. Eight or nine years ago there was an important event in your life. I cannot say if that event was a good or an evil, but it changed your life.*' (Excellent: my expulsion from China. It certainly changed my life, and for a while I myself was not sure if it was good or bad. Only today can I say it was good.) '*Until the end of your life nothing else of that kind will happen to you, nothing bad, no accidents. You will have a long life, very long; especially if you calm yourself and begin to meditate.*' (She too!) '*Give me three numbers under ten.*'

'Three, six, nine,' I replied without thinking. She took her rosary, put it around her neck and around her waist, did some calculations, separated a few beads, and then said: '*Your number is eighteen thousand. You must worship this number; you must never forget it. This number will help you throughout your life. If you are in trouble, if you feel yourself in danger, think intensely of this number and all will be well. Remember: eighteen thousand.*'

She stood up, took some peacock feathers and fanned the air around me, blowing on me very hard as if to drive away spirits.

'*What is your profession?*' she asked.

'I live by words, like you,' I said. Then, fearing that she might take me for a competitor and put the evil eye on me, I added: 'I write articles, books.'

'*Good. In the year of the pig,*' (did she mean 1995 or 2007, I wondered) '*your books will be successful,*' (I was about to believe her and feel delighted) '*because in the past your works have been banned, suppressed. But now there is more freedom and it is easier to circulate them.*' (Clearly she was looking not at my future, but at that of a Mongolian writer. Her prophecy, as I had noted in other cases, reflected local conditions.) '*You have a problem with your wife. She is against your profession, she is against your writing, she wants you to stop. But you must pay no attention to her. You must continue. Your wife is very jealous of you because you always travel.*'

After a splendid beginning, it seemed now that the woman was reading the wrong book, and that I could expect nothing more of interest from her. She made some more inaccurate comments about my relations with Angela, gave advice as to how my children should marry, and put me on guard against the alcoholism of Folco (poor boy, he doesn't touch even wine! But in Mongolia alcoholism among young people is one of the worst problems), and continued reciting other banalities I now knew by heart.

But aren't these the things people worry about most? If their wife or husband is unfaithful, if their daughter will marry, if their son will find a good job. Who goes to a fortune-teller to ask if the hole in the ozone layer can be repaired, if the world's population can go on growing unchecked? It has always been so. Even the great oracles of the past were faced with the same questions: 'Will I win the battle against my enemies?' Always survival, love, death. Our anxiety is for the immediate, for what closely touches us, our loved ones, our family. Curiosity about world affairs, about collective events, has always been limited.

The witch picked up her rosary, blew on it, put it around my neck, blew on my head as if to drive away dust or evil spirits, and said she would think of me, she would pray for me, and I would live happily to the age of ninety or a hundred.

I was annoyed with myself for having come so far to meet an ordinary soothsayer. In the kitchen there was a great sizzling of oil, and occasionally the aroma of burnt sugar came to my nostrils. I was thinking I would like to eat some of those doughnuts . . . now there was a powerful thought! A moment later the witch offered us some. The best part of the visit, I thought. But then, perhaps not. How else would I have come to the outskirts of Ulan Bator? How would I have entered one of those many identical houses? The thought consoled me.

I asked the woman if she believed in reincarnation. Of course! When she walked among the graves in a cemetery, she could feel who was reincarnated and who was not. That was a new idea for me – the unfortunate ones who are not reincarnated and have to remain in the putrefying cadaver. '*Therefore one must respect one's father and mother,*' said the witch. '*They are persons who have helped another human being to be reincarnated.*' That was another thing I had never thought of.

Before I left, she, like the lama, gave me some *arz* wrapped in a little packet to always keep with me for protection. She also presented me with two Chinese bowls to eat from; if they should break I must absolutely keep the pieces. Then, as something even more sacred, she gave me her photo, passport size, one of the old-fashioned ones with deckle edges, to help me think of her from afar.

I had a feeling that the sprig of scented grass drying between the pages of the book must have been pleasing to Ossendowski. It must have taken him back, as sometimes only odours can do, to the days he had spent in Urga. I would have liked to take another morning walk with him and revisit Hutuktu's throne room, but I had an appointment with the geologist-taxi-driver-head of faculty. He brought along, as interpreter, a stylish young man who spoke excellent French. He worked in the Foreign Ministry, but his dream was to go to a business school in Bordeaux and then become a businessman.

We were headed for the monastery of Ghisir, on the high plateau where the Gandan Temple also stands. Long ago Ghisir had been a school for monastic astrologers and fortune-tellers, and it had just been reopened to resume its old work, training a few young novices in the art of prophecy. 'The abbot is one who sees,' said the geologist-taxi-driver as he drove along. My young interpreter was very sceptical, and somewhat embarrassed to be part of this expedition. He was wearing a well-cut blue blazer with brass buttons, grey trousers, white shirt, striped tie and shiny leather shoes: all the right gear to mark him as a respectable person, not to be challenged by the bouncers at the doors of hotels where imported products can be bought for dollars. He was an up-and-coming young man with his eye on the international future, and here I was taking him back to the Mongol middle ages.

Practically nothing remained in the two remaining buildings of the old monastic complex. There was not one statue, one painting, one old piece of furniture. Grass was growing on the roofs, and even the stone steps leading to the terrace of the small pavilion where the abbot lived had been removed. It was hard to imagine the place in past times. Only certain sounds, perhaps, were the same as those of old. In a big bare room about ten novices, supervised by an elderly lama sitting on a high chair, were reading some sutras with obsessive monotony, to the rhythmic chiming of cymbals.

My young interpreter found it absurd that the novices were reading in Tibetan, a language they did not understand. The geologist-taxi-driver explained to him that lamaist Buddhism is Tibetan, that the originals of the sacred texts are in that language and the Mongol texts had been destroyed. 'But it's crazy,' said the young man. This crazy phenomenon, however, was becoming important: a huge number of young men were asking to be novices, said the geologist-taxi-driver, and the temples were reopening 'like mushrooms'.

Perhaps here too the failure of socialist modernity has induced a movement back to the origins. Someone who recently returned from the north of Mongolia told me that the few factories in the region were closing for want of raw materials, and many Mongols were happily going back to tend the flocks. It would not be surprising. What has modernity offered them to compensate for all it destroyed?

What has it substituted for the beautiful myths and legends it swept away? The myth of a business school in Bordeaux?

We had to wait for a while, as there was a queue of people outside the abbot's door who wanted to see him. After they had all been received – my young interpreter was annoyed that we did not have priority – our turn came.

The room was small and very dusty. The abbot was a tall, strong man of about forty, with a pockmarked face and eyes like two narrow slits. His skin was very dark, his arms muscular as those of a wrestler, his hands large and oddly shaped, with palms much longer than the fingers and oversized thumbs. He sat at a table on which was a wooden box about two feet long and a foot wide, containing some very fine grey dust: ashes of incense.

I was the first foreigner to have his future read by the abbot. His method was to ask first for my year of birth and then for a number under 109. With a silver chopstick he drew some complicated signs in the ashes, cancelled them, and drew some more. He traced a picture of my life that was there one moment and vanished the next, as with a simple movement of the box he restored the ashes to a perfectly smooth surface. I liked his truths because they were more ephemeral than horoscopes written on paper, to which one could later return.

That was precisely the secret, said the abbot: because every calculation was cancelled and he had to remember it by heart, he was forced to concentrate and therefore to 'see' better. At the end he traced a perfect circle in the ashes, inscribed some signs in it, and went to consult a sheaf of handwritten papers. The original basis of his system lay in the 108 volumes of the Ganjur, the sacred book of the Mongols; but what counted most were the registers with annotations on the events of the past, and those had disappeared. The lamas had reconstructed them from 1940 on, but could not go back earlier than that. Therefore my horoscope was difficult for him to work out.

'*Do you have heart trouble?*' he asked me.

'Not yet,' I replied.

He was sure that I would have it sooner or later – not serious, but definitely heart trouble. He said that if I wanted to stay healthy I should never cut down trees.

For the young interpreter all this was madness – and anyway, he had heard talk of a great seer, a blind woman called Vanga. 'Where?' I asked, once again ready to set off on the trail.

'In Bulgaria, in a little town on the Greek border,' he said.

I went back to the hotel for lunch. In the dining-room I found the usual situation – no free tables. At first I sat at one where an American was explaining something about China to his Mongolian guide. I got up before ordering and moved to a table with a Lebanese who was in Mongolia to sell French telephones. I told him about my morning and mentioned the marvellous seer of whom I had just heard.

'Vanga?' said a young man sitting opposite the Lebanese. 'Yes, she really is very powerful. I am Bulgarian, and I can help you get an appointment with her – otherwise you have to wait for months!' He said that the region where Vanga lived was, together with Tibet, one of the places in the world most charged with energy. From this came much of her power. I have heard the same thing said by faith healers in the Philippines.

The Bulgarian gave me the telephone numbers of some of his friends in Sofia, who would help me to find Vanga. One was the press attaché of the head of state. Chance or destiny? What had made me sit next to a man who knew about Vanga?

That evening I studied the railway map. Once I got to Warsaw I could easily turn south to Sofia rather than continue west to Berlin. The side trip would take only a few days.

CHAPTER TWENTY-TWO

The Peddlers of the Trans-Siberian Railway

In Ulan Bator the summer sunsets are slow and glorious. The mountains glow with beautiful pastel colours that change from green to blue to violet, like the colours of the silk sashes that Mongolian men and women wear around their waists like belts. I watched it for the last time, absorbing the lofty purity of the sky and the yearning sweetness of the hills. The sun never seemed to disappear, casting longer and longer shadows over the crowd that stood with raised arms to wave at the train, and over the pickpocket who, at the last moment, tried to steal my little Minox.

Unbeknown to each other, each with a good-luck charm to give me, they had all come to see me off: the geologist-taxi-driver-head of faculty with a bronze medal of Genghis Khan; the veterinarian-interpreter with a set of little plaster Buddhas glued to a wooden plate; the ex-Marxist reincarnation of a lama with three of the last pills given her personally by the Dalai Lama, to be taken with a sip of water in case of danger. Her husband, the high government official, was the most practical of all: he brought a plastic bag full of a very useful stock of beer and caviar. At such moments one would like the train to leave promptly, but this one pulled out of Ulan Bator half an hour late, prolonging the embarrassed conversation at the window.

The journey from Ulan Bator to Moscow takes five days. To me the term 'Trans-Siberian' has always suggested something *démodé* and romantic. In his book *Overland to China*, Archibald Colquhoun, who made the trip in 1898, describes *de luxe* carriages with bathrooms, a library, a gym and a music-room with a piano. I knew it was not like that any more, but the image remained in my mind, so when the ticket seller asked, '*De luxe*?' I automatically answered yes.

On boarding the train, however I found that in my *de luxe*

compartment there was hardly room to sit down. It was piled high with huge sacks and bundles, on top of which sat a corpulent red-cheeked Mongol of about thirty: my new travelling companion.

'Businessman?' I asked him in English, using the word that by now is everywhere a synonym for prestige.

He nodded. Thank goodness we discovered we could communicate in Chinese. The whole train was full of these businessmen. Every single compartment was crammed with bags and boxes, all jam-packed with goods. The space under the couchette-seats was taken up by more bundles and boxes, and so were the corridors and toilets. In the whole very long train there was apparently not a single ordinary traveller with just a suitcase.

It was a Russian train. Someone had warned me that in Russia everything that has to do with food is now in the hands of the Georgian mafia. Just to check, as soon as we started I went to inspect the restaurant car. And sure enough the head waiter, Vladimir, was from Tbilisi. I introduced myself, handing him a $10 bill, and asked him to look after me. It worked like a dream: for the whole trip I had a clean place at the table, fresh caviar and iced vodka.

As soon as the train had crossed the frontier into Russia I saw what the new Trans-Siberian Railway was like. At the first station the Mongols began to open their sacks and lean out of the windows, waving merchandise to attract the Russians: my romantic Trans-Siberian had dwindled to a prosaic travelling bazaar, assailed at every station by a crowd thirsting for bargains. Most of them were women: as if possessed they threw themselves against the sides of the train to grab the plastic overalls, raincoats, flip-flops and children's clothes which the Mongols dangled out of reach over their heads until they had the desired price in their hands.

For a long time the track ran along the shore of Lake Baikal, as big as a sea, very flat and calm. The night was lit by a splendid slice of moon that looked like shining mercury. We passed Irkutsk. Outside the windows the *taiga* continued, just like the day before – the same thin white birches, the same green meadows full of flowers, and little log houses with blue and white window frames. Every time the train slowed down and we felt it rumbling over the switches before a station the Mongols would swing into action, opening their sacks and pulling their reserve stocks out from under the seats.

'Krasnoyarsk!' yelled the woman in charge of the *de luxe* carriages, and we stopped in the radiance of another Siberian sunset. Ossendowski's city! It was from here that he had set out! On the platform a crowd flung itself on the train like a beast on its prey – pretty girls in mini-skirts, stout old women with headscarves – all scrambling to get hold of a sweater, a raincoat, a pair of plastic shoes. The only ones who did not join the fray were a few dirty and unshaven drunks who crouched at the feet of two electric pylons and smiled philosophically at the bargains they were missing.

Passing through Krasnoyarsk, where his odyssey began, I felt that my journey with Ossendowski had come full circle. Perhaps he would have liked to get off there, and go and see how little progress the people of the city had made since the day he fled for his life – since the revolution, so abhorred by the baron, had taken root. There, I thought, was the place for us to separate. I picked up the book, thanked it for the magnificent company it had kept me, and just for fun opened it at random, telling myself that what I read would be his farewell to me. My eyes fell on the first line of page 188: '. . . terrible bloody Baron. No one can decide his own fate.' I put the book into an envelope. I would post it home at the next stop.

Tomsk, Novosibirsk, Omsk: day after day, in every station, small or large, the same spectacle was repeated. As soon as the people heard the whistle of that train of wonders, they came pouring out of their houses and rushed excitedly to the station. At times it looked as if the whole population was running beside the tracks. Deals were clinched in seconds: grab the goods, hand over the money and off goes the train, leaving behind a few lucky purchasers to admire an ugly anorak or a pair of sandals, and the disappointed ones who had not managed to buy anything. For another chance they would have to wait two more days.

Between stops the Mongols drank and slept. Outside, the silver birches slid past monotonously.

Such is the strange destiny of the Trans-Siberian Railway. Built as a line of defence against China a hundred years ago, at the height of Russia's imperial ambitions, it has now become the supply line which enables the poor Russians, defeated by history, to dress in trashy Chinese clothes. Instead of the duchesses and spies and generals and adventurers of half Europe, today the Trans-Siberian carries the descendants of Genghis Khan along the path of ancient Mongolian conquests. But they too have come down in the world, travelling not as conquerors but as peddlers.

Waking up each morning I saw the endless *taiga* outside the window, and spread on a newspaper on the table the same old mutton-filled ravioli that stank up the compartment. 'It keeps, without going bad, more than a week,' said my businessman companion. He told me that in Ulan Bator, towards the end of October, every family buys a whole ox, skins it and puts it out on the porch. With the cold the meat freezes, and over the winter they eat it a bit at a time. They do the same with a couple of sheep.

Among the passengers in a nearby compartment was a beautiful woman, a former mining engineer, forced now to make a living buying and selling leather jackets; another was a student of French literature who travelled with a consignment of flip-flops, tracksuits and anoraks. Normally this was her brother's work, but their grandfather had read his future with stones and had seen that this trip would not be propitious for him, so the family had sent her instead. Each of the Mongols had invested something like $1000 in merchandise, and figured on returning to Ulan Bator with about $3000. They have no problem replenishing their stocks in China, and they do not require visas to enter Russia, so they profit from being in the middle.

At Marinsk, Vladimir, the head waiter, told me to lock the door of the carriage, and the compartment door as well: that was the station of the mafia and the gangsters.

'*Skolka? Skolka?*' yelled the faceless crowd in the middle of the night as the train entered the station of Ekaterinburg, where the tsar and his family had been slaughtered by the Bolsheviks. 'How much? How much?' they cried, without seeing what they were buying. Handfuls of money and plastic bags of goods changed hands in the darkness. My Mongol took the opportunity to get rid of some mismatched shoes and a raincoat with a big oil stain.

Halfway through the journey I realized that I was not the only European on the train. In the last carriage was a young Frenchman with his bride, a pretty girl from the Central African Republic. In the other *de luxe* carriage were a Bulgarian diplomat and an elegant Parisian gentleman of seventy-four who turned out to be an architect. He had spent two weeks in Mongolia. 'Interested in Buddhism?' I asked. Yes and no. His wife, he told me, was a famous clairvoyante. She had recently been paralyzed and had sent him to get 'recharged' with the energy which, she said, abounds in Mongolia. She used that energy to restore people to health.

'She doesn't claim to cure cancer, though she's been successful with some cases, but she is particularly good with mental illnesses,' said the architect. A session with his wife lasted at least two hours. Her method was to have the patient draw first a tree – because the tree is the source, the symbol of life, he said – and then a man and a woman. Each of us, he said, is protected by seven layers of skin, some of them luminous. He enthusiastically described his last journey with his wife to the 'high' places of France, those where something particularly spiritual had happened. There too she had gone to absorb energy. Once again, was it by chance that I met him?

The man was very warm and friendly, and felt much more at ease when I told him why I too was on that train. He said I must definitely go to Paris to meet his wife, and gave me his card. I kept it in my pocket for two days. Then one afternoon, watching the everlasting monotonous birches passing outside the window, it struck me that I might spend the rest of my life going from one place to another in search of fortune-tellers and seers. There would always be one who might be the best of all, always the next one. I let the wind whip the card from my hand. Watching it flutter away, I felt that I had reasserted my freedom of choice. I also decided not to go to Bulgaria to look for Vanga, and not to see any fortune-tellers in Moscow.

Another stop, another frightening mass assault on the train. It was the morning of a normal working day, but the whole town, including children who should have been in school and workers who should have been in the factory, seemed to be on the platform. Tremendous uproar, tremendous dealings. As the train began to move off again, a desperate old woman was weeping and vainly beating the door that had just closed. She screamed that she had paid but had not been given her tracksuit. The Mongols said they had given it to her but a thief had snatched it out of her hand. There was nothing they could do.

The crowd chased after the departing train, raising a cloud of dust that obscured the station. 'Africa! Africa!' said Vladimir. 'Russian people great history, but system, system no good,' and he laughed. As the train gathered speed I saw the old woman disconsolately readjust the kerchief on her head and disappear amidst the dust-covered crowd.

At Barabinsk I myself was infected with the selling bug. I asked my Mongol for a raincoat. How much should I sell it for? Twenty thousand roubles. I stood for a few minutes shouting that price to the crowds, who came, felt and dashed off again. Then a young man thrust two 10,000-rouble notes into my hand and I gave him the raincoat.

Back on the train, I proudly handed the Mongol his money. He burst out laughing: I had been tricked! These were 1,000-rouble notes to which someone had skilfully added a zero. All you had to do was to rub them with a bit of saliva and off it came.

In the long hours we visited each other, back and forth. The young Frenchman came to see me with his beautiful Central African wife. He too had a story of clairvoyance to tell. A friend of his in Africa had gone to have his diarrhoea cured by a witch-doctor, who drew some stylized figures of men in the sand, and told him that within fifteen days he would receive news that a woman very close to him was pregnant. He refused to believe it, but a week and a half later he had a letter from his sister telling him she was expecting a child.

What can one say? That everyone has a story in which he believes. 'My wife believes that in Africa there are men who turn into croco-diles,' said the Frenchman. 'For her, the creatures that eat children in the river cannot just be crocodiles. She has to believe they are evil men who have become crocodiles.'

Slowly the compartment emptied out. After the city of Perm my Mongol, whose cheeks got redder and redder from beer and vodka, had sold all he had. At the following stations Russians began boarding the train with things to sell to the Mongols, who by now were loaded with money. A man came with a case full of medicines, two girls brought German pistols. My Mongol bought one of them for $150, to defend himself against the 'Moscow gangsters'. Another young Russian had nothing but a pack of cards, but with that he organized a little gambling den. At the station of Daniloff two pretty, provocative Russian women got on with their pimp, and compartment 5 of my *de luxe* carriage was suddenly transformed into a brothel.

All night long the train panted its way up through the Urals, leaving Siberia and its birches behind at last. At dawn the landscape opened out in broad plains full of ripe grain and dotted with houses no longer built of logs.

The restaurant car filled more and more with young 'businessmen'. They boldly accosted Vladimir, ordered beer and vodka, drank, got red in the face and slumped over the tables.

Vladimir knew life, and held decided views about how the world went round. For him everything that was good, orderly, beautiful and clean was 'normal'. Freedom of enterprise? 'Normal.' Loving women? 'Normal.' What was no longer 'normal' was Russia, because there was no more order, no longer any difference between the mafia, gangsters and police – he waved his hand – 'all the same', one like another, all mixed up. 'Mafia? No normal. Democracy? No normal. Russian people need dictator. Big dictator for Russia is normal. Stalin for Russia is normal.' I do not believe he said this just because Stalin was a fellow-Georgian. He said it because, with the failure of Communism and the fall of the Soviet empire, people like him no longer know what to hope for; they see no one to whom they can entrust their fate.

Some tough-looking soldiers in camouflage uniforms, armed with big truncheons, boarded the train. Militiamen. They went back and forth collecting money from the Mongols. A thousand roubles for smoking in the corridor – or just to avoid trouble.

Gradually the hubbub subsided. Vladimir and one of his assistants dragged the drunken Mongols out of the restaurant car and dumped them in the corridor of economy class. A few men were still going in and out of compartment 5.

And then a new, long-awaited sound: the clickety-clack of the wheels assumed a more urgent rhythm, like a dialogue between various voices. The train slowed down, whistled, swerved as it negotiated a series of switches, and we entered a big city. The head conductor knocked on the doors of the drunks and sleepers, shouting in a joyous voice: '*Moskva! Moskva!*'

It was three in the morning and a fine rain was falling on the platform when, with enormous pleasure, I at last set foot on the ground. We were six hours late. My Mongolian companion shook my hand and vanished in the crowd. He was wearing an elegant dark jacket and blue jeans. In his hand he had a 'businessman's' briefcase, which I knew held stacks of roubles and a pistol.

From Moscow the rest of the journey was easy. A day to cross Belorussia. Then Brest, the last station of what used to be the Soviet empire. Again the carriages were driven into a shed and lifted to replace the wide-wheel trucks with some of narrower gauge. A last border guard watched us with binoculars as we crossed into Poland. In the distance, through the trees, I saw the shape of a church. Europe! The stations became tidier, the railwaymen's uniforms cleaner.

Soon I was home. I unpacked my bag and distributed all the oils, powders, envelopes, magic cards and other lucky charms I had accumulated *en route*. What I could not get rid of was the disquieting memory of those huge masses of humanity – desperate, disorientated, angry and ravenous – which, from Vietnam to China, from Mongolia to Russia, I had left in my wake. If I had travelled by air I would have seen none of it.

CHAPTER TWENTY-THREE

Better than Working in a Bank

My book *Goodnight, Mister Lenin* came out at exactly the right time, according to the Bangkok fortune-teller, to be a success. Just as she had prescribed, it was neither too long nor too short, the cover was in pastel colours, and there was a man's name in the title. But when I arrived in London, though the book was displayed in the windows, I found no queues outside the bookshops: another proof, if I needed it, that one should not put too much faith in fortune-tellers. At least not where details are concerned, because otherwise my visit to London was a great success. Just to arrive there by train, after crossing the Channel and seeing the white cliffs of Dover once again from the deck of the ferry, was a great pleasure. One that I owed to a fortune-teller.

But even that sensible separation, which for centuries has made the British British and the rest of us 'Continentals', has now disappeared because of a claustrophobic tunnel under the sea. Somewhere there is someone who is pushing to make the world turn faster and faster, and to make people more and more the same – in the name of something called 'globalization', the meaning of which few understand and still fewer have said they want.

In London I was in the hands of my publisher. Between one appointment and another I asked my 'minder' if she could help me to find a fortune-teller. She made an appointment for me at an address in Monmouth Street; I was to ask for Mr Norman.

I stepped out of the taxi somewhat embarrassed. It is one thing to visit an old lama in Ulan Bator as an explorer, a journalist looking for some truth, and another to go to a fortune-teller in the middle of London. There one feels the need of an alibi, even for oneself. But I had none.

My embarrassment increased when I found that the address I had been given was a shop with 'Mysteries' painted on the window. It was a sort of supermarket, or school, or temple, of the occult. It was surprisingly crowded with young 'alternative' people: punks, apprentice wizards and young witches on active service. For sale on the shelves were all the books of magic, miracles, mystery, all the tomes on Buddhism, Oriental philosophy, astrology and chiromancy, that one could imagine. Anything you might want to know was there. Everything which I imagined I had sniffed out myself could undoubtedly be found in one or other of those little books or those records and videos lined up on the shelves.

At the cash register was a girl with fiery red hair in great long curls. I paid her £15, went up a stairway covered with a straw mat, and arrived in a room divided into many cubicles, each with its fortune-teller and its posters of Indian or Buddhist divinities. In one I even saw a glass ball.

'I am Norman. Do you have an appointment?' The man was about sixty; he had a sallow complexion, a prominent chin, hair receding at the temples. He was wearing a black leather jacket and dark trousers. In his hand he held a lighted cigarette. He took me into his cubicle and had me sit across from him at a cheap little table. There were some psychedelic posters on the walls. I was entitled to half an hour of consultation, he said, and to get my money's worth we had better begin at once.

He handed me a pack of cards with pictures in bright colours and asked me to shuffle them three times. Then he took every seventh card from the deck, laid them out in a pattern, and began his analysis: *'You are beginning a new cycle of your life, and you are about to take some steps in the dark. As you are a man who likes challenges, you will meet with success. Great success, no doubt about it. Look – in this pack there are four powerful cards, and you have three of them here, all together. So I tell you: just do whatever you like and you'll succeed. Only you must take care of your health, because you are a man who uses a great deal of energy. At times too much. Try to keep your battery always well charged.'*

I interrupted to ask him to tell me everything, absolutely everything he saw, even if he saw horrible things.

'There is nothing negative in what I see in the cards. Of course you too will die one day, like me, like everyone, but the cards do not tell me when. I don't see your death here. Perhaps an astrologer could do it. You're a man who likes to be under pressure, to be in danger, to take risks; but if a bullet

comes along it misses you, perhaps by a fraction of an inch, and you survive. This is what the cards say. Your whole life is under a precise sign: "Lucky rather than rich". Here are the cards, see?' (I saw nothing but some pictures which meant nothing to me.) *'These are the cards of fortune, but there are none of the cards of wealth, not even one. In the cards I also see a woman, a woman with a strong character who plays a great part in your life.'*

Norman went on for twenty minutes, chain-smoking, reshuffling the cards, having me choose one and laying out his patterns again before pronouncing on various themes that I knew well by now. They were the same in Bangkok, in Ulan Bator and in London: the death of a person close to me in recent months or in the months to come; a person younger than me whom I should try to get along with during October; a friend who might betray me; long journeys between 10 October and 20 November, and so on.

I looked at my watch and decided to use the last ten minutes to talk about Norman rather than about myself. I interrupted again and asked him if he believed the things he said he saw in the cards.

'Not 100 per cent, otherwise we would no longer have any responsibility for our actions,' he said. *'The cards read the shadows of things, of events. What I can do is help people to change the position of the light, and then, with free will, they can change the shadows. That I really do believe: you can change the shadows.'*

This seemed one of the best descriptions I had heard of fortune-tellers' work: changing the shadows. Accurate too, if, as Pirandello and *Rashomon* have taught us, there is not one truth but many, depending on who looks at things and how he does so.

I told Norman why I was there, and in return, lighting yet another cigarette, he told me why he was there. For years he had been a teller in a bank. He couldn't stand it any more, and left. He went from one job to another, and none of them paid enough to live on or gave him as much satisfaction as reading the cards. Of the £15 fee half went to him, the other half to the shop. At the end of the day he felt he had truly helped at least a couple of people.

I liked Norman. By no means did he have special powers – if he had, he would have stopped smoking! – but he had a good deal of common sense. I felt that he was sincere, and that once in a while he really did help someone dispel a bit of shadow and bring more light into his life. Like the fortune-teller in Betong who could tell

by 'feeling' when a girl had AIDS, like the woman in H.
the witch of Ulan Bator.

I would have liked to board a ship in London and sail down the
Thames to the sea, like one of Conrad's voyagers, but the ship for
Hamburg departed from Harwich, so I had to take a train to the
coast. Even that was enjoyable, though, as it gave me time to take
in the beautiful, orderly English countryside, unspoiled by anything,
not even the usual high-tension pylons. It seemed as though particular
care had been taken of the landscape to preserve its naturalness. And
that was heartening. From the minute I arrived in Europe, I had
been struck by how well this continent carried its age. It had not
tried to give itself another face; it was proud of the one it had, and
made an effort to preserve it. After the Asian mania for self-
destruction this was a great relief.

The ship left Harwich in the early afternoon, and at dawn the
next day we reached the mouth of the Elbe. It was six more hours
before we docked at Altona, but they were six very pleasant hours,
slowly sailing between the elegant banks of this river which has seen
so much history, and which has brought Hamburg all its wealth.

Hamburg is a port: something I have always known but never
truly understood until, like a Hanseatic sailor returning after months
at sea, I saw on the horizon first the roofs of Cuxhaven, then the
small houses of the captains and the white mansions of the rich
merchants shining through the majestic trees at Blankenaese, and at
last the green copper church spires of the city. I had been in Hamburg
dozens of times, but it had taken a Hong Kong fortune-teller to
make me feel its true soul.

That was not the only surprise. When I went to see the chief
editors of *Der Spiegel* they said: 'We know you want to go and live
in India. Good. The job of correspondent will be free at the end of
this year. From 1 January we would like you to be in Delhi.'

Well, well. The old blind man in Bangkok was right, and so were
all the fortune-tellers who said I would move to another country in
1994. I said nothing, but the thing did seem strange. However, it
would be a problem for me to leave Bangkok so soon. And how
would I go? By plane? I remembered that one of my fortune-tellers
had said that a good time to move would be after 8 April. After

some discussion it was agreed that I would move to India on 1 May 1994, which would satisfy everyone's needs – even those of my destiny.

The Hong Kong fortune-teller, after all these years, continued to shower me with blessings. The next were eighteen long, restful days of silence and solitude on board a ship sailing from Europe to Asia, crossing the great seas of history: the Mediterranean, the Red Sea, the Persian Gulf, the Indian Ocean.

For some strange reason we tend to think of human events as taking place on land. We see the past in the physical solidity of monuments, in things that have been built, in the remains of things destroyed, in tombs. But much of history – often the most dramatic part – is written on the seas, where men have left no record of themselves, where everything has sunk without trace, and the water is just as it was a thousand or a hundred thousand years ago: illegible. The sea has inspired man's dreams of conquest; on the sea the fates of civilizations and empires have been played out. It was the promise of unknown lands beyond the sea that spurred the great navigators to entrust their lives to the waves.

Sea travel is one of the oldest and most enjoyable ways of moving about the world. But unfortunately, as I had already discovered, it is rapidly disappearing: another of those pleasures which, through our compulsion to be modern, we are wiping out. Ships still exist, and they all still have some cabins for passengers, but the rules of bureaucracies and insurance companies have made them inaccessible.

I was lucky. In Singapore I had had supper with Roberto Pregarz, who ran the old Raffles Hotel in its last years of glory, before it too was modernized and became a *de luxe* tourist supermarket. I had asked him if he knew anyone in an Italian shipping line that sailed to the Orient, and he had given me the address of a friend of his, a captain on the board of Lloyd Triestino. I wrote to him, and received an encouraging reply. If I would sign some papers releasing the company from liability for anything that might happen to me on board, I could travel – this time with Angela – on a container ship, the *Trieste*, that was sailing from La Spezia to Singapore at the end of September. A real gift.

The gift began with La Spezia itself. I knew the city only by name, and if it had not been for that ship, I probably would never have set foot there. I would have missed the pleasure of knowing a lovely nineteenth-century city, built by an admiral on the orders of Cavour, who had a strong aesthetic sense, when the newly united Italy needed an arsenal and a base for its navy. The departure of the *Trieste*, scheduled for a Saturday, was postponed first to the Monday and then to the Wednesday, so we had plenty of time for a side trip to Porto Venere and a whole day in Lerici, enjoying the gracious idleness of a seaside resort out of season.

Returning to La Spezia by bus along the coast, we saw the imposing, awkward form of the *Trieste* as it sailed into port. The ship was two hundred yards long, and its whole deck was occupied by stacks of containers. They looked like apartment blocks with a few narrow corridors between them; it was like a deserted city.

With the advent of containers, ships have lost their old shapely elegance, and ports have lost their lively swarms of humanity. The 'new' port of La Spezia looked like the set for a science-fiction film. Giant cranes moved back and forth, loading and unloading immense iron boxes of all colours, setting them down on lorries, on ships, on stacks of other boxes – all automatically, to the sound of a continuous alarm that did not alarm anyone. In all the vast quadrangles of the port we did not see a living soul, as if everything was manoeuvred by some distant computer, and men no longer existed.

It felt good to sail away and watch the lights of that spectral port merge with the others twinkling along the bay in the smoky darkness of the night.

For nearly three weeks we did not touch land. As the days passed, there was always some goal to look forward to: the sight of Scylla and Charybdis, the Strait of Messina, the Suez Canal, the stop at the Bitter Lakes, the entrance to the Red Sea. We had a spacious, comfortable cabin with a large porthole. The crew was reduced for economic reasons to a minimum of eighteen men who, because of the shifts of work below decks, we hardly ever saw.

The days went by quickly, punctuated by the ceremonies of lunch and dinner in the salon. We dined with the officers, elegant in their white uniforms – gentlemen in the old style, full of mariners' wisdom and sea stories to entertain their guests. The food, prepared by a Neapolitan cook, was excellent, and the menu was never repeated.

I got up with the sun and ran a dozen times around the ship each morning. Then for hours and hours I would sit at the stern, reading or dreamily looking out to sea, or watching a lone crew member scraping the rust off a capstan far away along the deck. In the silence, broken only by the creaking of the containers which shifted slightly with the rolling of the ship, I thought I finally understood sailors: they too were fugitives, they too were escaping from the world on land, from social commitments, from the weight of relationships, to live for weeks and months in that ever-changing universe of water and sky, to welcome the apparition of an island through the fog, or a lighthouse blinking in the darkness.

But sailors are a dying race. Already they are no longer called by the old names: able seamen, mates and boatswains have been abolished, and in their place, for trade-union reasons, there is a new category of *comuni polivalenti* – Italian bureaucratic jargon for all-purpose workers.

The same thing is happening with the marine knowledge accumulated over the centuries: the modern world has no more use for it. Now everything is done by instruments. Once a sailor had to train his eyes, to learn to discern the presence of a shoal of fish by a rippling of the surface, to assess a harbour's navigability or detect a reef. Now all this expertise has been supplanted by sonar and radar, which every year become more accurate. But what a fund of knowledge is being lost! How many natural antennae are falling from men's heads, to be replaced by electronic antennae!

'Everything is automatic. There's no more need to look at the sea,' said the captain sorrowfully. The sea, when you look at it, is so extraordinary! Different every hour, with different colours, different densities, sounds, movements, different spectacles: once it was dolphins swimming alongside the ship, once a whale diving quickly as if frightened by our monstrous size, or shoals of flying fish playing with the keel, or sharks on their way to mate and breed in the bay of Djibouti.

Every conversation in the salon ended with a lament for all that had changed in ships, and for the poetry which technology has stolen from life at sea. According to the chief engineer, it is the fault of the Americans: after spending so much money going to the moon they found nothing there to exploit, so now they're trying to recoup their investments by recycling the technology developed for that trip for civilian uses and hawking it all over the world. He was convinced that soon all large international shipments will be made by submarines entirely controlled by computers, with no crew at all and no need to face the difficulties and contrary forces that affect surface navigation.

The cook particularly objected to the telephone, because of which everyone had lost the habit of writing home. You spent a lot of money for three minutes of conversation a week in which all you said was, 'Hello, can you hear me?' 'Yes, I can hear you very well.' 'So can I.'

All the time on board we had a vague sensation of witnessing something that was ending. Then one day that sensation became precise: our voyage was a funeral. Shortly after we passed Cape Guardafui ('look and flee') the radio operator received a message from the trade unions urging the crew to go on strike: the state enterprise that owned the *Trieste* was negotiating to sell it. When it returned to Italy the ship would pass into the hands of some multinational company that would rename it, register it under a flag of convenience, and replace the Italian *comuni polivalenti* with Asian seamen, perhaps Chinese, paid less than $50 a month. So, this was the last voyage of one of the few remaining ships to fly the Italian flag.

Sitting at the stern, I wondered how much longer such a world can last, based exclusively on the inhuman, immoral and philistine criteria of economics. As I strained my eyes to make out the silhouettes of distant islands, I imagined one inhabited by a tribe of poets, held in reserve for a time when humanity, after this dark age of materialism, will begin once again to sustain its existence with other values.

One of the great pleasures of the ship was having time to let my thoughts wander unrestrained, to indulge in fantasies and play with the most absurd notions. At times I had the sensation of sifting through the whole ragbag of memories accumulated in my life.

Taking time for oneself is a simple cure for the ills of the soul, but one which people apparently find difficult to allow themselves. For years, in moments of depression, I had dreamed of sticking a note on my door saying 'Out to lunch,' and making that absence last for days or weeks. Now, finally, I had succeeded. I had all the time in the world to watch a flock of swallows that came aboard as we crossed the Mediterranean, flying out over the sea from time to time and then returning to hide among the containers. I had time to think about time, about how I instinctively always find the past more fascinating than the future, and how the present often bores me, so that only by thinking of how I will remember it later can I enjoy the moment.

For shipboard reading I had brought two books by Mario Appelius, a pre-war Italian journalist who has now been completely forgotten. He was put on the index for having been a supporter of Mussolini: another example of how, in these times of vaunted freedom of thought, heavy prejudices are still with us.

Appelius was a great traveller, with an instinct for history and a deep understanding of humanity's dramas. His descriptions of a meeting with an overseas Chinese in an opium den in Phnom Penh, or the crowning of a child emperor in the ancient city of Hué in Vietnam, are masterful. Appelius understood much about the character of colonialism, about the aspirations of Asian peoples and the consequences of modernity which in his time already threatened the survival of old cultures and civilizations. His sorrow for the disappearance of the Kas, mythical savages of the Laotian mountains, was quite authentic. But because he remained to the end a convinced fascist – it was his voice on the radio that repeated the famous wartime slogan '*Dio stramaledica gli inglesi!*' (May God super-curse the British!) – he became a non-person, an unmentionable name. In reading his book, I felt I did something to redress the balance.

At times, in those idle hours, I mentally reviewed the various fortune-tellers I had met, trying to find a common thread in all they had said. It seemed to me that the point of travelling is in the journey itself, not in the arrival; and similarly in the occult what counts is the search, the asking of questions, not the answers found in the cracks of a bone or the lines in your palm. In the end, it is always we ourselves who give the answer.

'Will I die in the war?' the soldier asked the Cumaean sibyl, and from her grotto she tossed out a handful of disconnected words that had to be arranged to give her answer. The soldier had to choose whether the '*non*' should go before his dying, making the prophecy read '*Ibis, redibis, non morieris in bello*' (You will go, you will return, and will not die in the war), or before his return, to produce '*Ibis, non redibis, morieris in bello*' (You will go, you will not return, you will die in the war).

As the days passed we watched for the points marked in pencil on the captain's charts. For three days we sailed through open seas towards the island of Minicoy, but when we passed it all we could see was the faint flashing of a lighthouse. The leprosarium on the beach which the officers had told us about was impossible to make out even with a telescope.

When we entered the Straits of Malacca we passed an island covered with palms, through which shone the white form of a Catholic church. This was the island of We', where Nino Bixio was buried. Bixio was Garibaldi's disillusioned companion, who came to Asia to seek his fortune and vent his frustrations after the Campaign of the Thousand. Once upon a time, passing Italian sailors would stand on the deck and salute, but that custom too has been abandoned.

We entered the Bay of Singapore in the middle of the night. A storm had broken. The Chinese pilot who came on board whispered his orders into a walkie-talkie. Despite the storm, the moment the *Trieste* tied up at pier number four the cranes began to unload the containers and replace them with others bound for Japan, where the ship was to call before returning to Italy. The crew were forbidden to disembark. The resupply operations would be finished in a few hours, and the ship would leave again at once, trying to make up time and avoid the fines imposed by international regulations.

When the police gave permission for Angela and me to go ashore, everyone was so busy working that the time for farewells and gifts was brief. The captain, in the name of the whole crew, handed us a paper bag with something light inside. I opened it when we got to the hotel. It was a flag: the flag of the *Trieste*, on which we had been the last passengers.

CHAPTER TWENTY-FOUR

The Rhymeless Astrologer

One gets used to everything. I was used to travelling slowly. Angela took the plane from Singapore, and in two hours she was in Bangkok, but I had two more days of travel ahead of me, by train. I stopped off in Kuala Lumpur, where my friend M.G.G. Pillai had managed to book an appointment for me with the famous fortune-teller whom I had not been able to see in April.

The meeting took place in his 'studio', which was in the shopping arcade of one of the big hotels, surrounded by souvenir shops, airline offices, tailors who made suits in twenty-four hours, a barber and a news-stand. It was because of his fame – he was so much in demand that one had to book months in advance – that I was so curious to meet him.

The minute I set eyes on the man I did not like him. He was small, about fifty, with thin curly hair, myopic eyes and a greasy forehead. I noticed at once that he had a tic – he kept jerking his right shoulder forward. My impression was of a weak person, not at ease with himself, certainly not one capable of 'seeing' into other people's lives. On his right hand he wore three rings. The most distasteful was a big one on his thumb, set with a coral. I do not know why, but I have an aversion to rings, and when I see them, even on a woman's hand, I instinctively want to draw back.

When I telephoned to confirm the appointment, the fortune-teller's secretary told me that before seeing him I must not drink alcohol, tea or coffee. This immediately struck me as a little trick to impress the clients and give himself importance – as if there were something religious about reading people's destinies in that hotel mezzanine, for a fee that depended on whether you wanted a forecast for three or six years or for the rest of your life.

Father Willem, the Dutch missionary in Indonesia, was right: there

322

is something in the invisible communications between people that has never been explained. You meet someone and take an instant dislike to him. Why? Why did I find that man, whom I had never seen before, absolutely unbearable? He had done me no harm – on the contrary, perhaps sensing my aversion, he went out of his way to be kind and accommodating. He tried hard to please me, and that annoyed me even more. Before he uttered a single sentence I already felt that he was a man without character, without inner calm, without wisdom. Perhaps I too, after seeing so many of these people who spend their lives meddling with the lives of others, had developed my own instinctive way of 'reading' them, and had learned to distinguish the ones who really tried to understand and help from the quacks – to tell the ones with some special gift from the impostors.

The famous fortune-teller told me he had been in his studio for twenty years. Before that he had been a teacher. I asked him if it had been some particular event, some trauma, that made him change his profession. He said no.

As he prepared his desk, lining up his pens and arranging papers with the manic punctiliousness of a petty bureaucrat, he explained that his system was an Indian combination of astrology and palmistry. This, he said, allowed him to see even into the lives of a person's parents, thus obtaining a more exact picture of the client's character and destiny. Every word he said got on my nerves, and so did his gestures, and the spots of dirt on his red carpet. When I told him the hour and date of my birth, he irritated me even more by informing me – as if it were good news! – that he and I were born in the same month of the same year, only a week apart.

So we were linked with the same animal. He, a tiger?

He went through the usual calculations, aloud (to impress me, I thought). With foreigners the calculations are more difficult, he said, because one must take into account the latitude and longitude of the place of birth. Then he launched into a preamble that I had never heard from anyone else. And that was stupid as well: '*I shall relate your past and your future on the basis of ancient Indian systems. What I tell you will remain absolutely between us. Discretion is very important. I shall tell you the whole truth, the good and the bad. I cannot be completely precise as to dates, because only God knows these things to the second. An astrologer can only be approximate. Have you seen any other astrologers in your life?*'

I nodded. He asked me what sign I was.

'Virgo,' I said.

'What? Haven't the other astrologers told you that you are not a Virgo? You are a Pisces. Yes: 80 per cent Pisces and 20 per cent Leo. Those astrologers were not great masters.'

The man was impossible. He took a big magnifying glass and a pocket torch and began to read my palm. After scrutinizing it for a long time he began: *'Mr Tiziano, in your family there are problems of diabetes, and you too suffer from it.'* (I do not, you fool! I wanted to say, but I held back to see how far he would go.) *'Your life is dominated by sex.'* (I really wouldn't say that!) *'You are attracted to women and women are attracted to you. With sex you have had many experiences – of course not as many as Casanova, the greatest lover in human history, but at least half as many.'* That pathetic line about 'the greatest lover in human history' suggested to me that this must be his own deepest wish: to be Casanova, not an astrologer! I had a fleeting impulse of compassion for this spindly, stooping, greasy-haired gentleman. *'This is absolutely certain: sex is very strong in your horoscope, and in your hand the Mount of Venus is prominent. To tell the truth, you can hardly even talk to a woman – what interests you is getting them into bed as quickly as possible. That is the spice of life for you, Mr Tiziano. Isn't that so?'*

I smiled, hoping to appear enigmatic and to encourage him to continue.

'In this respect you take after your father.' (My poor father, who met my mother, married her, and I think never knew another woman until he died at the age of seventy–seven.) *'Your father's still alive, isn't he?'* (I remained silent.) *'Don't be offended if I tell you this, but your father has always been a great ladies' man. Your horoscope is clear on this point. There, I see your parents. Your mother is sad, the two of them are quarrelling. When you were a child there were always quarrels in your house, about your father's lovers. It caused you much suffering. In the early years of your life you also had problems at school: you were at the bottom of your class, while your brothers and sisters were brilliant.'*

'I have no brothers or sisters. I'm an only child,' I said, as if to punish him for his inanities, but he recovered at once.

'Then that means that your mother must have had a number of miscarriages. That is why now you are interested in the occult, and why you have come to me to gain an understanding of your life. You bear the cross of all those souls.'

The man was hopeless, but by now I found him comic – just as when at the opera someone sings out of tune. The first false note hurts your ears, the second still worse, but then you start waiting for the next, to laugh. I began to feel a certain pity for him as he fumbled about with his papers, his calculations and his words. I almost felt like suggesting something right for him to say, but evidently he too had his destiny, and it was to make a fool of himself.

'*As a young man you wanted to pursue a military career.*' (It never crossed my mind, not even as a joke!) '*You wanted to be an officer, but you didn't succeed. Reading your palm, however, I see that now you often have to do with VIPs, important people in politics and the army. Recently you've had a hard time at work, because your bosses don't appreciate you enough. And then you had a big love problem. In 1991 there was a woman in your life – one with light skin, very light, perhaps a Chinese or Korean – who made you suffer very much. She is no longer on the scene, but now I see another, a woman about to enter your life, who will cause you many problems.*'

'What woman, soothsayer?' I asked.

'*I see her very clearly: she is a Muslim woman.*' (Not wearing a veil, I hope!) '*Yes, because you'll have more and more to do with Islam, and this woman is a follower of Islam. You must have had other Muslim women in the past,*' (No, but what a pity!) '*but this one is special. You've been married twice, haven't you?*'

'No.'

'*Then your marriage is unhappy, and therefore you've had many, many other women in your life. When was your wife born?*'

'9 April 1939.'

'*Ah, yes, yes! Your wife makes you unhappy: she is a* petite-bourgeoise, *a petulant, unbearable woman who never leaves you in peace. She is always worrying about what her friends and neighbours tell her.*' (Poor Angela, this idiot reads the exact reverse of every coin!) '*You have diabetes, don't you?*'

'No.'

'*Then you must have something wrong with your bladder, your liver . . . ah, yes, you've had hepatitis!*'

'No. Never.'

'*How many children do you have?*'

'You tell me.'

'*It's hard to tell about children, but it seems to me that the first one is
. . .* ' (Now it's a matter of luck) '*a girl.*' (He's wrong again!)

'No, a boy.'

'*Good, then you have two children, and the second one is also a boy . . .
and, forgive me for telling you this, but then your wife had several abortions.
Here, in your horoscope and in your hand, I see them clearly. Several
abortions. You will make great progress in the last years of your life because
in your hand there are two life lines,*' (That seems to be true, they all
see them.) '*and if you wish you could become a healer. Your twentieth year
was a disaster.*' (No!) '*But the really terrible year when everything went
wrong was 1971. You were confused and didn't know what to do.*' (On the
contrary, that was the year I decided to come to Asia.)

At that point I fell silent and just let him talk; I no longer wanted
to contradict him, but the facts did it for me.

'*I see from both your horoscope and your hand that you have a birthmark
on the sole of your foot, and that mole is significant.*'

My only mole is the one on my forehead, but I remained silent.
He had me take off my shoes and socks, and he looked and looked
with his flashlight. He found nothing. Anyone seeing the two of us
– me sitting on a chair with my feet in the air, and him with a
flashlight and magnifying glass looking for a non-existent mole –
would have burst out laughing.

He returned to a more serious subject: my previous life. He began
reciting a bizarre succession of reasonings and reckonings, with names
of planets, numbers, more names and more numbers, until he finally
reached his grand conclusion: '*Eighty-eight, five, sixteen . . . This is
clear: you were born Tiziano Terzani, in Florence, five years, five months
and sixteen days after your previous death.*'

'And where did I die?'

'*No, that I cannot tell. That I do not see, but if you wish I can give you
the address of someone who can. You see, I have had to specialize. The
great majority of my clients are Chinese, and if I started talking about their
previous lives I would go bankrupt. The Chinese do not care about past
lives, only this life; they are interested in making money, and what they
want to know is how far they can go in cheating their customers and deceiving
their friends. For them only this life counts, not the one before or the one
after.*'

My poor fortune-teller! Another victim of the prosaic character
of the times, and of the diaspora Chinese! Perhaps a hundred years

ago he would have been a better astrologer. Now he talked and
talked, but none of what he said could be made to rhyme with the
facts. I must have sent him a silent message of sympathy, because at
long last he began saying more sensible things.

'*In my sector I am good at my job, and I can tell you one thing for
certain: don't go into business, you'll lose everything. Never lend money,
you won't get it back. Don't guarantee anyone's loans and don't play the
stock market. Money is not made for you.*' He looked at my left hand
and said I had been in prison a couple of times in my life, and the
reason was that I had annoyed government authorities and the army.
There he was right.

According to his price list I had purchased a forecast for the next
three years, and he gave it to me with a plethora of dates and details.
Essentially, he said, my biggest problem was health. '*In 1979 you had
a skin disease,*' (No.) '*and it will come out again. Between now and your
fifty-eighth year you will have a sudden, very serious illness . . . perhaps a
heart attack. But I think you will survive. However, you must be very, very
careful.*' He said that in the next three years I would travel a great
deal, and that, apart from the Muslim woman, I would have many
lovers. I ran the risk of catching venereal diseases, perhaps even
AIDS.

He said that I would buy another house, and that I must be careful
of dangerous sports. There was a good chance that I would lose my
left eye. As for death, if I overcame the serious illness of the next
three years I might live to the age of seventy-six, but he was not
sure. He was sure that I would die far from Florence, probably in
Vietnam or China, but anyway in the Orient, not in the West.

I recalled a joke I had heard about fortune-tellers. 'For the next
ten years your life will be horrible, you will have great problems and
nothing will go well for you,' says the fortune-teller. 'And then?'
asks the client anxiously. 'Then? Then you'll get used to it!'

By this point I was used to the man's stupidities. I didn't want to
offend him, so I asked what he had learned from twenty years of
this work, and if in his opinion man had freedom of choice.

'*That is a question which has tormented Indian philosophers for six
thousand years,*' he said in the pontifical tone he adopted to lend
weight to his platitudes. '*Free will is an illusion. Much of life is predeter-
mined. We are born in a family, a country, a time which we have not
chosen, just as we have not chosen the body in which we are born.*' (He

glanced at his own with a grimace of disgust.) '*Knowing certain things in advance can help us to minimize the effects of our* karma: *light* karma, *that is, not the heavy kind. Heavy* karma *is like a typhoon striking a small island: you can't change it, you can only wait until it passes. But one can influence light* karma. *With stones, for example,*' and he displayed his rings, as if I had not already noticed them. '*The body,*' he said, '*has an aura of its own and that can be strengthened. A great deal depends upon the proper choice of stones.*'

So this was the fashionable fortune-teller of Kuala Lumpur, the one even his colleague Kaka in Penang had said was very famous (although he had told Kaka he would die of a heart attack at fifty-two, and he was already sixty-five!). He was also the dullest, the most banal, the least inspiring of all the odd characters I had met in my travels.

It was time. I felt that with him I could put an end to these encounters.

CHAPTER TWENTY-FIVE

TV for the Headhunters

Is it right that headhunters should abandon their rituals, however macabre, in favour of the more innocuous but equally inhuman practice of sitting for hours and hours in front of a box of illusions called television? Is it right that the warm, intimate light of oil lamps should be replaced by the flat, bluish glare of fluorescent tubes? That the sweet chiming of bells at the top of a pagoda, stirred by the sunset breeze, should be drowned by the screech of a discotheque by a lake on which plastic bags and empty imported beer cans float obscenely amid the shining expanse of lotus flowers?

'Progress' has spread to every corner of the earth – even where there are no roads or airports yet, a simple antenna on a pole will pick up the seductive messages and poisonous dreams of modernity. There are few places left where one can still ask questions like those above, even rhetorically. One of them was a remote corner of eastern Burma, between the town of Kengtung and the Chinese border. For more than half a century, because of Burma's internal events and the xenophobia of its rulers, the region had remained cut off from the rest of the world, and thus locked in the magic beauty of timeless things.

The spell is now broken. Twelve months after opening the road to Kengtung, built by the forced labour of chained prisoners, the Burmese, under pressure from Bangkok and Peking, have extended it from Kengtung to the province of Yunnan. This has transformed the whole region into a corridor between Thailand and China, and a free market for everything from heroin to virgins. One of the last sanctuaries of untamed nature has been sacrificed to the logic of profit. I was one of those who took part in that rape. At the beginning of December I rode in one of the forty-six cars of the convoy which inaugurated the link between Chiang Rai in northern Thailand and Kunming in southern China.

China and Thailand want to strengthen their economic ties, and they need a direct overland communication route. My 'Friendship Rally', advertised as a ten-day 'adventure tour', was meant to demonstrate that the Burmese mountains are no longer an obstacle to mutual development, and that the opening of the road is in everyone's interest. For the organizers, the trip was a great success. To me it was a continual cause for despair.

The crude, tortuous road from Mae Sai to Kengtung which I had travelled at the beginning of the year had already been doubled in width, and was about to be tarmacked. The prisoners had been sent off to work in stone quarries, so as not to spoil the view for the tourists. In their place were bulldozers, cranes and lorries from Thailand. In the villages I saw new brick houses which had been built with the money earned by girls in the brothels across the border. And Kengtung itself, after just a few months, already showed all the signs of the ineluctable victory of modernity over tradition, of the garish over the natural. Psychedelic haloes – concentric rings of multicoloured flashing bulbs – had begun to appear behind the heads of Buddhas in the pagodas; fluorescent lights could already be seen in many houses; and a deafening discotheque had been built on the shore of Lake Neung Ting.

The morning market was still a great adventure, with its fantastic collection of humanity – Meo hunters, Padaung women, the Lisu, the Karen, the Paò mountain people – each with something to sell or exchange. An Akka woman with a wooden pack-saddle held by a strap over her forehead showed some Thai tourists a beautiful blanket covered with embroidery in the old style. One of them offered her a 500-baht note. The woman signalled no. Another held up two 100-baht notes. She took them and gave him her blanket. Everyone laughed, even the poor woman who went away happy, confident that two notes must be worth more than one.

At the Italian mission, the only change in ten months was that there was one nun less. She had died in November, and they had buried her in the church.

*   *   *

The most truly 'adventurous' part of the trip began after Kengtung. The forest grew dense, and the road, barely opened by the bulldozers, ran up a steep slope. The villages we passed through were clusters of wooden huts grouped around pure white pagodas. The English writer Maurice Collis, who in 1938 was the last Westerner to travel in the region, described how the peasants would fall on their knees when they heard a motor car: it must be carrying a prince!

After a couple of hours we came to an old iron bridge over a little river. The convoy stopped.

'Is this the border?' I asked a Burmese official who seemed to be in charge of the place.

'No, that's thirty miles further on, but the border controls are here.'

'Why?'

The official did not answer, but simply handed back my passport as if from there onwards I and all the others were out of his hands. And indeed we were.

As soon as we crossed the bridge we were stopped again, and the cars were inspected once more, this time by some strange, small soldiers with lean, high-cheekboned faces, Chinese-style uniforms like those of the Khmer Rouge, and AK-47s. The striped flag that flew over their blockhouse, fenced with pointed bamboo stakes, was different from that of Rangoon. On maps the region is still part of Burma, but in reality we had just entered 'Wa Land', the territory of the headhunters. We were ordered not to get out of the cars and to keep our windows tightly closed. It was absolutely forbidden to take photographs. Nobody smiled at us or made a gesture of greeting. 'Adventure tourism' did not seem to interest the Wa, only a $15 tax per car which the organizers paid, after which we were allowed to pass.

The Wa are a mountain people. For years they fought alongside the Burmese Communist guerrillas against Rangoon; then the Communists lost the support of Peking, made peace with the government and started growing opium, and the Wa had no choice but to do the same. They obtained an autonomy of sorts for their land, and there, obviously with the consent of Burma on one side and China on the other, they have become full-time heroin producers. This has also turned them into competitors of Khun Sa, the great drug king who operates further south.

I am always curious at how the Western judicial system, which by now is formally the law of the world, has not taken root in Asia. Here the typically Western concepts of 'right', of 'state' and 'frontier', are adapted to local traditions and interests. The Chinese, for example, have always considered the fringe regions of the Middle Kingdom as 'subject areas' that owe tribute to the Son of Heaven, even though they are not officially part of China. Although the 'Wa Land' is technically in Burmese territory, its chief is the very Chinese Li Minxiang, an ex-Red Guard and former advisor to the Burmese Communist guerrillas. Now he too has been converted to the production of heroin. His headquarters are in the town of Monglà, the 'capital' of 'Wa Land', only a hundred yards from the frontier with China. We were absolutely forbidden to stop in Monglà, but it was not hard to recognize the house of Li Minxiang high on a hill, with a large satellite dish on the roof. In a sort of café by the roadside I saw about fifty young people sitting on wooden benches, glued to a television screen. The swift, dusty passage of our convoy distracted them for only a few seconds.

The Chinese are great actors, and several rehearsals must have been held for the arrival of the 'Friendship Rally'. A barrier, freshly painted red and white, was raised at the sight of the first vehicle, and policemen in brand-new uniforms recited: 'Welcome to China. You are pioneers. We hope that many others will follow you.' Since the end of the Second World War no Westerner had passed through there, and television reporters from Yunnan had been brought in to film the event. In the centre of the town of Daluò the authorities had laid on one of their standard receptions to celebrate 'friendship between peoples'. For me it was a good chance to take a walk around the place. Most of the houses were new or still under construction. A bank was prominent. From the telephone booths it was possible to call anywhere in the world. Everyone knew Li Minxiang, and they said he often came to Daluò. If I asked about opium and heroin they just smiled. A policeman said we had passed the refinery just before the border.

The set-up was perfectly suited to the interests of all the protagonists. By leaving part of its territory in the hands of the Wa, the Rangoon government could claim that it was in no way involved in the drug traffic carried out by those 'rebels', even if it undoubtedly took a percentage of the profits. The Chinese, for their part, could say they had neither plantations nor refineries within their borders, even if they undoubtedly profited from the fact that most of Li Minxiang's heroin passed through China *en route* to the rest of the world.

After Daluò the 'adventure tour' was entirely run by the Chinese authorities. Half a dozen police cars preceded and followed our convoy; in the villages and cities we drove through the whole population had been rounded up to stand by the road and manifest their 'spontaneous' enthusiasm for the 'Friendship Rally'.

The Chinese count on this road to export the products of their consumer industry through Burma to South-East Asia and India. The Thais are equally interested in the direct link with China for developing their depressed northern regions and extending their influence to those parts of Burma with populations related to the Thais, such as the Shan.

The city of Kunming was already famous in Marco Polo's time. He spent a few days there, and later described the local women's surprising custom of giving themselves to visitors with no opposition from their husbands. Now as our convoy approached the city it felt like arriving in Hong Kong, with brand new steel and glass buildings silhouetted against the sky. But on the roads, pushed to the side by policemen dressed like generals of a Latin American dictatorship, swarmed the usual enormous crowd of poor Chinese. Many still wore the blue outfits of Mao's time.

Mao. In Kunming he was far from forgotten. Every car I saw had a big medal hung on the rear-view mirror: on one side was the classic photo of the young Mao in Yenan wearing his green cap with the red star, and on the other the photo of Mao in old age, with the mole on his chin. 'It brings good luck. It gives protection against accidents,' I was told by one of the hotel drivers. From being the god of the revolution, Mao had become the god of traffic. Perhaps for the Chinese that was a wise and practical way of exorcizing the *phii*, the ghost, of a man who during his lifetime had weighed so heavily on their lives, and who after his death they certainly did not want returning to disturb their dreams. By honouring him as a divinity, they hoped to keep him quiet.

A strange fate, that of Mao. He began by trying to revitalize China by giving its civilization a new foundation and new values, and ended by wrecking what little still remained of the old. He tried to destroy the Chinese view that they were different because of their civilization, and to replace it with the idea that they were different because they were revolutionaries. When it became clear that the revolution was a failure, the Chinese were cast adrift to be swept away by the current of the times, to become just like all the others. Poor Chinese!

The fate of this extraordinary civilization saddened me. For literally thousands of years it had followed another path, had confronted life, death, nature and the gods in a way unlike any other. The Chinese had invented their own way of writing, of eating, of making love, of doing their hair; for centuries they had cared for the sick in a different way, looked in a different way at the sky, the mountains, the rivers; they had a different idea of how to build houses and temples, a different view of anatomy, different concepts of the soul, of strength, of wind and water. Today that civilization aspires only to be modern, like the West; it wants to become like that little air-conditioned island that is Singapore; its young people dream only of dressing like 'businessmen', of queuing up at Macdonald's, of owning a quartz watch, a colour television and a mobile phone.

Sad, is it not? And not just for the Chinese, but for humanity in general, which loses so much when it loses its differences and becomes all the same. Mao understood that in order to save China it had be closed to Western influence, it had to seek a Chinese solution to the problems of modernity and development. In posing the problem Mao was truly great. And he was great in being wrong about how to solve it. But always great, Mao: a great poet, great strategist, great intellectual, great murderer. Great like China, great like the tragedy it is now enduring.

If someone is able to look back at the history of humanity a few centuries from now, he will surely see the end of Chinese civilization as a great loss: because with it ended a great alternative, whose existence could perhaps have guaranteed the harmony of the world.

Not by chance was it the Chinese who discovered that the essence of everything lies in the equilibrium between opposites, between *yin* and *yang*, between sun and moon, light and shadow, male and female, water and fire. It is by harmonizing differences that the world works, reproduces itself, maintains its tension, lives. So in fact there is some reason to regret the end of Communism – not for itself, but as an alternative, a counterweight. Now that it no longer exists there is a great disequilibrium, and even the side that thinks it has won no longer has the tension that stimulated its creativity.

We left Kunming at dawn, and spent a day crossing a landscape of beautiful nature and forlorn humanity. The mountains, the rivers, the rice terraces and tea plantations were magnificent, but those who lived in the mud huts along the road were in a deplorable state – dirty, dusty, poor, dishevelled – the people who never figure in the statistics of economic growth.

I had heard that as a response to the rise of materialism in China, besides a renewed interest in the occult there had been a notable increase in the number of hermits. More and more people were abandoning society and seeking refuge in the mountains. Yunnan was one of the classical destinations. I saw a couple of hermits marching along with pilgrims' staffs at the edge of the road, dressed in the old style, their feet wrapped in cloth strips and their hair plaited and tied in buns on top of their heads. I would have liked to talk with them, but it was impossible to stop the convoy. For a long time those figures remained in my mind, like apparitions.

On the journey back the convoy stopped again in Kengtung. The first time round I had asked a Burmese woman to help me get in touch with the best fortune-teller in town, and she had made an appointment for me with a young man who was said to have exceptional powers.

He lived in one of the many wooden houses lining a beautiful cobblestoned street. When we arrived he was standing at the door waiting for us: a thin young man of about thirty, with a fine head of thick, rebellious hair and a look of exaltation. He took us up a rickety stairway to the first floor. We sat on wooden floorboards covered with a piece of green and brown plastic. After the usual questions and the usual calculations, he began talking about my life. He said that at fifty-five I was facing a major turn, that I had decisions to make, and that recently I had received a sum of money which had nothing to do with my salary. I said yes, thinking of a prize I had just been awarded, and this seemed to encourage him.

'*During the next two months you will meet a person at a much higher level than yourself, not in terms of power or money but of spirituality, and that person will improve your life. This will happen between the end of January and the beginning of February.*' (I thought of the meditation course I had decided to attend, just in that period. Was it I who told him about it, or was it he who 'saw' it?) '*In your hand there are two life lines. Both are very strong. You have the possibility of living long and of advancing spiritually. It depends on you, but you may still fail. In the next six months there will be many changes in your life.*' (Certainly, I thought, by May I have to be in India.) '*From next year on your life will continue to improve from day to day, from year to year, for a long period, until you die.*'

He took my hand and held his own an inch or two above it. He closed his eyes as if to concentrate, and after a few moments his hand began to tremble. '*I feel heat,*' he said. '*You have great strength. You have the capacity to become a seer. I feel it; we are in communication. You have something to do with India. Have you been there?*'

That was striking. I did indeed have something to do with India, but how did he discover it? I had just mentally formed the word 'India'. But how had he heard it?

'Yes, I've been there, but why do you ask?'

'*Because she is behind you. I see her,*' he said, still with his eyes closed.

'Who?'

'*An Indian goddess, a goddess who protects you, who is always with you. What is your religion?*'

'None, really.'

'*In your past life you were a Buddhist, and now you are tending to return to the* dharma, *the way of Buddha. When you arrive in India, make a donation at once. Not a charitable gift to the poor, but a donation to a Buddhist institution, to Buddhism. Do you meditate?*'

That too was a word that had just been in my mind. Was it I who suggested it to him?

'Not yet.'

'*Do it, because in this life, or at most in the next, you will reach* Shamballa *and you will have the power to help others . . . and then your life will lengthen and you will be able to control your death. Take care, everything will be decided in the next six months. It all depends on you. You have always had a sixth sense, an instinct that has always helped you. You have been in war zones and survived because you were able to see the danger in your future and avoid it, but now you have only a short way to go, and soon you will be able to see the future of others.'*

This was certainly one of the strangest characters – but also the most authentic – among the many fortune-tellers I had spoken to. And I myself felt that we were 'in communication'. But who was speaking to whom? And in what way?

'My children?' I asked, returning the conversation to something concrete so as to have a way of checking his capacities. He seemed to understand. *'You have two children. The first is a boy and the other a girl,'* he replied, after concentrating – or after having read that answer in my head?

'Do you see any problems in their future?' I asked.

'No, none. Not even that of your daughter worries me.'

'What problem?' I asked, knowing well that I was thinking of the witch in Bangkok.

'That she won't marry. But she will marry, fear not.'

It was remarkable how he seemed able to read my unspoken replies to the questions I asked aloud.

He was still holding his hand over mine, and at one point I too had the impression of feeling heat, something that passed from one to the other. Presumably it was a matter of suggestion. The place, the sounds and odours of the early evening, the smoke of cooking fires, the pleasant interlude of peace after days of cars and dusty roads, all put me in tune with the man. I certainly felt much more in common with him than with the 'adventure tourists' with whom I had spent the past week.

'Have you ever heard anyone speak of U Ba Khin?' he asked. *'He is a Burmese who founded a school of meditation that now has pupils all over the world. Follow his method. It is the best for people like you who want to go on living in the world – not to retire to a monastery, but to learn all the same.'* He told me he had been meditating for three years, but had only recently become aware of his powers. It had happened by chance: in a town in northern Burma the municipal safe had disappeared, and one day, by concentrating, he had managed to see who had taken it and where it was hidden. Since that time he had heard voices and seen into people's future. He no longer found it easy to work in the town's economic planning office, where he was employed.

He escorted me to the door, and as I took my leave he said that we would meet again. I could not imagine how. In less than a year I had been to Kengtung twice, and I had the feeling that for me this was a farewell, not only to the old Shan capital but to a kind of Asia which I loved, and of which Kengtung had become a symbol.

The convoy was to leave at dawn. I waited until everyone else had gone to bed and the discotheque on the lake had closed, and took a walk alone around the city. It was deserted, but alive with shadows and ancient sounds. I walked as far as the city gate that had remained sadly standing, with a piece of old wall, in the middle of the widened road; I heard again the divine tinkling of the bells of the pagoda on the hilltop, and among the silhouettes of the trees against the white monastery walls I saw the shadow of a man, cast by the moonlight. He walked slowly, his head bent, like someone absorbed in useless thoughts about the meaning of life as he follows a funeral procession. It was myself.

The rest of the trip was monotonous. The next evening we were back in Thailand. In Chiang Rai, in one of the new *de luxe* hotels for 'adventure tourists', they had organized a banquet to celebrate the success of the 'Friendship Rally', distributing medals and diplomas – the sort of situation I always avoid like the plague. I went straight to the bus station and on towards Bangkok.

I was lucky. If I had not arrived that night in Chiang Mai I would have missed a magnificent opportunity: an invitation to spend New Year's Eve with the Devil.

CHAPTER TWENTY-SIX

New Year's Eve with the Devil

All the message said was that I should go the next day to a certain inn in Maehongson, a town in north-west Thailand, and wait there for someone to contact me. That meant leaving immediately for another nine-hour bus ride through the mountains, but I didn't think twice. The message was the response to a request I had made through some intermediaries in Bangkok. Together with my Swedish colleague Bertil Lindner, a walking encyclopedia on Burmese affairs, I had asked to meet one of the most wanted men in the world: Khun Sa, the 'Prince of Darkness'. For decades Khun Sa has been the warlord of the Golden Triangle, the last great drug baron since General Noriega ended up in an American prison and Pablo Escobal in a grave in Colombia. Here was another story I could write without having to take a plane.

The generals of the Rangoon dictatorship, trying to appease international opinion after murdering thousands of students and arresting Aung San Suu Kyi, had just announced a military offensive against Khun Sa. He for his part had declared the secession from the Burmese Union of the territories he controlled, and named himself president of an independent state called the 'Land of the Shan'.

I used the long bus ride to get some sleep. In Maehongson I found the designated inn, took a room, and met up with Bertil, who had come directly from Bangkok. Of Swedish origin, he had come to Asia straight from university, and, rather like me, had found himself at home there. If ever there were a reincarnation of his compatriot Sven Hedin, the great explorer of a century ago, it might well have been Bertil. In 1985 Bertil walked for months through the mountains of northern Burma, married the telegraph operator of one of the guerrilla groups, and wrote the first of a series of books about the region.

Next morning, as we were having breakfast, a very Chinese-looking man of about thirty sat down at our table. He had the look of a pre-war Shanghai gangster: leather jacket, hair slicked back, thin moustache. He said everything was organized. We should expect to hike for eight to ten hours. Were we ready? We should follow him.

We drove for about twenty miles in Bertil's jeep on an asphalt road. The small compass I always carry indicated that we were going north. We came to a sort of farm surrounded by a high wooden fence, where we were handed over to some more strange characters, all apparently Chinese, who without saying a word showed us where to hide the car and offered us tea. Soon a young Shan appeared with three mules, and we set off. One mule carried our bags and water supplies, the other two were free in case we needed to ride. For the first few hours the going was easy. We passed a beautiful limestone mountain, then up and down a series of hills, crossing streams with water up to our knees. In the early afternoon we climbed a steep incline. The forest grew more and more dense, the trees taller. We followed a mule track, which made walking particularly difficult. The animals, sometimes in caravans of up to a hundred, all tended to put their hooves in the same places, producing a continuous series of holes. Along the way we encountered a *bandit krate*, a yellow-and-black striped snake, very poisonous but not aggressive, and some huge, brilliantly coloured millipedes.

At sunset we stood on the highest ridge, with a glorious, thrilling view to the west. The sun went down in a shower of fiery gold behind a succession of mountain ranges in shades of green, blue, violet and black. The nearest ones, covered with forest, had a soft and fuzzy look, while those further away had hard, precise outlines.

How deceptive beauty can be. The panorama was breathtaking in its vastness, its peace, its vitality. And yet there, under those trees majestic as cathedrals, under those bamboo thickets exuberant as fireworks, lay the origins of a trail of sorrow that knows no borders, that crosses every sea and penetrates every country to invade our homes and kill our children. What I saw before me was the heart of the Golden Triangle (what a deceptive name!), the source of much of the heroin produced in the world today. The man I was going to meet with so much effort was the ruler of that empire of death.

Night fell very quickly. The darkness echoed with bird calls, screams of monkeys, and the mysterious rustlings and scrapings of other animals that I could not see.

The last three hours, all downhill, were especially hard. I got cramps in my calves, a bad headache, and then – a sharp pain in the chest. Is that not how a heart attack begins? I thought of the abbot in Ulan Bator, who had seen problems with my heart in the ashes of incense; I thought of that clueless astrologer in Kuala Lumpur, who also foresaw a serious illness before I was fifty-eight. No use telling myself how many other things those fortune-tellers had got wrong. My hand instinctively went to the mole on my forehead – which according to the sorceress in Singapore was a sign that I would die in a foreign land. What could be more foreign than this forest! I would have to 'dictate my last wishes' to Bertil. When that expression popped into my head I had to laugh. And then I was really frightened, by the thought that one might take the words of a fortune-teller so seriously as to bring about what he foresaw, and make the prophecy come true. So instead of giving myself a heart attack, I took a good deep breath and went on walking.

The sky was crowded with stars, but at ground level the darkness was absolute. It was the night of the December new moon, when the Shan celebrate their New Year. Their 2088 was about to begin: they count from the year they were converted to Buddhism and built their first pagoda on the shores of the Dead Lake in Yunnan. The festivities last a week, and it was for these that we had been invited by Khun Sa. In two more weeks our 1993 would end. And my year without planes? Not quite. The Hong Kong fortune-teller was Chinese, and for him the year ends not on 31 December but with the first new moon of spring. In 1994 it would rise on 8 February. If I really wanted to heed his prophecy, I must hold out until then.

After nine hours' walking we came to a valley. I heard the rushing of a stream, and found myself walking through it before I saw it. On the opposite shore was a large, isolated wooden house. As we entered, by the dim light of an oil lamp I saw the shapes of a few people standing to one side. I heard a woman give some orders in Chinese, and a young man brought us hot tea.

'Where do you come from?' I asked him.

'From Yunnan.'

'To do what?'

'To work,' he replied. I did not feel I could ask him anything else. The woman spoke to someone over a walkie-talkie, and soon a small pickup truck came to collect us. We drove for half an hour along a dirt road, and at last, in the middle of a plain, surrounded by mountains even blacker than the sky, a town rose before us. In a large clearing was a fairground with crowds of people strolling, eating and playing various games at the stalls. Dozens of very young soldiers, in clean uniforms and carrying rifles, discreetly stood guard in the dark. We had arrived at Ho Mong – 'the Capital of Evil', as the newspapers call it. It was in Burmese territory, but only about six miles from the Thai border.

The sole warning we had been given before leaving was absolutely not to let ourselves be seen by the Thai army, which claims to control this border rigorously. They do not want in any way to give the impression – especially to foreign observers – of collaborating with the 'rebels' or having relations with the drug traders. Bangkok maintains cordial diplomatic and trade relations with the dictatorial regime of Rangoon, and officially denies having anything to do with Khun Sa and his Land of the Shan.

It was cold, and the 'foreign minister' of the Land of the Shan, who came to welcome us and take us to the 'government guest house', had a woollen skullcap on his head and an anorak over his pyjamas.

We spent five days in Ho Mong, and our stay was full of discoveries and surprises. The first came as soon as we got up the next morning, when we found that there are at least two direct roads from Thailand to Ho Mong, and that all of Khun Sa's other guests had arrived in comfort by car. Among them were Thai army officers in civilian clothes. Surprising, as since 1990 Khun Sa has been under investigation in the United States as a drug dealer, and both there and in Thailand there is a price of $20,000 on his head. We photographed one another smiling broadly. The other guests were Shan people who had come from territories controlled by the Rangoon government – I met two from Kengtung – or who live abroad. One was the daughter of the old *sawbaw* of Yawnghwe, the King of the Thousand Banana Trees, who had emigrated to America.

The General, as they all called him, did not keep us waiting. At breakfast time a pickup stopped in front of the guest house, six soldiers jumped out, armed to the teeth, and from the front passenger seat, elegant in a greenish-brown uniform with the flag of the Land of the Shan as the only decoration on his sleeve, Khun Sa slowly emerged.

The first impression was sympathetic. He was very Chinese in appearance and bearing, with a smooth, shining face, small lively eyes, teeth brown from nicotine; he was poised and at ease. Instinctively, from professional habit, I searched for some detail I would remember, something in his face, a gesture that betrayed who he was. I saw none. His face was no more inscrutable than those of other Asians, his eyes no more mysterious, indifferent, murderous, impassive, determined or cruel. If I had met Khun Sa in the market without his escort and his uniform, I would have taken him for just another citizen out shopping. But isn't that what is said about great spies?

Shaking Bertil's hand he said: 'I have heard much about you. Your words and my actions are arrows pointed at the heart of the dictators of Rangoon.' Bertil lit his pipe, embarrassed. For a journalist nothing is worse than being taken for an ally. By anyone, let alone Khun Sa.

He had come to invite us personally to the great New Year's Eve supper at his home. Theatrically, before he slowly climbed into his truck and left, Khun Sa gave his 'ministers' orders to show us everything, to explain everything to us, to let us go anywhere we liked.

Ho Mong is a town built entirely of houses with wooden walls and roofs of corrugated plastic. There are about twenty thousand inhabitants. The large square in the centre serves as a playing field, parade ground and market. All New Year festivities took place there. They had set up two theatres, a discotheque, some ranges for target shooting, and a catwalk for a beauty contest, the consolation prize in which went to a local transvestite.

Along the main street are barbers, tailors, jewellers, photographers and a couple of video rental shops. *Jurassic Park* was in great demand. All the goods come from Thailand. The currency used is the Thai baht, and even cars drive on the left-hand side of the road as in Thailand, not on the right as in the rest of Burma. Ho Mong has a Buddhist temple with four hundred monks, three hotels 'for commercial travellers', and a brothel with about fifteen girls.

On the houses of the well-to-do are satellite discs to pick up all the international programmes. At the entrance to a modest shop, selling everything from torches to nails to blankets, is a sign: 'Telephone'. Thanks to a special link with Thailand, from Ho Mong, the drug capital of the world, you can dial every corner of the earth, directly. In a telephone booth I overheard a Chinese girl telling someone in Taiwan to buy an air ticket from Bangkok to Hong Kong. Is that not the route the couriers follow? Is it not the Chinese gangsters who control the distribution of drugs all over the world? I did not dare ask these questions aloud.

The only brick building in the whole valley is the residence of Khun Sa: a white house, set apart on a height and surrounded by a vast garden, two tennis courts and a beautiful greenhouse full of orchids. From a distance it looked like a displaced Californian villa. Only from close up could you see it was also a bunker, protected by machine-gun emplacements, anti-aircraft batteries, and a whole barracks full of highly trusted guards.

For the New Year's Eve feast, Khun Sa opened his home to a few hundred officers of his army and officials of his administration. Along with mountains of food, the guests were offered karaoke. There too, in the middle of the Burmese jungle! The great attraction was a wonderful machine, very modern, with powerful speakers and a mega-television on which flashed the images and words of famous Chinese songs. As a polite guest, I ended up with a microphone in my hand to sing, tone-deaf as I am, a duet with the Drug King.

Nothing could have been more entertaining for that audience, and my reward for making everyone laugh was a guided tour of the house. The residence of Khun Sa, with a fireplace in the living room, pink carpeting in the bedrooms, imitation leather chairs with plastic sheets over them, and big bookshelves without one book but full of video-cassettes, was the fulfilment of the dreams of a *nouveau riche*, the status symbol of a bandit with a yearning for respectability. On the walls were souvenir photographs of foreigners: an English lord with his wife, the son of a New York police chief, a former American colonel of the Special Forces.

'Why are they here?'

'Friends,' was the reply.

'And drugs, General? Shall we talk about that?' I ventured.

'Another day, the interview another day. Today we celebrate,' said Khun Sa with a laugh.

The next morning Bertil and I were taken to the offices of the 'government' – a large wooden barracks overlooking the square, with hard earth floors – to meet the various 'ministers'. The minister of information, formerly a veterinarian, had the task of presenting to us the official position of the Land of the Shan. It was this: We Shan are a minority oppressed by the Burmese. After several attempts at guerrilla war conducted in the past by different groups, Khun Sa has united everyone under his leadership and is now fighting a war of liberation. Opium is our weapon in this war. We could easily grow other crops, mangoes for example, instead of opium poppies. It would take less work and nobody could accuse us of trafficking in drugs, which as we know well casts an ugly shadow over our struggle. The problem is that to grow mangoes you need peace, you need roads to take them to market. Whereas with opium we don't need anything. We sell it on the spot, because the buyers come even from very far away to get it. Thus growing opium is our only way of surviving. If we ordered our people to stop growing poppies overnight it would mean condemning them to hunger. The only way of stopping the production of drugs is to have peace and develop an alternative economy. Help us. We would like nothing better.

This argument was far from absurd. The 'foreign minister', no longer in his pyjamas and skullcap but dressed in a jacket and tie for the occasion, showed us some documents: several times since 1980 Khun Sa had made the West, and in particular the United States, an offer to sell or destroy his whole crop of opium. In return he had asked for economic aid of $300 million over a period of six years. There had been some contacts, but in the end nothing had been done. At the beginning of October Khun Sa had written directly to President Clinton reformulating his old offer, but, said the 'ministers', two months had already passed, and no reply had come from Washington.

'Why doesn't the West, instead of trying to eliminate us, help us to develop?' said the 'minister of finance'. 'Repression serves only to raise the price, and that makes the drug traffic more attractive.'

The figures bore him out. In 1948, when Burma became independent, the Golden Triangle produced thirty tonnes of opium. In 1988, despite billions of dollars spent on international police operations and several attempts to destroy the opium at its source – for example by spraying defoliants on the poppy fields – production had risen to three thousand tonnes. At the end of 1993 Khun Sa's men expected a harvest of over four thousand tonnes. As it takes ten kilograms of opium to make one kilogram of refined heroin, there must be four hundred tonnes of pure 'Chinese White' from the Land of the Shan going about the world. Never has humanity had such a quantity of drugs at its disposal, and never have the political and financial interests behind this traffic been so vast.

Khun Sa's power, according to his 'ministers', lies in the fact that the Shan people support him, and that he has an army of forty thousand men who are absolutely loyal to him. This army is efficient, with iron discipline. If a deserter is captured, his head is cut off. If he is not caught within three months his parents' heads are cut off and exhibited to his comrades as a warning. A soldier caught smoking opium or injecting heroin is sent to a re-education centre. The 'cure' is ten days in a hole in the ground ten feet deep, followed by months of forced labour. A second offence means execution.

Khun Sa was certainly not the Che Guevara of the Shan, the revolutionary idealist his men wanted me to think he was. But the longer I stayed in Ho Mong, the more I was convinced that there was something equally false, and perhaps unjust, in the way he is depicted as the great villain responsible for all the suffering caused by heroin in the world.

At dawn, as the chilly town emerged from the nightly blanket of fog, women squatted in the open, lighting small wood fires under smoke-blackened pots to prepare breakfast. It was hard to believe that this place hidden in the jungle was really the capital of the new 'evil empire', as the Americans called it. Were these people really malicious spreaders of the eleventh plague, or were they mere pawns in a game controlled by far more powerful forces?

Making Khun Sa the scapegoat is convenient for many people, especially the Americans, who in the past had their own role in the affairs of the Golden Triangle and the drug trade. It was the CIA who after Mao's victory helped the remnants of the Kuomintang army to settle in Burma and finance itself by growing opium. And it was the CIA, through the Thais, who supported Khun Sa when he joined the fight against Communist guerrillas in Thailand. Nobody in Ho Mong denied that the drugs were produced there, and that Khun Sa financed his army and his state by taking 20 per cent of the value of every transaction, from the purchase of opium in the villages to the export of heroin abroad.

How was the exporting done? They didn't tell me. Drug-control agents working in Western embassies in Bangkok are sure that most of Khun Sa's production passes through Thailand, and that plastic bags of 'Chinese White' often travel in military and police vehicles. They estimate that from five hundred to a thousand officials are involved in the traffic. But they are not the only ones. 'Most of these skyscrapers are built with money from drugs,' I was told by a European agent, pointing to the forest of new buildings rising in the centre of Bangkok. 'Drugs is one of the motors that drives this country's economic miracle. People at the highest levels of society have their fingers in that pie.' Now and then you see the tip of the iceberg. The man who was about to become Prime Minister after the fall of the government responsible for the Bangkok massacre had to withdraw when it was revealed that the US had denied him an entry visa on suspicion of being a drug dealer. A well informed person told me that the groups involved in drugs sponsor military and police cadets, so as to have them as accomplices years later when they become colonels and generals.

My interview with Khun Sa was fixed for the day before our departure. It took place among the orchids in the garden of his residence. I had the impression that he liked being interviewed by an 'international press representative', as I was called. He brought along a whole retinue of his men to enjoy the show, and his seraphic face opened in sudden laughter at my more provocative questions, no doubt partly for the benefit of his audience.

'General, you have had to do with drugs all your life. It was you, as a young man, who opened the first morphine factory in Burma. But now you present yourself as a fighter for the freedom of the Shan people. Is this not an excuse to go on doing your lucrative deals with drugs?'

Khun Sa lit a 555 cigarette. Speaking very slowly in Shan, which the 'foreign minister' translated, he replied: 'First of all, the deals are not so lucrative as they seem to you. A shipment of heroin which is worth $1 million here with us, by the time it reaches your countries is worth $100 million. Then who makes the big profits? Certainly not Khun Sa. Certainly not the Shan.' He took a long draw on his cigarette and continued. 'For over thirty years the truth about me and my people has been obscured by a curtain of lies about drugs, spread by our enemies. It is about time the truth came out. We have no secrets. You have gone everywhere freely, you have spoken to everyone, looked where you liked, haven't you? Well, then, do I seem like the devil to you?'

'Not the devil, General; I don't see the horns and the tail. But you can't deny that most of the heroin which floods our countries comes from the opium fields that your people cultivate, from the refineries that you control, and is exported under the protection of your army.'

Khun Sa's assistants appeared alarmed by the way I was talking to the General, but he seemed almost amused. 'It is not I who force my people to grow poppies. It is the Burmese who force them to, because they attack us, because they take away our best land and force us to live in the mountains. I don't control any refineries. The refineries are in the hands of foreign businessmen. As for transport, my army guarantees the security of the roads for everyone who uses them. I fight for the liberation of the Shan people. To finance this fight, I make those who profit from drugs pay taxes. That is all.'

I reminded him that a former American ambassador to Bangkok had recently called him 'humanity's greatest enemy'. I said, 'Noriega has been captured, Escobal was murdered; aren't you afraid your days may be numbered, General?'

'That ambassador, when he opens his mouth he doesn't speak, he farts,' exploded Khun Sa, and the audience burst out laughing. 'As for killing me – it's possible. I have already survived forty-three attempts. Certainly someone will try again. But do you really believe that the problem of drugs would be solved by my death? If that were so, I really would deserve to die. But drugs are an older problem than Khun Sa. In the last century it was you foreigners who brought drugs to Asia and imposed them on us. Now it is Asia that sends drugs to the West. Perhaps it is a question of *karma*. The West is paying for its past actions.' I couldn't say he was wrong.

'The growers and the addicts have nothing to gain from drugs. It is the dealers, the middlemen, who make the big profits.' Again I had to agree. I looked at him, trying to imagine what would happen if he really decided to stop the opium and heroin production. The dealers would kill him, I thought, and replace him with someone else who would serve their interests. The drug trade, like every other mega-business, has become part of the world system of investments and profits which knows no national boundaries and no morality.

In my mind I ran over the picture of international drug trafficking: the foreigners hanged in Penang for having a few grams in their pockets; the naive Englishwoman who agreed to carry a package for a 'friend' and who was now rotting away in a Bangkok prison; the poor addicts who, thinking they can make an easy profit, buy some drugs cheaply in the mountains around Chiang Mai only to be turned in by those who sold it to them, because if the police intercept a certain number of 'amateurs' every year, the professionals can move freely. All small fish compared to the sharks – the predators sitting safely on the top floors of banks, in insurance company boardrooms, in police headquarters or government offices.

When supper-time came Khun Sa invited me to dine with his people. He had me sit beside him, and without an interpreter, in Chinese, we ended up talking about his childhood. His father was Chinese, and had died when he was three years old. His mother had remarried, but she too died two years later. Khun Sa grew up without going to school, and it was only as an adult that he learned to read and write. He laid great emphasis on the fact that the recruits in his army studied from early childhood. At sixteen he stole some rifles and became a bandit. He opened a morphine factory to finance his gang. He had had many children with different wives, the last of whom had died not long ago. I asked him when he was born.

'22 February 1934,' he said.

'At what time?'

'In those days they didn't record the time, but I think it was in the morning.'

We ate at a round plastic table, served by some very young soldiers.

The food was Shan; very good, with lots of cooked vegetables. To drink there was only water. With age-old peasant courtesy Khun Sa occasionally wiped his chopsticks with his lips and put into my bowl some especially choice morsel which he picked out of the common pot.

As we parted he invited me, in the Chinese manner, to return again whenever I had time. The sympathetic impression I had of him that first day at the guest house remained.

The only thing I had not done by now in the Land of the Shan was to see a fortune-teller. I had heard that the abbot of the pagoda was a good astrologer, and on the last night I asked to see him. He was already in bed, but Bertil and I were unusual visitors and he was woken. Our interpreter was a monk who had worked in an American hospital during the Second World War.

When everything was ready the abbot sat, wrapped in a big orange blanket, in the lotus position in front of a low table, pen in hand for his calculations, and asked me the usual question. 'I was born on 22 February 1934,' I replied. 'I don't know the time, in those days it was not recorded, but I think it was in the morning.'

Nobody noticed anything, and the monk, after long calculations, began his litany: *'You had a difficult childhood, without a guide. Perhaps you lost your parents when you were very young. Your life is a life of adventures, of risks. You are generous with others, and people love you. In your heart there have been a number of women, and you have had many children. You yourself don't know exactly how many.'* (This was remarkable.)

'This is not a good year for you. It is a period of great tension. A critical period. You must take great care of your health; there is a chance that you may have an accident and that you will need an operation. The danger comes from the fact that you are a person who likes to move about in the dark, at night, and now you must be very careful about doing this. The greatest danger is between 24 September and 22 November. You must also be very careful of what you say. Even words may put you in danger. You have many enemies and you are always creating new ones. Your life has always been in danger.'

I was extremely impressed. The man whom the monk described was not me, it was the General. I had given Khun Sa's birth date instead of mine partly as a joke, partly because I was tired of hearing the same things again and again. I felt guilty about having deceived the monk, but it was too late to turn back.

'When will I die?' I asked.

'*You will not pass your sixty-seventh birthday,*' said the monk. '*You will die before it.*'

'How? Murdered?'

'*No. From an operation. Take care of your kidneys and your heart. You will be in great danger in 1996. If you survive 1996, then your life will become better afterwards.*'*

'What about money?' I asked.

'*You are one who has many expenses. Often you lose money because someone cheats you, and to get it back you have to cheat others.*' He studied his sheets of calculations, then looked at me as if something did not seem right. I was afraid he had seen through my trick. Then he said: '*Yours is a strange horoscope, a horoscope full of mysteries. Few people really know who you are, whether you are a good person or a bad one.*'

A shiver ran down my spine, and I could hardly take notes any more. None of the fortune-tellers I had seen had spoken of me with the precision with which the abbot unknowingly spoke of Khun Sa. Was it the date of birth? Or was it that I had mentally transmitted to him the three or four things I knew about Khun Sa? But in what language, given that we had none in common?

It was now Bertil's turn. He knew exactly at what time he was born. After doing the calculations, the monk began: '*Your mother is still alive, but I don't see your father. Perhaps he was already dead when you were born.*' Bertil was dumbfounded. It was true.

Intuition? Coincidence? Or perhaps this monk was a true, great astrologer, the best I had ever met. But as we took our leave I was pleased to think that for the sake of a joke I had eluded him.

A tiny sliver of moon shone over the valley as we returned to the inn. The cold was bone-chilling, but all around there was a wonderful peace. The black trees traced their embroidery against the starry sky.

---

* In 1996 Khun Sa, suffering from health problems, did a deal with the authorities. He left Ho Mong, and now lives peacefully in Rangoon. The generals have taken over his kingdom and the heroin trade.

On the big market square some of Khun Sa's young recruits were still shooting at tin cans by the light of little candles shielded from the wind by waxed-paper shades. It was an exquisite scene: the last image I would take away of the Capital of Evil.

Ahead of us lay another nine-hour march up and down the mountains. I went to sleep a little sorry I could not stop and join the game.

CHAPTER TWENTY-SEVEN

The Spy who Meditates

And so, in the end, I had come round to it. Sitting cross-legged on the ground, still as a rock, one hand on the other at navel height, palms upwards, back straight, shoulders relaxed and eyes closed, thinking about the tip of my nose and trying to catch the moment when my breath, slowly and lightly flowing in and out, touched a certain point on my skin. Hour after hour, day after day, never saying a word, eating vegetarian food – the day's last meal before noon – to bed at nine, without reading even one page of a book, to avoid distraction, striving constantly to be aware of every movement, every thought, every sensation.

Meditation: I had spent half my life in Asia and had never given it a thought. I had heard of people who practised it, who went on these courses, but I always felt it had nothing to do with me. I saw it as something for disturbed people, an escapist response to the problems of the world. Incredible, but true. In China, Japan, Tibet, Korea, Thailand, Indochina, I had visited perhaps hundreds of temples and spent whole days in Buddhist monasteries, but I had never thought about the question of meditation. What is its aim? How is it done? What is the sense of it?

Attracted by their beauty, I had collected dozens of statues of Buddha. I had lived in their company – a Burmese one in bronze had presided silently over my library for more than twenty years – but I had never asked myself what they were doing, sitting in the lotus position with that magnanimous smile and those half-closed eyes, one hand in their laps and the other touching the ground. I had truly never wondered about it, as one might never wonder about the meaning of a crucifix that has hung over one's bed since childhood.

But life is also a continuous waste. Think of how many wonderful

353

people we meet without realizing it, of how many beautiful things we pass every day on the way home without noticing them. It always requires the right occasion, a particular event, a person who stops you and draws your attention to this or that. The path that had brought me to the retreat in Pongyang was a labyrinthine one; but in the end, partly following the thread of the fortune-tellers – 'Meditate!' so many of them had told me – and partly the trail of white stones laid down by Chang Choub, I gave in. Leopold told me in November that his teacher, John Coleman, was coming to give one of his courses in Thailand, and urged me to go along. 'You must understand meditation,' he said, 'otherwise what have you been doing all these years in Asia?' The idea of learning to meditate from an American, a former CIA agent, seemed strange; but then, it often takes a Westerner to help one understand some aspects of the East.

The retreat was in Pongyang, in northern Thailand. On one side of a narrow green valley a sprinkling of straw-roofed wooden bungalows lay among drifts of flowers and thickets of giant bamboo and frangipani; across the valley stood the great trees of the ancient jungle, with their lush foliage. The meditation pavilion was a large wooden terrace, near a foaming waterfall that fed a small lake bordered with red and orange flowers.

The day began before sunrise with the striking of a gong on the high terrace whose sound echoed kindly but sternly over the valley. Promptly some thirty torches appeared, twinkling like fireflies as the participants walked up the hill in the darkness. Each took his place on a square cushion, and meditated for an hour facing a platform where the teacher meditated beside a small altar with a Buddha and flowers. Then came breakfast, then two hours of guided meditation, with a quarter-hour break, then lunch – vegetarian – at eleven, then two hours of rest and more hours of meditation. At sunset there was a lesson on *dharma*, the way of the Buddha. The booming gong lent its rhythm to the hours. Its last call, slow and warm, came at nine o'clock – time for bed.

It had taken me twelve hours by train and another hour by car to reach Pongyang, but I would gladly have left the minute I arrived. The other participants were already there. Most were middle-aged women, no longer beautiful, no longer loved, but intelligent, still curious, unwilling to accept the mediocre roles forced on them by society and hence at odds with life; women like those I had so often seen consulting fortune-tellers. Among the men there was not one with a real face. A Swiss said he was there because 'Health is my hobby'; another, a Canadian, hoped to improve his painting through meditation. And what was I doing there? I felt like a patient in a psychiatric ward trying to convince himself that he has been brought there by mistake, or that his condition is less serious than that of his neighbours. But I tamed my arrogance, and stayed.

John Coleman was a big man, tall and heavy, jovial, simple, with anything but the ascetic air of holiness that I expected from a meditator. His assistant – about sixty, thin, straight and elegant with white hair cut very short like a marine – looked like just what he was: a general in the police force.

John had met the general, then a captain, in Bangkok in the early 1950s when he himself was a young American secret agent. It was he who had introduced John to the first steps in the path of meditation. Over the years the captain had had a successful career and had become the king's aide-de-camp; he had retired not long before with a reputation of being one of the most honest police chiefs Thailand had ever known. A devout Buddhist, he had practised meditation for more than forty years, and now he had taken it upon himself to teach it to others.

The first days were very tough. When I first sat in the lotus position it seemed quite comfortable, but after a quarter of an hour it became unbearable, and after half an hour it was absolute torture. My knees were all pins and needles, my back was one big cramp, and the urge to move became overwhelming. Never, not for one second, did I manage to meditate. Instead of fixing my thoughts on the point where my breath touched my skin, my mind was 'a monkey jumping from branch to branch', as John put it, and I was unable, even for the briefest instant, to turn it into 'a strong, solid buffalo, to put a rope round its neck and tie it to a post'.

'Think only of that point, feel only that sensation of the breath touching your skin,' John repeated, very slowly, sitting on the platform like a great wax Buddha. 'At the moment when your breath touches the surface of the skin at the nose, the nerve tissues in the skin respond with a feeling, a sensation, an experience of touch. Be aware of that sensation. Be aware of the in-breath and the out-breath, and thus greed, hatred, and ignorance will be unable to arise. The fires of craving and aversion will be extinguished and your mind will be calm, peaceful, free of fears and anxiety.'

I kept my feet under my knees, my eyes closed, my hands still, but my mind, when it was not focused on the pain in my legs or on the desire to get up and scream, went rushing off in all directions; it fled, and I could not call it back. I did not dominate it; it was not mine. Useless. The pain became unbearable, and even before John announced the end of the hour, breaking the silence with his 'Amen' ('may all our merits be shared by all beings'), I gave up, changed position and opened my eyes. I was frustrated to see how some of the others carried on serenely.

At various times I was on the verge of leaving. What was the point of keeping one's eyes shut when surrounded by the beauty of nature? What was the point of thinking, only to expunge every thought, and of artificially inflicting upon myself some of the pain which life sooner or later deals out to everyone? I listened to the first 'sunset sermons' with irritation. 'Everything in life is suffering. We cause suffering when we are born, we die suffering, we suffer for what we want, we suffer for fear of losing what we have . . .' said John, sounding like a Bible salesman. I was annoyed by his talk of 'a higher level of energy', of 'refining the magnifying-glass of concentration'. The idea was that by spending the first three days thinking only of that point where the breath touches the skin, the mind would become calm – an exercise called *anapanaa*. Both the exercise and its rationale struck me as intellectually demeaning.

There were, however, some pleasures. One was the silence. In the opening ceremony we had formally pledged to observe, throughout the duration of the course, the Five Precepts: not to kill (that included any living being, even mosquitoes – hence no insecticides were used at Pongyang); not to lie; not to take what is not given; not to have sexual relations ('either with oneself or with others'); and not to take intoxicants (meaning not to drink coffee or smoke). We had also promised not to eat after midday, not to wear jewellery, not to use perfumes and not to sleep in an over-comfortable bed. And we had promised to keep the Noble Silence, not to speak or make sounds that might distract the others – and that was marvellous. When we met other participants between meditations there was no need to make conversation; a silent nod was enough. At table we did not have to talk merely to fill the at times uncomfortable vacuum with even more vacuous banalities. Each of us was alone with himself.

This silence was a great discovery. Without the foreground of other people's words, I realized that the glorious beauty of nature was in its silence. I looked at the stars and heard their silence; the moon made no sound; the sun rose and set without a whisper. In the end even the noise of the waterfall, the bird calls, the rustle of the wind in the trees, seemed part of a stupendous, living, cosmic silence which I loved and in which I found peace. It seemed that this silence was a natural right of every man, and that this right had been taken from us. I thought with horror of how for so much of our lives we are pounded by the cacophony we have invented, imagining that it pleases us, or keeps us company. Everyone, now and then, should reaffirm this right to silence and allow himself a pause, some days of silence in which to feel himself again, to reflect and regain a degree of health.

Another pleasure came from the effort. As the days went by, the commitment to the various prohibitions acquired more and more value, and gave a sense of increasing strength. That strength, John said, served to 'create a base of morality' for the next stage of meditation. Precisely by making the effort, one came to feel that one deserved some sort of reward. 'In the last days you will understand. Everything will make sense. Everything will find its place,' repeated John, giving hope that by concentrating on that point where the breath touches the skin we would gain control of our minds, and with that new horizons would open.

That was the real reason for my being there. During my year on the trail of fortune-tellers I had become fascinated by the mind's possibilities and powers. I had come to believe that in the West, for various reasons, the use of the mind has become more limited over the course of time, and a great part of its capacity has been lost. I wanted to rediscover that forgotten path, if it had ever existed. Could it be that the mind is like a muscle which atrophies if it isn't used to the full? I thought about myself. For years I have run a few miles every day, and exercised to keep fit. But when have I ever looked after my mind? When have I ever done exercises to strengthen it and allow it to reach its full capacity? The mind is perhaps the most sophisticated instrument we have, yet we do not even give it the attention we give to our leg muscles.

Alexandra David Neel, the extraordinary French explorer of the

357

Himalayas in the 1930s, tells of Tibetan lamas who could dematerialize themselves through mental effort alone, and of others who
could communicate with each other over long distances. All fiction?
Perhaps not. Perhaps in the human mind there really was something
that we have lost along the road. Some Europeans, supposing that
somewhere in the world there were still human beings able to use
their minds in that way, have gone to look for them in Asia. In 1924
a young Englishman, Paul Brunton, travelled to India to meet yogis,
hermits and fakirs. He tried to find out how, through the exercise
of the mind, they had attained a knowledge which he believed was
being destroyed by modernization. The first step in all the different
paths to that knowledge was meditation. Therefore it was worthwhile
trying to understand what it was.

I watched John meditate as he sat on the platform, wrapped in
a large white blanket, immobile as a statue. He was relaxed and
concentrated; his forehead was smooth and on his lips was a very
light, almost mocking smile, as if – or so it seemed to me – with
those closed eyes he saw something I could not see, as if with those
large, long-lobed ears he heard more than the silence of nature. John
had taken the step. I do not know towards what knowledge, but
certainly towards a peacefulness that hovered about him like a halo.

His was a peculiar story. He was born in 1930 in Pennsylvania
into a poor mining family. He began working as a mechanic and
then as a photographer. At the end of the Second World War he
joined the army and was sent to Japan, where he was given the task
of photographing accused war criminals as their death sentences were
read out to them. After his discharge he returned to the United
States, went to university and was recruited by the CIA. He was
trained to open and close any lock without being detected – locks
of houses, offices, embassies, safes. He would be sent to a foreign
city where for weeks he would study a building and work out how
to enter it, photocopy documents and get out again without leaving
a trace. In 1954 he was posted to Thailand to train the border police.
He became interested in Buddhism, and began to meditate. After a
few years the CIA obviously decided their agent had lost his wits,
and gave him premature retirement and an invalidity pension. For a
while John ran the Oriental Hotel in Bangkok; then he married and
had two children. He continued to meditate, and in the end made
it his mission in life.

In his third sunset sermon on *dharma*, 'the way of the truth, of purification, of detoxification' (my stomach turned at this language), John said that Buddha's great contribution was to have realized that the essence of the world lies in its instability, its impermanence – *anicca* – which is the origin of all suffering. To acquire knowledge of *anicca* is the only way of escaping from pain.

And so, after three days of *anapanaa*, we went on to inner meditation, *vippasanaa*. This means to direct 'that magnifying glass, that band of attention of the mind, sharpened by concentration', to the contemplation of one's own body. We were told to begin by fixing our whole mind on the point below the nostrils, and then to bring the mind up to the crown of the head – I finally understood why so many statues of Buddha have a flame at that very place. Then, from the highest point of the body, very slowly and without losing control, one moves the mind to the skin, under the skin, into the skull, into the brain, into the eyes, into the nose, and slowly down into the chest, into the lungs, the heart, the veins, the bones, the internal organs, down, down to the legs, the toes, the soles of the feet, never thinking of anything else. The mind is directed like a searchlight in a cave, constantly aware of every sensation and aware that all sensations are transient – pain, pleasure, sound, the touch of the wind, always fugitive. 'Know *anicca* . . . continue to know *anicca* . . . *anicca* is all,' repeated John in a slow, deep voice. Know *anicca*. Hour after hour, day after day. Never speaking a word to anyone; and even outside meditation, being always conscious of each movement, each step when walking, each mouthful when eating, feeling each sip of water as it descends in to the stomach and comes to rest.

John began his hours of meditation with a prayer which we awaited with joy:

> May all beings be peaceful and happy.
> May all beings be free of all ignorance,
>   all cravings and all aversions.
> May all beings be free of all suffering,
>   all sorrows and all conflicts.
> May all beings be filled with infinite loving kindness,
>   compassion and equanimity.
> May all beings be fully enlightened.

For my part, I awaited his 'Amen,' which put an end to the hour of torture. I made no progress. With great effort and pain I managed to sit still better than in the beginning, but my aim was to learn to meditate, and in that I was hopeless. One could say of me exactly what a famous monk-meditator had once told John: 'I have seen a hen hatch her eggs without moving for three days, but I've never seen an enlightened hen.'

As the days went by I found John more and more convincing. There was nothing false in him, no pretence. He was a simple man who believed he had understood a great truth. He was a layman who did an exercise, an exercise that was not necessarily religious, but spiritual. Entering and leaving the meditation terrace, he turned to the Buddha and saluted him with hands joined in front of his chest: a gesture of thanks for having shown the way, the *dharma*. In John there was nothing of that vulgar sanctimoniousness one sees in other converts.

Was he the 'superior person' whom, according to the young fortune-teller in Kengtung, I was destined to meet? The facts seemed to chime perfectly with that prophecy; and when John described in his sunset sermon how at first in Thailand no one wanted to teach him meditation, and how he had finally found his great teacher in Rangoon, my spine tingled. 'I learned from U Ba Khin,' he said. Yes, the very name! 'Follow his method,' the young man in Kengtung had said. 'It is the best for people like you.' And here I was following it!

U Ba Khin was born in Burma in 1899. He had entered the English colonial administration, and when the Burmese Union became independent in 1948 he was appointed Accountant General for the Ministry of Finance. A devout Buddhist, he had been interested in meditation since his youth, and he resolved to bring within the reach of laymen this spiritual practice which the monks had kept for centuries as a monopoly for themselves. Either one became a monk, or there was no way of meditating.

He began by giving courses to his subordinates in the ministry; then in 1952 he founded the International Meditation Centre in Rangoon. By his death in 1971, meditation had become a spiritual exercise accessible to everyone – as it was 2500 years ago in the temples of Buddha. U Ba Khin's method was to concentrate all the teaching in a ten-day course, so that afterwards the pupil could return to his normal life and continue meditating on his own.

According to one of the anecdotes John told to lighten his sunset sermons, U Ba Khin's first pupil was a stationmaster. While travelling in a remote part of Burma, U Ba Khin went with the manager of the only station in the region to pay his respects to a famous hermit monk – an *arahant*, or enlightened one, who lived deep in the forest. They came to a tall pole, at the top of which was a sort of nest-like hut made of bamboo leaves, where the monk had been meditating for days. A little door opened and a cloud of flies came out, followed by the head of the *arahant*.

'What are you seeking?' he asked.

'Nirvana,' replied U Ba Khin.

'And how do you expect to reach it?'

'By understanding *anicca*.'

'Excellent. Then teach it to others,' said the *arahant*; then he closed the door and returned to his meditation.

U Ba Khin immediately ordered the stationmaster to assume the lotus position and to breathe, focusing his attention on the point where the breath touches the skin. A new tradition had been born.

As meditation was brought within the reach of all, the practice spread to the West. John was one of the first pupils of U Ba Khin, who authorized him to teach, especially in Europe.

'Then, master, knowing the West, you won't be offended,' I told John when I was called to his bungalow to report on my progress in meditation, the only time I was allowed to break the Noble Silence, 'if I tell you that in all these days I have not meditated for a single minute. That my mind, instead of concentrating on my nose, has gone off in all directions, from repainting my house in the country to a plan for enlarging my library. Instead of thinking about breathing I've thought about things to write, and about how silly it is to be here. When you tell us to think of the throat I think of strangling yours, since you force me into this torture. When you say "legs" I think of those under the skirts of all the Thai women here, even the ugly old one in the back row.'

John laughed merrily. 'Don't lose hope,' he said. 'These things are transitory. They will come to an end. Perhaps for centuries your mind has never been brought under control. And now, all at once, you expect to master it in a few days? Wait. Hold on. Continue to know *anicca*.'

I really had to laugh at the idea that in 'all my previous lives' my mind had never been exercised. But who knows? It could be true. What I have always liked about Buddhism is its tolerance – the absence of sin, the absence of the dead weight that we Westerners carry with us, the cement that holds our civilization together: the sense of guilt. In Buddhist countries nothing is ever terribly reprehensible, no one ever accuses you of anything, no one ever preaches at you or tries to teach you a lesson. Hence these countries are very pleasant to be in, and many young Western travellers, seeking freedom, feel at ease there.

Buddhism leaves you in peace, it never asks anything of you – least of all to become a Buddhist. Among the various prohibitions – an interesting one forbids boasting about one's progress in meditation – there is one that forbids a monk to teach the religion to anyone who does not specifically request it. Buddhism always lets you be what you like. It says not to kill, but everyone kills. What about murderers? That's their business. Their next incarnation will not be a good one. Nobody tries to impose justice here and now: of all things, not that. It is not up to us. Charity, then, is not a moral obligation – on the contrary, by helping the poor one hinders their liberation from bad *karma*; caring for a leper impedes his redemption through suffering and his favourable rebirth. Is your neighbour's house burning down? It must have to do with his former life.

Even more than a religion, Buddhism is a way of life; it is an interpretation of the world from the point of view of a peasant society which is close to nature and needs to explain its absolute cruelty. In nature there is no justice, no reckoning. Then why look for it among men, who after all are part of nature?

Buddhism, then, has no aspirations for conquest, no sense of mission; it does not go fishing for souls. You want to be a Buddhist? Go right ahead. It's up to you. That is why they have never even taught meditation; and it is no accident that the spread of Buddhism today – apart from the Tibetan phenomenon – is mainly the work of Western converts who, not having lost their native crusading instinct, are opening centres for the spread of the religion throughout the world.

At the heart of Buddhism, if it is taken seriously and carried to its ultimate ends, lies a negation of civil society and, obviously, of progress. If everything is transient, if there is no escape from the law of cause and effect, and the only salvation is to acquire an indifference to life – to flee the terrible cycle of birth and death through meditation – then everything is irrelevant, everything is useless, everything should stop. It is a vision of great pessimism, with nihilistic consequences.

What kind of society would it be whose members followed these ideas to the limit? A truly Buddhist society could only be stagnant, inert. In practice there has never been such a society. Those that exist have survived thanks to a formula of great tolerance: they have left meditation to the monks (and usually to the less gifted among them, while the more intelligent devoted themselves to doctrine), and they have left the people to 'acquire merits' by making donations to support the monasteries. Ordinary mortals continued to live according to nature, while the monks set an example to remind them of all the virtues to which they could not aspire. This created an equilibrium which allowed society to move forward and forget the pessimism of the doctrine.

During the difficult hours of meditation I thought of all the Westerners I had come across in the course of the year who – as the Buddhists say – had 'taken refuge' in *dharma*: Chang Choub, the Dutchman Bikku, and all the meditators around me sitting on their feet. Was I like them? Twenty years ago I had come to Asia to try to understand Mao and Gandhi, and here I was attempting to meditate with an ex-CIA agent and a retired Thai police general. And not even successfully . . .

The first hour of meditation, before the sun rose, was the best. A cool, fragrant breeze blew up from the valley and wafted over the terrace, lightly touching the still, pyramidal, blanketed human forms, and disappearing into the forest, still very black, on the hill. John, his white blanket covering half his face, was an encouraging presence. Immobile at his feet, the general gave proof that meditation was possible: he was there, but in a sense he was far away. I would sit for a long time watching this scene of peace before I too closed my eyes. It seemed to me that the group emanated great energy, and that the common effort increased the strength of each one.

On the morning of the eighth day it increased mine too. My legs were hurting terribly and again I was on the point of giving up, but suddenly the agony began to dissolve, and then disappeared. I had made it. My mind was no longer a monkey leaping from branch to branch. It was there. It was mine. This was a great pleasure. Then I heard John's words: 'Let it go . . . Let it go. Attach yourself to nothing. Wish for nothing.' Even the joy of having tamed the mind, having conquered the pain, was transitory – *anicca* – and I let it go. I returned to the point where my breath touched the skin, and seemed to see myself from outside: my mind, separate, watched my body, now reduced to a numb skeleton through which I felt, through which I saw the dawn breeze blowing – a sensation I had never before experienced. I heard John's voice pronouncing the 'Amen,' I heard the breakfast gong, but remained immobile, feeling as if I had lost a little of my heavy materiality.

The following hours were not equally wonderful, but as the time passed I no longer waited impatiently for the end. Meditating was no longer a test of endurance, like staying underwater until the lungs burst. It had become what it should be: an exercise in concentration. I had the impression of having 'learned' something, like swimming or reading. Now it was up to me. I had put a rein on the beast that was my mind; the question now was in what direction to ride.

I used the midday break to go and meditate at the top of the waterfall. After *anapanaa*, I entered my skin, I lost myself in a cell, and the void opened before me. Golden images came to meet me, faces of people I knew: my mother, my father; then strangers; then beautiful colours. I had arrived!

I still had terrible cramps and difficulties, but now I knew they would pass, I knew I could go back to that door and walk through it. Above all I had understood the great wisdom of John and his method: to arrive at the idea of impermanence, the consciousness of *anicca*, by using the pain induced by immobility. Once one accepted the fact that pain, like everything else, was transitory, the great step was accomplished.

This experience reinforced my theory that our exclusive faith in science had cut us Westerners off from another sphere of awareness, that we had embarked on the high road of scientific knowledge and forgotten all the other paths we had once known. Here was the proof: pain was not merely a physical phenomenon to be controlled with a pill. By training the mind one could achieve the same result. I thought of Leopold's remark on the *Nagarose*, that travel makes sense only if you come back with an answer in your baggage. Was this relearning the use of the mind perhaps that answer, the thing that one day I will take back to Europe?

On the final day of the course, the last hour of meditation was given to the practice of 'loving kindness'. The idea was that, with the mind calm and purified, one turns towards all other beings to share with them the merits acquired by practice. It was a hymn to love, and John ended it by reading the magnificent words of St Paul's Epistle to the Corinthians: 'If I have the eloquence of men and angels, but speak without love, I am like a booming gong or a clashing cymbal. If I have the gift of prophecy, understanding all mysteries, and knowing all things, and if I have the faith to move mountains, but have not love, then I am nothing . . . Love is always patient and kind; it is never jealous, love is never boastful or conceited; it is never rude or selfish; it does not take offence, it is not resentful . . . Love never ends. But the gift of prophecy will come to an end and the gift of languages will not continue for ever. And knowledge, in time, also must fail. For our knowledge is imperfect and our prophesying is imperfect . . . When I was a child, I spoke as child, I thought like a child, I argued like a child, but now that I am a man, I have put away childish ways . . . In short, there are three things that endure: faith, hope and love: and the greatest of these is love.'

To this, twenty centuries of thought have added nothing.

Then John recited a long list of people to whom we sent our thanks and a share of the 'merits' for having contributed to the course. One of these was a woman who ran some of the most famous massage parlours of Bangkok, who had donated all our vegetarian meals. This too was Thailand!

We were released from our vows and from the Noble Silence. In the evening there would be a dinner – not vegetarian and with wine – to celebrate the end of the retreat and to allow the participants to talk and get to know each other. That was not at all what I wanted! I took my backpack and left.

Dan Reid's house was an hour and a half by car from Pongyang, and I got there at sunset. Wonderful. It was built entirely of wood in the old Thai style, on the bank of a river, with a wide terrace overlooking the water. Dan studied Chinese at Berkeley, lived fifteen years in Taiwan, learned tai qi chuan and kung fu, and has practised religions from Taoism to Lamaism. Dan, too, is a man engaged in a search. He is convinced that in the Chinese and Tibetan past lies a wisdom that has been lost, and he uses his deep knowledge of the language as a key to open that forgotten treasure-chest. He has written books on the Taoist methods for staying healthy and sexually active, and for achieving long life. Yuki, his wife, also practises Chinese occult sciences, and like Dan she is a great meditator.

Dinner consisted of three different kinds of rice and some tiny boiled cuttlefish. These were the first 'beings' I had seen on a plate for some time, and they made me cringe slightly. We talked about gems and stones which, if carried on the person, serve to attract energy and deflect dangers. Yuki said she believed in the dematerialization of certain objects. She told us she had two gold bracelets which a woman had put on her arm when she was small, bending the bones of her hand to force them on. One day she woke up to find that one of those bracelets had vanished. It could not possibly have slipped off. She searched high and low for it, but it was nowhere to be found. The only explanation was that it had dematerialized. It had become energy. Yuki said that the old Chinese legends are full of such tales.

Dan was writing a book on Chinese cooking. He described an evening he had spent in a new restaurant in Canton. The tables were set on three levels around an enormous iron cage containing dogs, snakes, monkeys, bears and other specialities. White-clad cooks would fetch the animal ordered by the customers. Some of the monkeys had no hands, because a client had wanted to eat only the palms. The wound would be cauterized with hot irons and the monkey thrown back in the cage, howling, to wait until another client wanted to eat, for example, its brain. The poor beasts, who knew what was in store for them, would begin screaming like banshees whenever someone in white walked by.

'In the next life,' I said, 'in that restaurant the monkeys will be the cooks and the cooks will be the monkeys.'

'Aha, you see,' said Dan, 'you're still a Westerner and a Christian. You have to believe there is justice in this world. For a Buddhist it's not like that.' I had to confess that ten days of meditation had not freed me from that desire to settle accounts with 'evil'.

I slept on the terrace. I woke at five, lit three sticks of incense in my hosts' Buddha room, and meditated facing the river for over an hour. I felt healthy, strong, purified. Those ten days of silence, abstinence and effort had sharpened me and ironed out the kinks.

It was 23 January, and according to the Chinese calendar there were still two weeks to go before the real end of 1993 and my flightless year. But I felt a strong urge to reassert my Florentine nature, to take my fate into my own hands again and defy that prohibition which had ruled my life for the past thirteen months. At breakfast I announced that I would go back to Bangkok by plane.

'You're right,' said Yuki. 'Today is a highly propitious day for you.' When she got up she had gone to meditate in the Buddha room and had seen my three sticks of incense. From the way the ashes had fallen she had read my future. 'You have no problem. Really, no problem,' she kept saying. That pleased me. Did I believe in the message of the ashes, then? Well, why not!

It was Sunday, and without a booking it wasn't easy to get a seat on a flight from Chiang Mai to Bangkok. I waited for hours at the airport. At last I was called for flight TG119. A good number? I wondered, as if by habit.

Suddenly everything was normal again: the piped music, the seatbelts, the take-off, the anonymity of the passengers. I shut my eyes, thought of the point where my breath touched the skin, and continued to get to know *anicca* until I felt the wheels touch the runway at Bangkok Airport.

I remembered – the general had said it in one of the sunset sermons – that if one dies while meditating, and in that last moment the mind is still, one will be reborn in a place of great peace and tranquillity.

I missed my chance that time.

And Now What?

I returned to Turtle House only to find that our dog, Baolì, was dying. It seemed he had been waiting for me, so we could go for that last run together. He writhed, trembled, whimpered. If I laid my hand on him he grew calmer. I spent a whole night like that, and then another chasing away the mosquitoes that persistently besieged his now sightless eyes. It was painful to see him suffer, and I remembered the Prozac. If one tablet could raise my spirits, an entire packetful would surely help Baolì! I gave him the whole lot, together with a little milk. And so that magic talisman, which I had always carried on my travels along with the other amulets to protect me in case of need, finally proved useful.

We buried Baolì in the garden, at the foot of a statue of the god Ganesh and in the shade of a bamboo. The staff of Turtle House and the street guards came and threw little wreaths of flowers into the grave, and planted a few sticks of incense in the fresh earth. With that dog there passed away a great constant in the nomadic life of the family: thirteen years, from Hong Kong to China, to Japan, to Thailand.

Who knows in what body he will be reincarnated? Perhaps in that of a superior being; perhaps in one of those who, as the police general-meditator would have it, finally reach the threshold of Nirvana after many a well-spent life, and then, when they are about to enter, come back down to live one life more. The last. *Bon voyage*, Baolì!

And I? Where next? What shall I devise for myself now that I no longer have to avoid planes? Another good opportunity will doubtless come my way. Life is full of them.

I have heard that in India, not far from Madras, there is a temple in whose recesses three thousand years ago a great sage wrote on palm leaves the lives and deaths of all men of all times, past, present and future. When a visitor arrives, a monk comes out to greet him, saying: 'We have been waiting for you.' From somewhere he takes out one of those yellowed leaves, on which is written all that has happened to the visitor, and all that will happen to him in the future.

Now, going to live in India, I shall seek out that temple. After all, one is always curious to know one's fate.

INDEX

Acquistapace, Father Angelo, 141
AIDS (and HIV), 20, 32, 52, 100,
    102–3, 108, 247, 314–15
Akka people, 56, 330
Albuquerque, Alfonso de, 139, 149
Altona, 315
Angkor, 22, 85, 111, 237–9, 251, 255
Angkor Wat, 238
Appelius, Mario, 320
Aranyaprathet, 15, 258
Al Arqam sect, 134–6, 154
Ashaari, Ustadz, 134–5
astrology, 58, 64–7, 73–7, 181–3, 323
Aung San Suu Kyi, 51, 55, 78, 231, 339
Auydhya, 58

Baikal, Lake, 305
Bali, 115, 195
Ban Noun, 23
Banda Hill, 147
Bangka, 201, 203
Bangkok, 15, 16, 32–45, 55, 58, 64–71,
    76–9, 82, 87–96, 180, 200, 228–9,
    233–4, 245, 315, 347, 358, 367, 369
Bantei Serei, 255
Bassac River, 252
Batak people, 187, 212, 220
Battambang, 230
Belawan, 220
Belitung Island, 205
Belorussia, 311
Bertil (journalist), 339–43, 350
Bertolucci, Bernardo, 86
Betong, 97–106, 314
Bikku (monk), 225–8, 363
Biltar, 192
Bintang, Evert, 211–14
Bixio, Nino, 321
Bolovens forest, 30
Bonetta, Father, 60
Brest, 311

Brunton, Paul, 358
Buddhism, 9, 35, 44–5, 48, 52–3, 55,
    60, 87–8, 124, 235, 251–3, 296, 301,
    336, 341, 353, 362–3
Bugis, 136
Bukit China, 138
Bulgaria, 303, 308
Bumiphol, King, 66
Bunyan people, 195–7, 201, 206, 210
Burma, 46–8, 62, 329, 332, 339
Butterworth, 109–10, 225

Cambodia, 5, 15–16, 85, 111, 230, 235,
    237–41, 242–58, 244–8
Cao Giao, 264
Celebes, 212
Chang Choub, Gelong Karma (Stefano
    Brunori), 79–84, 85, 87, 97, 119, 227,
    354, 363
Chao Paya River, 32, 87, 231–2
Chaplain, Ira, 113
Chatichai, 76
Chee Tong Temple, 170–6
Chen Ho, 139
Chiang Mai, 63, 338, 349, 367
Chiang Rai, 62, 330, 338
Chin Peng, 99
China, 8, 53–4, 71–5, 77, 91–2, 104,
    122–3, 160, 176–7, 195, 199–201,
    275–81, 298, 330, 333–5
Ching Ming, 138–9
Chou Enlai, 74–5, 199
Clinton, Bill, 345
Coleman, John, 233, 354–65
Collis, Maurice, 50, 331
Colquhoun, Archibald, 304
Cook's Travel Agency, 22

Dalai Lama, 56, 78–81, 83, 85–6, 285,
    296, 304
Daluò, 332–3

David-Neel, Alexandra, 77, 289, 357
Davis, Neal, 120–1
de Gaulle, Charles, 255
Deng Tiannuo, 172
Deng Xiaoping, 74–5, 200, 279
Dharamsala, 86
Dien Bien Phu, 240
Dili massacre, 245
Dong Dan, 275
Dong Mo, 275

East India Company, 169
École Française de l'Extreme Orient, 77
Eisenbruch, Maurice, 247
Ekaterinburg, 307
Erliang, 280–1
Escobar, Pablo, 339, 348

feng-shui, 8, 71–3, 117, 138
Foscolo, Ugo, 23
Foster, Norman, 72
France, Anatole, 149
Francis Xavier, 140–1

Gandan Temple, 286, 287, 301
Gandhi, Mahatma, 47, 84, 363
Gandhi, Rajiv, 221
Gansu, 279
Genghis Khan, 280, 296, 304, 306
Ghisir monastery, 301
Gobi desert, 279
Golden Triangle, 339, 340, 346
Goodnight, Mister Lenin, 41, 70, 312
Guilin region, 277

Hanoi, 200, 229, 265–75, 315
Hari Raja, 126, 128
Hedin, Sven, 339
heroin, 47–9, 175, 331–3, 340, 346
Hinduism, 220
Ho Chi Minh, 267
Ho Chi Minh City (formerly Saigon),
    263–5
Ho Chi Minh Trail, 20, 30–5
Ho Mong, 342–52
Hoc (journalist), 248–52, 261, 261–2
Holzgen, Joachim, 95–6, 112, 113
Hong Kong, 1, 14–17, 53, 72, 316, 341
Hongkong and Shanghai Bank, 72
Hua Hin, 227, 228

Hué, 71, 320
Huhehot, 280
Hutuktu Bodgo Khan, 285, 286, 288,
    291, 293, 300

India, 84–5, 131, 165, 180–3, 315–16,
    336, 370
Indonesia, 54, 136, 187, 199–200,
    212–13, 245
Ipoh, 123–4
Irian Jaya, 212
Irkutsk, 305
Islam, 106, 109, 127–9, 134–6, 187,
    189, 213, 220
Island of the Bees, 193

Jakarta, 156, 158, 163, 183, 198, 211
Japan, 53, 92, 216–18, 270
Javanese, 188, 213
Johore Barhu, 152

Karakorum, 294
Karen tribe, 48, 49, 330
Karmapa, the, 82
Karo tribe, 187
Kas, 320
Kengtung, 46, 52–62, 329–31, 335–8,
    360
Khieu Samphan, 244
Khmer Rouge, 15–16, 85, 230, 235,
    238–9, 242–3, 244, 249–53, 256, 258
Khun Sa, 49, 56, 331, 339–51
Kijiang, 206, 208, 209
Killing Fields, The, 236
Kim Lu, 267
Klang, 133
Kompong Som, 230, 234, 237, 239
Krasnoyarsk, 283, 305–6
Kroh, 107, 108
krus, 247
Kuala Lumpur, 123, 124–5, 126–37,
    187, 322
Kuan Lao Xiang Xian, 171–6
Kulen Mountains, 253
Kunming, 330, 333–5
Kwai, River, 108

La Spezia, 6, 316–17
Lam Son, 272, 274
Lamb, Charles, 229

Lanzhou, 278
Laos, 18–31
Lee Hsien Iong, 162
Lee Kuan Yew, 159–63, 164, 168, 169
Leopold, 230–4, 236–7, 239–4441, 243, 354, 364
Lerici, 317
Li Minxiang, 332–3
Lim Cheong Keat, 114–17
Lingga, 189, 195–6, 201, 206
Lisu people, 330
Little Buddha, 86
Lloyd Triestino, 6, 316
Lokman, Father, 202
Lon Nol, General, 254
London, 312–15
Loti, Pierre, 22, 238
Lua' tribe, 57
Luang Prabang, 17, 18, 20–1
Lungo, Pietro Maurizio, 222

Macao, 14, 53, 72
Madras, 369
Mae Sai, 47, 330
Maehongson, 339
Mahatir bin Mohamad, 126–8
Maitreya, Ananda, 226
Malacca, 133, 136–51, 208, 219–20, 225, 321
Malay Federation, 99, 107, 141, 159
Malaysia, 98–9, 106–10, 123–5, 126–37, 138–51, 152
Malraux, André, 255
Manzoni, Sister Giuseppa, 60–1
Mao Tse-Tung, 43, 47, 74–5, 80, 84, 194, 200, 276–7, 333–4, 363
Marinsk, 307
Maugham, William Somerset, 229–30, 233, 237
Medan, 208, 214, 220–5, 259
Mekong River, 18, 19, 21, 30–1, 252, 263
Meo people, 49, 56, 330
Mitterrand, François, 255
Mogellana, 88
Monde, Le, 113
Monglà, 332
Mongolia, 281–2, 283–303, 304–7
Monique, Princess, 254, 256
Moscow, 304, 308, 310–11

Mouhot, Henri, 22–3, 238
Muong people, 25–6
Mussolini, Benito, 320

Nagar Bankat Puri, 253
Nagarose, 230, 231–9, 363
Nam Khan River, 18, 21, 22–3
Nanning, 276–7
Ne Win, General, 47, 48, 58–9
Neak Leung, 263
Nehru, Jawaharlal, 256
Nerciat, Charles Antoine de, 46, 47, 63
Neung Ting, Lake, 330
Non, Ka, 147–50
Nordin (interpreter), 186–9, 193–7, 201, 206, 207
Noriega, General, 339, 348

Olivetti, 40, 154, 223
Ongaro, Sister Vittoria, 61
opium, 52, 53, 108, 320, 331, 345–7
Ossendowski, Ferdinand, 283–9, 293–6, 300, 306

Padaung, 'giraffe women', 49, 56, 330
Pakse', 29, 31, 32
Pancha Sila, 213, 214
Paò people, 330
Pathet Lao, 24, 26–7
Payroot, General, 64–5
Peking, 43, 54, 75, 85
Penang, 110, 114–23, 129–33, 225
Phi Phi, island, 12
Philippines, 303
Phnom Penh, 111, 112, 230, 237, 239–58, 260–1, 270, 274, 278, 320
Phongsovane, 27, 29
Pich Keo, 238–9
Pillai, M.G.G., 128–9, 134, 136, 158, 164, 322
Pintado, Father Manuel Joaquim, 145–6
Plain of Jars, 25–6, 29
Poipet, 15, 17, 230, 235, 258
Pol Pot, 47, 85, 236, 238, 240, 242, 246, 248, 250–2, 275
Polo, Marco, 333
Pomonti, Jean Claude, 113
Pongyang, 354–65
Porto Venere, 317
Potala Palace, Tibet, 21–2, 81

Pregarz, Roberto, 316
Premadasa, Ranasinghe, 221
Pulau Pinang, 183, 186–97, 198–214

Qin Shi Huang Di, 72

Raffles, Sir Stamford, 169
Rama the First, King, 66
Rama the Tenth, King, 66
Rangoon, 58, 76, 200, 229, 235, 360
Red River, 274–5
Reid, Dan, 365–6
Reid, Yuki, 366–7
Riau archipelago, 186, 188
Romance of the Three Kingdoms, 153–4
Rossett, Claudia, 95

Saigon, 6, 53, 230–1, 264; *see also* Ho
  Chi Minh City
Sam Neua, 27
Savannaket, 30
Sentosa, 185
Shan, 46, 49–50, 56, 60, 333, 338,
  339–43, 346, 348
Siem Reap, 111, 238, 240, 257
Sihanouk, Prince, 248, 253–8
Singapore, 129, 133, 152–85, 296,
  316–21, 341
Sisophon, 260
Sivaraksa, Sulak, 37
Soon, T.K., 171, 172, 176
Soviet Union, 6, 41, 154
Spiegel, Der, 3, 41, 92, 95, 112, 180,
  315–16
Sri Lanka, 221, 226
Stalin, Joseph, 310
Straits Times, 185
Strozzi, Piero, 146
Suchinda, General, 76–7
Suharto, Thojib N.J., 195
Sukarno, Achmad, 192, 212
Sumatra, 186, 188, 208, 220
Sungai Panchala, 134–5

Ta Prom, 237
Tachileck, 46, 47, 48–9, 63
Taiwan, 200
Takeck, 32
Tam Piu cave, 28–9
Tanizaki, Junichiro, 21

Tanjung Pinang, 187–8, 195, 198–206,
  211–14
Taoism, 77, 171, 176
Tashi Lama, 285
Terzani, Angela, 6, 13, 35, 46–7, 63, 79,
  84, 94, 109, 132, 149, 217, 272, 316–21
Terzani, Folco, 12–13, 15, 149, 155, 299
Terzani, Gerardo, 12
Terzani, Saskia, 12, 13, 42, 130, 155,
  132, 149, 337
Texiera, Michael, 143–4
Texiera, Nancy, 143
Thailand, 34, 47–9, 52, 75–7, 96, 98,
  100, 227–8, 330, 365
Tham Ting caves, 24
Timor, 213, 245
Tito, Marshal, 255
Tjong Ah-fei, 221–2
Tola river, 285
Trans-Siberian Railway, 304–10
Trieste, 316–21
Trikora, 209
Tibet, 21–2, 85–6

U Ba Khin, 337, 360–1
Ulan Bator, 280, 282–305, 307, 341
United Nations, 230, 240–1, 243–8,
  252, 257–8

Vanga, 303, 308
Vernon, Olivier de, 252–3
Vientiane, 17, 20, 24–6, 29
Vietnam, 104, 259, 270
Vietnam wars, 6, 20, 27, 28–9, 30, 53,
  264, 267
Vincent, Claude, 26–7
Vinh, 267
von Ungern Sternberg, Baron, 284–6,
  288–9, 291, 292, 295–6, 306

Wa tribe, 49, 52, 57, 331–3
Warren, Bill, 34
Wat Prakeo, 35
Wat Pusi hill, 18, 21
Wat Zom Kam, 55
We', island of, 321
Willem, Father, 201–5, 322

Xian, 71, 277, 278
Xianghuang, 27, 29

Yala, 97
Yang, Old, 198–200
Yang, Young, 200
Yawnghwe, 342

Yellow River, 279
Yuan Shu Shuan, 75
Yunnan, 329, 332, 341, 342